Romantic Dialogues: Anglo-American Continuities, 1776–1862

"How this study is received will say as much about the recovery of serious interest in literary history as about the work's quality. Learned, rigorous in testing its assertions, mordant and spirited in its expression, *Romantic Dialogues* makes an important claim: that American Literature of the nineteenth century knowingly attempted to fulfill the visionary promises of British Romanticism... What was reborn in the American Renaissance he writes, was 'as much Romanticism as America'. It is as if in the works of Whitman and Melville the ghosts of Blake, Wordsworth and Coleridge were posing a British alternative to Victorian conservatisms.... He makes one wonder how one ever read the American text at all without the British context. .... An extraordinary achievement...This is real work"

—Robert Weisbuch, *New England Quarterly:*

"Challenging the conventional notion that American literature emerged from Emerson's early essays, Gravil positions Blake, Wordsworth and Coleridge as its true progenitors: just as Locke's libertarian political writings bore their greatest fruit in Jefferson's famous manifesto, so the English romantics' most characteristic notions of liberty and selfhood were fulfilled in the United States and its literature. ... Gravil's deft and learned application of key texts in British Romanticism to works by Thoreau, Melville, Dickinson, Whitman and Hawthorne powerfully challenge the easy presumption of an autochtonous American writing."

—Kurt Eisen, *American Literature*

" ... a major study, alert to and at home with textual nuance and larger questions ... persuasively proving and describing a series of intricate, intertextual relationships: Gravil allows for uniqueness and difference; there is no 'Englishing' of his American authors, but a brimmingly revelatory stream of suggested connections. *Romantic Dialogues* is a ground-breaking study which bears witness to a generous, vigilant, and witty critical intelligence."

—Michael O'Neill , *Symbiosis*

ALSO BY RICHARD GRAVIL

Wordsworth: The Prelude, a Casebook (1972)

Swift: Gulliver's Travels, a Casebook (1974)

Coleridge's Imagination: Essays for Pete Laver
edited with Lucy Newlyn and Nicholas Roe (1985)

The Coleridge Connection: Essays for Thomas McFarland,
edited with Molly Lefebure (1990)

Wordsworth's Bardic Vocation, 1787–1842 (2003 and 2015)

Master Narratives: Tellers and Telling in the English Novel. Essays for Bill Ruddick (2001)

Wordsworth and Helen Maria Williams; or, the Perils of Sensibility (2010)

The Oxford Handbook of William Wordsworth
edited with Daniel Robinson (2015)

ROMANTIC DIALOGUES

ANGLO-AMERICAN CONTINUITIES, 1776–1862

Richard Gravil

2nd edition, revised and enlarged

𝓗𝐸𝐵 ☼ HUMANITIES-EBOOKS

© 2000, 2015 Richard Gravil

The Author has asserted his right to be identified as the author of this Work in accordance with the Copyright, Designs and Patents Act 1988.

Cover image: from William Blake, *America: a Prophecy*
© The Fitzwilliam Museum, Cambridge

First published by Palgrave-St Martin's in 2000.
Second revised edition published in 2015 by Humanities-Ebooks, LLP
Tirril Hall, Tirril, Penrith CA10 2JE.

Availability:
In Paperback from Lulu.com
As a library PDF from EBSCO, Ebrary and MyiLibrary.
In PDF from Google
In Kindle format from Amazon
In PDF, Mobi, and ePub from
http://www.humanities-ebooks.co.uk

The Paperback and PDF versions are recommended

ISBN 978-1-84760-348-7 PDF
ISBN 978-1-84760-349-4 Paperback
ISBN 978-1-84760-350-0 Kindle
ISBN 978-1-84760-351-7 ePub

Violetta Zara Turner
1914–2004

Contents

Introduction	11

Part 1: Revolution and Independence, 1775–1837

Chapter 1: The Anglo-American Revolution; or, 1776 and all that	27
Chapter 2: Romantic Americas	57
Chapter 3: Consanguinity and In(ter)dependence	91

Part 2: Redeeming the Promise of England, 1823–1862

Chapter 4: James Fenimore Cooper and the Spectre of Edmund Burke	129
Chapter 5: 'The Reign of Nature'; or, Mr Bryant's Wordsworth	159
Chapter 6: Stepping Westward: *Nature & Walden*	183
Chapter 7: Hawthorne & Poe, Romancing Romanticism	219
Chapter 8: The Whale and the Albatross: Melville and the Active Universe	249
Chapter 9: A Discharged Soldier and A Runaway Slave	283
Chapter 10: Emily Dickinson's Imaginary Conversations	315
Epilogue: The Escape from 'Locksley Hall'	341
Some Recommended Reading	365
Index	373

Acknowledgements

The first edition of this book was published by St Martin's Press at the behest of Marilyn Gaull. I am grateful to Professor Gaull for suggesting a revised edition and to Brigitte Shull of Palgrave-St Martin's for the reversion of rights, enabling me to produce this second edition.

For encouragement, criticism, and all varieties of assistance, material and transcendental, I owe thanks to Chris Ackerley, the late Robert J. Barth SJ, John Beer, Fred and Roswitha Burwick, the late Norman Fruman, the late Kate Fullbrook, Chris Gair, Colin and Jeanette Gibson, Cindy Hamilton, Stephen Hebron, the late Molly Lefebure, the late Thomas McFarland, Joan & Edward Ormondroyd, Robert Lawson-Peebles, Yvonne Pearson, Rebecka Persson, Nicholas Reid, Nick Roe, the late Ann Swyderski, Jim Wallace, the late Richard Wordsworth, Sylvia Wordsworth, and most of all to my wife, Fiona. It is a melancholy task to add the word 'late' so many times in updating this page fifteen years on. Bob Barth, who took me to Walden Pond and the Minuteman National Park and introduced me to breakfasting on blueberry muffins, during a memorable sojourn at Boston College, is an unseen companion on the first page of my Introduction.

While preparing the first edition of this book I was assisted, on regrettably brief and hurried visits, by staff at Dove Cottage Library, the Huntington Library, the Boston Athenaeum, Boston Public Library, Otago University Library, the Cornell Libraries, the Houghton and Widener Libraries at Harvard, the O'Neill and Burns Libraries at Boston College, the Bodleian Library and the British Library, as well as library staff at the College of St Mark and St John. Many passages of the book would have been very different but for my graduate students, especially Tony Hardie, Ann Oakins, Kathryn Rago, Doreen Smith, Ann Swyderski and Tim Worth.

Versions of three chapters in the first edition had previously appeared as follows, and were reprinted with permission of the editors: 'James Fenimore Cooper and the Spectre of Edmund Burke', *Romanticism on the Net*, 14 (May 1999); 'The Whale and the Albatross' in *The Wordsworth Circle*, 28:1 (1997) 2–10; and 'The Discharged Soldier and the Runaway Slave: Wordsworth and the Definition of Walt Whitman' in *Symbiosis: a Journal of Anglo-American Literary Relations*, 1.1 (1997) 48–68. Chapter 5, '"The Reign of Nature"; Mr Bryant's Wordsworth', new to this edition, appeared in *The Wordsworth Circle*, 46:1 (2015) 58–68, and a version of the Epilogue was first published as 'Emily Dickinson (and Walt Whitman): the escape from Locksley Hall', in *Symbiosis* 7.1 (April 2003)—a special issue entitled *The Republic of Poetry: Poetic Continuities from Bradstreet to Plath*, which constitutes a history of Anglo-American poetry by divers hands.

I thank Emma Darbyshire and the Fitzwilliam Museum for my cover image. It shows a detail from John Linnell's copy of *America: a Prophecy.* In this copy, executed on paper watermarked 1820—a year of much disappointing news from America—the facial colouring seems to make the Orc figure unusually vexed.

I am conscious of the topicality of this book, and in particular of the first four chapters, which are largely concerned with the entwined nature of republican discourses on either side of the Atlantic. A recent study of the 1790s asserts, without apparent irony, that America 'is a revolutionary country'. Yet, in these pages, Richard Price in 1785 and Harriet Martineau in 1856, lament the disappointing outcomes of the American Revolution, and Thoreau, in entwined meditations of 1849 and 1854, seems doubtful whether 'John or Jonathan' is the likelier—one day—to recognize and organize 'the rights of man'. Even Whitman wonders, in 1892, whether America's 'revolution' was more than a 'great strike'. As I complete this revision, Senator Bernie Sanders of Vermont is running for the Democratic nomination, and Jeremy Corbyn MP for Leader of the Labour Party. Neither is thought likely to overcome the hegemonic power of corporate capital, entrenched oligarchy, and—in the USA—dynastic alternation. But who knows? One of them might yet decide Thoreau's question.

Tirril, 4 July 2015

Introduction

> By the rude bridge that arched the flood,
> Their flag to April's breeze unfurled,
> Here once the embattled farmers stood,
> And fired the shot heard round the world
> —Emerson, 'Concord Hymn', 1836

The Minuteman Memorial park, where this famous shot was fired, offers its visitors unconsciously polarised narratives composed at differing distances from the event. In the brazen one, dating from the 1820s, the scene at Concord Bridge on the day hostilities began, was the heroic resistance of patriotic farmers against an 'invading army'. In an audio message, reflecting a subtler historiography, it was the moment in which, in fear and trembling, an American subject fired, perhaps involuntarily, on a soldier of his King. It is not my purpose to rewrite the history of what some call the American Revolution, others the War of Independence, and Whitman (in 'The Tramp and Strike Questions') came to see as merely a 'great strike', but it is appropriate to note these resonances.[1] They are related to differing interpretations of the 'revolution', as radical republican experiment or as conservative agrarian revolt, or indeed as an attempt to restore

---

[1] John McWilliams, 'Lexington, Concord and the "Hinge of the Future"', *American Literary History* 5:1 (1993) 129, offers a brilliant account of literary reconstructions of this scene. He examines Emerson's address for the dedication of Concord's Civil war monument (1867), Thoreau's battle of the ants, in *Walden* (1854), Hawthorne's *Septimius Felton* (1861) and Longfellow's 'Paul Revere's Ride' (1861) as rewritings of earlier patriotic narratives of the 'Concord Fight', which narratives include James Fenimore Cooper's version in *Lionel Lincoln* (1825)—as short on facts as it is long on patriotic gloss—and Emerson's own 'Historical Discourse at Concord' (1835).

the ancient status—royally conferred—of the yeoman freeholders of the Commonwealth of Massachusetts. And they are related to the problem which recurs for all the major writers of what Julia Power and F. O. Matthiessen termed the 'American Renaissance', the question memorably posed by Sidney Smith in 1820, as to what relationship should properly exist—fifty years after independence—between the United States and Great Britain.

My opening chapters address a variety of moments in what was a slow and painful amputation of Albion's republican limb. That 1776 was an Anglo-American event (in both senses of the term) is obvious enough, but discussions of Romanticism rarely acknowledge that the endlessly debated political dialogues of 1790–94 and 1815–19 are little more than belated echoes of the revolutionary utterances of James Burgh, Richard Price and John Cartwright and their friends Thomas Jefferson and Benjamin Franklin in 1775–76, or that the revolution which England failed to have in 1789 or so was not the French but the American. Modern discussions of the nascent American literature of the 1830s tend to treat it in isolation. Yet the fact is that that between 1776 and 1820 two intercontinental wars failed spectacularly to create an effectual breach between Whig England and New England; indeed it was necessary for the true architect of American literary independence, the New Yorker James Fenimore Cooper, to theorise and promote the desirability of such a breach in such works as *Notions of the Americans* (1828) and *Gleanings in Europe: England* (1837) and indeed throughout an fictional oeuvre which (with no effect on its popularity in England) lost no chance to emphasise American difference. In 1837, I suggest in chapter 3, the overtly antagonistic stance of Cooper, the ambivalently independent stance of Emerson, and the overtly 'one culture' stance of Elizabeth Peabody were equally viable stances for American literati.

The topics adumbrated in Part 1—some of the less familiar debates of the Revolution era, the residual and in some instances enhanced appeal of America to the English imagination in 1796–1819, and American concepts of in(ter)dependence in the 1830s—seem to me a necessary overture to my explorations in Part 2 of the continued Englishness of the American 'ear' in 1823–62. I necessarily rely on historians for much my data, which data will mostly be new to students of literature, and runs counter to much received opinion in literary circles on both sides of the Atlantic.[1]

The extent to which writers of the American Renaissance subscribe themselves in a Romantic diaspora, or indeed the extent to which what is reborn in that 'Renaissance' is as much Romanticism as America, was still, a decade ago, critically under-estimated. The Emersonian myth of an autochtonous American Literature had been very ably challenged, yet still enjoyed too wide a currency, thanks to our divided profession. Whereas English Romanticism has long been recognised as engaged with revising Milton and extending Shakespeare, with the sublimation of eighteenth-century loco-descriptive verse and Burkean aesthetics, with the critique of Rousseau, the application of Kant and the embodiment of Schelling, American Romanticism was too often been read as if Emerson conjured it from the soil itself, or more recently under definitions of context which suppose that literary currencies are of less account than those of merchant banking. In consequence, some key American texts still suffered a kind of critical incarceration quite at odds with their Atlantic genesis and their eager intertextuality. Yet as Julia Power put it, in her foundational study of Shelley's reception in America, the American renaissance 'was, in reality, the awakening of a people proud of their heritage, of their English tradition, and of their American independence',[2] and as Robert Weisbuch and Leon Chai have shown, New England writers in the 'Age of Emerson' were engaged in vigorous debate, correction, competition, and ultimately—in formal as well as existential terms—usurpation of the leading role of English Romantic writers and writing.

Cooper, Poe, Emerson, Thoreau, Hawthorne, Poe, Melville, Whitman and Dickinson were of course acted upon simultaneously by the cultural deposits of several generations of progressive European

---

1 In my first edition I advised those who felt sufficiently familiar with these matters to skip Part 1. The reviewer in *Romantic Circles* clearly took this advice as he ignored almost all Chapters 1 to 4 (i.e. 40% of the first edition) and concluded that the book showed 'scant concern with history or politics'.

2 Julia Power, *Shelley in America in the Nineteenth Century* (Lincoln, Nebraska: University of Nebraska Press, 1940), 10.

thinking, a fact superbly adumbrated by Barbara Packer, particularly, in her chapters in Sacvan Bercovich's monumental *Cambridge History of American Literature*. Eighteenth-century English and German rhetoric (the work of Blair, Lowth, Young and Herder particularly) predisposed them to look to art for the primitive, the original, the inspired, the prophetic. Aside from periodical revivals of Ossianic fever, this appetite was fed most satisfyingly by English Romanticism, especially as manifested by Wordsworth and Shelley, by German Idealism (filtered largely through Coleridge, De Stael and Carlyle) and by the visionary social challenges issued by their more immediate contemporaries, Ruskin and Carlyle.

What made the impact of the Romantic poets especially powerful, however, was that in numerous respects the situation of idealistic Americans in 1823–1862 (the years between Cooper's *The Pioneers* and Lincoln's draft Emancipation Proclamation) involved preoccupations and expectations strangely parallel to those of England in the period 1789–1819, the period between Blake's *Songs of Innocence* and Shelley's 'Ode to the West Wind'. As in Blake's *America: a Prophecy*, 'mind-forged manacles' and slavery manacles fused together for a generation appalled by the deadlock imposed upon social progress by a Constitution which they had been brought up to regard as the immaculate conception of demi-gods. The dark Satanic mills, too, were now in evidence. Emerson's generation perceived the corrosive effect upon solid American yeoman virtues of men crowded together in cities; the involvement of American governments in expansionist, arguably imperialist, wars; the possibility that even in America, Nature was not inexhaustible. Such factors occasioned, for more than one writer in the Age of Emerson, American equivalents of Wordsworth's long crisis in 1794–1807.

In 1819, of course, Wordsworth, Coleridge, Byron, Shelley, Keats, Carlyle, Emerson, Hawthorne and even Thoreau (aged two) were all contemporaries. It was clear from the rhetoric of both Shelley and Byron that English Romanticism was itself, imaginatively, of American stock and the popular Galignani edition which presented Coleridge, Shelley and Keats to America simultaneously in the twenties, confirmed an anglophone renaissance in precisely the terms likeliest to appeal to those who saw themselves as heirs to the values of both Commonwealths, as well as residents of the only surviving one. Keats's 'great spirits now on earth are sojourning' invokes Wordsworth pre-eminently—'he of the cloud, the cataract, the lake, / Who on Helvellyn's summit, wide awake / Catches his freshness from Archangel's wing'—and aligns him first with those who 'wear the chain for Freedom's sake', and then with that still younger generation 'standing apart / Upon the forehead of the age to come' whose role will be to 'give the world another heart and other pulses'. Shelley's mythologizing of the moment is grander still. Long before the 'Defence of Poetry' arrived in America in 1840 his preface to 'Laon and Cythna' had characterised the poet as a child of nature and the function of poetry as breaking through 'the crust of those outworn opinions on which established institutions depend'.

The sense of Wordsworth as Milton's heir, already promulgated in *The Friend* and *Biographia Literaria*, was reinforced by Shelley's significant allusions to him in 'Mont Blanc' and 'Ode to the West Wind' (Wordsworth's poem on the Wye is tutelary in both texts) and significantly glossed, in political terms, in the preface to *Prometheus Unbound*.

> The sacred Milton was, let it ever be remembered, a republican and a bold inquirer into morals and religion. The great writers of our own age are, we have reason to suppose, the companions and forerunners of some unimagined change in our social condition or the opinions which cement it. The cloud of mind is discharging its collected lightning, and the equilibrium between institutions and opinions is now restoring or about to be restored.

By the time of the major works of American Romanticism this politicised renaissance trope had been made even more explicit in Shelley's 'Defence', which proclaims that 'the literature of England, an energetic development of which has ever preceded or accompanied a great and free development of the national will, has arisen as it were from *a new birth*' and characterised the age as on the threshold or in the throes of a great 'awakening'.

Such terms could hardly fail to strike a chord in the Commonwealth of Massachusetts which had survived its English sibling and was prone to great awakenings of its own. Thoreau, for instance, saw the Wordsworth–Shelley–Thoreau continuum in these terms, agreed with Shelley in seeing no reason to suppose that the next institutional advance would take place on one side of the Atlantic rather than the other, and made this abundantly clear (as I show in Chapter 6) in the rhetorical structure of *Walden*. Writers on both sides of the Atlantic had believed in the 1770s that human nature was in the process of being reborn, under the aegis of nature, in a system that was itself the emanation of nature. Yet the imaginative consequences of that perception were first worked out not in America, where constructing a national infrastructure was of greater urgency than engaging in *belles lettres*, but in England. When Bryant, Emerson, Thoreau and Hawthorne looked about them for a model of what kind of literature might suit a new kind of nation, or energise a prematurely old one, they found it therefore—erected, one might say, in accordance with Emerson's law of compensation—in the old home. By then there had been ample time for a certain scepticism to have set in, in America, about what exactly 1776 had been about.

My aim in the second part of this book is to explore the intimacy of the dialogue which took place between the canonical American Romantics and their elective contemporaries—some rather older, some prematurely dead—particularly Wordsworth and Coleridge, occasionally Keats and Shelley. When I began work on the first versions of some of the following chapters, studies of the American writers were extraordinarily silent on the matter of continuing transatlantic awareness: Cooper's Burke, Hawthorne's Keats, Melville's Coleridge, were regularly left out of account in major studies, and even Thoreau's Wordsworth was seriously skewed. Some responsibility for this curious state of affairs must rest with that great scholar to whose work my title intends friendly rather than hubristic allusion. When he wrote his magisterial *American Renaissance* it could hardly have occurred to Matthiessen that anyone would read the writers he dealt with as if they functioned in cultural isolation. His references to English writing are few and understated because this context could at that date be taken for granted: he would not have envisaged the bizarrely separate development in the modern academy—especially in Britain—of English Literature and American Studies.

One reason of course for the sustained neglect of an Atlantic dimension in most twentieth-century criticism of American Transcendentalism is the degree of denial evident in some American writers of the period. Emily Dickinson is perhaps the only exception in the period in feeling equally comfortable with her contemporaries—Alfred, Emily, Charlotte, Elizabeth, Robert, Christina and 'George'—in part no doubt because the privacy of her creative process involved little risk of comparison. Whitman's note to himself, never to refer to any English writers, is a signal instance of anxiety and Emerson's 'The American Scholar', the laminations of which I address briefly and tactlessly in chapter three, is another. One explanation of Emerson's apparent lapses of memory, when it comes to acknowledging his sources—in an essay which proceeds from one borrowed thesis to another in a seamless web of unacknowledged allusion—may well be that offered by David Morse, in his *American Romanticism*. 'American Literature', says Morse in his provocative opening gambit, 'is born of excessive hopes and excessive claims, burdened from the start by an overblown national rhetoric. It is imperiously summoned into existence, like a genie out of a bottle, and expected to expand sensationally before the spectator's very eyes'. To envisage any more modest expectation 'is to gloss over the rancorous psychology of colonial status.'[1]

Robert Weisbuch, in his ground-breaking study, *Atlantic Double-Cross: American Literature and British Influence in the Age of Emerson*, argued that Emerson's generation was rapidly running out of excuses, after two centuries or so of waiting for the emergence of an American literature, so that 'frank acknowledgements of indebtedness became emotionally fraught and nigh impossible' (8). Arguing in terms familiar from Walter Jackson Bate and Harold Bloom, Weisbuch found the profound English influence upon American art expressed in 'a complex of acceptance, extension and completion, subtle misreading, cunning transformation, troubled refusal', and above all in a pattern of aggressive parodic response, with Melville and Whitman the most generally aggressive, especially as regards

---

1 David Morse, *American Romanticism*, 2 vols (Basingstoke: Macmillan, 1987) 1: 1.

18   Romantic Dialogues

their Victorian contemporaries. Motivations for that 'colonial rancour' and 'troubled refusal' had been much increased by the 1812 war and the subsequent wars of cultural attrition in the literary periodicals, for which reason I address some of the substance of this periodical war in chapter three.

Atlantic Double Cross has revitalised transatlantic romanticism as a field of critical inquiry, and will long remain the first recourse of anyone interested in transatlantic dialogue in this period. Nevertheless, I argue with it at points, as I do with Leon Chai's *Romantic Foundations of the American Renaissance*. I consider a narrower selection of writers than Weisbuch does, though at rather greater length, while challenging at points his application of the concept of 'cultural time', and indeed several of his readings. Tony Tanner's *Scenes of nature, signs of men* also provided signposts, as well as intimidation: both Weisbuch and Tanner offer blends of insight and sparkle at which it is much easier to aim than to arrive. A book published soon after the first edition of *Romantic Dialogues*, Paul Giles's *Transatlantic Insurrections: British Culture and the Formation of American Literature, 1730–1860* (2001) has been yoked with it by Lance Newman, who too kindly suggested that the two works established 'a new standard for empirical cultural analysis that is freed of nationalist distortions but closely attentive to the power of nationalism as one of the most fundamental structures of identity during the Romantic century'.[1]

In his Preface to 'Christabel' Coleridge remarked that 'there is amongst us a set of critics' who are inclined to attribute every seemingly original image to 'a perforation made in some other man's tank'. It really is not the purpose of the following chapters of this study, though it may well seem so at times because of the density of intertextures between the two literatures, to attribute every American rill to a perforation in an English tank, or to assume that without 'influence' there would be no transcendentalism, or no American Literature. It *will* be the assumption, however, that for Cooper, Emerson, Thoreau, Whitman, Melville, Hawthorne and Poe, paradoxically, one of their means towards cultural independence was their election of Romantic

---

1   Lance Newman, http://www.rc.umd.edu/praxis/sullenfires/intro/intro.html.

rather than Victorian contemporaries. To be a Romantic in America in the 1830s and 1840s and 1850s was one way of avoiding Augustan gentilities, without falling into Victorian ones. It had two other considerable advantages.

First, whatever one may think about the critical construction of something called 'Romantic Ideology', Romanticism represented adherence to a literary programme contiguous with England's abortive republican renaissance in the 1790s, a renaissance which led precisely nowhere (until Chartism, at least) but was itself inspired by America's example. Second, it affirmed what Robert Weisbuch calls American 'actualism' (the realisation of what others merely dream) in another way. Thoreau's remarkable tribute to Carlyle—'Carlyle, alone, since the death of Coleridge, has kept the promise of England'— provides one keynote of this book. I read American Romanticism as a sustained and brilliant effort to restate Romanticism in American terms, redeemed from the tentativeness, the doubt, the indirections, the failures and the compromises, of their English precursors, or to fulfil in America what was only promised in England—promised but not fulfilled, for instance, in the optimisms of 1789 and 1819. The Romantics are without doubt the instrumental precursors for all the American writers I have just mentioned but they are converted into prototypes, baptismal forerunners of a more liberated, more self-confident, and frequently more perfect, art. England sniffed at political revolution and passed by; so, politically, did America, as has been amply evident in recent decades. But England's intellectual rebirth found fulfilment in the New World, a point not lost on contemporary reviewers of Emerson. The vision and the faculty divine which Blake clearly found wanting in the America of the 1790s, emerged in the 1830s to accomplish imaginatively what had been fudged politically.

The change in tone, which my readings depict in chapters four to ten, from Cooper's deliberate alienation and Emerson's defensiveness, through Poe's combativeness, towards Thoreau's and Hawthorne's more genial sense of correction and collaboration, and Dickinson's habitual 'imaginary conversations', is precisely the kind of progress in transatlantic literary relations that one might expect. The change arises partly through a growing finesse. Hawthorne's mature tales, *Moby-Dick*, *Song of Myself*, read in the context of

Anglo-American Romanticism, take their confident place as technical masterpieces of an assurance which the English writers rarely achieved. For whatever the American writers set out to do, by way of creating a more 'early' art (a wilder art, in Thoreau's term) what they inescapably created was an art distinguished by precisely the contrary qualities. The raw materials of American Romanticism are to be found in fresh gobbets strewn around the creative shambles of English Romanticism. What is made of this—in Thoreau's artful diary, in Emerson's elegantly compressed and crafted exposition of Romantic theses, in Hawthorne's wonderfully enamelled miniatures, and above all in Melville's consummate Romantic Irony—is an art distinguished by a formal perfection, a completeness, and a confidence, which belie altogether the claims for 'earliness' which surround it and obscure it. To 'sublime' a thing, in Coleridge's curious and vivid notebook phrase, is to achieve a 'defecation' of the natural. Shakespeare, Milton and Bruno he cites as pure action, 'defecated of all that is material and passive'.[1]

What distinguished American art of the Transcendentalist period is precisely that it is 'defecated' of the tentativeness, the doubt, the indirections, the failures and the compromises, of those who in Blake's footsteps (as the author of *America*) created the possibility and set the terms of that American 'Renaissance'. By thus subliming its otherwise unfailing source American Romanticism handsomely repays its debt to the English Romantics.

I have for three reasons tended to take Wordsworth as a sort of synecdoche for English Romanticism. First because (as will amply appear) my ear is primarily attuned to him. The book could well be called *Wordsworth (& some others) in America*.[2] Secondly, because his pre-eminence as the purest emanation of the spirit of the age is amply attested by Keats, Shelley, Hazlitt, Thoreau, Peabody and Fuller, whose judgement in such matters has an authority no revision-

---

[1] *The Notebooks of Samuel Taylor Coleridge*, edited by Kathleen Coburn et al.(Princeton University Press, 1957–2002), ii, 2026.

[2] In this new edition, Wordsworth is usually cited from the closest thing to a complete Wordsworth now in print, *The Poems of William Wordsworth: Collected Reading Texts from the Cornell Wordsworth*, ed. Jared Curtis, 3 vols (Humanities-Ebooks, 2009–14). Hereafter, *CWRT*.

ary commentator can possibly claim. Thirdly, because the eminently desirable task of giving equal attention to all of Coleridge's contributions to the nascent American literary voice in the period 1830–55, following the precise impact of his greatest poems, and of *The Friend*, *Aids to Reflection*, and *Biographia Literaria*, and then doing the same for the collision of American mores with those of Byron, and the more slowly accumulating impact of Shelley and Keats, and the difficult question of how and when such writers as Emerson and Whitman and Dickinson acquired the awareness of William Blake that they so often appear to have, is work for a generation, not for a book. Since this book was first published, half a generation of remarkable work has already seen the light of day, not least in the pages of *Symbiosis*.[1]

One reason why, in reading Emerson, Thoreau, Hawthorne, Melville, Whitman, one seems to catch the accents of Wordsworth and Coleridge slightly transfigured is that this generation of American writers, like Gaskell and Dickens, had the inestimable assistance of that Romantic Victorian, Thomas Carlyle. In a longer book, I should like to have dealt more concentratedly with Carlyle's attempt in *Sartor Resartus* to 'build a firm bridge for British Travellers' over the 'medley of high and low, of hot, cold, moist and dry' to be found in transcendental speculations.[2] This celestial railroad metaphor implies, of course, that the thought of Teufelsdröckh is newly imported by Carlyle. But the disorder of Teufelsdröckh's writings, its entire want of method, is wittily and pointedly compared to the *Biographia Literaria*, that diasparactive product of the author of the 'Essays on Method'. And to be fair, it is Carlyle—making genial acknowledgement to Coleridge—who transforms the general sense of the authentic Romantic subject into the hero or able-man, and who first extracts from Coleridge the law of self-originating growth as the prime duty of man. In *On Heroes*, Carlyle observes that 'The meaning of life

---

1 Understanding of Emerson's dependency/originality ratio has been transformed by Patrick J. Keane and by Samantha Harvey, and Emily Dickinson's intellectual contexts by Richard Brantley. Less expectedly there has been a huge investment in understanding the 'Periodical Wars' broached in Chapter 3.

2 *Sartor Resartus*, ed. Kerry McSweeney and Peter Sabor (Oxford: Oxford University Press, 1987), 'Prospective', 61.

here on earth may be defined as consisting in this: to unfold yourself, to work what thing you have the faculty for. It is ... the first law of our existence. Coleridge beautifully remarks that the infant learns to speak by this necessity it feels.'[1] Carlyle's celebration of the awakening of his German Scholar (that more colourful precursor of 'The American Scholar') 'to a new heaven and a new earth', his awareness of man's saving infinitude, which is the happy cause of man's unhappiness, his insistence that 'not our logical mensurative faculty, but our imaginative one is King over us; I might say, Priest and Prophet to lead us heavenward; or Magician and Wizard to lead us hellward', his warning against the 'tatters and rags of worn-out symbols' which 'produce suffocation', his call for a bonfire of such symbols in a general conflagration so that 'we might find ourselves again in a living society', these are the retailored forms in which Americans of 'the Age of Emerson' first grasped as a unitary mythos the visions of Blake, Wordsworth and Shelley in their respective revolutionary moments of 1789, 1798, 1819. The idea that *Sartor Resartus*'s distillation of 'the promise of England' was pivotal in the development of American Transcendentalism and its literary products is assumed, rather than developed in this book. Between them, for their development is notably symbiotic, Carlyle and Emerson impose a plot on Romanticism, amplifying the Shelleyan motif of renaissance into a programme.

A further, and regrettable limitation of the first edition, is that I had to limit my treatment of Dickinson to a tentative footnote on current awareness of how extensively Dickinson interacted with the major Romantics, and how that interaction was coloured by Tennyson and the Brownings. She and Whitman were simultaneously heirs to Wordsworth and Coleridge and Keats, and contemporaries of Tennyson and Browning. Queen Victoria's favourite poet, the author of *In Memoriam*, shaped their developing poetics even more intimately than did any of their Romantic precursors, but that is not a matter capable of adequate exploration here. Just as Hawthorne and Dickens engage in a symbiotic exchange, with Hawthorne amply

---

1 *On Heroes, Hero-Worship and the Heroic in History* (London & Glasgow: Collins, n.d), 'The hero as King', 288.

repaying his 'debts' to Wordsworth, Coleridge and Keats by helping to form the composite of fictional styles we know as Dickensian; and just as Emerson assists Carlyle in transforming Romantic insights into Victorian—and then Nietzschean—forms of Transcendence; so Whitman and Dickinson reshape and re-equip the lyric tradition as it essentializes itself in Tennyson, preparing the modernity of Hopkins, Eliot and Lawrence. For the second edition I have included a further sketch, which glances at Whitman's prosodic response to Tennyson, but essentially addresses a single pregnant fact in Dickinson's oeuvre: that one of her best-known poems, often erroneously regarded as a melodic experiment in free verse, is written in a subtly disguised form of Tennyson's most haunting metre. My essay on 'The Escape from Locksley Hall' was intended as a pilot for a now-never-to-be-written full length study of the invention of free verse, the birth of modernism, and the writing of death, to be entitled *Crossing the Bar: Tennyson, Whitman, Dickinson, Lawrence*. I bequeath that title to anyone who fancies it.

I was tempted to add a further chapter on Fenimore Cooper, at the start of Part Two, to balance this enhanced attention to Dickinson. It is something of a scandal that literary history has allowed Ralph Waldo Emerson to usurp Cooper's claim to having declared America's literary independence. Unfortunately for Cooper, his generation-by-generation. nation-defining oeuvre requires a much greater investment than the evening or two required for a working acquaintance with Emerson, so the essayist looms much larger in the minds of modern readers than the prolific novelist, who is probably best known through the cinematic travesty of *Last of the Mohicans*. After the first edition of this book appeared I published essays on 'Regicide and Ethnic Cleansing: Fenimore Cooper's *The Wept of Wish-ton-Wish*' (*Symbiosis*, 4.2 October 2000), with further attention to Cooper's Burke, and 'The Wordsworthian Metamorphosis of Natty Bumppo' in *Wordsworth and American Literary Culture* ed. Joel Pace and Matthew Scott (2005) tracing the evolution of that character throughout the Leatherstocking saga. These fragments are all that ever materialized of a purposed study of Cooper's immense oeuvre under the (intentionally needling) title *James Fenimore Cooper: Anglo-American*. But instead of including more Cooper in this edition I have added a *mea culpa*. This takes the form of a recent lecture on Cooper's friend, America's first and now-almost-forgotten poet, William Cullen Bryant, who was relegated to a few asides and a somewhat belittling paragraph in the first edition of this book.

Part Two of *Romantic Dialogues* limits itself to certain aspects of Romantic poetic presence in the literature of New York and New England—mainly the latter—in the Age of Emerson: it looks at the importance in the articulation of American experience of new vehicles of expression which English Romanticism brought into being. From time to time, however, it hints at the existence of a lost continent of literary exchange which our artificially divided academic community is still only beginning to explore. My exemplars in Part Two are mostly canonical, though there is a much wider cast of characters in Part One (including the very remarkable American traveller, Estwick Evans).

Any study of Cooper, Emerson, Thoreau, Hawthorne, Whitman or Dickinson, which contents itself with a passing nod to English Romanticism, and the odd footnote to Coleridge, as most mid-to-late twentieth-century studies did, is both misleading and self-deluding. Blake, Wordsworth, Coleridge, Shelley and Keats shifted the English literary frontier too profoundly for that, and those who brought about America's 'Renaissance'—and her literary independence—enjoyed an intimacy with canonical Romantic texts that it would be hard to exaggerate, and hard for twenty-first-century readers to replicate. In Weisbuch's brutally candid summary: one could list 'every major tenet of Romantic thought as imported from Britain to America' (xviii). Equally, however, any study of English Romanticism which ignores the centrality of 'America' to Romanticism's self-definition—or any study of Gaskell, Dickens, Tennyson, George Eliot, Swinburne, Lawrence, Hughes, which treats 'English' at any date after *The Scarlet Letter* or 'Song of Myself' as immune to transatlantic renovations of literary practice—is offering a bowdlerised literary history. 'English', as Whitman and Carlyle both recognised, has its own frontier.

Part 1:

Revolution and Independence, 1775–1837

Under enlightened governors, [Britain's] North American colonies flourished, grateful for the blessings they enjoyed, and sincere in their attachment to the country whence they derived their origin. Had the liberal policy which her illustrious Chatham urged, been followed, Britain had not been charged with attempting to exercise tyranny and oppression; neither had her military and naval forces been humbled by surrender or defeat. Determined and successful in resisting all encroachment on their civil and religious liberties, the Anglo-Americans deserve respect from all who style themselves free-born Englishmen, and not that scurrilous invective which has been so liberally lavished upon them by the parasites of despotism.

—Isaac Holmes, *An Account of the United States of America*, 1823

While yet upon Columbia's rising brow
The showy smile of young presumption plays,
Her bloom is poison'd and her heart decays.
Even now, in dawn of life, her sickly breath
Burns with the taint of empires near their death;
And, like the nymphs of her own withering clime,
She's old in youth, she's blasted in her prime.

—Thomas Moore, 'To the Lord Viscount Forbes. From the City of Washington', 1806

Chapter 1:

The Anglo-American Revolution; or, 1776 and all that

> Great men have been among us; hands that penned
> And tongues that uttered wisdom—better none:
> The later Sidney, Marvell, Harrington,
> Young Vane, and others who called Milton friend
> (Wordsworth, 1802)

The notion that in 1776 the political fault-line within the Anglo-American community ran down the middle of the Atlantic cannot survive much acquaintance with the writings of the period. What happened in 1776 was a British and an American event which divided British and American subjects, and British and American families. Of those Americans who took up arms perhaps one in five did so as loyalists, facing obloquy, expropriation and exile as a result.[1] Of those British who were called to arms many responded without conviction, and some few refused the call at considerable cost to their careers. The impact of the event shaped the English response to the French Revolution. Indeed, the terms of political debate in the 1790s over France, and in the 1830s over reform, were set in large measure by the lines drawn in 1776: lines which were themselves predicated on that ancient fault-line in British politics between Republicans and 'True Whigs' on the one side, and Tories and Royalists on the other. The arguments deployed in America on the side of independence

---
1 See J. C. D. Clark, *The Language of Liberty 1660-1832: Political discourse and social dynamics in the Anglo-American world* (Cambridge: Cambridge University Press, 1994), 298.

28   Romantic Dialogues

were—inevitably, since until 1775 or so Americans were British subjects who happened to live in the colonies—as much English as American arguments. The arguments against—in the pamphlet wars between 'loyalists' and 'patriots' in what was universally referred to as British North America—were as much American as English.¹ Of the five republican gurus alluded to by Wordsworth, in the sonnet cited above, one was a former Governor of Massachusetts, one its adopted poet, and two constituted common political ground for the signatories of the Declaration of Independence.

The *Edinburgh Review*, looking back Whiggishly, and waggishly, in 1820, offered this short colonial history:

> The most important of their settlements were unquestionably founded by the friends of civil and religious liberty—who, though somewhat precise and puritanical, were, in the main, a sturdy and sagacious race of people, not readily to be cajoled out of the blessings they had sought through so many sacrifices, and ready at all times manfully and resolutely to assert them against all invaders. As to the mother-country, again, without claiming for her any romantic tenderness or generosity towards those hardy offsets, we think we may say that she oppressed and domineered over them much less than any other modern nation has

---

   1   For information on intellectual transactions between Republicans and Whigs in England and America see Bernard Bailyn, *The Ideological Origins of the American Revolution* (Cambridge, MA: Harvard University Press, 1967); H. Trevor Colbourn, *The Lamp of Experience: Whig History and the Intellectual Origins of the American Revolution* (Chapel Hill, NC: University of North Carolina Press, 1977); John Derry, *English Politics and the American Revolution* (London: Dent, 1976); Zera S. Fink, *The Classical Republicans: an essay in the recovery of a pattern of thought in seventeenth-century England* (Evanston, IL: Northwestern University Press, 1945); Stephen Foster, T*he Long Argument: English Puritanism and the Shaping of New England Culture, 1570-1700* (Chapel Hill, NC: University of North Carolina Press, 1991—especially illuminating on what spurred the emigration of such figures as John Winthrop); Caroline Robbins, *The Eighteenth-Century Commonwealthman: Studies in the Transmission, Development, and Circumstances of English Liberal Thought from the Restoration of Charles II until the War with the Thirteen Colonies* (Cambridge, MA: Harvard University Press, 1959); as well as the work of Virginia deJohn Anderson, Jack P. Greene, Philip S. Haffenden, Edmund S. Morgan, and Gordon S. Wood, cited hereafter.

done over such settlements—that she allowed them, for the most part, liberal charters and constitutions ... and although she did manifest now and then, a disposition to encroach on their privileges, their rights were, on the whole, very tolerably respected—so that they grew up to a state of prosperity, and a familiarity with freedom ... without parallel in any similar establishment.[1]

The sentiments might be those of John Dickinson, author of the much cited *Letters from a Farmer in Pennsylvania to the Inhabitants of the British Colonies*. Dickinson's perfectly authentic 'zeal' for the continuance of the British sovereignty—he argued and acted in the interest of conciliation until and beyond the outbreak of hostilities—not only coexisted with powerfully Lockean arguments against taxation without representation, but reflected his sense that British America benefited from its membership of an Empire founded on the most perfect set of constitutional principles then existing. He represented perfectly the gathering sense of Americans that while the British Constitution was the most perfect yet devised, it was in a state of abeyance in America, and a state of degeneration in England. Perhaps the commonest of articulated motives for asserting a degree of constitutional autonomy, some way short of wholly independent sovereignty—it was shared by John Adams, George Washington, and Thomas Jefferson—was the duty of preserving the integrity of British principles from the rampant tyranny of British Government under the malign influence of Lord Bute: 'Hitherto', says Dickinson, 'Great-Britain has been contented with her prosperity. But now, a generous humane people, that so often has protected the liberty of strangers, is enflamed into an attempt to tear a privilege from her own children, which, if executed, must in their opinion turn them into slaves.'[2] Dickinson could confidently suppose that English Whigs would share rather than reject the imputation. He is enunciating soundly Lockean principles, in soundly Whig terms. Indeed he cites Lord Camden's version of the matter, in the House of Lords,

---

[1] *Edinburgh Review*, May 1820, 397.
[2] *Letters from a Farmer in Pennsylvania to the Inhabitants of the British Colonies* (Philadelphia: 1768), 27.

TAXATION and REPRESENTATION are inseparable—this position is founded on the laws of nature; it is more, it is itself AN ETERNAL LAW OF NATURE; for whatever is a man's own, is absolutely his own; NO MAN HATH A RIGHT TO TAKE IT FROM HIM WITHOUT HIS CONSENT...; *whoever attempts to do it* ...THROWS DOWN THE DISTINCTION BETWEEN LIBERTY AND SLAVERY.[1]

Nature and Locke, it seems, are the same.

James Burgh's peroration in his *Political Disquisitions* of 1774–5 expresses perhaps, the representative radical sense of the crisis between governors and governed on both sides of the Atlantic:

> I have in these volumes laid before you a faithful and a dreadful account of what is, or is likely soon to be, the condition of public affairs in this great empire. I have exposed to your view some of the capital abuses and grievances, which are sinking you into slavery and destruction. I have shewn you, that as things go on, there will soon be very little left of the British Constitution, besides the name and the outward form. I have shown you, that the house of representatives, upon which all depends, has lost its efficiency, and, instead of being (as it ought) a check upon regal and ministerial tyranny, is in the way to be soon a mere outwork of the court ... to accomplish the villainous schemes of a profligate junto, the natural consequences and unavoidable effects of inadequate representation, septennial parliaments, and placemen in the house.[2]

Jefferson's *Summary View* had concurred: 'Single acts of tyranny may be ascribed to the accidental opinion of a day, but a series of oppressions, begun at a distinguished period [1763], and pursued unalterably thro' every change of ministers, too plainly prove a deliberate, systematical plan of reducing us to slavery'. Both writers deplore the ruin caused by what Jefferson calls 'the unseen hand [Lord Bute] which governs the momentous affairs of this great empire.'[3]

---

1 Dickinson, 38.

2 Burgh, *Political Disquisitions: or, an Enquiry into public Errors, Defects and Abuses*, 3 vols. (London: 1774-75), vol. 3, 277.

3 *The Portable Jefferson*, edited by Merrill D. Peterson (Harmondsworth: Penguin, 1977), 9, 11.

The Anglo-American Revolution 31

Burgh presented government policy in America as a substitute for reform at home:

> Before the taxing of the unrepresented colonies of America was thought of, the Ministry ought to have reduced exorbitant salaries, abated or abolished excessive perquisites, annihilated useless places, stopped iniquitous pensions, withheld electioneering expenses and bribes for votes in the House, reduced an odious and devouring army, and taxed vice, luxury, gaming and public diversions.

This, Catherine Macaulay agrees, 'would have brought into the treasury ten times more than could have been expected from taxing, by force and authority, the unrepresented Colonies'. Her argument is that the people of England and America have a common foe and that any further increase in the national debt would mean the end of English liberty. 'Rouse, my countrymen! rouse from that state of guilty dissipation in which you have too long remained.'[1] If renovation were to begin anywhere, as Paine put it, that place would have to be America. From an English radical perspective it was possible to agree, and many did, that separation was necessary, but that made it no less a matter of despair.

The Abbé Raynal also employed the rhetoric of reduction to slavery in the first of his pamphlets on the question, *The Sentiments of a Foreigner on the Dispute of Great-Britain with America* (Philadelphia, 1775), spelling out his reasoning more fully in *The Revolution of America* (London, 1781):

> The pretensions of the colonists rested on the nature of their charters and on the still more solid basis of that right of every English subject, not to be taxed without consent, expressed by himself or his representative. This right ... originated so far back as in the reign of the first Edward. From that epoch the Englishman has never lost sight of it ... it was in the defence of it that he has shed rivers of blood, that he has punished or dethroned his

---

[1] Catherine Macaulay, A*n Address to the People of England, Scotland and Ireland* (1775), cited from *The Magazine of History*, vol. 29:2, no. 114 (1925), 77–90, pp. 88–90.

kings. In short, at the Revolution of 1688, this right was solemnly acknowledged....[1]

America, in its passionate resistance to what Raynal called 'the fraud and violences employed by government to corrupt and enslave them',[2] represented a practical and effective version of the kind of awakening which every English oppositionist dreamed of, and would go on dreaming of, in 1789 and 1819 and into the Chartist era.

In the years since the end of the French and Indian Wars, however, British ministers had attempted to bring the colonies under tighter management than they had ever experienced. John Adams, Richard Price, John Dickinson, Thomas Jefferson, Edmund Burke, Samuel Williams all agree in dating disaffection from 1763. George Grenville in 1763–65 and Charles Townshend in 1766–67 had introduced a variety of new-fangled measures, from the prohibition of settlement West of the Appalachians, to a wide ranging set of customs duties, and a monopoly on the American tea trade, seeking to impose imperial control on what had been virtually self-governing states. British opposition to Government policy in America was divided, and rendered ineffectual, by two considerations. The first was a not unreasonable sense (it was shared by Raynal, at least) that Britain had just conducted an economically burdensome war with France mainly on behalf of the colonists, and that they ought to be a little more forthcoming in helping to pay for it. The second was the more puzzling question of how to support American opposition to governmental corruption without undermining the still fragile concept of the sovereignty of parliament. This, after all, was the jewel in the crown of 1688, a jewel which Edmund Burke, for one, felt worth defending. The notion that parliament must assert its right to govern British North America, while agreeing that these rights should not in practice be exercised, was not quite the answer the moment demanded, but was the only one such Whigs as Burke and Fox felt able to live with. Nor was this position limited to England: James Otis's *The*

---

1 Abbé Raynal [Guillaume Thomas Francois], *The Revolution of America* (London, 1781), 10.
2 Raynal, *The Sentiments of a Foreigner on the Dispute of Great-Britain with America* (Philadelphia: 1775), 13.

Rights of the British Colonies Asserted and Proved (Boston 1764) is merely one instance of a serious attempt to affirm the authority of the British Parliament in British North America while defining its limits. The contradiction fatally weakened Burke's appeal for conciliation. He could only appeal to self-interest, reminding parliament that England's trade with America was as extensive as her entire world trade had been at the start of the century, and amounted to a third of her imports and exports: he insisted that the needless alienation of America through the imposition of ill-considered taxes, the coercive acts, and belligerent garrisons to enforce them, would incense a people very passionate about their liberties, and bring about an avoidable amputation. In these nominal colonies, he warned, 'a love of freedom is the predominating feature' and indeed 'this fierce spirit of liberty is stronger in the English colonies, probably, than in any people of the earth.'[1]

He might also have reminded them, had it been politic to do so, that the intellectual commerce between the Whigs and Republicans of Old England and New England had always been as intimate as it was extensive. The literal 'alienation' of America was merely symptomatic of the political alienation of English political dissenters who, from the mid-seventeenth-century through to the end of the eighteenth, were prone to see American practice as the emanation (in a somewhat Blakean sense) of their own principles. That, indeed, may have been the monarchical point: American resistance had to be ended, by whatever force was required, and failure in the effort had to be contemplated, because a successful assertion of chartered liberties in America could only strengthen similar calls at home. In the eyes of too many English radicals America's cause was their cause: it was a revolt by proxy.

In England the 1770s, either side of the declaration of independence, saw much pamphleteering and agitation, inside parliament and out, for constitutional renovation. Obadiah Hulme's *Historical Essay on the English Constitution* (1771) had demanded a realisation of the myth of a Saxon constitution, with annual parliaments and univer-

---

1 'Speech on Conciliation with the Colonies', *Edmund Burke on Government, Politics and Society*, ed. B. W. Hill (Harvester Press 1975), 165–66.

sal male suffrage. Granville Sharp, more famous for his anti-slavery pamphlets, argued in *A Declaration of the People's Natural Right to a Share in the Legislature* (1774) that refusal of proper representation in America was a denial of natural rights and that 'every attempt to set the same aside in any degree, or in any part of the empire, or to corrupt it by undue influence of places and pensions, or bribes with public money, is *Treason against the Constitution*.'[1] Inspired in part by the proposed Constitution for the Commonwealth of Pennsylvania (which called for election by every freeman, by ballot, of representatives, to sit for districts, in annual parliaments, with rotation of office assured by allowing members to sit only four years in seven), John Cartwright's *Take Your Choice!* (1776) set out his stall for the agitations of 1819 and for what became the programme of Chartism half a century later: 'if you have a wish for reformation, either recollect or read what is proposed in the conclusion of [Burgh's] *Political Disquisitions*, concerning A GRAND NATIONAL ASSOCIATION FOR RESTORING THE CONSTITUTION.'[2] Obadiah Hulme's title-page epigraph 'Where annual election ends, there tyranny begins' had struck a chord, and in 1780 Charles James Fox led agitation in and around Westminster for the Cartwright programme of annual parliaments, universal male suffrage, equal electoral districts and paid MPs. For forty years, during which political progress was stalled, radical sensibilities were nurtured on a great succession of tracts demanding a restoration of the people's ancient liberties—tracts including Price's *Observations on the Nature of Civil Liberty* (1776), and *A Discourse on the Love of Our Country* (1789) and John Thelwall's *The Rights of Nature against the Usurpations of Establishments* (1796). The 'true whig' critics of English constitutional decadence, the proponents of American inde-

---

1 Sharp, *A Declaration of the People's Natural Right to a Share in the Legislature* (1774; New York: Da Capo Press, 1971), 14–15.
2 *The Legislative Rights of the Commonalty Vindicated; or, Take Your Choice!* 2nd edn. (London, 1777), 198. The rhetoric of this work is barely distinguishable from that of Jefferson's *Summary View* in its warning of what is to be expected from rampant tyranny. Cartwright aims at his own countrymen the argument being offered in American pulpits that 'an offended God hath suffered our nation, through forgetfulness of his law and hardness of heart, to bring itself to the brink of destruction' (229–30).

pendence or a Westward leaning federal empire, and the Jacobin sympathisers of the 1790s share a unitary discourse which stemmed—as Wordsworth makes clear—from Anglo-American republican theorists in the Age of Milton.

For many Americans, for most of the period between the first settlements and the first Continental Congress, the lines of literary, scientific and economic communication between their own colonies and London were more established and more used than those between the colonies.[1] Political links were still closer, and were so throughout the seventeenth and eighteenth centuries. One of Cromwell's parliamentarians, Sir Henry Vane, successor to Pym as Leader of the House of Commons, had been a youthful Governor of Massachusetts, if not a distinguished one. Another, Sir George Downing, a Cromwellian soldier who survived to become a prominent Restoration diplomat and financial expert, began his career as Harvard's second graduate (he also became distinguished for 'servility, treachery and avarice', according to the *DNB*, and therefore bequeathed his name to the residence of English Prime Ministers). A further Governor of Massachusetts, Thomas Pownall, who also served as Lieutenant Governor of New Jersey and Governor of South Carolina, would also sit in the British House of Commons, work closely with Franklin, and become prominent among British opponents of restrictions on American liberty.

Projectors of every kind found in America's social space, in Wordsworth's phrase, terrains as 'plastic as they could wish'. Maryland, as Jack P Greene, points out, was intended by the Lords Baltimore as not only a Catholic refuge but a sort of feudal utopia, an orderly mix of modest yeomen, and of great landlords who would work their estates with tenants and provide wise and judicial government. New York was destined by James, its royal proprietor, for the kind of absolutism preferred by Louis XIV and Charles II. Radical models predominated, however. Carolina was offered a Harringtonian

---

1 Two of the Mather brothers, for instance, Increase and Samuel, became respectively, President of Harvard and Chaplain of Magdalen College, Oxford, while Cotton Mather, like many other colonists, was elected as a man of science to the Royal Society. Marshall Walker, *The Literature of the United States of America* (Basingstoke: Macmillan, 1983), 20.

blueprint by none other than John Locke, while the ideals of *Oceana* were dominant also in Pennsylvania, where William Penn originally offered its citizens a complex Harringtonian constitution, alongside what Fanny Wright would call that 'beautiful penal code which is now the admiration of all enlightened political economists throughout the world.'[1] A plan for Georgia envisaged a slave-free colony of 'small independent landowners and producers'.[2] Quaker values not only found space for self expression, but exerted a reciprocal influence on England: the westward movement of George Fox and William Penn in the seventeenth century is matched in the eighteenth by the English mission of the travelling Quaker John Woolman, whose influence on Charles Lamb ran rather deeper than Bartram's on Wordsworth, Crèvecoeur's on Coleridge, or Joel Barlow's on William Blake.

The first touch of American soil, or even the anticipation of it, seems to have inspired Englishmen with egalitarian impulses. John Smith, in his *Description of New-England* (1616) emphasised the delights of a land where men would prosper if content to rely on their own merits, because rank, wealth, status and privilege did not exist. William Bradford's pilgrims had committed themselves while still aboard the *Mayflower* to establishing 'a civil body politic' on republican principles. Governor Winthrop followed suit, reminding his fellow settlers, while still aboard the *Arbella* in 1630 that they were by the act of embarkation pledged to establishing a society with communitarian priorities. Their mission was to show how brotherly love unites the divided remnants of humanity, 'knits them into one body again in Christ, whereby a man is become again a living soul' of which the evidence is preparedness to 'abridge our selves of our superfluities, for the supply of others necessities.'[3] Within a

---

1 Frances Wright, *Views of Society and Manners in America; in a series of letters from that country to a friend in England, during the years 1818, 1819, and 1820* (London: Longman, etc., 1821), 57.

2 Jack P. Greene, *The Intellectual Construction of America: Exceptionalism and Identity from 1492 to 1800* (Chapel Hill: University of North Carolina Press, 1993), 56.

3 *The Norton Anthology of American Literature*, ed. Ronald Gottesman, et al., New York and London: Norton, 1979. Volume 1, 37, 41.

generation Massachusetts was exerting a reciprocal influence on the English parliament and the formulation of English republicanism. The most radical such moment, perhaps is that in which Sir Henry Vane's *A Healing Question* (1656), drawing on a faith in colonial militias, proposes that since no other constituted authority existed, and since the army embodied the people in the most representative body then available, it should function as a Convention 'to debate freely, and agree upon the particulars that, by way of fundamental Constitutions, shall be laid and inviolably observed'. In this moment, Edmund Morgan suggests, we see the origins of an instrument used in the American revolution, when the rump of the colonial assemblies functioned as a federal convention: it is also the germ of the grand national Convention envisioned by English reformers, such as James Burgh, in his electrifying *Political Disquisitions* (1774–5).[1]

James Harrington's *Oceana* (1656) was itself inspired partly by the belief that what it presents as visionary is in the course of erection in America. The Harringtonian republic is based upon a bicameral system (such as most of the states and the union itself ultimately adopted), with its members elected by rotation (a third of the members being elected at any one time), a subtly graded system of property qualification for membership of the assembly and the senate (as practised at one time or another by most of the States), a limited franchise (such as Federalist leaders clung on to in New York and elsewhere until well into the 19th century), and a differentiation of function between the senate, whose business was to elaborate policy, and an assembly, whose right it was to accept or decline, after testing the public will, the senate's proposals. While *Oceana* recognised

---

1 Edmund S. Morgan, *Inventing the People.The Rise of Popular Sovereignty in England and America* (New York: Norton, 1988), 91. On the political maturity of New England, and its role in 1689 especially, see, especially, Philip S. Haffenden, *New England in the English Nation, 1689–1713* (Oxford: Clarendon, 1974): 'No earlier colony in history could claim among its founders a comparable galaxy of talented and educated men ... The consequence was a form of autonomy under which there had taken place in the half-century before 1684 a set of experiences particularly amenable to representation in clear and simple form. ... [T]he leaders of the bay colony after 1689 frequently spoke as if old and New England were on roughly equal terms as the pre-eminent members of a transatlantic polity' (38–9).

property as among the most fundamental human rights (any government disregarding property or failing to represent property proportionally will need to be maintained by force, Harrington believes), Harrington, like the Paine of *Agrarian Justice*, provided for a periodic redistribution of property.

For Harrington the relation between property and power was fundamental to his constitutional definitions. 'If one man be sole landlord' Harrington says, 'his empire is absolute. If a few possess the land, this makes the Gothic or feudal constitution. If the whole people be landlords, then it is a commonwealth.'[1] There are two ways of taking such a principle. The notion that there was an indissoluble link between property and representation appealed to the New York Federalists with their immense estates, and indeed became an insoluble element in the political schizophrenia of James Fenimore Cooper. Daniel Webster, Russell Kirk points out, argued from it that the English revolution of 1688 and 'our own immortal revolution' of 1776 were undertaken 'not to plunder property but to protect it' from monarchical actions which 'violated the rights of property'. But Webster also recognised the intrinsic radicalism of Harrington's position as a zealous promoter of that ideal of a commonwealth in which 'the whole people be landlords'. The unique social equality and social stability of the American republic, he thought, was derived from and secure in the ease which real estate became subdivided. It follows from this form of economic determinism that it only required a certain degree of such subdivision to create—*whatever* the political tendencies of the people and their ideologues—a stable popular government. '"If the people hold three parts in four of the territory", Harrington says, "it is plain there can neither be any single person nor nobility able to dispute the government with them; in this case therefore, except force be interposed, they govern themselves."'[2]

It is a consequence, perhaps, of such economic determinism, that

---

[1] James Harrington, *the Commonwealth of Oceana and a System of Politics*, ed. J. G. A. Pocock (Cambridge: Cambridge University Press, 1992), 12.

[2] Webster's 'The Basis of the Senate' and 'The First Settlement of New England' and his citations from Harrington are cited from Vernon Louis Parrington, *The Romantic Revolution in America, 1800–1860* (New York: Harcourt Brace, 1927), 307–8.

The Anglo-American Revolution 39

in 1783 Ezra Stiles, President of Yale, could claim that America had long realised all 'the capital ideas of Harrington's Oceana', with at least an 'equable' distribution of property, while Samuel Williams could claim in 1794 that 'Freedom has been the constant product and effect of the state of society in the British colonies' since the middle of the 17th century.[1] Despite the existence of great estates and huge plantations, observers of American society in the 18th century, both internal and external, display a remarkable consensus in ascribing a democratic quality, or a republican tinge, to American life. Crèvecoeur's *Letters from an American Farmer* (1782), the work of an English-educated Frenchman who settled in America in 1755, Benjamin Franklin's 'Observations Concerning the Increase of Mankind' (1751), and Adam Smith's *The Wealth of Nations* (1776) all attributed the phenomenal growth experienced in British North America during the seventeenth century in part to the cheapness of land, high wages, and the consequent social mobility. Such testimony might suggest that the actual American Revolution, as opposed to the War of Independence, was a gradual process brought about by a fortuitous marriage between economic conditions and constitutional ideals, and that it had taken place in the century or so following the English Revolution.[2]

Along with *Oceana*, the most influential political text of the seventeenth century was John Locke's *Second Discourse of Government*.

---

1 Ezra Stiles, *The United States Elevated to Glory and Honor* (New Haven, CT: 1783); Samuel Williams, *Natural and Civil History of Vermont* (1794), 2 vols. (Walpole, NH: 1794) 2: 415; cited in Greene, 183, 175. Another reason, perhaps, is that advanced by Virginia DeJohn Anderson. Emigrants were socially surprisingly homogeneous, with few very rich or very poor, and most were from urban backgrounds, used to participating in complex local government. *New England's Generation: the Great Migration and the Formation of Society and Culture in the Seventeenth Century* (Cambridge: Cambridge University Press, 1991), 34, 27-31.

2 Fanny Wright comments, in 1820, that the colonists lived for the most part under constitutions 'as essentially democratic as those of the present day' (*Society and Manners*, 323). Samuel Williams concurs: 'a free and equal government is best suited our infant and rising state. And such was the system of civil government that took place in these colonies, with a few exceptions, till the close of the last war [1763].' *A Discourse on the Love of Our Country; Delivered on a Day of Thanksgiving, December 15,1774* (Salem, New England: 1775), 17.

This essay, of 1680–83, by the former political agent of the Earl of Shaftesbury and Secretary to the Lords Proprietor of Carolina, has been cited as equally fundamental in the political formation of such federalists as John Adams, such democrat-republicans as Thomas Jefferson, such English Whigs as Edmund Burke, and the dissenting tradition of Richard Price and Tom Paine. It seems to constitute the common DNA in every variety of libertarian discourse in Anglo-American culture. 'In the beginning' said Locke, 'all the world was America.'[1] He meant, of course, the America of the Indian, before commerce, money and property took hold, and while it was still, as far as civility went, a tabula rasa on which any form of polity might be inscribed. Like Milton, Locke saw government as founded in the tacit consent of the governed and subject to natural laws which derive from a pre-political state of society, or the laws of nature. While Locke believed firmly in a balanced constitution—of monarchy, aristocracy and commons—he also believed that the powers of any sovereign were limited by the principle of consent, that taxation must be approved by the majority, and that rebellion was justified in case of infringement by government of such natural rights as life, liberty and property.

Such arguments underwrite, in the views of political animals as profoundly opposed as Richard Price and John Dickinson, the cry of 'no taxation without representation', and they constitute the philosophical foundation of Jefferson's *Declaration of Independence*. They unite a belief in the ultimate sovereignty of the people with a defence of the English constitution as the most perfect example of a balanced constitution yet achieved. In the summary of Joseph Towers, an associate of Richard Price:

> It is the doctrine of Mr Locke that all legitimate government is derived from the consent of the people; that men are naturally equal, and that no one has a right to injure another in his life, health, liberty, or possessions; and that no man in civil society ought to be subject to the arbitrary will of others, but only to known and established laws, made by general consent for the

---

1 John Locke, *Two Treatises on Government*, edited by Mark Goldie (London: Dent, 1993), 139.

common benefit; that no taxes are to be levied on the people, without the consent of the majority, given by themselves or their deputies.¹

Jefferson's 'We hold these truths to be self-evident: that all men are created equal; that they are endowed by their Creator with certain inalienable rights; that among these are life, liberty and the pursuit of happiness', differs from Locke only in its somewhat euphemistic substitution of 'happiness' for Locke's 'property'.

With the extraordinary growth of the American economy, through internal vigour and new immigration, it seemed obvious to Benjamin Franklin, Adam Smith and Edmund Burke that American power and wealth would equal that of the parent country within a generation. The dominion exercised by Britain was to Adam Smith already nominal, and could be only nominal. If such a country wished to remain with the empire that would be all to the good, but it was as apparent to Smith as it was to Benjamin Franklin that sometime during the nineteenth century America would become the hub of the English people, and that if the empire still existed its seat of power would move to the new world (Greene, 123). It was universally understood, outside the government benches in Parliament, that alienation through war threatened a virtual amputation of the British economy; that any attempt to make continued British sovereignty less purely notional than it had been in the early 17th century, would be a brake on development; that a free association of states was in Britain's own best interests.

Moreover, the nation now asserting its rights in this 'most important step in the progressive course of human development' was seen

---

1 *A Vindication of the Political Principles of Mr. Locke: in Answer to the Objections of the Rev Dr Tucker Dean of Glocester* (London: 1782), 96-7. Towers was vindicating these principles, rather humourlessly, from the assaults of the Dean of Gloucester who not only challenged a number of Locke's principles but argued that it was in Britain's interests to set America free since 'if we shall still submit to be fleeced, taxed, and insulted by them, instead of throwing them off, and declaring ourselves to be unconnected with, and independent of them, we shall become ... a Monument of the Greatest Infatuation.' Josiah Tucker, *The Respective Pleas and Arguments of the Mother Country and of the Colonies distinctly set forth* (Glocester: 1775), 51.

by Price as the home of 'forms of government more equitable and liberal than any that the world has ever known' and 'a place of refuge for oppressed men in every region of the world', the 'seat of liberty, science and virtue.' It was a place from which those blessings 'would spread until they become universal and the time arrives when kings and priests shall have no more power to oppress, and that ignominious slavery which has hitherto debased the world is exterminated.'[1] Thomas Pownall, MP, a highly experienced colonial administrator (he had been governor of three of the colonies) whose estimation of American democracy and potency is almost as eloquent as Price's own, alarmingly prophesied in 1780 that unless 'a Cherub with a flaming sword' could be stationed in mid-Atlantic (a curiously Blakean thought) there would be 'an almost *general emigration to that New World*', and that 'Many of the most useful enterprising Spirits, and much of the active property will go there also.'[2] Samuel Williams, a Massachusetts pastor, whose *Discourse on the Love of Our Country* (Salem, 1775) may have contributed to Paine's *Common Sense* and certainly gave more than a title to Price's more famous appreciation of the French Revolution, saw the flame of freedom being extinguished across Europe, and even in Britain, so that if freedom was to be kept alive anywhere, it must now be in America.[3]

---

[1] Richard Price, *Observations on the Importance of the American Revolution*, in Bernard Peach, *Richard Price and the Ethical Foundations of the American Revolution* (Durham, NC: Duke University Press, 1979), 182–83. Such rhetoric inspires John Adams to a delectable note of irony in writing to Jefferson in 1813: 'Many hundred years must roll away before We shall be corrupted. Our pure, virtuous, public spirited federative Republick will last for ever, govern the Globe and introduce the perfection of man, his perfectibility being already proved by Price Priestley, Condorcet Rousseau Diderot and Godwin.' *Heath Anthology of American Literature*, 3rd edn., edited by Paul Lauter et al. (Boston: Houghton Mifflin, 1998), vol. 1, 916.

[2] Thomas Pownall, *A Memorial, most humbly addressed to the Sovereigns of Europe, on the Present State of Affairs between the Old and New World*, 2nd edn. (London: 1780), 87. For the following quarter century there was a 'flaming cherub' in the form of war, but in the 1820s Pownall s prophecy began to come true. The social status and wealth of the new wave of emigrants after Waterloo—including Morris Birkbeck and his recruit George Keats—had much to do with the acrimonious treatment of emigration propaganda in the British reviews.

[3] *Samuel Williams, A Discourse on the Love of Our Country, 21–22.*

Both the future of liberty, and the future of the British nation, now seemed to many to belong to America. In the words of Samuel Adams, Boston's notorious agitator, it required little discernment 'to foresee, that providence will erect a mighty empire in America; and our posterity will have it recorded in history, that their fathers migrated from an *island* in a distant part of the world.' That island's inhabitants, once revered for wisdom and valour, became 'absorbed in luxury and dissipation' and finally, after being deserted by their industrious emigrants, 'sunk into obscurity and contempt'.[1] Adams's unfilial observation is cited by Edwin G. Burrows and Michael Wallace in their magisterial essay on 'The American Revolution: The Ideology and Psychology of National Liberation' as part of an enormous body of evidence regarding the sense in 1776 that a rupture was taking place between two nations who had been (or had been thought to have been) until that point in the relation of parent and child.

The notion that a set of vigorously expanding colonies thousands of miles away with a rising population soon to exceed that of the home country, could remain content with a subordinate relation to an ageing parent, was tenable only to those who found themselves able to retain the comforting illusion that the vehicle and its tenor have some necessary relation to each other. Many employed such figures routinely, arguing that, if the analogy held, Britain must now expect its children to set up for themselves, or that sending troops was equivalent to infanticide, or that the rebels were attempting parricide. Paine was rather pedestrian: 'even brutes do not devour their young.'[2] Burke in his last ditch attempt to persuade Parliament to conciliate the colonies in March 1775 by repealing those acts which had caused most offence, played startlingly with the possibilities of the metaphor when asking what would have happened in Britain during its recent famine, 'if this child of your old age, with a true filial

---

[1] Samuel Adams, *Writings*, 3:101-2, cited in Burrows & Wallace, '*The American Revolution: The Ide*ology and Psychology of National Liberation', *Perspectives in American History* 6: (1972), 167–306, 207.

[2] Thomas Paine, *Common Sense*, edited by Isaac Kramnick (Harmondsworth: Penguin, 1976), 84. Charles Inglis, *The True Interest of America Impartially Stated, in Certain Strictures on a Pamphlet Intitled Common Sense. By an American* (Philadelphia: James Humphreys, 1776).

piety, with a Roman charity, had not put the full breast of its youthful exuberance to the mouth of its exhausted parent.'[1] In the same year John Cartwright's *American Independence, the Interest and Glory of Great Britain* reminded the nation that parental authority 'totally ceases when the child arrives at years of maturity', which maturity the deliberations of the first American Congress in that year had exhibited.[2] As Burrows and Wallace conclude, the parent-child analogy, by which Britain justified her continuing authority in America was used in England and in America to legitimate three quite divergent conclusions: that 'the colonial "children" should be coerced into submission as unnatural ingrates, enticed back to obedience by a return to policies of leniency and affection [which was essentially what Burke and Dickinson hoped], or given their independence for having at last come of age' (Burrows and Wallace, 250).

What Burke, Raynal and (ostensibly) most Americans wanted in 1774 was a continued state of virtual rather than actual independence. Even John Jay's *Address to the People of Great Britain* (1774) and Thomas Jefferson's *A Summary View of the Rights of British America* (1774) purport to envisage a perpetual union as the 'greatest glory' (Jay) of both countries and one that 'may continue to the latest end of time' (Jefferson). An 1821 review of Botta's history of the American revolution took issue with the author's view that independence had been long contemplated, citing Franklin on the matter. Quizzed by Lord Chatham in August 1774 on whether Americans wanted an independent state Franklin replied:

> 'I assured him that having more than once travelled almost from one end of the continent to the other, and kept a great variety of company, eating, drinking and conversing with them freely, I never had heard in any conversation from any person, drunk or sober, the least expression of a wish for separation, or a hint that such a thing would be advantageous to America.'[3]

---

1 Burke, 'Conciliation', 168.
2 Cartwright, *American Independence, the Interest and Glory of Great Britain* (1774; 2nd edn., London: 1775), 8
3 F. C. Gray, *North American Review*, 13: (1821), 186. Dr Franklin, says Gray, 'had the best possible means of learning the temper of all classes of men in the col-

Perhaps the presence of the amiable Franklin was enough to create an atmosphere in which anyone seriously disaffected would keep such sentiments to themselves.

There is little doubt, however, that some British writers were clearer about the need for autonomy than were some Americans. Adam Smith argued for a friendship between equals, as far more profitable than any attempt to coerce continuing submission. John Cartwright argued for independence followed by a 'an effectual union of interests, by means of a league in which America would be a free, voluntary contracting party.' His brilliant and impassioned manner of framing the issues at stake left little, in reality, for Paine and Burke to do in 1789 when debating the notion of entailed liberties. Liberty, he argued, is not 'an estate or a chattel' proved by 'grants and charters, custom and usage'. Mankind's title to liberty

> is not established on such rotten foundations: 'tis not among mouldy parchments, nor in the cobwebs of a casuist's brain we are to look for it; it is the immediate, the universal gift of God, and the seal of it is that free-will which he hath made the noblest constituent of man's nature. It is not derived from anyone, but original in every one; it is inherent and unalienable.[1]

Cartwright proposes an act declaring each American colony to be a free and independent state, but one in which 'his Majesty is, and shall be held to be the sovereign head, in like manner as he is of the legislature of Great Britain' and guaranteeing the independence both of the colonies and of 'the rights and independencies of the several tribes or nations of Indians'. His concept of 'a firm, brotherly and perpetual league ... for mutual commercial benefits and joint security' (63) was not, in essence, much different from what Jefferson was proposing in the *Summary View*, though by the time both texts were in circulation events had rendered such proposals a little belated.

Richard Price, in his *Observations on Civil Liberty* (1776) was more imaginative. He envisaged nothing less than a United States of the British Empire, with sovereign governments in each nation

---

onies, and ... did not want sagacity to penetrate their wishes and designs.'

1 Cartwright, *American Independence*, 7.

but all supra-national functions ceded to a senate representing all of the nations of Britain and her overseas possessions. Price, like Cartwright, was worried about the psychological effects of continued domination, when 'the meanest person among us is disposed to look upon himself as having a body of subjects in America', and looked to a different kind of pride as preferable. 'The case of a free country branching itself out in the manner *Britain* has done, and sending to distant world colonies which have there, from small beginnings, and under free legislatures of their own, increased, and formed a body of powerful states, likely soon to become superior to the parent state—This is a case which is new in the history of mankind'.[1] Samuel Williams had agreed: 'No instance can be found in the annals of mankind, in which such a universal and steady attachment to, and dependence upon the mother-country has been kept up, as the North-American colonies afford'. 'We looked to the mother-country with a reverence ...which ... was new among mankind', thanks mainly to 'the free and equal government on which they had placed us with themselves.' Such liberality during a century and a half had produced 'such an attachment to, and dependence upon the Parent-State, as has no parallel in human affairs.'[2]

Price's interest, of course, is in what America represents for the future of mankind, and the future of England. If the kind of union he envisaged had proved possible, 'The Liberty of America might have preserved our Liberty; and under the direction of a patriot king or wise minister, proved the means of restoring to us our almost lost constitution'. Even now, rather than an imposed subjection 'Ought we not rather to wish earnestly, that there may be at least ONE FREE COUNTRY left upon earth, to which we may fly, when venality, luxury, and vice have completed the ruin of liberty here?'[3] Again, the vision is one he shares with Williams: 'To our own country then we must look for the biggest part of that liberty and freedom, that yet remains, or is to be expected, among mankind.... the North-American provinces yet

1 Richard Price, *Observations on the Nature of Civil Liberty, the Principles of Government, and the Justice and Policy of the War with America* (London: T. Cadell, 1776), 36, 32, 33.
2 Williams, *A Discourse on the Love of Our Country*, 18.
3 Price, *Observations on the Nature of Civil Liberty*, 40.

remain the country of free men: the *Asylum*, and the last, to which such may yet flee from the common deluge'[1] More pugnaciously, Catherine Macaulay, in 1775, wondered whether 'The Ministry ... have raised a spirit beyond the Atlantic, which may ... recover the opportunities we have lost of restoring the breaches which for near a century have been making in our constitution.'[2]

In America itself in 1775 the debate was between those who still saw the conflict as an attempt to restore the rights of Englishmen, as the birthright of all American yeomen, and those who were already, or would be as soon as Paine's *Common Sense* was published, hot for independence. There is an astonishing consensus, which the events of Concord and Lexington did not essentially disrupt, that the ties between England and America were almost indissoluble. Jefferson, for another fifty years, whatever Gallican policy he pursued in foreign affairs, would regard himself as part of the current phase of the great Saxon diaspora, an inheritor, from the Saxons, of the finest set of constitutional principles ever imagined, and as one who had actualised the ancient British dream, of ridding itself of the Norman yoke. From 1776 through the eighteen-twenties his letters show the impact of the republican staples of his various libraries—Locke and Sidney on government, the true whig arguments of James Burgh and Trenchard and Gordon, the radical history of Catherine Macaulay. Most interestingly, they show the indelible impression made by that remarkable exposition of the Norman Yoke reading of English History, Obadiah Hulme's timely utterance, *An Historical Essay on the English Constitution* (London, 1771).

Despite Hulme's argument that Americans did not need to be directly represented in London his work was well received and widely disseminated in America.[3] What sold it to Americans was its

---

1 Williams, *Discourse*, 21–22.
2 Macaulay, 81.
3 Thomas Whateley's argument that the colonists were just as well represented in parliament as the nine-tenths of Englishmen who could not vote (see Morgan, 240) was rightly ridiculed on both sides of the Atlantic. Yet 'virtual representation' is in essence an idea of Algernon Sidney. Since legislators are, as Sidney had argued, responsible to all of the people, Obadiah Hulme argued that Americans, though choosing not to exercise their rights of residence, were represented in

vivid representation of Saxon liberties and Norman encroachments, a transparent allegory, in American eyes, of events since 1763. Writing to Cartwright in 1824, to congratulate him on his own constitutional work, Jefferson praised him for having 'deduced the Constitution of the English nation from its rightful root, the Anglo-Saxon'. 'It has ever appeared to me that the difference between the Whig and the Tory of England is, that the Whig deduces his rights from the Anglo-Saxon source, and the Tory from the Norman'. Hulme's sentiment—that 'if ever God Almighty did concern himself about forming a government for mankind to live happily under, it was that which was established in England, by our Saxon forefathers' (*Historical Essay*, 20)—was promulgated by 'Demophilus' under the title *The Genuine Principle of the Ancient Saxon or English Constitution: Carefully collected from the best authorities; with some Observations, on their peculiar fitness, for the United Colonies in general, and Pennsylvania in particular* (Philadelphia: 1776). It animated not only Jefferson but Ezra Stiles, President of Yale College, who cites the Saxon 'wittenagemot' as a model for the republic, in his 1783 election day sermon, *The United States elevated to Glory and Honour*.[1]

Ironically, all this transatlantic Greater Saxon harmony was breached most effectively by an incendiary pamphlet by a former staymaker of Norfolk, with an immense chip on his shoulder about his record of failure in England, and now enjoying success as a vibrant journalist in America, at the invitation of Ben Franklin. *Common Sense* is credited not only with igniting bourgeois Boston and converting a loyalist majority into a revolutionary majority, almost overnight, but with having converted the role of one George Washington from that of reluctant rebel to that of first President of the United States. Its circulation, Fanny Wright would observe, almost half a century later, was as instantaneous as 'the electric fluid' (Wright, 95). For a time, also, *Common Sense* changed a War of Independence into something closer to a revolution. It replaced the deeply bourgeois cogitations of Dickinson, whose anxieties seem essentially

---

Westminster. Hulme, *An Historical Essay on the English Constitution* (1771), 194.

1 Ezra Stiles, *The United States Elevated to Glory and Honor*, 2nd edn., (Worcester, MA: 1785), 29.

The Anglo-American Revolution   49

concerned with taxes and property values, with a radical agenda.[1] It persuaded people that it was possible to think of a constitution on some other pattern than the British model; that a constitutional balance involving monarchy was not indispensable to liberty; and that they should seize the moment of hostilities to establish a convention to create an entirely new constitution, rather than a transatlantic replica of England's. Paine expected such a constitution to be based on unicameral government and the widest possible franchise. So did French observers: indeed Mirabeau, Turgot and Condorcet, in 1778-86, prior to the French Revolution, criticised American determination to reproduce British bicameralism, seeing it as superfluous in a state without royalty.[2] The ignorance, as he saw it, of such critiques led directly to John Adams's highly Burkean three-volume *Defence of the Constitutions of Government of the United States of America* (London—paradoxically?—1794).

When the great Federalist trio of Adams, Hamilton and Madison had had their say in the 1780s, the system that emerged managed to reconcile ultimate popular sovereignty with a bicameral system

---

[1] Farmer Dickinson's most impassioned complaint is that 'Our chief property consists in lands. These would have been of much greater value, if such prodigious additions had not been made to the British territories on this continent' (Letter 8, p. 40).

[2] 'If Cicero and Tacitus could visit the earth', Adams argued, 'and learn that the English nation had reduced the great idea to practice, and brought it nearly to perfection, ... and that the Americans, after having enjoyed the benefits of such a constitution a century and a half, were advised by some of the greatest philosophers and politicians of the age [Turgot, Price] to renounce it, and set up the governments of the ancient Goths and modern Indians—what would they say?' John Adams, *A Defence of the Constitutions of Government of the United States of America* (Philadelphia, PA: 1787), xv. Adams notably takes J. L. De Lolme as his most recent authority. De Lolme's *The Constitution of England* (1784) was dedicated to the King by his "Subject by Choice" (De Lolme was a citizen of Geneva) eight years after Paine had declared that England had no Constitution, a judgement which in Jefferson's view showed that he had not read enough. For the French debate see Gordon S. Wood, *The Creation of the American Republic, 1776–1787* (Chapel Hill, NC: University of North Carolina Press, 1969), 236. Those who imagine that the primary influence on the American constitution was French, from Montesquieu (as taught in American high schools), forget that Montesquieu was a Lockean, whose writing was proscribed in France because it was English.

in a way that left a route for Adams's 'natural aristocracy' to head the senate ('the first necessary step' Adams had argued in his earlier *Thoughts on Government*, 'is to depute power from the many to a few of the most wise and good').[1] Ideologically, then, the divide in 1776 was between figures like Paine, Price, Cartwright, Sam Adams, on the one side, as clear-minded proponents of a democratic revolution; and Chatham, John Adams, Franklin and Washington on the other hand, anxious mainly to ensure the survival of Lockean liberalism. The tensions between the generally sceptical John Adams and the intermittently radical Jefferson, which will take two decades to work themselves out (they took similarly polarised views of France's prospects in 1789), are a naturalised version of the English debate between Burke and Price, one celebrating the republicanism of the 17th century revolution, the other defending the entailed liberties of the Glorious revolution of 1688. The fact that it is not, other than incidentally, a transatlantic divide, is symbolised in the fact that the figure who successfully articulated an unabashed demand for independence was a dissident Englishman, and that the net result was a good British constitutional compromise. That compromise combined a remodelled British Constitution, founded more on Blackstone's theory of checks and balances than on Winstanley's or Lilburne's revolutionary demands, with a de facto Federal structure, powerless to diminish entrenched state rights. The compromise was worthy of the gradualism of Burke, who was always prone to prefer (as in his speech on Conciliation), 'profitable experience' over 'mischievous theory'.

Numerous apparently radical distinctions between British and American political forms and practices, which generally turn out to be a matter of gradation rather than absolute opposition, are rooted in 1770s revivals of debates of the 1660s.[2] Among these, the most obvi-

---

1 Adams, *Thoughts on Government*, cited in Wood, 208.
2 Jefferson's assertion of the right to bear arms is rooted in the arguments of Sidney that an armed militia is a powerful guarantor of liberty: the twentieth-century manifestation of this is an anachronistic gun lobby. Yet, had Sidney's defence of 'virtual representation' prevailed, corporate America might have had a less easy ride. Adams, Burke, and Jefferson all assumed that an elected member, once elected, was a member for the country, not merely a locality, and had some responsibility to those unborn.

The Anglo-American Revolution 51

ous is the substitution of an elected Presidency for a hereditary monarchy. Although America repudiated monarchy, for some generations coronation prospects seemed not far off: they are feared by Jefferson, dreamt of by Hamilton, satirised by critics of Jackson (a.k.a. King Andrew I), and allegorised by Melville in the person of Ahab. Few seriously disputed that the American system was a simple translation of the ideal form of the British balanced constitution. When Sydney Smith in 1820 envied the cheapness of America's 'King and Vice-King' he alluded playfully to numerous expressions of this idea. The formulae of Harrington and Sidney were everywhere familiar. 'A Commonwealth', says Harrington, 'consists of a Senate proposing, a people resolving, and the magistracy executing: whereby partaking of the Aristocracy in the Senate, of the Democracy in the People, and of Monarchy in the Magistracy, it is complete.' 'There never was a good government in the world,' says Sidney, 'that did not consist of the three simple species of monarchy, aristocracy, and democracy.'[1] Even Sir Henry Vane, at his trial, while asserting that kings accept their powers on trust from an assenting people, commended Charles I for recognising that the constitution was a mixture of Monarchy, Aristocracy, Democracy, 'having the conveniences of them all without the inconveniences of any one, as long as the balance hangs even between the three estates.'[2] Both John Milton and John Adams accepted this model without supposing that it necessarily entailed an hereditary monarch, and Adams in 1775 explicitly compared the British system to 'a republic, in which the king is first magistrate'.[3] Algernon Sidney supposed that ideally kings were elected. He glossed hereditary kingship as an error we must be at liberty to correct, and insisted—in what could be taken as the first argument for a directly elected President—that 'the People, for whom and by whom the Magistrate is created, can only judge whether he rightly perform his office or not.' After all, the Saxons 'acknowledged no human laws but their own, received no kings, but such as swore to observe them,

1 Harrington, 25; Algernon Sidney, *Discourses on Government* (London: 1775), 74.
2 T. B. Howell, *A Complete Collection of State Trials*, 21 vols. (London: 1816) vol. 6, *The Trial of Sir Henry Vane*, 158.
3 Adams, *Thoughts on Government*, cited in Wood, 206; Adams, *Defence of the Constitutions*, 208.

and deposed those who did not well perform their oaths and duty.'[1]

In the course of the War of Independence, and the constitutional debate that accompanied and followed it, more radical measures, such as those proposed by Harrington to ensure a periodic adjustment of property, or by Cartwright, Price and Paine, to deal with the slavery issue promptly and on a nationwide basis, were set aside. Property dilution would have been anathema to the Federalists of Virginia, Massachusetts and New York, whose greatest interest was to ensure the non-dispersal of landed estates, and of course a proper political influence for their owners. Notwithstanding the arguments of Obadiah Hulme and Joseph Towers, ascending property qualifications, for voters, congressman, senators, governors, were required in several of the state constitutions.[2] Considerably less was achieved, then or since, in the way of redistribution or of preventing oligarchy, than was envisaged by Harrington. Abolition of slavery took place in Pennsylvania and elsewhere in the North with considerable alacrity, rectifying an abuse imposed and sustained by Britain, and many voices in England and America were raised in support of prompt action to eradicate it altogether.[3] There was considerable optimism in

---

1 Sidney, *Discourses on Government*, 225, 170.

2 Property qualifications were an innovation of Queen Anne's ministry, Hulme argued, and changed a government of the wise into a government of the rich (*An Historical Essay on the English Constitution*, 126–28). Towers pointed out that 'that able and upright senator, Andrew Marvell, could not have been a member of parliament in the present age (*A Vindication of the Political Principles of Mr Locke*, 79, 82). On American debates and practice regarding qualifications see, for example, Morgan, 250–53, and Wood, 434.

3 Granville Sharp warned that while 'the Congress have acted nobly in forbidding the iniquitous importation of more slaves', the business is but half done, 'till they have agreed upon some equitable and safe means of gradually enfranchising those which remain,' for 'American liberty cannot be firmly established until this is done.' *The Just Limitation of Slavery in the Laws of God, Compared with the Unbounded Claims of the African Traders and British American Slaveholders* (London: 1776), 56, 61. Benjamin Rush (*On Slave-Keeping*, 1773) argued that 'The plant of liberty is of so tender a nature that it cannot thrive long in the neighborhood of slavery.' Samuel Hopkins, in *Dialogue Concerning the Slavery of Africans* (1776) exclaimed against 'This gross, barefaced, practiced inconsistence': the slavery we complain of 'is lighter than a feather compared to their heavy doom.' Rush and Hopkins cited in Bailyn, 239, 244.

the 1790s that it would soon or very soon, disappear altogether from the union. Such optimism, however, would look decidedly complacent to Estwick Evans, Sydney Smith and Frances Wright in 1820, by when the slave population had increased tenfold, from 400,000 to 4,000,000, and the complacency looked revoltingly rebarbative to the generation of Frances Trollope, Harriet Martineau, and Charles Dickens. In the 1840s Emerson (whose family in 1776 was polarised between a slave-owning revolutionary and a loyalist abolitionist), Melville, Thoreau, Twain, and Whitman would still be able to experience over this issue what Wordsworth had called, referring to 1792, 'a novel heat of virtuous feeling.' Enough had been achieved to make America the model, for several generations to come, of a popular democracy; not quite enough to establish the perfect republic.

From the Mayflower compact to the *Declaration of Independence*, the Idea of America is crucial to English Whigs and Dissenters as: (a) a *test-bed* for ideas of constitutional reform fundamental to Sidney, Harrington, Locke & co; (b) a place of ultimate refuge should the liberties of the 1688 settlement be eroded; (c) the place in which English liberties might survive, should they disappear altogether from England, and from which they would ultimately be reimported, and (d) in Price's visionary eyes, the major component of a future united states of the English-speaking world. The 'revolution' one might argue, was more an emanation of 1688 than of the 1640s, except in the emphatic act of Counter-Restoration. The major *revolutionary* component is to be found in the fact that there existed in such centres as Boston, New York and Philadelphia an artisan class, personified in such figures as Paul Revere, Samuel Adams and Tom Paine, and the impact of that element is almost as significant in England as in America.

Adams was founder of the Committees of Correspondence which spread out from Boston in 1772–73 to co-ordinate resistance to the British. In England, many of those not too absorbed in luxury and dissipation—these had been the code words for royalists from the time of Sidney to those of Cartwright—followed his example and set up Corresponding Societies in London and elsewhere, calling among other things for a national convention to press for reform of parliament, and offering a flickering hope of a revolution at home before the War of Independence ended. The London Corresponding Society and the Society for Constitutional Information (formed during the War of Independence) lived on to focus Jacobin opposition in the 1790s, when Paine's next incendiary, *The Rights of Man*, became their bible, and when once again there was widespread expectation of an imminent restoration of English liberties. In 1792, for instance, Joel Barlow, the American poet, delivered to the French Convention an address from the London Society for Constitutional Information, and expressed their hope that after the French example, 'It would not be extraordinary if, in a little while, congratulations were to arrive to a National Convention of England'. To which sentiments Henri Gregoire, as President of the Convention, replied, 'The spirits of Pym, of Hamden, and of Sidney hover above your heads, and *without doubt* the moment is at hand when the French Nation will send its own congratulations to the National Convention of Great Britain'.[1]

Of course, no such moment arrived. English dissent failed to convert itself in 1776, or in 1792, or 1819, or at any time before Chartism reaffirmed Cartwright's principles, into anything approaching a mass revolutionary movement. 1776 is, nevertheless, a crucial component in the rise of English Romanticism, especially in the mythic utterances of William Blake, in whose *America* one sees, as in the prose tracts of the American revolution, the trace of such figures as Algernon Sidney and Obadiah Hulme, blended with the American voices of Ezra Stiles and Joel Barlow. Romanticism, frequently viewed as an internal compensation for the human failure of the French revolution, is quite as much a response to the different failures of the American revolution—its partial failure, in some respects, to *be* a revolution, and its more lamentable failure, from an English standpoint, to bridge the Atlantic. The loss of America reverberates in the work of Burke, Price, Cartwright, Southey, Byron, Shelley, in different ways, but for all of them, given their own investment in realising the ideals of the

---

[1] *Reimpression de l'Ancien Moniteur depuis la reunion de Etats-Generaux jusqu'au Consulat, Mai 1789–Novembre 1799*, 31 vols. (Paris: 1840–7), xiv, 594, cited in Nicholas Roe, *Coleridge and Wordsworth: The Radical Years* (Oxford: Clarendon, 1988), 82. My emphasis.

seventeenth-century Commonwealth, it is a colossal amputation.

It is therefore a form of poetic justice that when the generation of Emerson, Hawthorne, Melville, Whitman, began to suspect that 1776 had been less a revolution than (in Whitman's phrase) a 'great strike', some of the primary constituents of the literary response to that disillusionment—a delayed variation upon the literary awakening occasioned in England by the loss of America—should have been drawn from the literary revolution effected in its stead by Blake, Wordsworth and Shelley. By then, of course, there had been ample time for a certain scepticism to have set in, in America, about what exactly 1776 had been about and what had become of this new kind of man and nation. One abolitionist work of 1840 expressed such scepticism in peculiarly rancid terms. The author of *Despotism in America* analyses America at the time of independence as a union of slave-owning aristocratic despotisms 'of the sternest and most odious kind' in Virginia and Carolina; land-owning oligarchies in New York, New Jersey, and Pennsylvania, where the masters lorded it over rude and ignorant yeomanries; and the New England clerisies of New England, where clergymen and lawyers dominated their simple fellows until democratic ideas from the South (in the person of Jefferson) gained favour. But as the anonymous author points out, 'The democracy which [Jefferson] preached at home was democracy among the aristocrats; and the perfect equality of all the members of the privileged order, has ever been a popular doctrine of all aristocracies.'[1] Only because Jefferson fomented greater democracy in other states than he practised at home, had America progressed.

In 1836, the year of Emerson's *Nature*, and four years before *Despotism in America*, Congress had passed a gagging act, to prohibit further divisive discussion of papers relating to slavery. By the time of *Walden*, *Moby-Dick* and *Song of Myself*, the American writer was likely to find himself in the position of Wordsworth in 1793, an unpatriotic 'patriot'. The twin failures of the 'Revolution', its failure to discourage oligarchy and its enshrinement of slavery, had become both institutionalised and endemic: as Harriet Martineau, once an

---

1 *Despotism in America; or An Inquiry into the Nature and Results of the Slaveholding System in the United States* (Boston:Whipple and Damrell, 1840), 16.

enthusiast, complained, 'Idolatry of the Union is one chief cause of the apparent pusillanimity and complicity in guilt; and Mammon-worship is another'.[1] Some eighty percent of American wealth was in the hands of five percent of the population (as against 70% in 2010). A dispossessed underclass, reminiscent of the slave population of earlier 'republics' was rapidly developing. A land-hungry imperial state had engorged itself on Louisiana, Texas, and Oregon. Systematic expropriation of the indigenous population had become identified by Jacksonian democracy as 'true philanthropy', and the slave states had multiplied. The historic moment in which Jefferson's administration gave tacit consent to Napoleon's snuffing out of the liberties symbolised by Toussaint L'Ouverture had become all too symbolic. In numerous ways, the disenchantments of Blake, Wordsworth, Coleridge and Shelley—disenchantments which gave rise to the most passionate epoch in English art—were being revived in a new world where the old Adam was newly rampant.

---

[1] *A History of the American Compromises* (London: John Chapman, 1856), 32. Walt Whitman had to work through the first of these for himself.

Chapter 2:

Romantic Americas

> Everything in this wilderness of woods being totally different from an old world, almost worn out ... the settlers reason, not from what they hear, but from what they see and feel. They move not but as Nature calls forth their activity ... and take the direction of their courses by that line only, where Truth and Nature lead hand in hand.
>
> —Thomas Pownall, *A Memorial, most humbly addressed to the Sovereigns of Europe*, 1780

1. BLAKE'S AMERICA

Whether or not Blake's preoccupation with severed emanations stems from what he treats in *America: a Prophecy* as 'the American War', he was intellectually rooted in both English and American accounts of ancient English liberties and their corruptions. His work at around the time of French revolutionary terror, when it would have been natural enough to reflect upon what the American moment had *really* meant, is impregnated with the discourses of Richard Price and Tom Paine and Benjamin Franklin and Joel Barlow, as one might expect. Figurative echoes, at least, suggest that he was also drawing on Algernon Sidney, and a variety of more obscure figures whose names have occurred in the previous chapter, such as Obadiah Hulme and Thomas Pownall and Ezra Stiles.

A lengthy discussion of the laminations within Blake's own revolutionary discourse would lead me away from the purpose of this chapter, which is first to delineate some English Romantic images of America, and next to trace the lineaments of an American Romanticism contemporaneous with the outbreak of English Romanticism. But the kinds of material treated in chapter 1 suggest lengthier genealogies for some of Blake's tropes than might be apparent. When Blake cautions his readers to 'expect poison from standing water' John Cartwright's sense that English legislative authority is poisoned at its source perhaps combines with Obadiah Hulme's more elaboration figuration concerning the efficacy of annual elections: 'As standing water soon stinks, and a running stream throws out all impurities, so a standing house of commons will ever be a standing pool of corruption; but an annual current, through that house, will restore it to its pristine purity, and preserve it incorrupt for ever'. Blake's implied deconstruction of peace as oppression in 'The Human Abstract' certainly stems, through whatever indirections, from that well of republicanism, Algernon Sidney: 'It is ill that men should kill one another in seditions, tumults and wars; but it is worst, to bring nations to such misery, weakness, and baseness, as to have neither strength nor courage to contend for any thing ... to give the name of peace to desolation' until at last 'every rascally collector of taxes extorts, without fear, from every man, that which should be the nourishment of his family.[1]

Blake's seeming idiosyncratic conviction that all action stemming from impulse is virtue, and that apparent actions which harm another are not action but 'hindrance' (a version of Sartre's optimistic 'kingdom of ends') may well have the same pellucid source. Sidney writes: 'reason injoins every man not to arrogate to himself more than he allows to others, not to retain that liberty which will prove hurtful to him; nor to expect that others will suffer themselves to be restrained, while he, to their prejudice, remains in the exercise of that freedom which nature allows'. Those famous 'mind-forged manacles' in 'London', associated as they are with charters and corporations,

---

[1] Cartwright, *Take Your Choice!* 2nd edn. (London: 1777), 229; Hulme, *Historical Essay*, 149; Algernon Sidney, *Discourses on Government*, 146, 147.

certainly have something in them of Paine's *The Rights of Man*, but perhaps something more *specifically* aligned with Thomas Pownall's sense of the relative liberty of America in matters of craft and work: let us, Pownall counsels, 'abolish all those useless *bonds* of slavery, which operate in corporations and corporation-laws; which fix down the activity of a human being, as if it were a plant, to a local vegetable life, where its real powers are *fettered* and locked up, which repell all equality and competition'. Similarly, Blake's curiously mythological representation of personages in the American War, while characteristic of his later proceedings, may not be unconnected with the vivid scriptural imagination of Ezra Stiles. In Stiles's election address of 1783, George Washington appears not surprisingly as the American Joshua, divinely formed by a peculiar influence of the Sovereign of the Universe, and as one whose name perfumes the universe; a similar transformation befalls those lesser personages, Hancock, Greene & Co, in whose doings Blake manifests a surprisingly similar interest. Was it to Stiles's vision of the future, as transformed by America, rather than to Barlow's rather cooler one, that Blake's imagination first warmed? Stiles, anyway, prophesies to his Harvard congregation that the knowledge of human potential 'being here digested and carried to the highest perfection, may reblaze back from *America* to *Europe*, *Asia* and *Africa*, and illumine the world with TRUTH and LIBERTY'.[1] Blake's transcontinental odyssey follows the same apocalyptic map.

America: a Prophecy, engraved in 1793, ten years after the peace which occasioned Stiles's euphoric celebrations, and at the start of a European war, has been read in a bewildering variety of ways. Its proximity to *The Marriage of Heaven and Hell* and to *The French Revolution* suggests that it should be read as the product of Blake's most optimistic period, a suggestion supported by the engraving and colouring of some of Blake's most energetic plates. In broad terms, S. Foster Damon and Harold Bloom agree on its celebration of the American revolution as 'the outward and visible sign of the

---

1 Sidney, 98; Thomas Pownall, *A Memorial to the Sovereigns of Europe*, 106; Ezra Stiles, *The United States Elevated to Glory and Honor* (New Haven, CT: 1783), 62, 89.

Millennium, the first proof that mankind was, after all, indomitable'.[1] Northrop Frye strikes this note from time to time, seeing the work as celebrating the victory of a Promethean Titan over repressive conventions. But his argument is careful to suggest that Orc, the revolutionary principle, is revolutionary in both senses. He is partly, perhaps dominantly, in *America*, the titanic rebel, but he is also Blake's Adonis, 'the dying and reviving God', and already represents the pessimistic thought that social tyranny being endemic, requires 'periodic overthrow'.[2] This gloomier cyclical implication is developed in David Erdman's '*America*: New Expanses', a reading much more open to the barren designs of the final plates of the poem in which the signs of renewal are limited to miniscule figures surrounding the earthbound figure of America.[3]

The implication that despite the promise of renewal in the early plates, America remains isolated and absorbed in material cares is developed in Minna Doskow's 'William Blake's *America*: the Story of a Revolution Betrayed.' Doskow argues that the poem reflects 'the isolationist policies ... enunciated in Washington's first inaugural address, and the limited social aims of the revolution itself.'[4] Consequently the glimpses of revolutionary possibility, which account for the vibrancy of the work, belong to the realm of dream rather than to that of historical actualisation (Doskow, 181). James McCord shares this disenchanted reading: in place of an apocalyptic cleansing the poem emphasises that revolution 'is by nature cyclic not apocalyptic'. In any case, Blake's draughtsmanship (like his draft title) leans towards The American War, rather than the American Revolution as his presiding image.[5] This may well be, as Erdman

---

1 S. Foster Damon, *William Blake* (1924; reprint, Gloucester, MA: Peter Smith, 1958), 110, and Harold Bloom, *Blake's Apocalypse* (Garden City, NY: Doubleday, 1963), 129.

2 Northrop Frye, *Fearful Symmetry* (1947: repr. Boston, MA: Beacon Press, 1962), 219, 207.

3 '*America*: New Expanses', in *Blake's Visionary Forms Dramatic*, ed. David V Erdman and John E Grant (Princeton, NJ: Princeton University Press, 1970), 92–114, 104.

4 Minna Doskow, 'William Blake's *America*: the Story of a Revolution Betrayed', *Blake Studies*, 8:2 (1979) 176–86, 184.

5 James McCord, 'West of Atlantis: William Blake's Unromantic View of the

has pointed out, because his focus in 1793 is in fact on England rather than on America: for Blake's generation the ultimate sadness of the American War was not merely that England fought against liberty, but that 'it ended with tyranny still enthroned in Britain and the rest of Europe' (Erdman, 99). This would certainly be sufficient to account for the gloom of the last five plates, and to explain why the only optimistic images are those situated West of Atlantis. These Western plates affirm John Adams's germinal metaphor, turning the world upside down: 'Light spreads from the day-spring in the *West*; and may it shine more and more until the perfect day'.[1]

It is not all gloom. As Stephen Behrendt argues, the American Revolution, viewed merely as the overthrow of a colonial regime and a disgrace for George III, remained for Blake a 'paradigm' of the overthrow of outmoded models of 'patriarchal' tyranny.[2] Nonetheless, Blake's mood in 1793 seems close to that of Richard Price in 1785, as one would expect. Few Englishmen were closer to the American colonists than Price, who engaged in frequent correspondence before and after 1776 with such figures as Charles Chauncy, John Winthrop, James Bowdoin, John Adams, Thomas Jefferson, Benjamin Rush, and 'My dear Friend' Benjamin Franklin. In 1778 Congress had offered him American citizenship and a role in regulating the finances of the new republic. Now, while reaffirming that 'the independence of the English colonies in America is one of the steps ordained by Providence to introduce these times'—the apocalyptic times that is, when in the words of Isaiah 'nation shall no more lift up a sword against nation'—Price nonetheless finds himself 'mortified more than I can express by accounts which have led me to fear that that I have ... deceived myself with visionary expectations'.[3] The accounts which have distressed him concern the still

American war', *Centennial Review* 30:3 (1986) 383-99, 390, 392-5.
 1 I cite this letter of Dec 18, 1782, from Ezra Stiles, 90.
 2 Stephen C Behrendt, '"This Accursed Family": Blake's *America* and the American Revolution', *The Eighteenth Century* 27:1 (1986) 26–51, cites Wordsworth's remark in his *Concerning the Convention of Cintra*: 'In the course of the last thirty years we have seen *two wars waged against liberty*—the American war, and the war against the French people in the early stages of their Revolution', 27.
 3 Richard Price, *Observations on the Importance of the American Revolution*,

manacled portion of America's population.

A 'Song of Liberty', final plate of *The Marriage of Heaven and Hell*, makes it clear that whether or not 1776 saw a genuine revolution, it did unambiguously inaugurate an apocalyptic overthrow of oppressive regimes throughout Europe: the Bastille, the Inquisition and the Papal State tremble alongside the Hanoverian dynasty in this ecstatic draft. But when Blake came to treat the American theme more fully, his verbatim transposition of so many lines and images and plot motifs from the shorter prospectus for a 'bible of hell' into a mythological account of the American War does draw attention to some textual half-heartedness alongside the iconographic ambivalence of the later poem.

The remarkable frontispiece to *America: a Prophecy* shows the walls of the city breached, but Orc still bound, the shadowy daughter of Urthona still lamenting and the children orphaned. It overshadows the vibrant plates which make up the first half of the poem and makes the narrative stance of the poem ironic, indicating that the vision of liberation will *remain a vision* at the end of the 'prophecy'. Given the fact that the first decade of American liberty was dominated by legal minds devising constitutional restraints, to ensure that the right people came out on top, the text-focused elders occupying the space between AMERICA and PROPHECY on the title page may well account for the desperation of the woman's attempts to breathe life into the fallen warrior at the foot of the page.[1]

Contrariwise, the 'Preludium', and the opening plates of the Prophecy offer visionary figures rising from states of manacled woe (Plate 1) to states of ascendancy (Plates 2, 3). Orc rises titanically from earthen roots in Plate 2, and flies above birds of paradise in Plate

---

in Bernard Peach, *Richard Price and the Ethical Foundations of the American Revolution*, 184, 214. Compare Harriet Martineau: 'We supposed the American character and policy to be represented by the chiefs of the revolution, and their declaration of Independence and republican constitution; and now we find ourselves mistaken in our supposition.' *Autobiography* (1855), 3rd edn., 2 vols. (London: Smith, Elder, 1877), 2: 456.

1 All references are to *'America: A Prophecy' and 'Europe: A Prophecy'* (NY: Dover, 1983), while I have, like everyone, made use of David Erdman's commentaries in *The Illuminated Blake* (London: Oxford University Press, 1975).

3, while textually the 'warlike men', 'Washington, Franklin, Paine & Warren, Gates, Hancock & Green' meet on the blood-stained coast to outface the Guardian Prince of Albion. Spiritually, the dragon-angel form of George III is reduced to a trembling bare-forked animal (Plate 4), and hurled into the vortex (like the Simoniac Pope alluded to in the 'Song of Liberty') between the scales and the sword of justice on plate 5, by a figure who seems uncannily prescient of Shelley's Hercules casting out the doomed Jupiter in *Prometheus Unbound*.

The problem is that the falling monarch in Plate 5 mirrors all-too-closely the ascending rebel of Plate 2, just as the reclining Urizen in plate 8 mirrors the Orc of Plate 10. Moreover, the scaly dragon on Plate 4 suggests a petrific and wrathful stage of the lithe and playful serpent on plate 11, while the swan-borne Paul Revere in Plate 11 is not merely looking the wrong way, but already sports a coiffure identical to that of the aged man in plate 12 who is meekly entering the darkness from which Orc has so lately emerged. Optimism may read this aged man as entering the tomb to be reborn, but cyclicity and interchangeability are signalled everywhere, and the least compromised signs of life and energy (plates 14–15) are still underground. To reinforce these disturbing implications, text and image are cacophonously out of sync: the Arcadian scene imaged so tantalisingly in Plate 7 illustrates only the concluding echo of Isaiah on plate 6 ('For Empire is no more, and now the Lion & Wolf shall cease'; the same text which Price had appealed to in 1785 in praying that 'nation shall no more lift up a sword against nation'). Its text, however, introduces the wrathful monarch, whose image is delayed until Plate 8, where it not only accompanies a speech by Orc, but assumes Orc's earlier stance. These curious 'dissolves' appear to prophesy that Orc shall become Urizen; or perhaps does become Urizen in the moment of pronouncing the end of time.

Joel Barlow's version of events, from which Blake probably drew his basic plot and imagery of Albion's war on the colonies, had represented matters somewhat more simply. In *The Vision of Columbus: A Poem in Nine Books* Columbus, rather like Milton's Adam, is granted a vision of the future of America, from the arrival of 'the noble Baltimore' and 'heaven-taught Penn' to the onslaught of an irascible George III on his turbulent children. Urizen's dark clouds rise first in this passage of Barlow:

> When, borne on eastern winds, dark vapours rise,
> And sail and lengthen round the western skies,
> Veil all the vision from his anxious sight,
> And wrap the climes in universal night.
>
> When Albion's prince, that swayed the happy land,
> Shall stretch, to lawless rule, the sovereign hand;
> To bind in slavery's chains the peaceful host,
> Their rights unguarded, and their charters lost.[1]

The cherished charters, that is, of the colonies.

All is not lost, however. Thanks to the solidarity of the colonies in resisting tyranny, the plagues visited upon them by the wrathful Prince of Albion recoil upon England in Blake's last three plates. Otherwise,

> Then had America been lost, o'erwhelmed by the Atlantic,
> And Earth had lost another portion of the infinite (Plate 14).

Momently, even, the revolutionary warmth reaches the matrons of the metropolitan capital:

> The doors of marriage are open, and the Priests in rustling scales
> Rush into reptile coverts, hiding from the fires of Orc,
> That play around the golden roofs in wreaths of fierce desire,
> Leaving the females naked and glowing with the lusts of youth.
> For the female spirits of the dead pining in bonds of religion
> Run from their fetters reddening, & in long drawn arches sitting
> They feel the nerves of youth renew, and desires of ancient times

---

1 *The Vision of Columbus: A Poem in Nine Books* (Hartford, New England and London: 1787), 148. Fiona Robertson reads Barlow and some British Columbiads, by William Bowles, Robert Southey, and Samuel Rogers in 'British Romantic Columbiads', *Symbiosis* 2:1 (April, 1998), 1–23.

Over their pale limbs *as a vine when the tender grape appears.*
(Plate 15, my italics)

This penultimate plate's allusion to the staple imagery of the *Song of Solomon* echoes that of the dark virgin in Plate 2 of the Preludium ('I know thee, I have found thee, *and I will not let thee go*', an allusion noted by Michael Ferber).[1] It also reminds that revolution for Blake is both universal and all-encompassing. The 'stern Americans,' though Blake refrains from depicting them in powdered wigs and military costume or inhabiting Greek temples as a tribute from one slave-owning democracy to another, seem as unready as Urizen himself for the sensuous, imaginative and visionary rebirth that their Declaration of Independence implies. The poem thus ends with prophecy rather than enactment: Urizenic repression reasserts itself in pouring forth its stored snows,

> Hiding the Demon red with clouds & cold mists from the earth
> Till Angels & weak men twelve years should govern o'er the strong;
> And then their end should come, when France receiv'd the demons light. (Plate 16)

Textually the poem ends in a promise that France, Spain and Italy will, as in the 'Song of Liberty', be unable to 'shut the five gates of their law built heaven' as the fires of Orc burn 'round the heavens, & round the abodes of men'. In a rare concert of text and design, a newly hatched serpent makes its way Eastwards across the bottom of the final plate, announcing 'Finis' (in some copies; implying perhaps the end of Urizen, as well as the poem) amid the opening rose-buds which constitute the first floral tribute in the poem.

Interpretations of the poem diverge upon the name and nature of Orc, and also upon the name and nature and conduct of the 'shadowy daughter of Urthona', embraced, raped, impregnated by Orc in

---

[1] Michael Ferber in 'Blake's America and the Birth of Revolution', in *History and Myth: Essays on English Romantic Literature*, edited by Stephen C. Behrendt (Detroit: Wayne State University Press, 1990) 73–99, 87.

Plate 1 of the *Preludium*. 'Crowned with a helmet and dark hair' this 'nameless female' and 'dark virgin' must be called America, and her 'quiver with its burning stores' suggests an Indian daughter of Britannia. Orc, at least, appears to suppose that her 'father' is Urizen or Albion, who 'rivets my tenfold chains': he may be mindful of those native American nations which supported their English 'father' in 1776. Against the proposition that the shadowy female embodies white America, whose selfish proclamation of liberty in one country arouses Blake's suspicions, Julia M Wright, in a brief and richly suggestive essay of 1992, has suggested that she is instead native America. Her rape by 'the champion of the oppressed' manifests Blake's awareness—shared of course with Tucker, Sharp and Price—that 'the revolutionaries were ... in the ideologically contradictory position of trying to conquer one group while crying for liberty from another'; that 'Orc's colonists liberate a nation from imperial rule, but it is a nation that they have themselves "seiz'd"'.[1]

In Blake's political cosmology whatever results in the erection of a warlike state, devoted to its own hegemony, is at war with the spirit of universal revolution. His own text indicates in the praise it offers to the unison of the colonies, and its discontent with a sundered Atlantic community, that his political vision was that of Richard Price and Joseph Priestley: liberty and nationhood are incompatible. The apocalyptic objective, as it recurs throughout Blake's oeuvre, is of course the great harvest and vintage of the nations, a united states of the world, a condition for which the newly united states of Britain's former colonies provide a model, not an alternative. The secession, as an instance of the further division of fallen humanity mythologised in *The First Book of Urizen*, can only be seen as marking an indefinite postponement of Albion's resurrection.

Blake's text, while offering in Plate 6 what many have routinely referred to as 'a visionary paraphrase of the declaration of independence', is exceedingly pointed in that paraphrase. The fact that Orc has been in waiting for fourteen suns at the start of the poem has been associated with his emergence into puberty, and with the fact that

---

[1] Julia M. Wright, '"Empire is no More': Odin and Orc in America', *Blake: An Illustrated Quarterly* 26:1 (1992), 26–29, 28.

fourteen years have passed between Rousseau's *The Social Contract* (1762)—universally known to have affirmed that 'Man was born free, and he is everywhere in chains'—and Jefferson's declaration of 'self-evident' truths (1776).

> Let the slave grinding at the mill, run out into the field:
> Let him look up into the heavens & laugh in the bright air;
> Let the inchained soul shut up in darkness and in sighing,
> Whose face has never seen a smile in thirty weary years,
> Rise and look out, his chains are loose, his dungeon doors
>   are open.
> And let his wife and children return from the oppressors
>   scourge;
> They look behind at every step & *believe it is a dream...*

The effect, in a poem of 1793, is to counterpoint the loosened fetters of the Bastille and the swelling choruses of Beethoven's *Fidelio* with the continued manacles of Virginia.

Was it 'a dream'? Price had been asking himself the same question in 1785. Thanking Jefferson for sending him his *Notes on Virginia* Price comments on reports of the unfriendly reception in Virginia of his own *Observations on the Importance of the American Revolution*.

> Should such a disposition prevail in the other united states, I shall have reason to fear that I have made myself ridiculous by speaking of the American Revolution in the manner I have done; it will appear that the people who have been struggling so earnestly to save themselves from slavery are very ready to enslave others; the friends of liberty and humanity in Europe will be mortified, and an event which had raised their hopes will prove only an introduction to a new scene of aristocratic tyranny and human debasement.[1]

To Benjamin Rush, three weeks later, Price writes that he has not given up his hope 'that the American Revolution will prove an introduction to a better state of human affairs and that in time the United States *will* become those seats of liberty, peace, and virtue which the enlightened

---

1 July 2, 1785. In Peach, *Richard Price and the Ethical Foundations of the American Revolution*, 330–31

and liberal part of Europe are ardently willing to see them'. Either way, it seems, America has become an introduction rather than the book.[1]

2. WHIG AMERICAS

A potent paradigm it remained, however. Coleridge, in *Religious Musings* and his sonnet 'On the Prospect of Establishing a Pantisocracy in America', Byron, in 'The Age of Bronze', *Childe Harold* and *Don Juan*, Mrs Barbauld in *Eighteen Hundred and Eleven*, Southey and Shelley all contributed to the mythologising of America as the remaining home of liberty, from which reanimation might be expected to emerge. As might be expected, Mary Shelley alone of the Shelley coterie remained resistant to the mythos.[2] For whatever reasons, neither Price nor Blake seems to have been under any illusion that emigration offered the solution to anything. Yet the year after *America*, Robert Southey, Samuel Taylor Coleridge, their fiancées, the fiery James Watt the younger, and twenty other young idealists were well advanced in preparations to try out what Coleridge called an 'experiment of human perfectibility on the banks of the Susquehanna.'[3] Even in 1801 Coleridge told Poole that he was still attracted to the idea of settling near Priestley, if he could encourage Wordsworth to go with him. 'It fills me with indignation to hear the croaking accounts which the English Emigrants send home of America', a land where 'there is no poverty but as a consequence of absolute Idleness' whereas in England 'the laborious poor are dying with Grass in their bellies' (To Thomas Poole, 23 March 1801).

In 1796 Coleridge had written of America in mythic terms in *Religious Musings*. In these lines he gives verbal expression to

---

1 Peach, 332. Barlow sees Price's Universal Government (an extensive prose note credits Price's *Observations*) as the true end of what has started in America.

2 Fiona Stafford, 'Lodore: a tale of the Present Time?' (*Romanticism* 3:2 (1997), 209–19) argues that in contradistinction to her friends Frances Wright and Edward Trelawny (who was in Mary Shelley's words 'America-mad'), Shelley herself was influenced by a 'growing consciousness of social inequality in the United States'.

3 *Collected Letters of Samuel Taylor Coleridge*, ed. Earl Leslie Griggs. 6 vols (Oxford 1956), 1: 126.

Blake's lightning image, musing on:

> That blest triumph, when the PATRIOT SAGE
> Call'd the red lightnings from th'oer-rushing cloud
> And dashed the beauteous Terrors on the earth
> Smiling majestic.[1]

Byron, too, was inspired to mythologise the ever-practical Franklin in 'The Age of Bronze' invoking 'stoic Franklin's energetic shade, / Robed in the lightnings which his hand allayed' along with 'Washington, the tyrant-tamer', as inspirational symbols for 'outworn Europe'. Franklin-worship seems to have been a serious inducement to emigration.

The seriousness of the Pantisocracy project, and of Coleridge's expectations that the new utopians, inspired by Brissot, Gilbert Imlay and Thomas Cooper, would link up with Franklin's disciple Joseph Priestley as part of a continuing brain drain to the New World, has been treated by Stuart Andrews and by Ian Wylie and others.[2] As Stuart Andrews points out, the three authors whose works on America inspired Coleridge and his associates were themselves in personal contact:'When Captain Gilbert Imlay arrived in Paris in January 1793—the month of Louis XVI's execution—he was carrying a letter of introduction from Thomas Cooper to Jean-Pierre Brissot'.[3] In 1792 Cooper and the young James Watt had marched together 'in a Jacobin procession, the one carrying a bust of Algernon Sidney, the other a British flag'. They reported back to the Manchester Constitutional Society that the British flag 'united and entwined with the three-coloured flag of France and the thirteen stripes of the brave Americans, is suspended from the roof of every patriotic society in

---

1 Coleridge, *Poems*, ed. John Beer (Dent, 1974), 71, lines 247–50.
2 See Ian Wylie, 'Coleridge and the Lunaticks', in *The Coleridge Connection*, edited by Richard Gravil and Molly Lefebure (Basingstoke: Macmillan, 1990), 25–40, and Stuart Andrews, 'Fellow Pantisocrats: Brissot, Cooper and Imlay', *Symbiosis* 1:1 (1997), 35–47.
3 For their works see Gilbert Imlay, *A Topographical Description of the Western Territory of North America* (London 1792); Thomas Cooper, *Some Information respecting America* (London 1794) and J-P. Brissot de Warville *New Travels in the United States of America* (London 1792).

France' (Andrews, 36.)

What writers from Richard Price to Fanny Wright and the *Edinburgh Review* asked for in their Whig reading of the mission of America, Shelley expressed symbolically in what has emerged in recent years, since Dr Leavis had his wicked way with it, as one of the very greatest of lyric poems, his 'Ode to the West Wind'. Now in the winter of our discontent, with repression re-established in every land of Europe, there is only one place to look. Shelley's wild west wind, destroyer and preserver, sweeping across the Atlantic, cleaving the Atlantic's level powers as if to reveal the long-lost Atlantis still barred out in Blake's poem, building the storm-clouds from which Franklin's lightning will again discharge its accumulated force, shattering the reflections of Imperial villas in the Bay of Baiae, charioting the seeds to their wintry beds, where they await the apocalyptic trump of renewal, blowing up the faint sparks of liberty, promising the long-awaited conflagration, is the most eloquent expression of liberal Europe's faith in its own American dream. In the same year as the 'Ode to the West Wind' Shelley set out in *A Philosophical View of Reform* perhaps the most eloquent exposition of what America was to the English left of that date. It was to Shelley, as it was to the leader writers of the *Edinburgh Review* (whose parallel 'reading' of America I shall glance at in chapter 3) 'the victorious example ... of a highly civilized community administered according to republican forms'.

> It has no king; that is, it has no officer to whom wealth and from whom corruption flows. It has no hereditary oligarchy; that is, it acknowledges no order of men privileged to cheat and insult the rest of the members of the state and who inherit a right of legislating and judging which the principles of human nature compel them to exercise to their own profit and to the detriment of those not included within their peculiar class. It has no established church; that is, it has no system of opinions respecting the abstrusest questions which can be topics of human thought founded in an age of error and fanaticism and opposed by law to all other opinions....[1]

---

[1] *Shelley's Prose*, ed. David Lee Clark (London: Fourth Estate, 1988), 234.

Also, though far from a state of ideal excellence in this respect, 'it has no false representation, whose consequences are captivity, confiscation, infamy and ruin, but a true representation'. It is, in short, the successful embodiment of the state of enlightened opinion that existed throughout Europe at the time of its 'successful rebellion', but which, in Europe, has not yet resulted in a corresponding state of institutions.

That Shelley's 'Ode to the West Wind' should be contemporaneous with James Kirk Paulding's *The Backwoodsman* is perhaps something which it would be more tactful not to mention, if it were not that the conjunction epitomises the complex and reciprocal nature of the transatlantic time-lag in 1818–20. To claim that a juxtaposition of Shelley and Paulding represents the comparative states of British and American poetry in 1818/19 would be grossly unfair. A decapitated Romanticism—one without Blake, Wordsworth, Coleridge, Shelley, Keats—would strike no-one as markedly in advance of Dwight, Barlow and Paulding. Compare Paulding with the epic productions of Cottle, Southey, Thelwall, Campbell and Rogers, or the effusions of Mary Tighe, and one understands why his work was received with something more than courtesy in the English reviews which were scorning Shelley. In a contest between Freneau, Halleck and Bryant for the new world and More, Southey and Campbell for the old, one would very probably go for the finesse and irony of the Americans. But American literary culture in 1819 was in no condition to offer Europe the renovation it sought. Before it could do so it would first have to make up for over a century of poetic somnolence, since Anne Bradstreet wrote the last poetry which bears comparison with the *best* of contemporary work in England.

Joel Barlow did his best to celebrate signs of cultural vitality in his *Vision of Columbus*, but the best example of American art he could come up with was Benjamin West, and the manner of his celebration is sufficiently diagnostic of the problem:

> See West with glowing life the canvas warms;
> His sovereign hand creates impassioned forms
> Spurns the cold critic rules, to seize the heart,

And boldly bursts the former bounds of Art.[1]

Not even the single reversed foot, to energise 'spurns', does much to loosen the iambic manacles. A generation later, though one would hardly suspect it, this is Paulding:

> Neglected Muse! of this our western clime,
> How long in servile, imitative rhyme,
> Wilt thou thy stifled energies impart,
> And miss the path that leads to every heart?
> How long repress the brave decisive flight,
> Warm'd by thy native fires, led by thy native light?
> Thrice happy he who first shall strike the lyre,
> With homebred feeling, and with homebred fire.[2]

To call this Pope in deerskins would malign Pope, whose lines never broke with such artless monotony. The final 'servile imitative rhyme' recalls Whitehead's catalectic tetrameters in 'Verses to the People of England' half a century earlier:

> But when War's tremendous roar
> Shakes the isle from Shore to Shore,
> Every Bard of purer fire
> Tyrteaus-like should grasp the lyre[3]

Paulding at his best is quite capable of the kind of verse that stirred the sentimental reader of the eighteenth-century Celtic revival. He knows what he is supposed to feel, and indeed offers a sort of romantic manifesto in his 'Nature and Art: a Fable', but despite the facility of Freneau and Bryant, who are already writing with a sense of what a nineteenth century poet is supposed to do, has no idea how to say it:

> 'Tis Nature, and 'tis she alone
> That gives the bright celestial zone,
> Which virgin Venus blushing wore,
> When first she touch'd gay Cyprus' shore;

---

1 Cited from the Chadwyck-Healey *American Poetry Full-Text Database*.
2 *The Backwoodsman* (Philadelphia: M.Thomas, 1818), 8.
3 *Verses to the People of England* (London: R. & J. Dodsley, 1758).

> And ere she sought her destin'd skies
> Charm'd every wondering gazer's eyes.
> (*The Backwoodsman*, 193)

Does nature do this? Really? In 1819? And (of all places) *in America?*

According to Mrs Barbauld, of course, that is exactly what he should be doing. The work of a woman of sixty-eight, Barbauld's *Eighteen Hundred and Eleven* looked back to her own 'thirties in recycling the (then) current theme of America's future as the only receptacle of England's fading glory. It looks back also to the poetics of that date: the 'electric life' which Shelley detected in works of his great contemporaries is not to be found. Oddly, for an erstwhile associate of Joseph Priestley and George Dyer, Barbauld seems unable to imagine that the American future will or can be any different from England's past. Her imperial and deeply patronising vision is one of endless repetition. Addressing her native country she declares:

> Nations beyond the Appalachian hills
> Thy hand has planted and thy spirit fills;
> *Soon as their gradual progress shall impart*
> *The finer sense of morals and of art,*
> *Thy stores of knowledge the new states shall know,*
> *And think thy thoughts, and with thy fancy glow;*
> Thy Lockes, thy Paleys shall instruct their youth,
> Thy leading star direct their search for truth;
> Beneath the spreading Platan's tent-like shade,
> Or by Missouri's rushing waters laid,
> 'Old father Thames' shall be the poet's theme,
> Of Hagley's woods the enamoured virgin dream,
> And Milton's tones the raptured ear enthrall,
> Mixed with the roar of Niagara's fall;
> In Thomson's glass the ingenuous youth shall learn
> A fairer face of nature to discern. (my emphases)[1]

One hardly knows whether to wonder more at recent critical endeavours to recuperate such poor stuff, by people seemingly

---

1 *Eighteen Hundred and Eleven* (London: Joseph Johnson, 1818), cited from Duncan Wu, *Romantic Women Poets* (Oxford: Blackwell, 1997), 12.

unaware how stale her arguments are, or at the fact that a protégé of Priestley could decline into such myopia. Apart from the stumble over 'Niagara' (pronounced Níagára perhaps?) the verse proceeds as somnolently as one would expect from a compeer of Hannah More, with almost unvaried iambs breaking routinely after the fourth, fifth or sixth syllable, without a single original image, developing its deeply dispiriting vision of an America slowly developing towards moral sense, aspiring to the learning of the Mother country, and at last, at some future date, aspiring to the sensibility of Thomson. Just how dispiriting the verse is, to anyone with an interest in the life of verse, would take too long to demonstrate. Suffice it to say that of the brilliant arguments and dramatic imagery in the pamphlet wars of the 1770s and 1780s, reviewed in Chapter 1 (Hulme, Pownall, Cartwright, Price, and Burke) there is no trace.[1]

If plodding verse and outdated argument are bad enough, the poem's timing was even worse. 'Bravely, though vainly, [Britain] dares to strive with Fate' Barbauld writes in her fifth line of the peninsular war. In January and March 1812, either side of the publication of her poem in February, Sir Arthur Wellesley and his allies took Ciudad Rodrigo and Badajoz, inaugurating a series of allied victories that would culminate in Waterloo and the beginning of what might be termed the British century. A few hundred veterans from those battles would burn Washington in 1814, in the expansionist war that America declared in June 1812, hoping to annex Canada while Britain was engaged in liberating Europe. (The primary result of this shabby affair was to stimulate Canadian nationhood).[2] But Barbauld can hardly be blamed for knowing none of that. Or even, arguably, for writing in this antique manner twelve years after Wordsworth's

---

1 Current interest in the writings of Barbauld, More, Paulding and other purveyors of flatulent verse does little to persuade me that the canon is essentially wrong in these cases: Felicia Hemans, Helen Maria Williams and Fitz-Greene Halleck are another matter.

2 For a Canadian view of the War of 1812 see The Reverend John Bethune, *A Sermon preached at Brockville, Upper Canada on the 18th day of June 1816, being a Day of General Thanksgiving to Almighty God for his great goodness in putting an end to the war in which were engaged against France* (Montreal, 1816), 17–19. Available on Google Books.

'Poem upon the Wye' and just eight before Shelley's 'Ode to the West Wind'. Altogether, if she had not had the good fortune to be reviewed by John Wilson Croker, who patronises her almost as much as she patronises America, and does so to the understandable fury of modern readers, this tedious poem would have remained in richly deserved obscurity instead of boring and befuddling innumerable unfortunate students. Barbauld, by the way, was herself *ineffably* patronising in reviewing for the *Monthly Review* the 1808 *Poems* of Felicia Hemans. These were announced as 'the genuine productions of a young lady, written between the age of eight and thirteen years' and Barbauld cannot resist advising the young lady to 'content herself for some years with reading instead of writing' (*Monthly Review*, LX, 1809, 323). At twelve, Hemans wrote two lengthy poems inspired by the peninsular war, *England and Spain*, and *War and Peace*—both of which poems compare exceeding well in point of life and originality with Mrs Barbauld's turgid moralising. But I digress.

One curious effect of America's secession was that English poets from the 1790s onwards had effected an imaginative compensation. They had vigorously colonised American space, jostling aside America's own producers, Barlow, Freneau and Dwight, in such works as James Moore's *The Columbiad* (1798), Southey's *Songs of the American Indians* (1799) and *Madoc* (1805), William Lisle Bowles's *The Spirit of Discovery* (1804), Thomas Campbell's *Gertrude of Wyoming* (1809) and Samuel Rogers's *The Voyage of Columbus* (1812).[1] Through such works, the English and American reading publics became thoroughly conversant with Jefferson's idealisation of Indian character and oratory, with the complex role of native American nations in the French and Indian wars, the War of Independence, and the war of 1812, and—in the more serious works—the ineluctable moral questions posed by British/colonist/native American relations. By the time James Fenimore Cooper took possession of this imaginative territory in the Leatherstocking tales

[1] Freneau and Southey are treated in Astrid Wind, '"Adieu to all": the Dying Indian at the Turn of the Eighteenth Century', *Symbiosis* 2.1 (1998) 39–655; and Thomas Campbell, in the context of political and cultural representations of Indians, by Timothy Fulford in 'Romantic Indians and Colonial Politics: the Case of Thomas Campbell', *Symbiosis* 2.2 (1998) 203–223.

he was addressing in England a nation which had, on the well-known evidence of such authorities as Benjamin Franklin, Cadwallader Colden and Thomas Jefferson, though contested by settler's complaints and parliamentary debates, developed a proto-Cooperian map of native America. On the one hand, honourable, naturally republican Indians whose beliefs and oratory represented a vanishing cultural ideal; on the other hand, remorseless, treacherous, bloodthirsty savages; and in between, romantic individuals capable of blood brothership with the noble variety, and a ruthless state exploiting the savage sort for its own military purposes.

None of this poetic literature, however, whether of British or American manufacture, represents the energies of canonical Romantic writing. The Indian lyrics of Wordsworth and Hemans, like those of Freneau and Bryant are very much livelier, but no reader of these longer artefacts is likely to be 'startled' as Shelley promises readers of the new poetry 'with the electric life which burns within their words' and whatever that 'electric life' consists in did not, it seems travel well. The ironies and symbolic texture of Blake, the imagination-teasing communicative strategies of Wordsworth and Coleridge, the sudden refreshment of blank verse with rhythms and harmonies unheard before, the subtle psychologising which displaced platitudinous moralising, the multiplication of lyric forms and experimental genres, the rampant mythopoeia of Blake, Keats and Shelley found no immediate echo.

In America, in the eighteen-teens-and-twenties, with the exception of William Cullen Bryant and the best of Fitz-Greene Halleck, the literature that should express America—an innovative, consciousness-expanding literature of freedom, spontaneity, natural feeling and democratic aspirations—was still being imported, rather than home-grown. And conservative canons of taste, derived from the Scottish reviews, preferred imitations to originals, for instance in Byron's translation of Wordsworth's poetry of nature into the borrowed thoughts and rhythmic clichés of *Childe Harold*. F. W. P. Greenwood implied as much in the *North American Review* of 1824: the alert reader, he said in one of America's first significant appreciations of Wordsworth, knows that 'however this poet may have been disregarded, he has borne a most important part in giving its character to the poetry of the age; he knows that many of the poets, with whose writings this country is so familiar, have borrowed some of their sweetest minstrelsy from strains which have reached us but rarely and faintly from the mountains of Westmoreland; and he is continually detecting plagiarisms, both in spirit and in letter, made from the volumes of Wordsworth, by those who have joined to depress him.'[1]

3. ROMANTIC AMERICANS

Yet America did share in the genesis of Romantic ideology, and not only by inspiring the English Romantic poets. By Romantic ideology I mean (contra Jerome McGann) a commitment to human liberty, a millennial set of social expectations, a faith in the human imagination, *and* a sense of nature as not merely a storehouse of symbols but an aspect of human being. Since 1776 did little to sever cultural homogeneity, and since Romanticism is in large part the poetic compression of new world ideology, and since Americans of the era were nurtured on precisely the same literary inheritance as their English counterparts and had lived through the same debates, it would be surprising if there were not, in America, numerous instances of Romantic sensibility, contemporaneous with the birth of Romanticism as such.

To make the point, I would nominate four very diverse and little-known Americans as proof of the existence in America of something approaching an indigenous American Romanticism—lacking only the appropriate poetic form—contemporaneous with each phase of Romanticism in England. These are the Massachusetts pastor and Vermont historian, Samuel Williams; the remarkable plagiarist, seducer and adventurer, Gilbert Imlay; the Boston pastor, William Ellery Channing; and that most remarkable of American travellers, Estwick Evans.

Williams I have alluded to in chapter one, as an American who combined the political sentiments of Richard Price with an added, and prescient, sense that Nature could mean something other than

---
1 *North American Review*, 18 (1824): 371.

short-hand for enlightenment ideas. His arguments in *A Discourse on the Love of Our Country* and in *The Natural and Civil History of Vermont* provide one of the era's most remarkable instances of someone other than Wordsworth finding 'in nature and the language of the sense, the nurse, the guide, the guardian of his heart and soul of all his moral being'. Williams's work attributes the independence of the United States to nothing other than nature's education of man.

Gilbert Imlay is a more difficult case, who had much to do with the way European Romanticism developed. He deserves somewhat more than his notoriety as the archetypal confidence-man who swindled Daniel Boone, plagiarised John Filson, and deserted Mary Wollstonecraft.[1] It is something, after all, to have inspired Chateaubriand's *Les Natchez*, provoked Coleridge and Southey to form their Pantisocracy project, and persuaded liberal Europe to take him for 'an unspoiled child of nature, an incarnation of Rousseau's Emile'.[2] Imlay's *Topographical Description of the Western Territory of North America* (London, 1792) has much wider ambitions than its short title suggests, comprising, as the sub-title promises, such matters as 'an accurate statement of the various tribes of Indians that inhabit the frontier country', 'a delineation of the laws and government of the state of Kentucky', and a prophecy of 'the probable rise and grandeur of the American Empire'. Its author presents himself as an emigré from a state of innocence to the realms of artifice, bringing messages of the patriarchal simplicity of the American wilds. In his account, America is an actualisation of Blake's 'Ecchoing Green', where, in the sugar-making season:

> The business of the day being over, the men join the women in the sugar groves where enchantment seems to dwell...; [and] while our rural Nestors ... contemplate the boyish gambols of a growing progeny ... they recount the exploits of their early age, and in their enthusiasm forget that there are such things as

---

[1] James D. Wallace, *Early Cooper and his Audience* (NY: Columbia University Press, 1986), 7.

[2] For a negative view of Imlay see Wallace, 7 and Richard Slotkin, *Regeneration through Violence*. For a more sympathetic view see Stuart Andrews, 37–9.

decrepitude and misery.¹

The laws and government of this land are based 'on the natural and imprescriptable rights of man', for in an enlightened commonwealth 'the genius of freedom is enthroned in the heart of every citizen', in contradistinction to Europe where life is enslaved by 'forms and authorities' and where 'mystery' is reverenced as wisdom (Imlay, 158).

Like a young Orc, casting Jefferson in the role of Urizen, Imlay situates himself well to the left of Jefferson's *Notes on Virginia*, describing Jefferson's doubts about the potential despotism of unicameral government as worthy of Burke, and wondering how Jefferson could possibly compare the government of reason with 'a dark aristocracy which has rivetted upon the minds of their citizens the most diabolical superstition'. The critique of Jefferson is in fact the most impressive aspect of Imlay's work, allowing for his desire to ingratiate himself with his audience and to burnish his own merits at the great man's expense. Referring to the constitutional compromise over slavery he writes: 'We have disgraced the fair face of humanity, and trampled upon the sacred privileges of man, at the very moment that we were exclaiming against the tyranny of your ministry.'² Bogus and self-interested Imlay may be, but he attunes his account admirably to the cultural expectations of the English in Paris (Thomas Cooper and James Watt, Wordsworth, Helen Maria Williams, Mary Wollstonecraft), Brissot and Crèvecoeur of the Gallo-American Society and the *Société des Amis des Noirs*, and a rising generation of emigration-minded poets, including Coleridge and Southey.

Mindful of Imlay's treatment of Wollstonecraft (she was pregnant when he deserted her, though Imlay accorded her some protection by registering her as the wife of an American citizen), and of Wordsworth's friendship with Godwin, at the time of Godwin's *Memoir of Mary Wollstonecraft*, and mindful, too, of Wordsworth's

---

1 Gilbert Imlay, *A Topographical Description of the Western Territory of North America* (London: J Debrett, 1792) 138–9.

2 Imlay contests Jefferson's view of black Americans being ill-formed, defends the poet Phillis Wheatley from Jefferson's negative judgement, and in a coup-de-grace, points out that it is illogical to express a cultural preference for the Indian over the black American, while leaving out of account that the Indian is not enslaved.

long association with Coleridge, one may wonder how much the feckless young officer in Wordsworth's 'Ruth' owes to Imlay. The poem has often been noted to incorporate aspects of Bartram's depiction of American flora and fauna, but the gallant and seductive youth who tells of them has suggestions of Imlay about him:

> There came a Youth from Georgia's shore —
> A military casque he wore,
> With splendid feathers drest;
> He brought them from the Cherokees;
> The feathers nodded in the breeze
> And made a gallant crest.
>
> From Indian blood you deem him sprung:
> Ah no! he spake the English tongue,
> And bare a soldier's name;
> And, when America was free
> From battle and from jeopardy
> He cross the ocean came. (*CWRT* 1: 421–2)[1]

The notion that wild landscape has any necessary connection with virtue is one that Wordsworth is more sceptical about than his reputation suggests. America in Wordworth's poetry is no panacea for human ills, and no guarantee of virtue. Deserted by her Georgian adventurer Ruth finds herself restored by her natal scenes:

> Among the fields she breathed again:
> The master-current of her brain
> Ran permanent and free;

Coleridge's admiration for this poem (he claimed that he would rather have written it than anything of his own) often seems exaggerated: the admiration may be rooted in the awareness that he, if anyone, could read it as a critique of the notion that mere transplantation could achieve what Tom Paine appears to suggest it can—an environment in which human evils cannot live. Coleridge's projected Pantisocracy

---

1 *The Poems of William Wordsworth: Collected Reading Texts from the Cornell Wordsworth*, ed. Jared Curtis, 3 vols (Humanities-Ebooks, 2009–14). Cited hereafter as *CWRT*.

foundered on the discovery that Robert Southey, at least, proposed to take his European class consciousness with him, in the form of servants, thus repeating the original sin of the first colonies in their reliance upon bondsmen. It may well be Coleridge's infatuation, or rather the infatuation of a generation of would-be Pantisocrats, that accounts for Wordsworth's return to the subject in 'The Female Vagrant' and (rather presciently, given the impending boom in emigration literature) in *The Excursion*. The fact that *The Excursion*, published in 1814, reopens the emigration issue a year before the peace provoked a new tide of emigration, might or might not be attributed to Wordsworthian prescience, but it does serve to remind one that throughout the lifetimes of the English Romantics three questions were associated with the American idea: the big Godwinian question whether the American constitution would create a new kind of human being (Godwin himself appears to have given up on that by the time Fenimore Cooper visits him in 1829); the question whether happiness was to be found by transplanting old stock in virgin soil; and the curious psychology of the returned emigrant, or deracination. The careers of William Cobbett and James Fenimore Cooper provide notable instances of characters whose patriotism seems to grow in proportion to their distance from their native land, and whose radicalism is refreshed by repatriation. Wordsworth's 'solitary' serves as an archetype of this ubiquitous phenomenon.

Despairing of social renovation in Europe, the 'Solitary' emigrates in search of that purer humanity promised by Paine. Disappointed by the colonies he then enacts the westward drive of Cooper's Leatherstocking, in *The Prairie*, only to find the Western wilds defiled:

> Let us, then, I said,
> Leave this unknit Republic to the scourge
> Of her own passions; and to regions haste,
> Whose shades have never felt the encroaching axe,
> Or soil endured a transfer in the mart
> Of dire rapacity. There, Man abides,
> Primeval Nature's child ...
> But that pure archetype of human greatness,

> I found him not. There, in his stead, appeared
> A creature, squalid, vengeful, and impure;
> Remorseless, and submissive to no law
> But superstitious fear, and abject sloth.
> (*Excursion*, 3: 922–28, 960–64; *CWRT* 2: 388–9)

'The encroaching axe' suggests, irresistibly, the sons of Cooper's Ishmael Bush causing havoc in *The Prairie*, but the 'squalid' and 'remorseless' figure deplored by Wordsworth's disillusioned Solitary is most probbaly a (most un-Wordsworthian) native American.

There is, perhaps one reason why Wordsworth was relatively immune to the emigration fever. His view of Cambridge, and London, and France was that of a young man who claims never to have experienced a class-ridden society until he left Westmoreland. What he praises in the economy of the lakes, and defends in 'Michael', is the relative equality of its yeoman culture, in effect its Americanness. The point is made by Margaret Fuller, obliquely, in one of her despatches to the *New York Daily Tribune* in 1846. Commenting on the seventy-six year old Wordsworth's apparent distance from his country's sufferings she observes that 'Living in this region, which is cultivated by small proprietors, where there is little poverty, vice or misery, he hears not the voice which cries so loudly from other parts of England'.[1] To Wordsworth, the Cumbrian republic of his childhood, with its democratic worth and its sturdy freeholders, already *was* America, in any sense likely to be realised this side utopia. Visitors to Rydal often thought Wordsworth rather American, Bryant comparing him to a southern planter, and Theodore Ledyard Cuyler reporting that he looked 'more like a New York farmer than an English poet'.[2]

Had the Solitary persisted, however, or taken less misanthropy with him, he might have found congenial company. William Ellery Channing (1780–1842), for instance, has distinction of being a thorough-going American Romantic in both of the *anni mirabili* of

---

1 Margaret Fuller, *New York Daily Tribune*, 29 September 1846. Cited to different ends in Joseph J. Moldenhauer, 'Walden and Wordsworth's Guide to the English Lake District', *SIAR* (1990): 261–92, 284.

2 Cuyler, *Recollections of a Long Life* (NY: 1902), 14 for which reference I thank Joel Pace.

English Romanticism. In 1798 he was thoroughly Romantic in his own experience of nature and in his democratic optimism; and he was a still more conscious Romantic in 1819, by when he was— like Shelley and Keats—a disciple of Wordsworth and Coleridge, and a student (through Coleridge's *The Friend* and Mme de Stael's *De l'Allemagne*, in the first instance) of Fichte, Schiller and Herder. Educated in a Harvard syllabus which involved the study of Blair, Locke and Lowth, and devoted especially to the works of Priestley and Price, Godwin and Wollstonecraft ('I consider that woman as the greatest of the age ... her sentiments are noble generous and sublime'), Channing, at nineteen, was a critic of slavery, fiercely Anti-Jacobin (he served briefly as a private tutor in Jacobin slave-holding Virginia), and an 'enthusiast for liberty.'[1]

He was more than capable in 1798 of his own version of the Romantic trope of escape from the city:

> View me, pent up in a school for eight months, and then let loose in the fields, free as the air I breathe, and emancipated from the frivolous punctilious and galling forms of society. I snuff up the fresh breezes; I throw myself on the soft bed of grass which Nature has formed for her favourites; I feel every power within me renewed and invigorated. (Channing, 1: 76.)

Aware at an early age that such moods must not end in delirium, he counsels a friend that it is not enough 'to seek in unreal worlds what the actual world cannot give', or to weep at 'at fictitious misery; at tales of imaginary woe'. The task is to realise the vision in active benevolence, and 'form benevolence into a habit of the soul' (77, 78).

> I find *avarice* the great bar to all my schemes, and I do not hesitate to assert that the human race will never be happier than at present till the establishment of a community of property.
> I derive my sentiments from *the nature of man*'. (1. 82)

Like Coleridge in 'On leaving a Place of Retirement', Channing feels impelled to enlist his energies 'in the cause of virtue and science' and

---

[1] *Memoirs of William Ellery Channing*, 2 vols (London: George Routledge & Co, 1850), 1: 32, 47, 75, 61, 62, 65.

conceives the notion of serving as pastor to a Scottish 'pantisocracy': Walter and Ellery Channing, appalled at the influence of Godwin on his young relative's sensibilities, cautioned him against the temptation of engaging in what Walter calls some 'imaginary republic of Coleridge and Southey ... in the backwoods, or ... some South Sea island'.[1]

Channing, however, held to his early reading of Wollstonecraft and Godwin, staunchly promoting women's property rights, and remained sceptical in his forties of what Wordsworth habitually called 'mere rights of property', or the notion that a legal framework is enough to secure liberty. There is a particularly Godwinian note to this argument in his forties:

> Liberty is the great social good,—exemption from unjust restraints,—freedom to act, to exert powers of usefulness. Does a government advance this simply by establishing equal laws? The very protection of property may crush a large mass of the community, may give to the rich a monopoly in land, may take from the poor all means of action... A poor man in the present state of society, may be a slave, by his entire dependence. (1: 499)

Pastor and educator, Channing had been visiting Wordsworth and Coleridge in 1822, shortly before he wrote this passage. Wordworth remembered his visit vividly, and the tenor of Channing's European Journal that winter may well reflect his conversations both with the poet of *The Excursion* and with the author of *Church and State*. He asks himself:

> has not every state of society a spirit, a unity? Do not its parts cohere? Can we judge of one habit, one trait of manners, one institution alone? Must not the system be understood, the central principles, the great ends to which the community is working? ... The intellectual education of the poor is talked of. Can the poor, as they are now situated, be taught much? What idea does the poor child get in a common school? The true school of human nature is the sphere opened to its faculties and affections in our conditions in daily life... (1: 496, 497)

---

[1] Channing, 1: 85–86.

If there were such a thing at the time as an American Romantic movement, Channing's parallel development with Wordsworth and Coleridge, his impact upon them and theirs upon him, his intellectual possession of the primary elements of the Romantic prospectus, would surely have qualified him for membership, considerably before Emerson left school.

In theory, America was the most appropriate terrain for Romanticism to develop: it was synonymous with self-reliance, the overthrow of Aristocratic oppression, a passion for democratic equality, a sense of social justice, and, since Paine at least, an imaginative association of liberty with nature. The land of Benjamin Franklin, Samuel Williams and Daniel Boone, as a colossal social experiment in perfectibility, seemed intrinsically Romantic, long before Whitman dubbed his country essentially 'the greatest poem'. Yet not until the late 1830s, under the explicitly Wordsworthian guidance of Greenwood, Bryant, Channing, Emerson, did such germs develop into a coherent American Romanticism. Ironically, the political nationalism of the American monthlies did not extend to literary independence and they were as dismissive of England's new spirit in poetry as Jeffrey himself. When Romanticism did take root, beginning with Bryant and—somewhat oddly, Cooper—it founded itself on Wordsworth, as a writer who discovered how poetry could go beyond a mere depiction of landscape and celebrate that transcendent interaction of the mind with nature which, for half a century it had seemed the destiny of America to express.

To cite Greenwood again, 'the great distinction and glory of Mr Wordsworth's poetry is the *intimate converse* which it holds with Nature. He sees her face to face' and his work unravels 'those secret influences which we had always felt, but hardly understood'. Not merely describing objects, 'he causes them to live, breathe, feel' so that through his work 'Our intercourse with Nature becomes permanent.... We are convinced that *there is more mind, more soul about us, wherever we look.*'[1] The core of *Nature*, already articulated in the experience of William Ellery Channing, is here formulated by Greenwood a decade before Emerson's voyage to Europe in search

---

1 *North American Review*, 18 (1824) 366–7.

of an American renaissance and an American poetry.

While 'Romanticism' failed signally to get itself airborne as a literary movement in America until the generation of 1848 there were, I have been suggesting, numerous entirely authentic specimens of *Homo Romanticus Americanus*. Samuel Williams theorised the American Revolution in terms which are entirely consonant with the nature philosophy of 'Tintern Abbey', Gilbert Imlay symbolised, briefly, the new Adam, and Channing's development from Godwinism, through nature worship to a preoccupation with the spiritual form of the state suggests a personal porfolio consonant with the entire Romantic prospectus.

Estwick Evans (1787–1866), a lawyer whose social idealism led him to work for the needy rather than the prosperous, is an exemplary case, and since he is little known he deserves rather more space. Evans had, as far as is known only one point of contact with European Romanticism: wishing to fight in the Greek War of Independence, he arrived too late either to fire a shot in anger or to shake Byron's hand. Evans's Romantic sense of nature led him to undertake a journey which he recorded in a classic of travel writing, *A Pedestrious Tour of Four Thousand Miles, through the Western States and Territories during the Winter and Spring of 1818*.[1] Evans's second-generation Romanticism—his *Pedestrious Tour* is contemporaneous with Shelley's 'Ode to the West Wind', the Odes of Keats and the fourth Canto of *Childe Harold*—is expressed in a fascination with Indian culture, an abhorrence of slavery, a Byronic admiration for Napoleon 'this king of men', and above all in a frank and disarming love of his country: Americans, he concludes from his travels, 'possess the greatest virtues and the fewest imperfections' of any people on earth.

Not that he is uncritical of the improved variety of the English stock brought about by transplanting. He has trenchant words, for instance (as trenchant than those of Sydney Smith in the *Edinburgh Review* of 1818), for the national adulation of General Jackson, barbed with reference to Julius Caesar, another military hero who 'became a tyrant'. Anchored East of New Orleans, Evans watches

---

1 Concord, NH: 1819; reprinted in *Early Western Travels, 1748—1846*, edited by R. G. Thwaite (Cleveland, Ohio: Clark, 1904), vol. 8.

'a black and ragged little schooner' pass by. This vessel of darkness proves to be that 'from the foreyard of which the Indian Chief Hemattlemico, and the Indian Prophet Francis were hung, by order of General Jackson' during his campaign against the Seminole Indians in April 1818.[1] Rebutting the notion that Indian savagery, in the execution of prisoners, justifies this stain on America's national honour, Evans indicts him further for the summary execution of the Indian traders Alexander Arbuthnot and Robert Ambrister eleven days later. Even if they were guilty of inciting Indian incursions, a country which wishes to appear 'exemplary in everything', Evans argues, will not seek to justify Jackson's fondness for blood, or allow its statesmen to invoke the laws of less enlightened nations to justify its actions (351–4). His patriotism demands that the values of republican institutions should transcend those of despotic and aristocratic governments.

This demand for a transcendent greatness, such as he sees demeaned by the future President's 'unmanly' fondness for blood and by Adams's 'undignified' 'justification' of him,[2] is matched by a thoroughly Romantic sense of transcendence achieved through nature. Transcendence of ordinary 'customs and manners' he suggests in his prologue, was the motive of his tour. 'Civil society is not without its disadvantages ... it lessens the vigour of [man's] mind, and the generosity of his heart. He no longer experiences the sublime inspirations of Nature.' (101) In a Thoreau-like agenda, he writes:

> I wished to acquire the simplicity, native feelings, and virtues of savage life; to divest myself of the factitious habits, prejudices and imperfections of civilization; to become a citizen of the world; and to find, amidst the solitude and grandeur of the western wilds, more correct views of human nature, and of the true interests of man. (102)

More like Cooper's Leatherstocking than Thoreau, however, Evans

---

[1] Compare Wordsworth's concern that Nelson's career was stained 'with one great crime', namely a similar shipboard hanging in Naples, for which cause (it is believed) Wordsworth cancelled his association of Nelson's name with his poem 'Character of the Happy Warrior'.

[2] For 'manliness' at this date see my *Wordsworth's Bardic Vocation* (2nd edn , 2015) 254–66.

sets out in deerskin moccasins, 'a close dress consisting of buffalo skins', around his neck 'a double leather case, with brass chargers for shot and ball', about his waist 'an Indian apron', while 'on my shoulder I carried a six-feet rifle', with which to defend 'the privileges of the traveller and the rights of the man'.

Thus accoutred, Evans desires to find in an examination of his own heart a minuter knowledge of 'the secret springs of action', for 'he who is ignorant of his own heart must be ignorant of human nature'. His tour begins in traversing the heights of New Hampshire and Vermont, terrain where men still learn peace from their rural avocations, and are reminded by mountain storms of 'the blasts of tyranny and of the unconquerable spirit of freedom.' It is hard to believe that he set out without first reading Wordsworth's 'The Influence of Natural Objects', or Canto 3 of *Childe Harold* and the alpine drama *Manfred*, perhaps even the alpine scenes of *Frankenstein*, though other motivations might determine his invariable choice of the most alpine routes from A to B. From his 'native hills' he traverses 'tremendous mountains' in New Hampshire while dreaming of Wallace and Tell. Traversing snow-bound slopes in New York, he imagines himself a 'chamois hunter' in Switzerland (157). Lost in a snowstorm in the land of the Tuscarora Indians he reflects on the 'force of thought ... which the wilderness inspires': 'here man feels, at once, humble and exalted. Silence, with a voice of thunder, maintains the cause of virtue, and the human soul experiences the tranquil ardour of immortal hopes'(156). In the frozen wastes, even nature is mute: 'I looked towards the Lake, but it spake not. I asked a reason of the trees, but even their branches did not whisper to me.' (186). Alone and benighted on the precipitous frozen shores with 'the ice of the lake cracking in every direction, and producing a noise like distant thunder', Evans finds in himself in a situation truly enviable: 'There is a charm in desolation; and in the season of danger, the human soul triumphs in the conviction of its own indestructibility.'

Evans's enthusiasm for Nature is Romantically integrated with an ongoing lament for what man has made of man. He laments, in particular, the importation of slavery into Kentucky, 'where all was nature, and all was liberty' before the arrival of the Virginians with the 'foul stain' of slavery.

> Why do we boast of liberty, when, every day, we violate its most sacred principles? ... Should a slave endeavour to obtain his freedom, which, no doubt, he has a right to do, the law of the land,—the whole power of the union, would enforce his obedience and again rivet his chains. Oh, cruel nation! Oh, detestable system! (323)

He demands that Congress should purchase every slave, granting full manumission when each slave has worked to pay off his purchase price: it is essentially a union-wide version of the project soon to be put into effect by Fanny Wright on a private scale:

> Should the government act upon the supposed plan, she would greatly increase her reputation and security; relieve an unfortunate and oppressed portion of the human race, and remove forever this dark stain upon her glory.

He has no truck with 'colonisation' in Africa to avert the prospect of black dominance, but demands the full admission of an oppressed people, as capable as any other of being 'great philosophers, physicians, legislators and warriors', to 'the privileges of citizenship'. Evans's zeal in the matter reminds one of the heritage suggested by his surname and shared by Richard Price. Detailing the atrocities he has observed on his tour he denounces the silence of the pulpits: 'Stand forth ye ministers of our holy religion, ye viceregents of a righteous God, and speak the truth in behalf of the slave' (333). Had many written thus in 1818, Shelley's invocation of the 'wild West Wind' (symbolising the spread of freedom from across the Atlantic) would have had a less Autumnal tone.

Chapter 3:

Consanguinity and In(ter)dependence

The American who should write a close, philosophical, just, popular and yet comprehensive view of the fundamental differences that exist between the political and social relations of England and those of his own country would confer on the latter one of the greatest benefits it has received since the memorable events of July 4, 1776. That was a declaration of political independence only, while this might be considered the foundation of the mental emancipation which alone can render the nation great.

—James Fenimore Cooper, *Gleanings in Europe: England* (1837)

We will walk on our own feet; we will work with our own hands; we will speak our own minds. ... A nation of men will for the first time exist, because each believes himself inspired by the Divine Soul which also inspires all men.

—Ralph Waldo Emerson, 'The American Scholar' (1837)

I have been led to feel more vividly than ever before, that our government has truly quite another foundation than a paper constitution of mere human device,—that it grew from living roots—and that in fact the Revolution was only a change of form—and of quite outward form—leaving the heart of society unscathed and unchanged. ... Although this may not appear in political papers.

—Elizabeth Palmer Peabody, letter to Wordsworth (1838)

92   Romantic Dialogues

1. THE SYDNEY SMITH AFFAIR

In 1846 Margaret Fuller found herself wondering why, many decades after independence, she could detect only 'the first faint streaks' of a literary dawn, and why though her compatriots have produced numerous books, 'there still wants a distinctively *American* book'.[1] Twenty-six years before Fuller posed this question, Sydney Smith found himself growing a little impatient with the compendium of American statistics he was reviewing, and allowed himself a gentle dig at American preoccupations with material matters, in the almost identical question, 'Who ... reads *an American book*?'

By the time E. A. Duyckinck published *The Wit and Wisdom of the Rev. Sydney Smith*, the 'jibe', as this sally is generally called, had presumably been forgiven. But by 1858 we were all Victorians. In the coming decades George Eliot and Henry James would again be 'English' writers, rather than British or American writers, Bryant was one of Macmillan's 'English Men of Letters' and the Brownings' friend William Wetmore Story could write in 1891 of James Russell Lowell being mourned 'by this double nation of our English speech'. In the 1820s, however, with memories of two Anglo-American wars still fresh, the jibe was unforgivable: instantly mythologised as the first shot in what became a lengthy periodical war. Its reverberations can still be heard in the academic world. It was the subject of the very first article in the first issue of the now prestigious journal of *American Literature* in 1929.[2] Between 1981 and 1991 it was referred to in scholarly work as 'one example of a tradition of blunt insult', 'this so-called review', 'Sydney Smith's often-quoted attack on all things American', and as exhibiting 'a determination to deny American culture any possible avenue of expression'.[3] I probe an

---

[1] 'Modern British Poets', 38, 'American Literature', 358, in *The Writings of Margaret Fuller*, ed. Mason Wade (NY: Viking Press, 1941).

[2] Robert E Spiller, "The Verdict of Sydney Smith," *American Literature* 1:1 (1929), 3–13.

[3] Robert Weisbuch, *Atlantic Double Cross: American Literature and British Influence in the Age of Emerson* (Chicago and London: University of Chicago Press, 1986), 12; Allison Lockwood, *Passionate Pilgrims: The American Traveler in Great Britain, 1800–1914* (New York and London: Cornwall Books and

open wound, clearly, and with some trepidation, but as the periodical war of 1820, rather like the military war of 1812 which primed it, is not much remembered in England, it is worth recovering its main events and justifications.

Smith's first mistake was to review in December 1818 an assortment of travel books by Francis Hall, John Palmer, Henry Fearon and John Bradbury, published in 1817–18, a small sample of the flood of such books produced in the twenty years following the peace, to encourage or discourage intending refugees from England's wartorn economy. Such works frequently offered hasty impressions of their authors' very brief exploration of the new world, and reviewers in the Tory *Quarterly* relished the opportunity to retail discouraging depictions of a land of smoke-filled saloons and ubiquitous spittoons. Smith was not above quoting such passages, either, but the Whig *Edinburgh*, like the Unitarian *Monthly Magazine* and the radical *Westminster Review*, generally commended such books more warmly, the more they espoused republican ideals, and rebuked illiberal criticisms of American government and principles. Smith took issue, for instance, with Fearon's sneers at political 'caucuses' which Smith sees as a proper forum for the exercise of persuasive talents: 'What other influence', he asked, 'can the leading characters of the democratic party in Congress possibly possess? Bribery is entirely out of the question—equally so is the influence of family and fortune.'[1] He makes wry comparisons with the burden of government at home:

> One of the great advantages of the American Government is its cheapness. The American king has about 5000*l* per annum, the vice-king 1000*l*. They hire their lord Liverpool at about a thousand per annum, and their Lord Sidmouth (a good bargain) at the same sum. Their Mr Crokers are inexpressibly reasonable,— somewhere about the price [of] an English door-keeper or bearer of a mace. Life, however, seems to go on very well, in spite of

---

Fairleigh Dickinson University Press, 1981), 198; Gary Williams, in his introduction to James Fenimore Cooper's, *Notions of the Americans* (Albany, NY: State University of New York Press, 1991), xviii; James D. Wallace, *Early Cooper and his Audience* (NY: Columbia UP, 1986), 12.

1 *Edinburgh Review*, December 1818, 135.

these low salaries; and the purposes of Government to be very fairly answered. (134)

Gallantry, patriotism, kindness and religious liberty he approves, and illustrates. Literary culture he warns his readers not to expect.

> They had a Franklin, indeed; and may afford to live for half a century on his fame. There is, or was, a Mr Dwight ... a small account of Virginia by Jefferson, and an Epic by Joel Barlow—and some pieces of pleasantry by Mr Irving. But why should the Americans write books, when a six week's passage brings them, in their own tongue, our sense, science and genius, in bales and hogsheads? Prairies, steam-boats, grist-mills, are their natural objects for centuries to come. Then when they have got to the Pacific Ocean—epic poems, plays, pleasures of memory, and all the elegant gratifications of an antient people who have tamed the wild earth, and set down to amuse themselves.—This is the natural march of human affairs. (144)

Is Robert Spiller is right to find 'lurking antipathies' in these sentences? American writers at the time, and for some time later, offered much the same explanation for the slow emergence of a national literature: American monthlies were still looking anxiously for signs of the coming efflorescence throughout the 1840s. Most agreed that the time for a literary efflorescence would come when the business of development was more advanced and there was leisure for a different kind of cultivation. The major difference between Smith's view and that of such Federalist Americans as Benjamin Silliman and Fisher Ames is that Smith neither accuses America, as Silliman does, of *having no reading class*, nor assumes as Ames does, that a literary culture presupposes replacement of the republic equality by a stratified social system.[1]

Smith was probably unconscious of any slight, as regards literature. His real complaint comes when he turns his attention to the inev-

---

[1] Wallace, *Early Cooper and his Audience*, 14, 15. Addressing the first U. S. Congress, Fisher Ames argued, as James Wallace puts it, that 'one way or another the unstable egalitarianism of the early republic would have to yield to great concentrations of wealth in a few hands, and a golden age of art would ensue' (15).

itable references to slavery in the volumes he is appraising. Citing Jefferson on the corrupting effects of slavery, as involving 'unremitting despotism on the one part, and degrading submissions on the other', and quoting advertisements requiring the return of fugitive slaves, as Dickens would later do, Smith warms to the theme:

> That such feelings and such practices should exist among men who know the value of liberty, *and profess to understand its principles*, is the consummation of wickedness.... We wish well to America—we rejoice in her prosperity—and are delighted to resist the absurd impertinence with which the character of her people is often treated in this country: But the existence of slavery in America is an atrocious crime, with which no measures can be kept—for which her situation affords no sort of apology—which makes liberty itself distrusted, and *the boast of it* disgusting. (emphases added)

There is reason to credit Smith's final note in this passage.[1] Like Martineau and Dickens, later, Smith seems motivated less by enmity than by mortification that the great experiment in political liberty should prove so profoundly flawed: as we shall see, their collective disillusion is in many ways echoed still later in the political lucubrations of Thoreau and Whitman.[2]

Smith's second mistake was bad timing. Henry Fearon's *Sketches of America*, which he was reviewing with all due scepticism, gave great offence in America. It was no defence, in America, to point out that Fearon merely set out to counter the commercially motivated propa-

---

1 Pun intentional. The 'note' recurs in his angry treatment of American financial perfidy, in 1842, when Philadelphia and Pennsylvania repudiated entire bond issues in one case, and interest payments in another, and when he was joined in his denunciations of such perfidy by Wordsworth and Dickens. By this date, admirers of America found that her practices were bringing into disrepute the entire notion of popular government. It was, of course, one thing to say this as an American, and quite another if the writer was English. A recurring problem is the English writers' psychological inability, after two intercontinental wars establishing the fact, to regard America as altogether a separate country.

2 Smith reverts to the matter in a further review of July 1824, intimating that this disgrace, 'if not timously corrected, will one day entail (and ought to entail) a bloody civil war [between] slave states and states disowning slavery'

ganda of such writers as Morris Birkbeck or George Courtauld, considerable property owners who had a vested interested in encouraging emigrants—including George and Georgiana Keats in Birkbeck's case—to buy their land or staff their businesses. Fearon's work (that of a 'journeyman stocking-weaver' as Edward Everett disdainfully put it in the *North American Review* when rebuking Earl Grey for referring to its author as a 'gentleman') provoked Robert Walsh, hitherto a warm admirer of Great Britain, to assemble evidence of what he saw as two centuries of literary calumnies of America by English writers. Such calumnies he insisted (at some cost to his argument) went back to the 1620s.[1] They culminated in the use made by British periodicals, the *Quarterly* in particular,[2] the *Edinburgh* by association, of Fearon and other 'illiterate and interested slanderers' of the Republic. Walsh's book, *An Appeal from the Judgements of Great Britain Respecting the United States of America* (1819), appears to have brought American discontent with English attitudes to fever pitch just in time to ensure a hostile reception for Smith's insufficiently critical review of Fearon, and for his next mistake.[3]

---

[1] Compare Thomas Dudley's adverse criticism in 1631 of the 'too large commendation' of New England by Francis Higginson in 1629 and John Winthrop in 1630 as leaders of Naumkeag and Plymouth plantations. See David Cressy, *Coming Over: Migration and Communication between England and New England in the Seventeenth Century* (Cambridge: Cambridge University Press, 1987), 12–15.

[2] John Bristed's *The Resources of the USA* (New York, 1818) had greatly alarmed the Tory *Quarterly* in 1819 with its contemplation of the day when 'the great Republic of the United States is to rule the destinies of the Globe'. The *Quarterly* consoled itself with the inspired thought that the American Constitution only works because the Senate is in effect 'the concentration of the aristocracy of the state governments which it represents'. Henry Fearon, too, in the *Quarterly*'s eyes, is a 'patriophobe' and lover of America, redeemed only by his rapid disenchantment (*Quarterly*; January 1819, 2).

[3] A slightly later instance of the genre, Adlard Welby's *A Visit to North America and the English Settlements in Illinois* (1821; ed. Reuben Gold Thwaites, Cleveland, Ohio: Clark, 1905) fared no better than Fearon's. Welby travelled to examine the truth of recent reports of a land flowing with milk and honey. He praises such signs of real progress as the remarkable achievements of the German-led 'Harmony Commune' but this is not enough in the eyes of American or British reviewers to outweigh his 'slanders' and 'calumniations' on anything from high prices to the punishment of slaves by burning alive. Welby also noted such irritants as frequent

This was to review Adam Seybert's *Statistical Annals of the United States of America* (Philadelphia, 1818) in the January 1820 issue of the *Edinburgh*. A model critic, Smith patiently devotes seven of his eight pages to telling his readers what Seybert has to say about population growth, trade and commerce, imports, the army and navy, government expenditures, etc. When he departs from this agenda it is to draw comparisons between American and British practice, wonderfully larded with satirical stabs at Britain's expense, except where he detects that 'Jonathan' is becoming almost as enamoured as brother John with naval glory. Even here, his prose recalls Gillray's satirical depiction of John Bull being melted down into taxes to pay for military adventures, and is turned against 'Jonathan' only in its final warning. 'Every wise Jonathan should remember this, when he sees the rabble huzzaing at the heels of the truly respectable [Stephen] Decatur, or inflaming the vanity of that still more popular leader [Andrew Jackson] whose justification [by President Adams] has lowered the character of his Government with all the civilized nations of the world.'

'Thus far', he concludes, 'we are the friends and admirers of Jonathan.' And thus far he has summarised with considerable patience Seybert's statistical eulogy, which he characterises sagely as designed to 'teach us how to appretiate that country, either as a powerful enemy or a profitable friend'. Like many sympathetic observers of America, Smith was aware of half a century of confident predictions that America's economic power would soon rival that of England, and that with her rapid population growth America would become the new great power, with a decisive role in world history— along with eulogies of the nascent power as the greatest emanation of political virtue the world had ever seen. His infamous peroration must be read in this context. Bearing in mind the time which has passed since 1776, and their descent from the race of Bacon, Shakespeare, Newton, together with Franklin and Washington and other heroes of the revolution, '*all born and bred subjects of the King of England*',

---

money exchanges (270), expensive inns expecting people to sleep two or three to a bed (272), and such blemishes as the admission of Missouri to the Union, without restriction as to slaves (311).

what has been done by Americans, he asks teasingly, 'to show that their English blood has been exalted and refined by their republican training and institutions?' What is the proof that the Republic, *as Republic*, has exalted humanity? And before he reverts, as Price and Blake and Evans and Channing had done, and as Martineau and Dickens and others would do, to the sore point of slavery, he retaliates on Seybert with a different kind of enumeration (to which time has, in some instances, not been kind):

> Where are their Foxes, their Burkes, their Sheridans, their Windhams, their Horners, their Wilberforces?—where their Arkwrights, their Watts, their Davys?...—their Scotts, Campbells, Byrons, Moores, or Crabbes?... In so far as we know, there is no such parallel to be produced from the whole annals of this self-adulating race. In the four quarters of the globe, who reads an American book? Or goes to an American play? ... What does the world yet owe to American physicians or surgeons? What new substances have their chemists discovered? ... What new constellations have been discovered by the telescopes of Americans?—what have they done in the mathematics? Who drinks out of American glasses? Or eats from American plates? Or wears American coats or gowns? Or sleeps in American blankets?—Finally, under which of the old tyrannical governments of Europe is every sixth man a Slave, whom his fellow-creatures may buy and sell and torture?[1]

The enduring response to this sally I have indicated above: Smith exhibits (it is true) a culpable ignorance of American achievement,[2] attacks (it is said) all things American, and denies to Americans (it is

---

[1] *Edinburgh Review*, January 1820, 79–80.

[2] William Cobbett, currently in one of his pro-American phases had already penned the appropriate retort in his *A Year's Residence in the United States of America* (London: 1818–19; New York: Kelley, 1969). The learning of the US, he says, 'is proclaimed in something better than books; in the grandest canal in the whole world; in bridges over rivers, more than a mile wide; in ships, by far the finest and best the world has ever seen; in steam-boats (an American invention) compared to which our very best are beggarly things; ...in house building; in legislation; in law; in surgery and medicine; in every science useful to man; and, indeed, in every science cultivated by man, the Americans are our equals.'

Consanguinity and In(ter)dependence   99

said) any possible avenue of expression. In short it has not been much 'appretiated', these last one-hundred-ninety-odd years.

The *Edinburgh* now had to review Robert Walsh's *Appeal from the Judgements of Great Britain*, which Francis Jeffrey did in the most conciliatory fashion possible, in May 1820, well aware of the great importance of the question, 'What are, and what ought to be, the Dispositions of England and America towards each other?'[1] The thirty page review offers a history of the *Edinburgh*'s own writings about America and reminds Walsh that he had himself, in 1810, argued passionately for Americans to back England in its struggle against France, as the country from which 'we derive the principal merit of our own character—the best of our own institutions—the sources of our highest enjoyments—and the light of Freedom itself' (425).[2] The review's importance, however, lies in the evidence it gives of liberal British attitudes, as they stood in 1820, towards Anglo-American consanguinity, despite two Anglo-American wars, the first of which, the War of Independence, terminated 'as the friends of Justice and Liberty must have wished it to terminate', while throughout the second, 'the opinions of her people, as well as our own, were deeply divided' (the Whigs of England and New England, generally, assumed in 1812 a stance of neutrality amounting to constructive treason).[3]

Walsh's motive, the *Edinburgh* recognises, is to retaliate for what he sees as 'excesses of obloquy' and 'paroxysms of spite and jealousy' motivated by the prospects of large-scale emigration to the United States. In the social conditions after 1815 (worsened considerably by the war with France) the emigration issue produced a plethora of travel books, of the kind Smith reviewed, some of scientific

1 *Edinburgh Review*, May 1820, 397 ff.
2 James Fenimore Cooper, in the *Literary and Scientific Repository*, in 1822, accuses the English of revising their estimate of Walsh when he revised his estimate of England.
3 William Ellery Channing, who saw England as the only barrier to Napoleon's project of universal dominion—'England, once fallen, and the civilized world lies at his feet'—appealed to his Boston congregation on 23 July 1812 to consider 'against what nation' war would be waged: 'We have selected for our enemy the nation from which we sprang . . . and which is now contending for her own independence and for the independence of other nations, against the oppressor of mankind.' *Memoir of William Ellery Channing*, 1: 258.

pretensions, others written simply to encourage or discourage potential emigrants. Such emigration could be perceived as valuable safety valve, removing the disgruntled and disadvantaged to greener pastures, or as posing a de-skilling threat to the British economy while magnifying the power of a potential transatlantic rival.

Aware of such issues and motivations, the *Edinburgh* agrees with Walsh that America has indeed been assailed with scurrility by 'a portion of the press in this country', which speaks for 'a powerful and active party in the nation', but not for the nation itself. The party to which it refers is 'decidedly hostile to all extension of popular rights' and 'holds the only safe or desireable government to be that of a pretty pure and unincumbered Monarchy ... obeyed by a people just enlightened enough to be orderly and industrious, but no way curious as to questions of right—and never presuming to judge of the conduct of their superiors' (399–400). That party has never forgiven the success of America's war of independence, and the spectacle of her republican prosperity 'is unspeakably mortifying to their high monarchical principles'.

It is easy to conceive, Jeffrey argues,

> that the splendid and steady success of the freest and most popular form of government that ever was established in the world, must have struck the most lively alarm into the hearts of all those who were anxious to have it believed that the people could never interfere in politics but to their ruin.

It irritates the *Edinburgh* very considerably to be 'confounded and supposed to be leagued' with the same party scribblers by whom it has been vilified for the praise it sees itself as having heaped upon America. More momentously it foresees the long-term effect of Walsh's efforts. It dreads (giving the 'special relationship' its first authoritative utterance?) the *isolation* of America from the 'momentous contest impending' between the principles of Reform and Liberty and those of 'Established Abuse'. The next fifty years will be crucial, and the question is whether the new world will step forth with all its power and might—though its 'prodigious power' is Jeffrey's less Churchillian term—to help redress the balance of the old, or whether it will 'stand aloof, a cold and disdainful spectator'. It will be a tragedy if, on grounds so slight as those alleged by Walsh, America 'should nourish such animosity towards England, as to feel a repugnance to make common cause with her, even in behalf of their common inheritance of freedom'. The moment is at hand for the good old cause to triumph, and not only America's *example* but her *influence* 'will be wanted in the crisis which seems to be approaching'. It is an astonishing appeal.

The Edinburgh, that is to say, interprets the proper relations of England and America in terms of a continuous political evolution which in Whig mythology runs from the days of Henry Vane (champion of two Commonwealths), through to the War of Independence (ignited by Tom Paine with the ideas of Sidney and Harrington, Hulme and Price). Although that War of Independence had failed to lead to a third English Revolution on the same principles, its success will culminate, at some time in the nineteenth century, in the re-assimilation by the mother country of principles exported to America and triumphantly demonstrated there (by 'born and bred subjects of the King of England') to be not merely operable but successful.

The War of 1820; or, Colonel Gardner's Campaign[1]

But the periodicals war of 1820 was repeating the conflicts of 1776 and 1812. In 1776 Chatham's conciliatory Bill coincided with the outbreak of hostilities. In 1812 Brougham's successful agitation to repeal the Orders in Council—which involved the stopping and searching of American shipping as part of the blockade of France—came just too late to prevent President Madison's declaration of war. In 1820 Jeffrey's conciliation came too late to prevent a literary war. This took the form of the launch by Colonel Charles Kitchell Gardner (an old naval colleague of Midshipman James Fenimore Cooper) of New York's *Literary and Scientific Repository*. This

---

1 Much has been written on the periodical wars since my brief treatment in this chapter, including the essays by Robin Jarvis, Will Kaufman, Nicholas Mason and Susan Oliver listed in my *Symbiosis* Appendix. In the light of such work, readers may find my next five pages on one obscure Journal eminently skippable.

short-lived periodical (1820–22) seems to have had as its primary mission the widest possible dissemination in America of British literary 'calumnies', though it failed to supplant the conservative *North American Review* which adopted the same stance. In some ways the first issue of Gardner's *Repository*, rather than Cooper's consequential *Notions of the Americans* (1828) or Emerson's very belated essay 'The American Scholar' (1837), constitutes America's real 'declaration of intellectual independence'. If so, Sydney Smith may well claim (he probably did) to have fathered the American 'renaissance'.

It might be a useful exercise for students of post-colonial psychology to study how Gardner went about the business of promoting that alienation of sentiments which James Fenimore Cooper later pronounced to be so necessary to a proper independence. His *Repository* now has the unintended effect of making one realize just how much attention British reviews were paying to the literary and commercial achievements of America, and to how their own views were received in America.

Pride of place in Gardner's first issue was given, of course, to ensuring that nobody missed the significance of Sydney Smith's 'jibe'. It also reprinted from the *Edinburgh*, *Blackwoods*, the *Eclectic* and *The New Monthly Magazine*, their friendly commendations of Brockden Brown's 'dark mysterious power of imagination', and Washington Irving's 'singular genius', and a more than charitable account of Paulding's *The Backwoodsman*. Blackwood's encomium of Brown and Irving in February 1820 (describing Irving as 'one of our first favourites among the English writers of this age') was especially fulsome and in tune with its prior commendation in March 1819 of the wisdom of Congress and of the Federalist Papers, and of Jonathan Edwards 'the very Euclid of divines'. By way of contrast, Gardner included three British reviews of Shelley that ranged from hostile to horrified. The effect is to indicate American literary prowess and British critical ineptitude at one and the same time.

Some of Gardner's issues contained nothing but pirated articles from London and Edinburgh, not because these were unobtainable (the circulation of the *Edinburgh* and the *Quarterly* in America has been estimated at over 4000) but to ensure by pointed annotation that New York's readers missed no sign of calumnious intent. The years 1814–1820 had seen such symbolic events as the burning of the Capitol by veterans of the Peninsular War, Andrew Jackson's defence of New Orleans in 1815, English echoes of American protests at the war crimes of Andrew Jackson, and American echoes of British protests at imperial follies in India. To nationalist opinion in the United States it was clear that the development of an American identity depended upon the deliberate fostering of precisely that alienation which Channing and the *Edinburgh* deplored, so as to neutralise the achievements of Adams and Monroe in demilitarising the Canadian border, and agreeing Anglo-American cohabitation in Oregon.

The *Repository* published its own review of Walsh's *Appeal from the Judgements of Great Britain*, larded with savage quotations from the *Quarterly*, supported by extracts from the *North American Review*, and (contra Estwick Evans, who we met in the last chapter) takes up the cudgels on behalf of General Jackson's summary execution of two British citizens—Ambrister and Arbuthnot—during his campaign against the Seminole Indians. As Walsh aptly points out, this action, described by the Marquis of Lansdowne in the House of Lords, in May 1819, as conduct 'unparalleled in the history of civilized nations' is surely rather more than paralleled by the execution by a British commander of Indian prisoners following the surrender of Fort Talneir, in British India, a 'horrible circumstance' cited by the same Marquis of Lansdowne in the same House of Lords just two months previously (*Literary and Scientific Repository*, Volume 1, No 2, 481).

Volume 2 of the *Repository* consists largely of items from the *Edinburgh*, to which it adds reviews of Walsh's *Appeal*, and John Bristed's *The Resources of the USA* (New York, 1818) from the *Eclectic Review* (May and July, 1820). It is interesting mainly for its editorial procedure in excerpting the *Eclectic*. The *Eclectic* handled Walsh's *Appeal* quite neutrally, while objecting to the sophistry involved in comparing slavery to apprenticeships as morally equivalent forms of servitude, and wondering whether such arguments advanced or injured Walsh's case. Colonel Gardner intervenes at the point where the *Eclectic* turns from Walsh to Bristed, to make sure that its readers know that while one writer is incapable of misrepresentation, the other is capable of nothing else. Mr Bristed, the *Eclectic* says, offers a 'rambling descant', exhibiting rather mixed prejudices, and is 'neither a furious hater of England, nor a devoted worshipper of America', though his affection towards his adopted country seems wayward and 'liable to frequent disgusts'. 'Citizen Bristed', Colonel Gardner interjects, if not a 'furious hater' of America is certainly 'a devoted worshipper' of England. And where the *Eclectic* candidly draws attention to Bristed's irritability and expresses the hope that he 'calumniates, or at the least, that he misrepresents his countrymen' in some of the views he attributes to them, the Colonel responds by calling attention to the work's real intention, too subtle for the English reviewer's comprehension, which is to 'excite ... an alarm in his beloved government of England at the extending power and growing ambition of America.'

Similarly, when *The British Critic* cites John Bristed as an authority for its view of the national vanity of the United States (as shown by Congress debating for three days on the proposition 'that America was the most enlightened nation on earth'), Colonel Gardner again interjects by divorcing citizenship from nationality: 'Mr. John Bristed is an Englishman—and though he has become a citizen of the United States, he has not, it is seen, changed his character.'

Volume 4, number 7, in January 1822 turned its attention to Campbell's *Monthly Magazine*, which had in February 1821 reviewed Edward Everett's *North American* review of Walsh (what single book ever enjoyed so much attention?). W. H. Curran, in the *Monthly*, is aghast at the charges of 'systematic [British] hatred and contumely' levelled both by Walsh and by the *North American*: 'The Boston reviewer [Edward Everett] derides the notion of the endearing influence of consanguinity; but we feel it in all its force. We have not enough of his philosophy to forget ... that our fathers were the countrymen of Washington and Franklin. We can never bring ourselves to consider the land of their birth as absolutely foreign ground.' (It is Gardner's point, of course, that after two wars fought to establish the fact that America is foreign ground it is high time they did.) Rejecting

Everett's description of Sydney Smith as 'malignant', Curran first enumerates the criticisms of Britain in Smith's review of Bradbury, Hall, and Fearon, and the conspicuous pleasure he takes in their praise of Jefferson and Adams, then wonders why Americans should find it offensive to be treated occasionally with the same levity, irreverence, and downright hostility, which Englishmen have to endure from their 'scribblers'. It does not occur to Curran that forty-six years after the *Declaration of Independence*, Americans expected to be treated with the courtesy due to a foreign country. Warming to his theme, Curran passes to disparaging remarks on the boastfulness of American travellers and thus ends by providing more evidence of the 'calumniation' he sought to deny—including a parting shot on slavery. His article, entitled 'On the Complaints in America against the British Press' is indexed by Colonel Gardner as 'British Calumnies against America'.

In the December issue of the *Monthly*, Thomas Campbell set out to make amends, apologizing for publishing Curran's piece, and praising 'the fair and temperate reply' Everett made to it. In a pacific gesture, Campbell confesses that a people who benefit from slavery, and pay taxes to maintain it in the West Indies, are in no position to reproach America with its continuance. With this 'amende honorable', as Colonel Gardner concedes it to be, some of the heat goes out of the *Repository*. A year later Campbell was making amends again, this time to 'the Mohawk Chief Ahyonwaeghs commonly called John Brant' for calumniating Brant's father in his own *Gertrude of Wyoming* (February 1822).

Volume 4, number 8 of the *Repository* (1822) reprinted the *Monthly*'s sympathetic review of Frances Wright's encomiastic *Views of Society and Manners in North America 1818–20*, and the *Eclectic*'s stingingly critical review of Adlard Welby's *A Visit to North America*—the work, it says, of 'an insufferable coxcomb and slanderer'. It also carried, without comment, three further notices from *The Monthly Review*: a serious discussion of George Courtauld's *Address to Emigrants*; a sympathetic notice of William Tell Harris's enthusiastically pro-American *Remarks Made during a Tour through the USA, 1817–18*; and a curt dismissal of James Strachan's *A Visit to the Province of Upper Canada in 1819*, with what the *Monthly* calls its 'scurrilous abuse' of America. In these five notices, as even Gardner can hardly have failed to notice, commendation of America is commended in the British reviews, and abuse is contemptuously dismissed.

And there the paper war of 1820 might have ended. In 1824, however, Edward Everett allowed himself to be stung by the *Quarterly*'s attention to another travel book, William Faux's *Memorable Days in America ... By an English Farmer*, 1820, which the ever-disdainful Everett characterizes in the *North American Review* as 'the slanders of The Somersetshire Clodhopper'. Faux's comments show him little qualified to comment on, or indeed to follow, the intricacies of American constitutional practice, and his poor command of English allows Everett to find calumnies where none are intended. For instance, Faux walks several miles under a hot sun in the hope of seeing the President, 'but he passed by me in the tumultuous crowd, quite unobserved': it is clear enough what Faux means, but the prickly Everett takes him—or affects to take him—to be implying that the President was so rude as not to notice him (*North American Review*, n.s. 19, [1824] 99). Faux also has the temerity to pronounce on slavery, and in dealing with this, Everett first recalls and quotes Campbell's 'manly' attempt at atonement two years before. Now he will not be mollified, however. He dissects Campbell's words as masking a deeper hypocrisy, and accuses the English nation of 'sinning against the cause of freedom as deeply as the most heinous despotism of which the memory exists'. In a superb blend of truth, bad faith, and sophistry, he concludes that America is 'overwhelmed with abuse, because it is impossible to throw off the slavery which they have entailed upon us.'

What Edward Everett and Colonel Gardner could not (or would not) see, was that for Sydney Smith, as for Fanny Wright (who would in 1824 quietly set about 'throwing off slavery', however impossible Everett deems this to be), and such later travellers as Harriet Martineau and Charles Dickens, any blemish on the perfect achievement of the young republic—any failure which might give ammunition to the enemies of progress—is felt not as ground for self-righteous condemnation, but as a threat to their own liberal and republican

Consanguinity and In(ter)dependence 107

identity, a slur on their own American Dream, and an impediment to the political credibility of reform.

3. MENTAL EMANCIPATION

In a postcolonial era, all Americans had to decide for themselves on appropriate models of dealing with siren calls from 'the Old Home'. I will broach, in the remainder of this chapter, three obvious models: Emancipation, Appropriation, and Identification—the modes adopted respectively by James Fenimore Cooper, Ralph Waldo Emerson, and Elizabeth Palmer Peabody.

The *Edinburgh*'s question, what should be the relations between Britain and Anerica, and Margaret Fuller's question, as to when an American literature would arise, also dominated the literary career of James Fenimore Cooper. Born in 1789, the year in which the fires of liberty returned to Europe from America, Cooper came of age as a midshipman in the United States Navy at a time when war with Britain, for supremacy in American waters, was felt to be imminent. As a naval officer and naval historian, greatly exercised at the outset of his career by Britain's habit of searching American ships for British deserters (or in American eyes, impressing American seamen), Cooper was particularly devoted to the notion that America should maintain a fleet capable of ensuring that the British could never exercise Atlantic hegemony. His fictional career was no less patriotic. Cooper's America, for much of his lifetime, was still surrounded by British dominions in Canada and the West Indies, supported by commercial presences along the West Coast from Oregon to California. Not only his patriotic sea stories, but also his fictional histories of America's westward expansion reflect the consciousness of the United States that such expansion—at one time prohibited by the British, whose interests dictated a network of littoral colonies communicating solely with the Mother Country—is essential to the assertion of a new American identity.

When Cooper arrived in London from France, in February 1828, he did so as the author of *Precaution* (1820), *The Spy* (1821), *The Pioneers* (1823), *The Pilot* (1824), *Lionel Lincoln* (1825), *Last of the Mohicans* (1826) and *The Prairie* (1827). He had been in France for eighteen months as the friend and collaborator of the midwife of American Independence, the Marquis de Lafayette, at whose instigation he had written a robust defence of American institutions from the kind of calumny about which Walsh and Gardiner complained. He was in London to arrange the publication of this work, *Notions of the Americans* (1828) and to be lionised. His experiences are recorded in the English volume of his *Gleanings in Europe* (written 1828, published 1837).

The first person to lionise him—under the mistaken impression that he was related to Thomas Cooper the Pantisocrat—was William Godwin, once celebrated as the author of *Political Justice*, now a virtual nonentity.[1] 'I cannot recall any one, who, on so short an acquaintance, so strongly impressed me with a sense of his philanthropy', says Cooper, but 'I could not consider him a friend. He regarded us as a speculating rather than as a speculative people.' Clearly, by 1828, Godwin had forgotten the early impact of America's social experiment on his own theories of perfectibility. Disappointed by the conversation of Coleridge, of which he gives one of the most entertaining accounts, Cooper reserves his warmest praise for Sir James Mackintosh, 'the best talker I have ever heard' (*Gleanings*, 61). Yet Mackintosh, too, was deficient in his view of America: 'it was quite evident that he thought us a people who might yet do prodigies, rather than as a people who *had* performed them' (62). Cooper cannot easily forgive those who like him for himself, rather than because he is an American, and this resentment is almost the keynote of the book: 'I cannot recall a single man, who, I have had the smallest reason to think, has ever given me his hand more cordially and frankly because I was an American!' (10). Sir Walter Scott, with whom he had been

---

1 *Gleanings in Europe: England* (1837), edited by Robert E. Spiller (New York: Oxford University Press, 1930), 29. As Hazlitt had said of him in 1825, 'Mr Godwin's person is not known, he is not pointed out in the street, his conversation is not courted, his opinion is not asked, he is at the head of no cabal, he belongs to no party in the State, he has no train of admirers, no one thinks it worth his while even to traduce and vilify him' *Lectures on the English Poets & The Spirit of the Age* (London: J. M .Dent, 1910), 182–3. Cooper attributes the isolation to Godwin's anti-aristocratic views.

Consanguinity and In(ter)dependence 109

co-lionised by friends of the Princess Galitzin, in Paris in 1826, and about whom he was rather complimentary at the time[1] also fares rather badly in *Gleanings*. 'The bias of his feelings, of his prejudices, I might almost say of his nature,' says Cooper, 'is deference to hereditary rank.' Such deference condones 'feudal and conventional laws', and if Sir Walter Scott is right it follows that the American system is wrong, and '*one of the first duties of a political scheme is to protect itself*.'

In each of these appraisals, of Godwin, Mackintosh, Scott, a personal feeling which is broadly benign, is subordinated to a national differentiation in which the Englishman or Scot is found to be either anti-American or inimical to the American spirit. At times this prejudicial construction beggars belief. A young lady of no particular distinction has the temerity to venture the surely innocent remark that a country with rattlesnakes 'could not be agreeable to walk in', provoking Cooper to this fierce retaliation: 'I do not believe that the annals of the world can present another such instance of a people, so blindly, ignorantly, and culpably misjudging a friendly nation, as the manner in which England, at this moment, in nearly all things, misjudges us' (337).

The personal portraits are designed to underwrite Cooper's insistence that cultural independence must follow political independence, and—fifty years on—has not done so. Personal antipathy and constitutional incompatibility must both, therefore, be projected in the most extreme lights, at whatever cost to candour. Thus, 'In America, an election ought to be, and in the main it is, an expression of the popular will for great national objects; in England, it is merely a struggle for personal power, between the owners of property.' Cooper's father, it is known, used every sanction to ensure that his indebted tenants voted for the right candidate, and once imprisoned a man for inciting those tenants 'to question their landlord's politics.'[2] His son, nevertheless, continues unblushingly his ideal antithesis: 'The voter with

---

1 Robert E. Spiller, *James Fenimore Cooper: Critic of his Times* (New York: Minton, Balch, 1931), 118.
2 Charles Hansford Adams, *The Guardian of the Law* (University Park and London: Pennsylvania State University Press), 1990.

us is one of a body which controls the results; in England, he is one of a body controlled by direct personal influence' (271).

Some of Cooper's chagrin, it may be thought, may well have resulted from his choice of company. At home one of his favourite pursuits, Susan Cooper records, was reading about heraldry. In Europe he enjoyed the society of the Marquis de Lafayette, the Princess Galitzin, the Count Pozzo di Borgo, the Marchese Gino Capponi, the Marquese Giuseppe Pucci, and the Bourbon King Louis Philippe.[1] Where else, then, could the creator of Leatherstocking reside in London but 33 St James's Place, where his neighbours included not only Samuel Rogers, but George IV, the Bishop of London, and the Earl Spencer? He knew, of course, that there was a radical working class culture in England, and indeed refers briefly to such a class of men 'among what are called the operatives' (*Gleanings*, 190) but the company he sought was that of Earl Grey, Lord Lansdowne, the Duke of Devonshire, Lady Holland and Lord John Russell. Though sometimes shocked by the informality of young men in such company, Cooper missed the democratic character of life in his New York club or among Parisian refugees. Nor did the 'persons of quality' and 'ladies of condition', whose 'deportment' he praises always accord him the deference he expected. Placed at the foot of a dining table, having been delayed in conversation with another guest, he finds this painful matter worthy of record. [2]

Gleanings is a strange and testy work, but to say this is to miss its function and its significance in the culture wars. It is a sort of appendix to *Notions of the Americans*, in which even the corruptions of the American press are attributed to British influence, and as an exer-

---

1 '"You have visited many countries" said the Queen, "which do you prefer?" "Italy, in which Your Majesty was born, for its nature"' replies Natty Bumppo's courtly creator, '"and France, in which your Majesty reigns, for its society."' (Spiller, 164).

2 Thackeray, in a one paragraph review of *Gleanings*, complained that Cooper enjoyed the 'deference paid by the aristocracy of title and wealth to the aristocracy of genius' yet quitted England as 'a hater and despiser of everything connected with the land in which he had experienced so much misapplied hospitality'. George Dekker and John P McWilliams, eds., *James Fenimore Cooper: The Critical Heritage* (London and Boston: Routledge & Kegan Paul, 1973), 229.

cise in disenchantment it will meet its match in Dickens's *American Notes* (1842). Half way through the work Cooper notes that 'until we do enjoy a manly, independent literature of our own, we shall labour under the imputations which all foreigners urge against us ... that of being but a second hand reflection of English opinions' (154). At the end, thanking the *Quarterly Review* for alienating the feelings of America from Great Britain he comments:

> When I rejoice in the alienation of the feelings of America from England [it is because] we must pass through some such process of alienation, before we shall ever get to consider the English in the only mode that is either safe or honourable for one independent nation to regard another. (364)

The curious phrasing seems to imply, as the conspicuous chip on Cooper's shoulder already has, that this process of alienation is not yet accomplished even for himself, and that he does not feel entirely 'safe' from identification with the 'old home'. Ironically, by the time *Gleanings* was published in 1837 Cooper was well beyond the phase in which he wrote it and his own identification had strengthened. He had already been back in America for five years, and was about to publish his first stinging critiques of American egalitarianism in *Home as Found* (1838). Park Benjamin noted the psychology of the returned emigrant when reviewing the latter work: 'when in England he blackguarded the English; now he is at home, he blackguards his own countrymen.'[1]

The underlying purpose of Cooper's career is expressed with the utmost clarity in the opening sentence of his *Gleanings in Europe: England*. It was to foster 'mental emancipation'. Such fostering is particularly evident in *Lionel Lincoln* (1825), which deals directly with the events in and around Boston in 1776, his sea trilogy, *The Pilot* (1823), *The Red Rover* (1827) and *The Water-Witch* (1830), which as Thomas Philbrick says, depict 'the separation between England and America and the slow awakening of an American consciousness,' and the European trilogy, *The Bravo* (1831), *The Heidenmauer* (1832) and *The Headsman* (1833) in which, as McWilliams says, Cooper

---

1 *The Critical Heritage*, 22.

'hoped to free America from any present deference to aristocratic polities.'¹ His writing is inspired by a belief, reinforced by the writings of Mme de Stael and Lafayette, and shared by the *Edinburgh Review*, that America's literary dawn will be an event of supreme moral importance to the world.

The Wept of Wish-ton-Wish (1829), dealing as it does with a seventeenth-century Puritan settlement, has necessarily to recognise that the republican spirit of this settlement is either transplanted from England or produced in symbiosis with it. But the narrator still finds signs of a separate consciousness, in a passage which amounts to a rephrasing of Cooper's cultural manifesto: 'The colonists had not yet severed all those natural ties which bound them to the eastern hemisphere.... But different circumstances, divided interests, and peculiar opinions, were gradually beginning to open those breaches which time has since widened, and which promise soon to leave little in common between the two peoples, except the same forms of speech and a common origin'.²

Only in his last decade did Cooper's sense of American degeneracy neutralise his fundamental stance as midwife to a separate American consciousness. In *The Ways of the Hour* (1850) Cooper strikes one his most self-doubting notes, situating his concluding wedding scene 'in one of those little chapels reared by our fathers in the days of the monarchy, when, in truth, greater republican simplicity really reigned among us in a thousand things, than reigns today'.³ The wistfulness of this variation upon Wordsworth's 'Milton thou should be living at this hour' reminds one, rather poignantly, of Mark Heathcote's patriarchal republic in Wish-ton-Wish. It implies, perhaps, that by 1850 both parts of the Anglo-American community could wonder where and when the genuine republican moment might arrive. At about the same moment, as it happens, Henry David Thoreau was asking him-

---

1 Thomas Philbrick, *James Fenimore Cooper and the Development of American Sea Fiction* (Cambridge, MA: Harvard University Press, 1961), 58. John McWilliams, *Political Justice in a Republic: James Fenimore Cooper's America* (Berkeley, CA: University of California Press, 1972), 144.
2 *The Wept of Wish-ton-Wish* (Chicago, New York, and San Francisco: Belford, Clarke, n.d.), 311.
3 *The Ways of the Hour* (London: George Routledge, 1889), 451.

self the same question, in explicitly Wordsworthian terms.

4. APPROPRIATION: THE ANGLO-AMERICAN SCHOLAR

It is something of an irony, after Cooper's strenuous efforts in *Notions of the Americans* and elsewhere, that Emerson's 'The American Scholar' (1837) should ever have been lauded by Oliver Wendell Holmes as America's declaration of literary independence.[1] It is equally ironic that Emerson's belated declaration should depend so much upon the major figures of English Romanticism. Earlier reviewers of Emerson, before the academic segregation of the two literatures set in, praised Emerson precisely for recognising and absorbing and articulating, as English writers of the period had not, the vital significance of Wordsworth and Coleridge, or as a latter day Shelley.[2]

Such recognition is hardly surprising. 'The American Scholar' begins by adopting a Keatsian faith that poetry will revive and lead in a new age', as the pole star of a new millennium; proceeds to a Platonic fable revived by Boehme, Swedenborg, Blake and Shelley, of the race of men as One Man, divided in his social state; and elaborates, in the manner of Robert Owen and Thomas Carlyle on the further reduction of these divided men to particles of labour.[3] Next, Emerson asks his audience what is the value of nature to the human mind? The answer is an optimistic (Wordsworthian rather than Kantian) view of how exquisitely the things of the world are fitted to laws of the mind, to such an extent that 'So much of nature as he is ignorant of, so much of his own mind he does not yet possess.' Not only nature instructs the mind: so (as Wordsworth teaches) does that second nature, in the creations of man. A Blake-like determination

---

[1] Since Holmes, elsewhere, recognised Emerson's *Nature* as essence of Wordsworth, he may have meant that the essay owed as much to Romanticism as the *Declaration of Independence* did to Locke and Hulme.

[2] See references to Emerson's early reception in Chapter 5.

[3] *Collected Works*, 1: *Nature, Addresses and Lectures*, edited by Robert E. Spiller and Alfred R. Ferguson (Cambridge, MA: The Belknap Press of Harvard University Press, 1971), 52–53. Hereafter CW. Owen's *A New View of Society* was published in 1813, and Emerson numbered him among the modern prophets.

to construct his own system rather than be enslaved by another's, is announced in a striking trope: 'I had better never see a book than be warped by its attraction clean out of my own orbit, and made a satellite instead of a system' (*CW* 1. 55, 56).

Despite this comprehensive raid on Romanticism, Emerson's first reference to any English poet is to support his view—a view transparently influenced by Edward Young's *Conjectures on Original Composition*—of the dangers of influence. Young had warned that 'illustrious Examples *engross, prejudice* and *intimidate.*'[1] 'The English dramatic poets', Emerson thunders, have Shakespearized now for two hundred years' (57). It is a merited rebuke, and one which Melville of course, will turn to brilliant account, in *Moby Dick*, drawing the discourses of *Hamlet* and *Lear* into the orbit of his own Ahab to show that however feebly the degenerate English might echo Shakespeare, an American writer could treat with him on equal terms. After all, says Emerson, in a fiercely democratic, if self-deluding sentence, 'each philosopher, each bard, each actor, has only done for me, as by a delegate, what one day I can do for myself' (66). Or as Young had already put it, with equal democratic fervour a mere eighty years earlier, the true imitation of Homer was to 'tread in his steps, …drink where he drank, at the true Helicon, that is at the breast of Nature' for 'then, if you write naturally, you might as well charge Homer with an imitation of You.' 'Born Originals', Young had concluded with proto-Emersonian pithiness, 'how comes it to pass that we die Copies? (Young, 21, 42).

Carlyle on work, Newton on polarity and Coleridge on method are the next three cisterns to be drained ('first one; then another, we drain all cisterns' Emerson boasts). But the most striking appropriation is Wordsworth. A major theme of the essay is a curiously retrospective appraisal of 'the auspicious signs of the coming days', starting with a Wordsworthian espousal of 'the literature of the poor, the feelings of the child'. Where Hazlitt had said in 1825 that Wordsworth's poetry is part of the spirit of the age, and his muse a levelling one, Emerson adopts a somewhat flabby periphrasis: 'the same movement

---

[1] Edward Young, *Conjectures on Original Composition* (1759; reprint, Leeds: Scolar Press, 1966), 17.

Consanguinity and In(ter)dependence 115

which effected the elevation of what was called the lowest class in the state, assumed in literature a very marked and as benign an aspect.' Adopting Wordsworth's persona, the Emerson who had once derided the lyrical ballads as 'the poetry of pygmies'[1] now exclaims, none too convincingly: 'I embrace the common, I explore and sit at the feet of the familiar, the low' finding spiritual sublimity in 'these suburbs and extremities of nature'. Blurring this manifest paraphrase of the most famous of Romantic manifestos with his next point, that the world has 'form and order', and that 'one design unites and animates the farthest pinnacle and the lowest trench', Emerson first attributes 'this idea' to Goldsmith, Burns, Cowper, Goethe, Wordsworth and Carlyle (Hugh Blair, one might feel, is a striking omission from this promiscuous lineage) then appears to attribute 'this philosophy of life', to a man of genius 'whose literary value has never yet been rightly estimated—I mean, Emmanuel Swedenborg'. Swedenborg, Emerson claims, 'saw and showed the connexion between nature and the affections of the soul. He pierced the emblematic or spiritual character of the visible, audible, tangible world.' One reason for Emerson's apparent attribution of a clearly Wordsworthian point to Swedenborg, and his quiet slide from England to Europe, is that the passage originates, characteristically, in a quite accidental notebook transition from poetry's interest in the common man, to Swedenborg's interests in the lower strata of nature (*JMN*, 5: 365-6). Nevertheless, the procedure seems less than candid.[2]

---

[1] *The Journals and Miscellaneous Notebooks of Ralph Waldo Emerson*, edited by William H. Gilman et al., 14 vols. (Cambridge, MA:The Belknap Press of Harvard University Press, 1960), 1:162. Hereafter *JMN*.

[2] I think of the bizarre suggestion, earlier in the notebooks, that 'the doctrine of the amiable Swedenborg and the subtle Goethe is that "we murder to dissect"' (*JMN*, 5: 256). Did Emerson genuinely believe that Wordsworth was in some way contiguous with Swedenborg? Or is it that even in the notebooks he feels the need to use continental figures to mask English influences? Of course, the Goethe of *Werther* is quite properly associated with the cult of simplicity, along with Goldsmith and MacPherson (Wordsworth's modern pre-eminence should not prejudice one's judgement here) but an acknowledgement as slight as this, given the terms of Emerson's passage, constitutes concealment. In the same month as 'The American Scholar', Emerson wrote in his Journal: 'Carlyle and Wordsworth now act out of England on us' (August 20, 1837).

'We have listened too long,' Emerson concludes, reminding his 1837 audience perhaps that some English poets had ceased to do so several generations back, 'to the courtly muse of Europe'. The lecture's most Emersonian sentence is that which reduces Plato, Shakespeare, Newton and Locke to 'delegates' of Ralph Waldo Emerson. Emerson's personal contribution to this vivifying digest of Plato, Young, Blair, Wordworth, Coleridge, Keats, Shelley, Hazlitt, Owen, and Carlyle is not really in what he himself sees.[1] It is rather the inspirational quality of the belief—without the qualifications that surround it in Wordsworth—that what *one* is, *all* may become. Otherwise the essay is best understood as the re-animation of the headiest moments of the 1770s, when the world watched as a new kind of nation, on an entirely new social principle, and composed of an entirely new kind of person—as Price, Raynal, Pownall agreed—took its place in the world order; or as a re-germination upon American soil of the Jacobin 1790s when Jefferson in correspondence, Wordsworth in poetry and Paine in best-selling prose led their revolt against what Paine called 'the manuscript assumed authority of the dead' and Wordsworth called 'those barren leaves.' Emerson had already used the same tactic in 1836, in his *Nature*. 'Our age is retrospective' Emerson opines in the famous opening to that essay; why should not we, like foregoing generations, 'enjoy an original relation to the universe?' The succeeding question in *Nature*, 'why should we grope among the dry bones of the past, or put the living generation into masquerade out its faded wardrobe'[2] directly paraphrases Carlyle's *Sartor Resartus*—which Emerson has just been instrumental in publishing—while reiterating the question Jefferson posed to Madison in 1789, and with which Paine ignited the revolution controversy the following year, and which Wordsworth made the substance of numerous provocative lyrics (from 'Expostulation and Reply' to 'At the Grave of Rob Roy'), the question 'who is to decide, the living or the dead?'

---

1 He confided as much to his Journal in 1836: 'I go to Shakespeare, Goethe, Swift, even to Tennyson, subject myself to them ... and thus a Proteus enjoy the Universe through the powers of a hundred different men.' (*JMN* 5: 178).

2 *Collected Works*, 1: 7.

Consanguinity and In(ter)dependence 117

What though, did Emerson's 1837 audience make of this attempt to announce a national vision made up so overwhelmingly of borrowed insights, or of his quietly damning implication that Boston culture was half a century out of date? Would Emerson have assumed that his audience picked up the echoes and allusions, already shared his allegiance to Romantic aspirations—together perhaps with his sense that England had not lived up to them, and so had no title to them—and approved his procedure? Does the pre-penultimate sentence of the work—the gratuitous dismissal of the Romantics from whom he been plagiarising throughout, as purveyors of pity, doubt and sensual indulgence—legitimise this appropriation? The manoeuvre offers a particularly sharp instance of one of the techniques Robert Weisbuch sees as characteristic of 'the Anglo-American contest'. In the struggle between 'British lateness and American earliness', Weisbuch says, the American strategy is 'to make decrepitude and its signs the characterisation of Britain and its writers, and to contrast with this British anxiety, the promise of a free American future'.[1] The illustrious poets of the recent past must now be set aside; their hour of vision was short; each of them has merely done for me, 'as by a delegate', what I can do for myself. And since 'a man rightly viewed, comprehendeth the particular natures of all men' acknowledgement would be superfluous. On this principle, paradoxically, one can see the concluding prophecy of 'The American Scholar'—that in America 'A Nation of men will for the first time exist, because each believes himself inspired by the Divine Soul which also inspires all men'—both as a sentence that only an American could write, and as a sentence that such Englishmen as Price, Pownall, Cartwright, alongside such Frenchmen as Crèvecoeur, Raynal and Chateaubriand, had already written. 'Free of all restraints', Thomas Pownall had claimed of Americans, 'their souls are their own': and he added: 'The genuine Liberty on which America is founded *is totally and intirely a New System of Things and Men*, which treats all as what they actually

---

[1] Weisbuch acknowledges John Lynen's concept of cultural time in *The Design of the Present: Essays on Time and Form in American Literature* (New Haven and London: Yale University Press, 1969).

are.'[1] The force of Emerson's essay, surely, and perhaps its ultimate rhetorical motivation, is that it returns its audience imaginatively to a moment *before* the birth of Romanticism. It pretends, in effect, that the intervening sixty years have not happened and summons in its audience a very belated, but perhaps instrumental, sense of earliness.

5. IDENTIFICATION: ELIZABETH PALMER PEABODY AND 'THE COLUMBUS OF POETRY'

What makes the attempted occlusion of Wordworth in 'The American Scholar' all the more striking is that by this date New England Transcendentalism—at least in the figures of William Ellery Channing, Richard Henry Dana, Elizabeth Peabody and her sisters Mary and Sophia, and Amos Bronson Alcott, to be followed by Margaret Fuller, Anna Cabot Lowell and Thomas Chase—had for ten years or so been in full voice for Wordsworth as *'the father of Modern poetry*—the founder of an era'.[2]

William Ellery Channing had been an early convert. His early experience of Wordsworth's poetry led him to make his way, on his first visit to Europe, directly from Liverpool to the Lake District. From Ullswater he writes of having spent days surrounded by 'scenes of grandeur, and wildness, and beauty'.[3] The 'sacred spot' of Grasmere—made sacred by Wordsworth's 'mingled reverence and freedom, loyalty and independence, manly simplicity and heroism' and his 'all-vivifying imagination' (299) inspires a rhapsodic description of its tranquillity, experienced as foretaste of the afterlife, surrounded by bold, rugged and precipitous mountains, 'which

---

1 *Thomas Pownall, A Memorial to the Sovereigns of Europe,* 42; *To the Sovereigns of America* (London: 1783), 54.

2 Elizabeth Palmer Peabody, Dove Cottage MS, A/Peabody/8, May 15th 1845. Peabody's eight letters to Wordsworth are dated December 9th, 1825 [1], March 27th, 1829 [2]; September 7th, 1835 [3]; February, 1838 [4], April 20th, 1839 [5]; March 29th, 1841 [6], May 7th, 1842 [7]; May 15th, 1845 [8] and are cited hereafter by the DCMS number 1–8. They are transcribed by Margaret Neussendorfer in 'Elizabeth Palmer Peabody to William Wordsworth: Eight letters, 1825–1845', *Studies in the American Renaissance* (1984) 181–211.

3 *Memoirs of William Ellery Channing,* 2: 485.

Consanguinity and In(ter)dependence   119

surpass all others which I have seen in expression and spirit' (490). Walking from Rydal to Grasmere towards sunset with the poet talking and reciting at his side, he experienced 'a combination of circumstances such as my highest hopes could never have anticipated' (493). One factor, especially, makes for this surprising experience. With the possible exception of Washingston Allston, Channing was almost certainly the first New World visitor to hear Wordsworth reading from the manuscript of *The Prelude*. George Ticknor, the first American pilgrim to Rydal Mount only three years earlier, experienced the same warm reception, but had been treated to the much parodied *Peter Bell* and *The Waggoner*.[1]

Channing's familiarity with Wordsworth's poetry, especially the poetry dealing with early childhood, made him a crucial figure in the development of Elizabeth Peabody's discipleship. She was twenty-one when he spent time with her in Brookline, just outside Boston, and introduced her to the work of this 'still persecuted prophet' of the new moral order.[2] Ten years later, she and Bronson Alcott would make Wordsworth central to their Boston teaching activities, inviting their young pupils (mostly under twelve) to discuss texts as various as *Peter Bell* and the *Ode: Intimations of Immortality*: 'how I wish you could have seen how like the breeze of Spring the first stanzas [of the Ode] passed over these opening blossoms of Life—the very sound of wakening nature seemed to breathe from their lit-up faces, as their whole natures responded to the "thronging echoes", the "trumpet cataract", the "shouting Shepherd boy".'[3] Prefiguring the more famous therapeutic self-administrations of John Stuart Mill and Matthew Arnold, Channing and Peabody read Wordsworth to each

---

1 Elizabeth Peabody, *Reminiscences of Wm Ellery Channing* (Boston: Roberts Brothers, 1880) 80–81, reveals that Channing heard *The Prelude*. For Ticknor and other American pilgrims, see Mark Reed, 'Contacts with America', *William Wordsworth: 1770–1970*, ed, Nesta Clutterbuck, Dove Cottage: 1970, 32–36.
2 *Reminiscences*, 80.
3 Dove Cottage MS, A/Peabody/3. Boston, September 7th, 1835. These readings are treated in her *Record of a School: Exemplifying the General Principles of Spiritual Culture* (Boston, NY and Philadelphia, 1835) 110–13, 198–9. The imagery of awakening suggests Bryant's similar experience when he first read the *Lyrical Ballads*. See Chapter 5.

other, in the Spring and fall of 1825, the pastor using Wordsworth's poetry as medicine for his young associate's perturbed state of feelings, and as a corrective to the egotism induced by education and addressed in Wordsworth's opening poem in *Lyrical Ballads*, 'Lines left upon a seat in a Yew-tree'.[1]

As a leading practical and theoretical educator, translator, bookseller-librarian (and importer of the most recent English and continental publications),[2] purveyor of homeopathic remedies, writer and editor (Thoreau's 'Civil Disobedience' was first published in her *Aesthetic Papers*), communitarian (she helped with the prospectus of the Brook Farm Utopia), editor and sponsor of *The Dial* (produced in her bookshop), Elizabeth Palmer Peabody is a much under-rated figure in Boston transcendentalism. The model for Henry James's 'Miss Birdseye' (as she rather cruelly became in *The Bostonians*) she was also a remarkable correspondent with a penchant for allusion.

She first wrote to Wordsworth in December 1825 at the age of 21, thanking him for his *Poetical Works* because they had enabled her to relive 'sensations and emotions and sentiments which were strongly in my soul' in youth, but which 'might never have revived again had not your Spirit ... called me forth from the *dissecting* room into "the light of things".'[3] They had also confirmed her sense that the theory and practice of the education she had experienced was defective, that only poetry of genius—particularly that of a poet 'with a heart / That watches and receives' (citing Wordsworth's 'The Tables Turned')—could 'develop the nobler part of their nature'. This first letter addresses Wordsworth in phrases permeated with the language of the Preface to *Lyrical Ballads*, the Intimations Ode, the 'Ode to Duty', *The Excursion*, and that especially germinal poem

---

[1] See Neussendorfer, 181, 186n.

[2] The *Catalogue of the Foreign Circulating Library, No 13 West Street, Boston, kept by E P Peabody* (Boston, 1849) listed twelve pages of continental titles, including forty volumes of Goethe and sixty of Herder; poetry by Bryant and Byron, Coleridge, Channing, Hemans and Longfellow; *Aids to Reflection, The Friend, The Spirit of Hebrew Poetry, Sartor Resartus, Women in the Nineteenth Century*; and such new fiction as *The Deerslayer, Vanity Fair, Jane Eyre* and *Wuthering Heights*.

[3] DC MS A/Peabody/1. She had bought and 'feasted upon' the four-volume Boston edition of 1824 with her sisters (Neussendorfer, 185 n).

'The Tables Turned'. Her later letters will allude to a wider variety of Wordsworth's poems than any casual reader would recall, including some unnoticed by the anthologists.[1] In her third letter the 'disciple' praises him as one who has 'done all that Milton left undone', thanking him 'for all you have sung of women' as well as for his work as 'fosterfather to young spirit' (Peabody/3, September 7th, 1835) In the fourth he becomes her 'own dear spiritual father' (February, 1838).

But she is also self-consciously American, appealing to this 'Columbus of poetry' (Letter 3) not to shirk his duties to his fosterchildren across the pond, more than willing to criticise where she sees him failing in a proper sense of his position as 'the poet not of the English nation but of the English language' (Letter 2). Where she fails to understand him, she says in her second letter, this is sometimes because his poems lament circumstances which may be 'the peculiar heritage of Europe'. In the new world, thankfully, there is 'nothing equal to that *weight of custom*—which you lament'. In America, 'everything in the forms of society & almost in the forms of thought is in a state of flux' so that 'all that is not founded in the nature of things is swept away continually' and 'whatever be our faults, imitation & submission to established forms are not strongly our characteristics'. Her correspondence balances its news of his reception in the new world with expectations that he will delight in that new world's own productions. In 1838, after he had commented 'obligingly' on her *Record of a School*, she sends the sixty-eight year old poet Emerson's *Nature* and 'the American Scholar', which he seems not to have received, followed in 1841 by the *Essays: First Series* 'of which I am greatly proud—for it seems to me to sound as an American book ought to do'. Wordsworth's reply is untraced but he let his American editor, Henry Reed, know that he was profoundly

---

[1] They include 'Lines written in early Spring', 'The Farmer of Tilsbury Vale', 'Simon Lee', 'Peter Bell', 'the Russian Fugitive', 'She was a Phantom of Delight', 'Song at the Feast of Brougham Castle', 'The Norman Boy', 'At the grave of Burns' ('I hardly know anyone who always goes so to the heart with Burns', Peabody/7, May 17th 1842). Joel Pace, in 'Wordsworth in America; Publication, Reception and Literary Influence, 1802–1850' (D Phil dissertation, Oxford, 1999) shows that having Wordsworth by heart was a not uncommon feat in New England.

unimpressed by 'what passes for philosophy at Boston'.[1] More promisingly, except that there is no evidence that they arrived, she sent Hawthorne's *Twice-Told Tales*, introducing their author, her future brother-in-law, as 'a very retired young man', one whose 'daily teachers have been woods and rills—/ The silence that is in the starry sky / The sleep that is among the lonely hills', these haunting lines being from Wordsworth's 'Song at the Feast of Brougham Castle'.

An undercurrent of the later letters concerns Wordsworth's troubled views of America. In 1838 she writes 'I hear that you have small hopes for this country' (Letter 6): he appears to have replied encouragingly in the following year, in an untraced letter sent via Montreal, for she comments in 1839 that she is 'glad to read all you said about our country—I knew it must be so—or else you were labouring under some erroneous information' (Letter 7). Commenting on Dr Channing's repudiation of 'Mr Clay's bad speech in Congress about slavery' she says she rather agrees with Wordsworth that 'our people ... will have to suffer—as you intimate—in order to learn that there is something more than the material interests which have been so greatly promoted hitherto'. Had Wordsworth made to her the point he was by now in the habit of making, especially to people who came to Rydal and tried to convert him to the slave-owners point of view, that the contradictions in American society had reached a point soluble only by civil war? In 1842 Wordsworth published in *The Dial* a furious denunciation of the perfidy of Philadelphia and Pennsylvania, in repudiating state development bonds, and defrauding innocent investors such as his daughter Dora.

In her last letter, of 1845, Peabody recalls this protest against 'the bad faith of one of our States', and asks him to realise that while there ought to be a *'moral solidarity'* in the Union, the American states are *'separate sovereignties'* like those of Europe. Turning the tables rather adroitly, she remarks: 'I hope you have some hope in the spiritual strength of the *Idea of Freedom*—to console you for the regret you must feel as an Englishman to see your government making common cause with absolutism in Europe' (Letter 8). But, return-

---

[1] *Letters of William and Dorothy Wordsworth, Later Years*, ed. Alan G Hill. (2nd edn, Oxford: Clarendon Press, 1979). 4: 231.

ing to her theme of Wordsworth as the poet of the English language, she restates the presiding theme of her letters: 'I would not have him despair of any of the natural domain in which he is to work forever with his inspired word.' As she had said in 1839, in her fifth letter, 'Whereas your audience was once as *few* as *fit* in this country—now it is coextensive with the country—and nowhere have you a deeper power'.[1] The Wordsworth she is addressing in 1839 is, clearly and poignantly, that of 1798–1802: a poet whose days are connected each to each in a chain of natural piety, the young poet, in effect, whose works Hawthorne and Thoreau were reading at this date.

This personal and national adoption of Wordsworth as 'my own dear spiritual father' (Peabody/4), and 'the prophet of a new moral order' (Channing), accords to Wordsworth a role in the development of an American consciousness which suggests a very different reading of Anglo-American relations from that of James Fenimore Cooper, one shared by Margaret Fuller in her essays of 1846. Fuller, too, feels a need for an American literature, and looks anxiously for the first signs. 'We have no sympathy with national vanity. We are not anxious to prove that there is as yet much American Literature.' Such a genius will rise, but despite the work of Cooper and Emerson and Halleck, and of Hawthorne—'the best writer of the day'—only 'the first faint streaks of that dawn are yet visible'.[2] Fuller wants an American Literature, clearly, and means by this something other than the production of 'English' books by American writers. They must justify their existence by offering something an English writer cannot offer, or has not offered. But there is no sign that she feels English writing to be alien. She treats Campbell, Moore, Scott, Crabbe, Shelley, Byron, Southey, Coleridge and Wordsworth, in that order, which is more or less the same as Hazlitt's in his 1818 lecture 'On the living poets'; in both cases, a rising order of merit. A quarter of Fuller's essay is devoted to an appreciation of Wordsworth—'beloved friend, how shall I speak of thee?'—in terms which confirm the Channing, Peabody, Chase estimation of Wordsworth, and suggest the role his work must have in fer-

---

1 Compare Thomas Chase in 1851: 'No country contains a larger number of intelligent admirers of Wordsworth's genius than our own' (cited, Mark Reed 33).
2 'American Literature', *The Writings of Margaret Fuller*, 358.

tilising the kind of writing that will be worthy of America.

The nature of that significance emerges clearly in two of Peabody's letters. As she wrote in her letter of 1838, after reading Carlyle, she has come to believe that 'the Revolution was only a change of form—and of quite outward form—leaving the heart of society unscathed and unchanged'. It is not that she opposes the notion of a revolution, rather she doubts (as Whitman would come to do) whether it has yet happened. In her second letter, of 1829, before Emerson or Hawthorne or Thoreau were active, she had already argued that if only poetry could be brought to 'mould the people',

> we might see grand souls indeed; which would do in the republic of letters, in the temple of lofty sciences, what they did fifty years since in politics. And it is necessary to that this more interior revolution should take place, to give life to—or even to perpetuate those forms of freedom which Washington & his friends left to us.

This 'more interior revolution' which is necessary 'to give life to—or [ominously] even to perpetuate' that of 1776, is clearly one of which Wordsworth is the designated prophet. When it arrives, it will at last realise the moral significance of the American Revolution. George Washington remains the father of his country, of course, but it lacks a godfather. More playfully, Peabody's last letter concludes:

> I would that you might in harmonious numbers welcome America (Alleghania as they propose to call it) upon the shores of being—You might name it—and christen it—and be its godfather 'for a Song'—the true prophet is the instrument of accomplishing the prophecy (Peabody/8).

For Cooper, the necessary condition for an American Literature is the alienation of American feelings from Great Britain. For Emerson, in his public utterance at least, the impression must be given that an American Literature will be self-generating. For Channing and Peabody and Fuller and Chase, however, an American Literature will grow when other young writers, like Hawthorne, have found the courage to enter the new era, and to emulate, not imitate, England's poet of National Independence and Liberty.

Peabody, having fewer axes to grind, was considerably more right than either Cooper or Emerson. Wordsworth had *already*, through Bryant and Byron, formed the sensibility of Natty Bumppo. Emerson could not have dethroned the 'courtly muse' without the assistance of Wordsworth's 1800 Preface and the 1815 postscript— both crucially formative in 'The American Scholar'. *Nature* would not have been *Nature*, nor Emerson Emerson, without Wordsworth's 'Poem upon the Wye' and 'Ode: Intimations of immortality'. 'The Boy of Winander' hooting to Lakeland owls originates the call with which Thoreau endeavours to awaken America and return the nation to its early self, while 'The Thorn' provides the grit around which Hawthorne's characteristic style forms itself. In Hawthorne and Thoreau Wordsworth found his most creative American readers. The 'Lucy' poems and 'Intimations' are, however, almost equally formative in the various arts of Poe, Whitman and Dickinson. In the Ode and the Lucy poems Poe encountered his characteristic topoi. Imitating 'We are seven' Whitman took his first manuscript steps in poetry, and his 'Song of Myself' answers *The Prelude*. *Moby-Dick* defines one pole of its 'high argument' with the aid of 'Intimations' and *The Excursion*. Even the ageing Wordsworth's premature burn-out, becomes for Thoreau a symbol of the American compromise and its gathering deafness to the still sad music of humanity.

For some of the writers treated in Part 2 of this study—particularly Cooper, Emerson, and Whitman—becoming an author involves a struggle between their sense of Americanness and their sense of belonging to an English literary tradition. It is marked by pugnacity in Cooper's case, a pugnacity uncomfortably at odds with his epigraphic raids upon the entire corpus of English poetry, and by transparently inefficaceous denial in Emerson's, and a policy, on Whitman's part of pretending most of the time to be quite untouched by the English canon. That no such struggle seems to exist for Elizabeth Peabody, Margaret Fuller or Emily Dickinson, may need no comment. Harold Bloom's famous theory of oedipal contestation is, after all, heavily gendered. Yet Bryant, Thoreau, Melville and Hawthorne, too, seem relatively untouched by the testosterone-driven confrontations in which Cooper, Emerson and Whitman feel obliged to engage, inscribing themselves with much less anxiety—indeed with evident delight—in an Anglo-American dialogue.

PART 2:

REDEEMING THE PROMISE OF ENGLAND, 1823–1862

Carlyle alone, since the death of Coleridge, has kept the promise of England.

—Henry David Thoreau

Generation after generation ... passes away, but the vital principle is transmitted to posterity, and the species continue to flourish. Thus also do authors beget authors, and having produced a numerous progeny, in a good old age they sleep with their fathers, that is to say with the authors who preceded them, and from whom they had stolen.

—Washington Irving

First one; then another; we drain all cisterns, and waxing greater by these supplies, we crave a better and more abundant food. The man has never lived that can feed us ever.

—Ralph Waldo Emerson

The American poets are to enclose old and new for America is the race of races.

—Walt Whitman

Chapter 4:

James Fenimore Cooper and the Spectre of Edmund Burke

> Man cannot enjoy the rights of an uncivil and of a civil state together. That he may obtain justice he gives up his right of determining what it is in points the most essential to him. That he may secure some liberty, he makes a surrender in trust of the whole of it.
>
> —Edmund Burke, *Reflections on the Revolution in France*

1. THE PIONEERS

The Pioneers, George Dekker has said, 'is one of a handful of great novels which deal so profoundly with *American* experience in the context of *American* social history that no *American* literature or history course can be sound without them' (my italics).[1] True; but its intellectual context is, nonetheless, transatlantic. Written in 1823, the novel opens with a reflection on the condition of upstate New York as a place still rejoicing in 'unfettered liberty of conscience' and 'exhibiting how much can be done, in even a rugged country, and with a severe climate, under the dominion of mild laws, and where every man feels a direct interest in the prosperity of a commonwealth, of which he knows himself to form a part'.[2] This complacent note

---
1 George Dekker, *James Fenimore Cooper the Novelist* (London: Routledge & Kegan Paul, 1967), 63, my emphases.
2 *The Pioneers*, ed. James D. Wallace (Oxford: Oxford University Press, 1991), 15-16.

is reminiscent not only of Rousseau's 'volonté générale' but of the numerous celebrations of republican prosperity written throughout the period from the 1780s to the 1830s by Crèvecoeur, Adam Smith, Paine, Chateaubriand and De Tocqueville. Lafayette, too, attributed American prosperity to 'institutions founded on the rights of man and the republican principle of self-government'.[1] The point is reinforced—and related to the Federalist interpretation of the Revolution—by an immediately subsequent reference to the permanent improvements being made by a hereditary 'yeomanry', though no such 'yeoman' republic existed in New York, which was still at the time of writing, governed by an aristocratic elite whose power sprang, as Paine had complained, from its enormous landholdings.

The confident opening note is perhaps a little shadowed by Cooper's reference, in the following paragraph, to the swelling population of 'a million and a half inhabitants' (that is, in 1823) 'who are maintained in abundance, and can look forward to ages before the evil day must arrive, when their possessions shall become unequal to their wants'. As it happens, for much of the novel, the leading citizen, Judge Temple, founder of Templeton, will be in ineffectual dispute with his Sheriff and his Law Officers and Deputies, who cannot be brought to see what Temple and Natty can see very clearly, that what Natty calls their 'wasty ways' already threaten the destruction of the paradise whose bounty they exploit with all possible speed and the least possible restraint. The irony is deepened when one remembers that the action of the novel is set in 1793, when Europe 'was in the commencement of that commotion which afterwards shook her political institutions to the centre ... and a nation, once esteemed the most refined among the civilized peoples of the world, was changing its character, and substituting cruelty for mercy' (chapter 8, 96). In 1794, inspired by this commotion, Condorcet would ask: 'Must there not arrive a period ... When the increase in the number of men surpassing their means of subsistence, the necessary result must be either a continual diminution of happiness and population, a movement truly retrograde, or, at least, a kind of oscillation between good and evil?'

---

1 *Notions of the Americans*, edited by Gary Williams (Albany, NY: State University of New York, 1991), 375.

Citing this passage in 1798 while discussing the inequality between population and production Malthus would find that 'the argument is conclusive against the perfectibility of the mass of mankind'.[1]

It is perhaps stretching a point to note that in 1793 one Tom Paine, author of *Common Sense* and of *The Rights of Man*, was imprisoned for ten months in Paris for displeasing the Directory. Natty Bumppo is somewhat luckier: he spends merely an afternoon in the stocks for colliding with the new edicts of Judge Temple. M. Le Quoi, who is in Templeton as a refugee from the Terror, finds it safe to make his way back to French possessions in the milder climate of late 1794 (when, as it happens, Paine was released). But it is surely pertinent to note that 1793 is the year of the first edition of William Godwin's *Political Justice*, the most reflective of all the replies to *Burke's Reflections on the Revolution in France* (1790) and that in the historical epoch in which the novel is set, the terms of political debate had already been set by the two English figures whose names were most popularly linked with American liberty—Edmund Burke and Tom Paine.[2] Until the publication of *Reflections*, Burke's liberal reputation was such that Paine expected his friend to lead pro-French opinion in England, and Mirabeau cited him regularly in the Constituent Assembly. In England, after its publication, and that of Paine's reply in *The Rights of Man* you were either a Burkean or a Paineite. In America it remained possible, or so the career of James Fenimore Cooper suggests, to be both. Certainly, when writing in 1823 a novel set in his childhood home in the period of his own boyhood, and

---

1 Marquis de Condorcet, *Esquisse d'un tableau historique des progres de l'esprit humain* (1794) cited in Thomas Malthus, *An Essay on the Principle of Population* (1798), p 123, both cited in Thomas McFarland, *Paradoxes of Freedom: the Romantic Mystique of a Transcendence* (Oxford: Clarendon, 1996) 115.

2 In private correspondence, Adams and Jefferson were engaged in much the same dispute. The next Leatherstocking novel, incidentally, is set in the year of Burke s *Philosophical Enquiry into the Origin of Our Ideas of the Sublime and the Beautiful*, 1757. Cooper's interest in this text is recognized by Steven Blakemore in '"Without a Cross": the Cultural Significance of the Sublime and Beautiful in Cooper's The Last of the Mohicans', *Nineteenth-Century Literature* (1997): 21–57. For Cooper's blend of the sublime and the political Burke, see my 'Regicide and Ethnic Cleansing: Edmund Burke in Wish-ton-Wish', *Symbiosis* 4:2 (October, 2000) 187–203.

contemplating the justice of his father's polity, Cooper combines the mind of Burke, the heart of Paine, and the language of both, in surprisingly evocative ways.

It is usual to see Cooper developing an American historical novel out of the Scott model. In Wa*verley*, for instance, the hero has to choose between a romantic identification with the Highland clans and a future within the new British constitutional settlement. Similarly, Cooper's young hero Oliver Effingham has to choose between marrying into the prosaic future of the new settlements, and their painful progress towards order, or remaining loyal to the past. In disguise for much of the novel as Oliver Edwards, he appears to be mysteriously related to two figures who represent that past, Natty Bumppo, the Leatherstocking, and Chingachgook, or Indian John Mohegan. Actually, he is the grandson of the loyalist Major Effingham whose estates—originally conferred on him by the gift of Chingachgook, and passed on to his son—were confiscated after the American Revolution and acquired by Marmaduke Temple, who (though Oliver is not aware of this) has always regarded himself as merely holding them in trust for his lost friend or his issue. The plot may be somewhat obscured by these Shakespearean disguises and surprises, as it leads towards the union of Oliver Effingham and Temple's daughter, but is designed to suggest simultaneously the ultimate legitimacy of this young American couple's possession of land which was once Indian, and the healing of the wounds of 1776 when loyalist (or 'Tory') estates were—in part at the suggestion of Tom Paine—confiscated by the victors for the benefit of 'patriots'.

This, however, is neither the sole, nor emotionally and imaginatively, the primary plot. Templeton, the scene of the action, is a settlement run by its somewhat feudal but nonetheless modernising and constitutional proprietor, Judge Temple (a compound of Cooper's father, William Cooper of Cooperstown and the equally enterprising Governor De Witt Clinton) whose laudable ambitions are to temper the rape of the land by its pioneers and to establish a system of lawful governance. The legitimacy of this ambition is challenged not only by the claims of the expropriated Effinghams, but by the presence of two relics of the past. Natty Bumppo, whose presence on the lake long predates that of Temple, now appears an out-of-place squatter with no foot in this world of property and law; his blood-brother, Chingachgook, is the last representative of the Mohicans, the original owners of the territory. The question for the reader is not whether the Temples or the Effinghams are the legitimate owners, but whether a world of title deeds can justly supplant a world of natural rights.

The novel opens with a parable of legality of which the tenor is that of Blake's Paineite poem, 'London'—namely, what is a 'chartered' liberty? Blake's denunciatory voice in 'London' focuses on the monopolistic implications of charters which reserve for the benefit of a 'titled' few what was once the liberty of all:

> I wander through each chartered street
> Near where the chartered Thames does flow
> And mark in every face I meet
> Marks of weakness, marks of woe.

Cooper became aware of such 'mind-forged manacles' in London in 1806, as a merchant sailor. Encouraged to exercise his 'right' to enter a Royal park, he understood for the first time, he says, the difference between genuine liberty and mere 'franchise'.[1] Judge Temple, on his way home with his daughter, stops his sleigh to fire twice at a fine buck in flight from the hounds of the Leatherstocking. His shots miss, but the buck is mysteriously brought down by two further shots, fired it transpires by Natty and by Oliver. The Judge persists in claiming it as his own, on the grounds that it is in his woods, whether he has shot it or not, until he realises that he has wounded Oliver. The dispute takes several pages to resolve, because a variety of claims have to be asserted and the Judge is determined to establish 'title' by purchase if not by deed or by shot. Natty is unwilling 'to give up my lawful dues in a free country.—Though for the matter of that, might often makes right here, as well as in the old country for what I can see' (1: 22). Oliver believes that his own shot killed it, and proves that the Judge's did not, since he miraculously detects four of the Judge's five shots in a nearby pine tree, and the fifth in his own body. At this the Judge

---

1 *Gleanings in Europe: England* (1837), ed. Robert E Spiller (New York: Oxford University Press, 1930), 248–9.

cedes 'title' in the venison, but also declaims in feudal grandeur:

> 'I here give a right to shoot deer, or bears, or any thing thou pleasest in my woods, for ever. Leather-stocking is the only other man that I have granted the same privilege to; and the time is coming when it will be of value' (25).

Natty, who has never heard of any law that a man shouldn't kill deer where he pleases, stands on the rights of man in a state of nature.

> 'There's them living who say, that Nathaniel Bumppo's right to shoot on these hills is of older date than Marmaduke Temple's right to forbid him'.

The Judge's rule, of course, is not quite absolute, nor is he the big bad baron. He functions as an odd blend of old baron and new whig, with a considerable admixture of the archetypal liberal. At a later point, when the potential for rapport seems to exist between Natty and Temple on the matter of wasteful felling and wasteful fishing, Temple tells Natty that laws have been passed controlling use of seines and the cutting of timber and adds, '"I hope to live to see the day, when a man's rights in his game shall be as much respected as his title to his farm."' Natty is unimpressed: '"Your titles and your farms are all new together," cried Natty; "but laws should be equal, and not more for one than another."' (14: 134). Refusing Temple's equation of broad ecological management with hunting rights (he knows nothing of his interest in developing mining rights), Natty sees Temple's notion of establishing proprietorial rights in game as restoring old-world inequalities between gamekeeper and poacher.

Precisely such inequality is a principal indictment against the ruling class in Obadiah Hulme's *Historical Essay on the English Constitution*, that exposition of the 'norman yoke' theory of English history which exercised such influence in 1776 on such writers as 'Demophilus' and such persons as Thomas Jefferson. As Hulme complained:

> They have engrossed, within a line of their own drawing, all hares, wild fowl, and fish, that are natives of this kingdom; which, in their own nature, being wild and wandering, and not

subject to restraint, are, therefore, the natural right of the first man that can catch them.¹

That feudal game laws should be a live issue in upstate New York some ten years after the close of the War of Independence suggests a concern with notions of liberty somewhat wider than purely American social history.

Temple's arguably self-interested law-making will bring about the major parable of the novel. At a later point, when it is established that the Judge has created a close season, Natty again shoots a deer, as a result of a ruse set up by one Hiram Doolittle, a corrupt legal officer who, for reasons of his own, wants an excuse to search Natty's hut. Doolittle has released Natty's hounds, which start a deer. Natty and Chingachgook, unable to resist the call of the wild, intercept the deer on the lakeshore, and Natty kills it. Doolittle acquires a search-warrant, on the pretext of looking for the carcass or the hide. Natty resists the execution of the search warrant, is tried for both crimes, and sentenced to the stocks and to a fine and/or imprisonment (the stocks, Cooper points out, were a legacy of the common law, which Paine— unlike Cooper—was particularly anxious to extirpate in favour of a new republican code). His dignity is outraged, he has no money, and of all men in the novel, cannot abide the loss of liberty. He is also, of course, the one figure in the novel whose relation to the natural world does not need to be controlled by the laws Judge Temple has found necessary for the rest of the settlers. In terms of abuse of the resources of Lake Otsego, every law officer in Templeton is far guiltier than he.

Much of the novel—including all of its greatest and most poetic scenes—is devoted to establishing Natty as innately ecological and responsible. In a drawing room or a court room he may appear clumsy and out-of-touch, though his misunderstanding of court procedure have the possibly unintended effect of bringing legal process, not himself, into ridicule (Cooper's ambivalence shows itself here in particularly confusing strength: his sympathy for Leatherstocking

---

1 Obadiah Hulme, *An Historical Essay on the English Constitution* (London, 1771), 131. Jefferson, in writing to Major John Cartwright in 1824, rehearses Hulme's views with evident familiarity.

undercuts quite fatally the theme of needful legitimacy). With a rifle or a fishing spear in his hand, or steering a slender canoe across the waters, he is not merely in nature but of Nature, and the heart of the novel consists of successive narrative and descriptive passages whereby Cooper (as Donald Davie has shown most effectively)[1] shows his incipient Wordsworthianism in the unobtrusive shift from literalism to symbol.

Natty's touchstones are Billy Kirby, a robust and good-natured woodcutter whose business and pleasure is the destruction as efficiently as possible of virgin forest; and the Sheriff, who uses cannon to shoot pigeons and a seine to dredge the lake of its fish, in scenes that amplify Wordsworth's 'Nutting', but without the saving recognition. Natty, who in his own environment has no need of law, since he embodies justice, and is the fearless guide and protector of anyone weaker than himself, which—in his own habitat—means more or less everybody, becomes the helpless victim of an unjust law, triggered by villainy. In an abstract sense the law is necessary, Temple strives to administer it fairly, and Templeton will be the better for it: concretely, its only casualty is the most Adamic person on the scene, persecuted by the law's corrupt or compromised agents.

Almost any work on political theory from Aristotle to Locke would furnish passages pertinent to Natty's situation, but Edmund Burke expresses its irony particularly well:

> One of the first motives to civil society, and which becomes one of its fundamental rules, is, that no man should be judge in his own cause. By this each person has at once divested himself of the first fundamental right of uncovenanted man, that is, to judge for himself, and to assert his own cause. He abdicates all right to be his own governor. He inclusively, in a great measure, abandons the right to self-defence, the first law of nature. Man cannot

---

[1] Donald Davie, *The Heyday of Sir Walter Scott* (London: Routledge and Kegan Paul, 1961), 135–43. In part thanks to William Cullen Bryant, Cooper's Wordsworthianism developed by leaps and bounds in the Leatherstocking saga, on which see my essay 'The Wordsworthian Metamorphosis of Natty Bumppo' in *Wordsworth in American Literary Culture*, ed. Joel Pace and Matthew Scott (Palgrave, 2005), 43–58.

James Fenimore Cooper and the Spectre of Edmund Burke 137

enjoy the rights of an uncivil and of a civil state together. That he may obtain justice he gives up his right of determining what it is in points the most essential to him. That he may secure some liberty, he makes a surrender in trust of the whole of it.[1]

This, at least, is how Judge Temple, scourge of Jacobin excess— 'these Jacobins are as blood-thirsty as bull-dogs' (14: 133)—might put the case, in explaining the matter to his more Romantic daughter, whose heart inclines her towards Natty's position, and not merely because he has just saved her life.

It is a persuasive case, partly because it was penned by the man who provided in his first published work, *A Vindication of Natural Society*, the most eloquent statement of its contrary. Natty himself, were he gifted in philosophical disputation, might well reply to Temple as follows (he habitually appeals to God as the author of a right state of things):

> We will not place the State of Nature, which is the Reign of God, in competition with Political Society, which is the absurd Usurpation of Man. In a State of Nature, it is true, that a Man of superior Force may beat or rob me; but then it is true, that I am at full liberty to defend myself, or make Reprisal by Surprize or by Cunning, or by any other way in which I may be superior to him. But in a Political Society, a rich Man may rob me in another way... and if I attempt to avenge myself, the whole force of that Society is ready to complete my ruin.[2]

Or, if not familiar with what Gilbert Imlay called 'Burke's paradoxical book', he might cite Paine, whose 1791 translation of Lafayette's 'Declaration des droits de l'homme', in defining 'the natural and imprescriptible rights of man', observed that 'Political liberty consists in the power of doing whatever does not injure another. The exercise of the natural rights of every man has no other limits than those which

---

1 Burke, *Reflections on the Revolution in France* (1790), ed. Conor Cruise O'Brien (Harmondsworth: Penguin, 1968), 150.
2 Burke, *A Vindication of Natural Society: or, a View of the Miseries and Evils arising to Mankind from every species of Artificial Society*, 2nd edn (London: 1757), 87.

are necessary to secure to every other man the free exercise of those rights...'. There is, however, a further clause, or Catch-22, which Natty has not hitherto noticed: '... and these limits are determinable only by the law'.[1]

Since the *Vindication* is the first item in Burke's *Complete Works* (Boston 1806) and as Gilbert Imlay refers to it as early as 1792, it is reasonable to assume that Cooper knew it.[2] That being so, it may also be relevant to note that Natty's claims on the Judge's interest include the fact that he welcomed the Judge to these parts, despite seeing Temple's interests as inimical to his own; gave him his own bear-skin to sleep on, fed him (on '"the fat of a noble buck ... Yes, yes—you thought it no sin then to kill a deer!"'); and has just saved his daughter from a panther—a point not lost on Elizabeth or Oliver. Natty might well feel, in the words of the youthful Burke, that 'it is an incontestable truth, that there is more havoc made in one year by Men, of men, than has been made by all the Lions, Tygers, Panthers ... since the beginning of the world... But with respect to you, ye Legislators, ye Civilizers of Mankind!... your Regulations have done more Mischief in cold blood, than all the Rage of he fiercest Animals in their greatest Terrors, or Furies, has ever done or ever could do!' (*Vindication* 35). What he does say, more temperately, is 'there's them that says hard things to you, Marmaduke Temple, but you an't so bad as to wish to see an old man die in a prison because he stood up for the right. Come friend, let me pass; it's long sin' I've been used to such crowds, and I crave for the woods ag'in' (ch 33).

In Templeton, Natty has come to believe, Might is Right. At the close of the book Natty will say to Elizabeth and Oliver, symbolically descended from Quaker and Indian sires respectively, 'bless you and all that belong to you, from this time till the great day when the whites shall meet the red-skins in judgement, and justice shall be the law, and not power.' Like every comment Natty makes, this under-

---

1 Thomas Paine, *The Rights of Man* (Harmondsworth: Penguin, 1984), 111.
2 In his *Topographical Description of the Western Territory of North America* (London, 1792) Imlay attributes Jefferson's anxieties concerning unicameralism, as expressed in his *Notes on the State of Virginia* (1787), to the influence of 'Burke's paradoxical book'. Since Jefferson's *Notes* predate the *Reflections*, the 'paradoxical' book seems likeliest to be the *Vindication*.

James Fenimore Cooper and the Spectre of Edmund Burke 139

mines Temple's law as having anything to do with natural justice, just as Cooper's emotional commitment to Natty makes nonsense of his intention to celebrate the progress of civil society.

When Burke wrote his *Vindication of Natural Society*, with its impassioned critique of all forms of human government ('In vain you tell me that Artificial government is good, but that I fall out only with the Abuse. The Thing! the Thing itself is the Abuse!', 68), he intended its irony to be recognised. His purpose was to represent the anti-civil case as it might be put by a Bolingbroke, in order that its speciousness might be recognised. Yet, as Adam Phillips says of the *Vindication*, 'He had so successfully identified with the writer he opposed—and the theory, derived from Rousseau, of a natural as opposed to a civil society—that he had become stylistically indistinguishable from the object of his contempt. Nine years later, in the Preface to a second edition, Burke had to explain his ironic intentions.'[1] Similarly, Cooper, when he created Natty Bumppo, and gave him the toothless grin and silent laugh and nose-wiping uncouthness of the comic outsider, did not intend that he should be a wholly persuasive spokesman for Paine's sansculotte views. The Leatherstocking, initially, is meant to be a touching irrelevance, an archaic hangover. Instead he not only walks away with the novel, but commands his creator to write four further novels, each of which takes us further from any sense of the moral superiority of white civilization or civil law and provides further vindications of a state of nature.

Natty's age disguises the fact that in terms of civil society his is an adolescent resistance to lawful authority that must be overcome, but his force of character undermines any sense one is meant to derive from the novel that the ways of the settlers represent moral progress. Thus, the Paineite or ironically Burkean sansculottism of the Leatherstocking is lent an authority which is quite at odds with the author's fixed views and intentions.[2] Nor is the theme of historical progression

---

1 Edmund Burke, *A Philosophical Enquiry into the Origins of our Ideas on the Sublime and Beautiful*, ed. Adam Phillips (Oxford: Oxford University Press, 1990), xiv.
2 Henry Nash Smith argues persuasively that Natty is created as a kind of antidote to Judge Cooper: 'all the aspects of authority ... are exhibited as radiating from the symbol of the father. But if the father rules, and rules justly, it is still

and legitimacy—the *Henry V* theme—much helped by the patently false fictional manoeuvres to which Cooper resorts. Chingachgook decides to allow himself to die during a forest fire brought about by the greed and carelessness of the settlers, and expires to the accompaniment of a thunder clap bringing rain. This sublime death, combined with the miraculous rescue of Elizabeth, and the brief reappearance of Major Effingham (named the Fire-Eater by the Mohicans who gave him the lands Temple now occupies) is meant to legitimise the act of dispossession that has now been completed by this rapacious white society. Mohegan—friend of Effingham—recognises in Elizabeth Temple the 'Miquon', or Quaker heritage, which he admired, and blesses the forthcoming union of the Royalist and Republican strains. He has remained quietly confident that Temple, in whom he sees the heritage of William Penn, will willingly divide with Oliver the lands which he, Chingachgook, once gave to Major Effingham. In any case he himself articulates to Elizabeth the fatalistic view that 'the Great Spirit gave your fathers to know how to make guns and powder that they might sweep the Indians from the land'. Judge Temple's polity is meant to represent the future, but since neither Temple, nor ultimately his daughter and son-in-law, can command the reader's confidence, the myth of progress whereby in Chateaubriand's words 'this liberty of the United States replaces the liberty of the Indian' is felt as a myth of regress.[1]

Not for the last time, Cooper uses a gravestone motif with an effect which may or may not be ironical. Chingachgook (the Great Sarpent) whose splendid prime will be celebrated throughout three of the subsequent novels, is known for much of the novel as Mohegan, or John Mohegan or merely as Indian John. This progressive renaming, Fiona Stafford points out, mimes not only his loss of identity and status but

---

true that in this remembered world of his childhood, Cooper figures as the son. Thus he is able to impart real energy to the statement of the case for defiance and revolt.' Henry Nash Smith, *Virgin Land: The American West as Symbol and Myth* (Cambridge MA: Harvard University Press, 1970), 62. Compare Leslie Fiedler, *Love and Death in the American Novel*, 2nd edn (Harmondsworth: Penguin Books, 1966) 165.

1 *Travels in America*, tr. David Switzer (Lexington: University of Kentucky Press, 1969), 191.

the extinction of the Mohican people, and symbolically the Indian race.[1] At the end of the novel Natty contemplates the gravestones which Oliver Effingham, the Young Eagle, has erected for his Tory Grandfather and his Indian Godfather. A paragraph records the name and rank and the numerous martial and Christian virtues of Major Oliver Effingham. On Chingachgook's headstone, erected by Oliver, *to whom Chingachgook has bequeathed the lands of his nation*, his name is mis-spelled and posterity is told merely that 'his faults were those of an Indian and his virtues those of a man.'[2]

Natty no more notices the irony, and the slight, than he does the beautifully prepared irony in his own disappearance from the novel in flight from the face of man: 'He had gone far towards the setting sun,—the foremost in that band of Pioneers, who are opening the way for the march of the nation across the continent.' The reader must have wondered from time to time, when we are to meet the 'pioneers' referred to in the title, rather than the motley assortment of settlers, exploiters, shopkeepers and landowners who make up the cast of the novel—which, without Natty, would be a thoroughly English social novel concerned with the foibles of a squire and his neighbours. The close of the novel, with its affirmation that Natty is the Pioneer, leaves one with a bitter irony. Templeton, exemplary frontier settlement, cannot be home to the one figure who has bodied forth the values of natural justice America itself exists to realise.[3] 'Yes— yes', Natty will recognise as soon as he arrives in the opening pages

---

[1] Fiona Stafford, *The Last of the Race: The Growth of a Myth from Milton to Darwin* (Oxford: Clarendon Press, 1994), 250.

[2] Cooper recycles this technique of monumental obliteration in *The Wept of Wish-ton-Wish*, which also ends with a graveyard. Mrs Heathcote's grave is marked with the sort of detail accorded to Major Effingham, 'Ruth, daughter of George Harding of the Colony of Massachusetts Bay, and wife of Captain Content Heathcote'. The Indian Conanchet is treated rather as Chingachgook was: he is buried as 'The Narragansett'. Even greater anonymity befalls his white bride Narra-Mattah (Ruth Heathcote). Her grave is marked merely 'The Wept of Wish-ton-Wish'. The child of this miscegany is not mentioned. *The Wept* is intriguing also for its treatment of a fugitive regicide and the quality of its irony in depictig whte attitudes to native Americans.

[3] *The Pioneers, or the Sources of the Susquehannah*, ed J. F. Beard, Lance Schachterle and Kenneth M Andersen Jr (Albany: SUNY Press, 1980), xlviii.

of *The Prairie*, 'the law is needed, when such as have not the gifts of strength and wisdom are to be taken care of',[1] but for those who have such gifts, it represents too unpalatable a departure from the first principles of liberty. Of course, the reader recognises, waking from the anarchic dream into which Cooper's imagination has wandered, since all men are not Natty Bumppo, the civil law is needed. But this is the last of the Leatherstocking novels in which that case will get so fair a hearing. The truly representative American is not Natty Bumppo but the proto-Jacksonian Billy Kirby, his natural antagonist, whose very occupation spells death to Natty Bumppo, Chingachgook, and their ways of life. 'I earnestly beg you will remember' says Judge Cooper of the trees in which Kirby makes 'such dreadful wounds':

> 'that they are the growth of centuries, and that when once gone, none living will see their loss remedied.'
> 'Why, I don't know, Judge,' returned the man he addressed: 'It seems to me, if there's a plenty of any thing in this mountaynious country, it's the trees.... I've chopped over the best half of a thousand acres, with my own hands, counting both Varmount and York states; and I hope to live to finish the whull, before I lay up my axe.'

In *The Prairie*, Donald Davie points out, Cooper has to conjure up a grove of trees on the treeless prairie so that Ishmael Bush and his sons may symbolically fell them: 'here, too ... the sound of the axe is for Cooper the sound of doom'.[2]

The Pioneers has had three major thematic concerns: America's embodiment of political justice; landscape and its resources; and Indian dispossession. The first of these proved more tangled than Cooper may have supposed when he began the novel, and he returns to it equally indecisively in *The Prairie* and if anything more despairingly in *The Wept of Wish-ton-Wish*. Each of these novels, together with *The Last of the Mohicans*, *The Pathfinder*, and *The Deerslayer*, also develops Cooper's landscape art. Natty is, as George Sand noted, an unparalleled observer of landscape, the unobtrusive eye through

---

1 *The Prairie*, ed. Donald A. Ringe (Oxford: Oxford University Press, 1992), 27.
2 *The Heyday of Sir Walter Scott*, 135.

which Cooper's reader experiences the virgin lands, and even on his debut in *The Pioneers* (Chapter 26) he devotes three pages to a depiction of remembered vistas and waterfalls in the Catskills which will become the stuff of the Hudson River School of Painting. Cooper thus joins with the consciously Wordsworthian Bryant and their friend the unconsciously Martinesque Thomas Cole in associating American liberty with the wildness of American landscape. The well-travelled Cooper was well aware, as he will point out in the opening sentence of *Wyandotté* (1843), that while the world attaches to American scenery 'an idea of grandeur ... the scenery of that portion of the American continent which has fallen to the share of the Anglo-Saxon race very seldom rises to a scale that merits this term.'[1] The lush rolling forests of the Susquehannah are, if anything, reminiscent rather of Surrey than the Alps, which Cooper came to associate with genuine sublimity. But it was of course Thomas Paine who most famously established the conjunction between the Romantic sublime and American Liberty. Introducing Part 2 of *The Rights of Man,* Paine deftly turned the young libertarian Burke against the older counter-revolutionary one:

> As America was the only spot in the political world where the principles of universal reformation could begin, so also was it the best in the natural world.... The scene which that country presents to the eye of a spectator has something in it which generates and encourages great ideas. Nature appears to him in magnitude. The mighty objects he beholds act upon his mind by enlarging it, and he partakes of the greatness he contemplates. ... In such a situation man becomes what he ought. He sees his species, not with the inhuman idea of a natural enemy, but as kindred; and the example shows to the artificial world that man must go back to nature for information.[2]

---

1 *Wyandotté, or the Hutted Knoll* (1843; London: George Routledge, 1887), 5. To the European eye, Cooper goes on, its scenery is 'tame and uninteresting as a whole, though it certainly has exceptions that carry charms of this nature to the verge of loveliness'.

2 *The Rights of Man*, edited by Eric Foner (Harmondsworth: Penguin, 1984), 160.

The Pioneers, by making all but three of his characters entirely impervious to such effects, adds to the scepticism about human perfectibility that his book conveys. It also sees American society as incipiently a second edition of the artificial society of Europe, and creates in Natty a child of nature whose very existence is a critique of that artificial society.

Unlike Burke, Cooper never explained his ironic intentions—never, perhaps, fully recognised that his intentions and performance were so discrepant. Despite the author's lack of sympathy for the Paineite dimension of Jeffersonian Republicanism, the sansculotte leatherstocking is the one figure in the book who fully engages Cooper's Romantic imagination and the one character with whom every reader's fullest sympathies engage. Unlettered, ignorant of law, with limited vocabulary and syntax ('anan?' is his invariable way of requesting a simpler paraphrase), unimaginable within a polite drawing room—and tactfully *never placed in one throughout the saga*—Leatherstocking is the antithesis of almost everything that Cooper values, except natural justice. Yet without the Leatherstocking there would have been no saga, and while his sansculotte status may represent an impossible dream, that dream becomes the more commanding through every successive treatment, and attracts to it other impossible dreams—among them that of miscegenistic union of white and red (*The Last of the Mohicans* and *The Wept of Wish-ton-Wish*), or absolute patriarchal authority (*The Prairie*, and *The Wept of Wish-ton-Wish*), or the reconciliation of frontier values and unspoiled virgin land (*The Pathfinder* and *The Deerslayer*). As Cooper's politics become more Burkean, his discontent with democracy the more extreme, Natty Bumppo, that personified *vindication of natural society*, moves deeper into wilderness and/or backwards in time.

Regressing, as Cooper's greatest readers—from D H Lawrence to Yvor Winters and Donald Davie—have said he does, Natty if he pursues the journey far enough will rendezvous with Sigmund Freud, analyst of *Civilisation and its Discontents*, and finally recognise that:

> What makes itself felt in a human community as a desire for freedom may be their revolt against some existing injustice, and so may prove favourable to a further development of civiliza-

tion.... But it may also spring from the remains of the original personality, which is still untamed by civilization and may thus become the basis in them of hostility to civilization. The urge for freedom, therefore, is directed against particular forms and demands of civilization *or civilization altogether*....[1]

Leslie Fiedler and D. H. Lawrence both intuited in Cooper such a hostility. 'Men live by lies', Lawrence observes:

> In actuality, Fenimore loved the genteel continent of Europe, and waited gasping for the newspapers to praise his WORK.
> In another actuality he loved the tomahawking continent of America, and imagined himself Natty Bumppo.
> His actual desire was to be: Monsieur Fenimore Cooper, le grand écrivain américain.
> His innermost wish was to be: Natty Bumppo.[2]

And so, haunted by this alter ego, he writes the Leatherstocking Saga, pursuing as Lawrence says, 'a *decrescendo* of reality, and a *crescendo* of beauty' (317). The idealisation, which after the attempt at a social novel in *The Pioneers*, sets in throughout the Leatherstocking Saga, does indeed represent a flight from American reality. In subsequent novels, curiously, the American characters often refer to themselves not as frontiersmen but as 'borderers', as if they have walked out of a Scott novel or Wordsworth's frontier play, and have not quite registered the new territory, or as if to remind us of the border between reality and the dreamscape of the books. In its positive dimension, Cooper is a great mythmaker. His Leatherstocking, as Yvor Winters says, becomes 'a great national myth, with a life over and above the life of the books in which he appears, a reality surpassing that even of a historical figure such as Daniel Boone.'[3] Boone was celebrated by Byron as the child of nature and

---

1 Sigmund Freud, *Civilization and its Discontents* in *The Complete Psychological Works*, edited by James Strachey et.al., 24 vols. (London: Hogarth Press, 1966–74), 21: 96.
2 D. H. Lawrence, *Studies in Classic American Literature* (London: Heinemann, 1964), 45–6.
3 Yvor Winters, *In Defence of Reason* (NY:The Swallow Press, 1947), 186.

critic of artificial society, whose strength was drawn from the very wilderness and seclusion his followers—the William Coopers and other pioneers of the Susquehannah (among them, but for the grace of God, Samuel Taylor Coleridge)—destroyed. In mythologising the youthful spirit of America as already aged in 1793, and as fated to experience perpetually the irreconcilability of freedom and law, Cooper dealt a fatal blow to the idea that America and freedom were synonymous. Pursuing that elusive freedom back to its source, his works, oddly enough, find themselves impelled to regress, towards the truly republican moment of the earliest and colonial settlements.

2. COOPER'S POLITICAL PROGRESS

As the son of a pioneer and Federalist—William Cooper of Cooperstown, disciple of the great Governor De Witt Clinton—and as the friend of Lafayette, early admirer of Washington, and belated admirer of the 'sansculotte' Jefferson,[1] Cooper was never altogether sure where to situate himself *vis-à-vis* the revolution debate of the 1790s. Socially, and to some extent politically, he belonged to the party which feared and was prone to vilify the side of Tom Paine and William Godwin, as, for instance, did President John Quincy Adams:

> I know not whether any man in the world has had more influence on its inhabitants or affairs for the last thirty years than Tom Paine. There can be no severer satyr on the age. For such a mongrel between pig and puppy, begotten by a wild boar on a bitch wolf, never before in any age of the world was suffered by the poltroonery of mankind, to run through such a career of mischief. Call it then the Age of Paine.[2]

Paine must be counted one of the fathers of the revolution, and perhaps the only unreluctant one, but Cooper never identifies with him, either

---

1 Cooper came to admire Jefferson only after seeing him in Sully's portrait, 'not in red breeches and slovenly attire, but a gentleman ... without any of the repulsive accompaniments of a political "sans culotte".' *Letters and Journals of James Fenimore Cooper*, edited by James Franklin Beard (Cambridge, MA:The Belknap Press of Harvard University Press, 1960), 1: 95.

2 Cited by David Freeman Hawke, *Paine* (New York: Norton, 1974), 7.

socially or ideologically, any more than did President Adams. He grew up in a culture in which Burke rather than Paine was the culture hero. Two of Burke's essays on American rights—'On American taxation', 'On Conciliation with the Colonies'—were schoolroom texts, and his works were published instantaneously in American editions (a major six volume edition was published in Boston in 1806).

'There are many "manors" in New York', Cooper explains in *The Pioneers*, 'though all political and judicial rights have ceased'. He grew up on one such manor or 'patent', comprising some 100,000 acres originally ceded under an Indian deed to Colonel George Croghan in 1770, and energetically developed by William Cooper who took possession of what became known as 'Cooper's Patent' in 1786. The novelist, in his childhood in Cooperstown, where William Cooper's home was the local meeting place of the Federalist squirearchy, had ample opportunity to observe how in reality, political power belonged to the great landowners and was exercised through influence over tenants which was little diminished from pre-Revolutionary days.[1]

In 1820–21 Cooper still opposed the liberalisation of voting rights, and, like his father, held aloof from the Jeffersonian Republicans, supporting instead the more moderate faction of Governor De Witt Clinton. As he moved away from his roots, and mixed with the more liberal intelligentsia of New York City, to which he moved in 1823, Cooper came to reject, as a good Republican, and still more when he became a good Democrat, the social stake theory into which Jay and others had perverted the association between property and republicanism in Harrington's *Oceana*. Internationally, Cooper was

[1] See Robert E. Spiller, *Fenimore Cooper: Critic of his Times* (New York: Minton, Balch & Co, 1931) 6–23. For Cooper's political bearings see Charles Hansford Adams, *The Guardian of the Law* (University Park and London: Pennsylvania State University Press, 1990); James Franklin Beard, 'Cooper and the Revolutionary Mythos', *Early American Literature*, 11 (1976) 84–104; George Dekker, *James Fenimore Cooper: the Novelist* (London: Routledge & Kegan Paul, 1967); Russell Kirk, *The Conservative Mind: from Burke to Eliot*, 7th revised edition (Chicago: Regnery Books, 1986); Vernon Louis Parrington, *The Romantic Revolution in America 1800–1860* (NY; Harcourt, Brace & Co, 1927), and especially John P. McWilliams's indispensable *Political Justice in a Republic* (Berkeley: U of California Press, 1972).

of course an active partisan of liberation, like his immediate English Romantic precursors, Shelley and Byron, and the continental revolutionaries whose causes they and he espoused. He had been radicalised in mid-career, in part by his New York friendships with Bryant and the Byronist Halleck, in part by his European experiences with Lafayette, Kosciuszki, Mickiewicz and the English Reform Movement, and in part by his chosen role as the American patriot-at-large. But domestically he espoused successively the causes of Federalism, independent Republicanism, Clintonian Republicanism, Jacksonian Democracy, and his own peculiar brand of American Conservatism. From *Home as Found* (1838) to *The Crater* (1847) his essential role as the American Burke predominates.

In a manuscript left at his death, 'The Towns of Manhattan', later published as *New York*, Cooper reflects on the unattainability of a perfect polity. In any comparison of differing systems, he says,

> We are far from saying that our own, with all its flagrant and obvious defects, will be the worst ... though we cannot deny, not do we wish to conceal, the bitterness of the wrongs that are so frequently inflicted by the many on the few. This is, perhaps, the worst species of tyranny. *He who suffers under the arbitrary power of a single despot, or by the selfish exactions of a privileged few, is certain to be sustained by the sympathies of the masses. But he who is crushed by the masses themselves must look beyond the limits of his earthly being for consolation and support. The wrongs committed by democracies are of the most cruel character;* and ... carry with them in their course all the feelings that render injustice and oppression intolerable.[1]

The Burkean quality of this late Cooper utterance becomes evident when we place it beside what is surely its original:

> Of this I am certain, that in a democracy, *the majority of the citizens is capable of exercising the most cruel oppressions upon the minority*, whenever strong divisions prevail in that kind of polity, as they often must; and that oppression of the minority

---

1 James Fenimore Cooper, *New York* (New York: Payson, 1930), 58–9. My emphases.

will extend to far greater numbers, and will be carried on with much greater fury, than can almost ever be apprehended from the dominion of a single sceptre. In such a popular persecution, individual sufferers are in a much more deplorable condition than in any other. *Under a cruel prince they have the balmy compassion of mankind to assuage the smart of their wounds ... but those who are subjected to wrong under multitudes, are deprived of all external consolation.* They seem deserted by mankind; overpowered by a conspiracy of their whole species.[1]

Strikingly, Burke's final sentence epitomises the condition of Natty Bumppo, exhibited in the stocks, made exemplary victim of the people's court, and punished for taking a single deer—as a result of the actions of an *agent provocateur*—within the borders of a polity in which for chapter after chapter the most wasteful carnage and destruction of every kind of natural resource has been perpetrated remorselessly by the Sheriff, and remorsefully by the Judge, over the protests of that same Natty Bumppo, who is, as Dekker has put it, 'the only just man in sight' (Dekker, 89.)

Burke, famous up to the moment he published his *Reflections* as a liberal, and thereafter as a conservative counter-revolutionary makes an interesting touchstone. Today, Burke's *Reflections on the Revolution in France* is read almost always through the eyes of Paine, as somewhat tendentiously represented in *The Rights of Man* (Paine learned this brilliantly reductive strategy from Algernon Sidney's *Discourses* where it is deployed against Robert Filmer's *Patriarcha*.) Its argument, according to Paine, is that the living are and always must be subjected to the will of the dead, from whom we receive our liberties as an entailed inheritance. A fairer summary might be offered in the words of James Madison who wrote to Jefferson in the same year, that 'The improvements made by the dead form a charge against the living who take the benefit of them .... All that is indispensible in adjusting the account between the dead and the living is to see that the debits against the latter do not exceed the advances made by the former'.[2]

---

1 Burke, *Reflections*, 229. My emphases.
2 Jefferson, writing to Madison in 1789, had raised the question whether

In Cooper's eyes, one of the great merits of the American Constitution, though created by a constitutional convention at a particular moment, was that it respected and institutionalised the received wisdom of the participant states and accepted the theoretically absurd notion that a majority of states containing a minority of the national population could impose its will on the majority of Americans. The only power the federal government possessed, or ever would possess, Cooper argued, was that explicitly delegated to it by 'the states then in *existence*'—which alone could ratify it—and not by that vague entity enshrined in its preamble 'we the people'.[1] Given that Cooper, in 1838, already looked back upon 1788 as America's Golden Age, and his treatise on American democracy is an attempt to restate the principles of *The Federalist* for his own brazen one, it is evident that he takes considerable comfort in the extent to which American practice must be always circumscribed by the 'entailed liberties' inherited from John Jay, James Madison and Alexander Hamilton.

It is true that Cooper recognises that 'no country can properly be deemed free, unless the body of the nation possess, in the last resort, the legal power to frame its laws according to its wants. This power must also abide in the nation, or it becomes merely an historical fact' (*American Democrat* 112). But Burke, too, is perfectly aware that a nation must have the right, as it clearly does have the power, to abandon one system, when it has grown oppressive, and choose another. In *Reflections* his specific complaint is *not* that the French abandoned an absolute monarchy for democracy. In 1789, he says explicitly, 'the absolute monarchy was at an end. It breathed its last, without a groan, without a struggle, without convulsion. All the struggle, all the dissension arose afterwards upon the preference of a despotic democracy to a government of reciprocal controul. The triumph of the victorious party was over the principles of a British constitution' (*Reflections*, 241). The difference between Burke and Cooper is in their view of

---

'one generation of men has a right to bind another,' proposing that 'the earth belongs in usufruct to the living.' *The Portable Jefferson*, ed. Merrill D. Peterson (Harmondsworth: Penguin, 1977), 445. I cite Madison's 1790 reply from John P. McWilliams, 298.

1 James Fenimore Cooper, *The American Democrat*, ed. George Dekker and Larry Johnston (Harmondsworth: Penguin, 1969), 84.

James Fenimore Cooper and the Spectre of Edmund Burke 151

the reality of British polity. To Burke, the British Constitution is the very prototype of the principle of checks and balances, whereas to Cooper it is an Aristocracy, tempered by franchises and masquerading as a Monarchy.

Cooper's theory of government is, nevertheless, aligned with Burke's and John Adams's grasp of the traditional view from Aristotle to Montesquieu. In this view, summarised in both *The American Democrat* and *A Vindication of Natural Society*, there are three kinds of government: despotisms, aristocracies and democracies. Despotisms, or monarchies, if just and benevolent, which they usually are not, may provide the most harmonious of societies, but they suffer from flattery and vice and rely on the unrealistic expectation that the despot will represent the perfection of human nature. Aristocracies are as expensive as monarchies, and tend to be more soulless and ruthless, lacking the personal feelings of responsibility that temper despotism (*American Democrat*, 125). As Burke puts it, 'an Aristocracy and a Despotism differ but in name; and ... a people, who are in general excluded from any share of the Legislative, are to all Intents and Purposes, as much slaves, when twenty, independent of them, govern, as when but one domineers' (*Vindication*, 49). Nominal 'republicks', both authors agree, may in practice be elective despotisms or hereditary aristocracies. Nor is pure democracy an acceptable device, because it is the most prone to abuse by the demagogue. The Greek democracy of Solon was soon overset because 'an artful man became popular, the People had power in their hands, and they devolved a considerable Share of their Power upon their Favourite, and the only use he made of this Power, was to plunge those who gave it into Slavery' (*Vindication* 55). In large democracies, 'the people are peculiarly exposed to become the dupes of demagogues and political schemers' and 'in a country where opinion has sway, to seize upon it, is to seize power' (*American Democrat*, 128, 208).

These are commonplace agreements, deriving ultimately, as Burke points out, from the ancients, who saw absolute democracy as no more legitimate than absolute monarchy. What Cooper describes in *The American Democrat* is the proper functioning of a stable republic designed to guard against this corruption and degeneration, for 'no tyranny of the one, nor any tyranny of the few' is worse than that of 'the publick' when it assumes 'the powers that properly belong to the whole body of the people, and to them only under constitutional limitations' (130). Genuine liberty cannot exist, Cooper says, 'without many restraints on the power of the mass' (117) and 'it ought to be impressed on every man's mind, in letters of brass, "*That in a democracy, the publick has no power that is not expressly conceded by the institutions, and that this power, moreover, is only to be used under the forms prescribed by the constitution. All beyond this, is oppression.*"' (197 Cooper's italics). 'We are to understand by liberty,' Cooper argues, 'merely such a state of the social compact as permits the members of a community to lay no more restraints on themselves, than are required by their real necessities, and obvious interests.' For liberty, says Burke, 'is secured by the equality of Restraint; a Constitution of things in which the liberty of no one Man and no body of Men and no Number of men can find means to trespass on the liberty of any Person or any description of persons in the society.'[1]

One major distinction between Burke and Cooper is that, writing in America, Cooper sounds a good deal hotter on the necessity and *beneficence* of material and social *inequality*. Inheritance of parental acquisitions is essential to a dynamic society, 'an inducement to great and glorious deeds' (138). Without this (though Cooper does not quite say this in *The American Democrat*) America would no longer have the great landed estates which alone could produce the disinterested political leadership she needed. And 'social inequality … is as much a consequence of civilized society, as breathing is a vital function of animal life' (140). Another, perhaps the definitive differentiation between the two, is that Cooper insists that because wealth confers its own privileges and status, the nation must deny any 'hereditary claims to trusts and power.' Burke saw himself as 'no friend to aristocracy', which when undiluted led to 'austere and

---

[1] *The Correspondence of Edmund Burke*, ed. Thomas W. Copeland, 10 vols. (Cambridge: Cambridge University Press, 1958–78), 6: 39–40.

James Fenimore Cooper and the Spectre of Edmund Burke 153

insolent domination',[1] but persuaded himself that the Constitutional settlement of 1688 had created a balance between crown, aristocracy and bourgeoisie which reflected real interests and worked in favour of liberty. Cooper, though believing in a democracy based, as he put it, on numbers, not property, was already doubtful in 1838 whether a country as unstable as the United States could really allow people without 'permanent and fixed interests' in their constituency an influence on government (194) and within a few years would be advocating a restricted suffrage and fewer elections. He had in fact advocated a moderate property qualification for France in 1831.[2] In 1847 in *The Crater* he produced a dystopia in which social collapse is brought about by the propertiless divesting the propertied of political power—thus endorsing, implicitly, the notion that property has a constitutional rights—and in 1850 he would argue that American democracy is not obligated 'to admit any but a minority of her whites to the enjoyment of political power'[3]

Read through the mesmerising eyes of Tom Paine, Burke's *Reflections* makes us all slaves of the dead. Read in itself, however, *Reflections* has a rather different thesis which may be summarised as follows. France in 1789 had the opportunity to replace a thoroughly discredited absolutism by a carefully counterweighted constitution on the British model. That such a model guaranteed the optimum balance of stability and liberty was axiomatic, not only to Burke, but to such of his disciples as de Tocqueville and John C Calhoun.[4] Such a balance may grow, but is not easily achieved by fiat. Adams and Burke shared the conviction that 'The moment you abate any thing from the full rights of men, each to govern himself, and suffer

---

1 *Edmund Burke on Government, Politics and Society*, ed. B. W. Hill (Brighton: Harvester Press, 1975), 93.
2 Spiller, *Fenimore Cooper: Critic of his Times*, 167–68..
3 McWilliams, *Political Justice*, 394.
4 Calhoun argues that the king, who is in effect the tax-consuming power, can act only through ministers who are responsible both to the lords, 'as constituting the high court' and the commons who represent the tax-paying interest and possess 'the impeaching power'. So the acts of the government 'may be fairly considered as the result of the concurrent and joint action of the three estates'. *A Disquisition on Government* (1853; NY: Peter Smith, 1943) 101–103.

any artificial positive limitation upon those rights, from that moment the whole organization of government becomes a consideration of convenience. This it is which makes the constitution of a state, and the due distribution of its powers, a matter of the most delicate and complicated skill. It requires a deep knowledge of human nature and human necessities.' Like the Federalists Burke believed that government was a complicated contrivance for maximising 'genuine liberty' without licensing government by fickle passions. The Revolutionary sympathisers in England, he thought, 'are so taken up with their theories about the *rights* of man, that they have totally forgot his *nature*' (156). Whatever system is adopted must be based upon the recognition that those who rule exercise a trust: 'All persons possessing any portion of power ought to be strongly and awefully impressed with an idea that they act in trust; and that they are to account for their conduct in that trust to the one great master, author and founder of society.'

Both Burke and Cooper are aware that 'all political power is strictly a trust, granted by the constituent to the representative' though to Cooper this is the 'leading distinctive principle' of America (*American Democrat*, 91). But Burke's criticism of the structure being created in France in 1790 (he was writing long before this structure gave rise to any remarkable excesses and when only Adams took a similarly pessimistic line) is that it was centred on a National Assembly 'with every possible power and no possible external controul' (*Reflections*, 315). 'Your all sufficient legislators, in their hurry to do everything at once, have forgot one thing that seems essential, and which, I believe, never has been before, in the theory or the practice, omitted by any projector of a republic. They have forgot to constitute a *Senate*, or something of that nature and character .... Such a body ... seems to be in the very essence of a republican government. It holds a sort of middle place *between the supreme power exercised by the people, or immediately delegated from them,* and the mere executive' (316). In short, France was not American enough.

The case is made the worse, Burke felt, because of an indirect electoral system, based upon a scale of property qualifications, which annulled any direct personal connection between elector and elected.

'To elect someone you must know 'the fitness of your man ' and then 'retain some hold upon him' (305): the French system made it impossible for the elector to discharge what Cooper also felt to be 'a sacred publick trust', namely that of voting only for one whom he knows, and knows to be honest (*American Democrat* 142). Having done so, Cooper recognises, in a principle indelibly associated with the name of Burke, 'no constituency has a right to violate the honest convictions of a representative' (161).

While Sir James Mackintosh could temporarily persuade himself, in *Vindiciae Gallicae*, that France was designing a proper division of powers, a constitutional balance of the representatives of the people, a hereditary first magistrate and a judiciary unconnected with either,[1] Burke professed to be puzzled what kind of polity France was in process of becoming. 'I do not know under what description to class the present ruling authority in France. It affects to be a pure democracy, though I think in a direct train of becoming shortly a mischievous and ignoble oligarchy' (228). He was confirmed in this opinion by the system of escalating electoral qualifications. In a rarely quoted passage of great vehemence, Burke comes remarkably close to expressing the complex of suspicions which drove Cooper, when he returned to America in 1833, into the arms of the Jacksonian Democrats.

> One thing only is certain in this scheme [of electoral qualifications], which is an effect seemingly collateral but direct, I have no doubt in the minds of those who conduct this business, that is, its effect in producing an Oligarchy in every one of the republics. A paper circulation ... must put the whole of what power, authority, and influence is left ... into the hands of the managers and conductors of this circulation (307).

Cooper would concur with Jackson's populist war against the

---

[1] James Mackintosh, *Vindiciae Gallicae* (1791), 223. Mackintosh soon changed his mind. Wollstonecraft, too, critiques the failure to move swiftly enough to a balanced constitution as the Americans had done (*An Historical and Moral View of the French Revolution* [1795], 399–400). Jefferson, who in 1789 thought that the French would retain an executive monarchy, later confessed to Adams that he had been wrong and that the false dawn had cost 'eight or ten millions of human beings' (*Portable Jefferson*, 443, 551).

banks on the grounds that they undermined real value (which was agricultural) and therefore undermined the *producers* of real value, or as Burke puts it a page or so later,

> few can understand the game; and fewer still are in a condition to avail themselves of the knowledge. The many must be the dupes of the few who conduct the machine of these speculations.... Those whose operations can take from, or add ten percent to, the possessions of every man in France, must be the masters of every man in France.... The landed gentleman, the yeoman, and the peasant [the first two of which terms define Cooper's constituency] have none of them, habits or inclinations, or experience, which can lead them to any share in this the sole source of power and influence now left in France (311).

It would be absurd to suggest that this passage helped to stimulate Jacksonian abhorrence of the Whigs, since detestation of oligarchy is at least as old as the English revolution, but it is very likely, since Cooper seems to have re-immersed himself in Burke in the year Jackson came to power (*The Wept of Wish-ton-Wish*, 1829, is replete with complex echoes of both the *Philosophical Enquiry* and *Reflections*) to have stimulated Cooper to share in that abhorrence.[1]

Cooper was nothing if not paradoxical. A firm believer that Aristocratic power should be overthrown, and politics divorced from heredity, he also believed in the necessity for a landed elite, a leavening twentieth, drawing sufficient wealth from their estates to enjoy a life of intellectual cultivation and public service, and whose business it was to govern at the behest of a deferential electorate. Critical of Sir Walter Scott for an ingrained deference to aristocracy, Cooper, having been born to quasi-feudal power, married into a particularly grand strain of the New York aristocracy and mixed as of right in almost exclusively titled circles during his years in Europe. Believing in theory that sovereignty resides in the people, who must be constitutionally free to change their constitution, he also believed that the

---

1 See Marvin Meyers, *The Jacksonian Persuasion: Politics and Belief* (Stanford: Stanford University Press, 1957), 12–20 for an appraisal of the Jacksonian case against bank-led oligarchy.

James Fenimore Cooper and the Spectre of Edmund Burke   157

Constitution as the guarantor of liberty was in all practical respects above criticism, and that change should be gradual: 'One of the chief merits of all our political innovations is that they have been gradual', he wrote, in phrasing highly suggestive of George Eliot, 'and have rather followed than preceded opinion.'[1] During the agitations of the 1840s, which threatened the extinction of a privileged landed gentry, Cooper could take this principle to extremes, arguing that if righting the wrongs of tenants damages the power of the gentry, the wrongs must remain unrighted. Mid-nineteenth-century tenants, however impoverished, must remain bound by contracts entered into by their ancestors a century before. As James Grossman summarises the point, in an appropriately Burkean phrase (although he refers it to Cooper's 'secular Calvinism') 'the tenants' choice is decisive not only for the profitable rent-free years but *for all time*.'[2]

Such a paradoxical political portfolio goes some way to explain how the creator of Natty Bumppo, the most powerful mythological personification of natural justice, cross-cultural friendship and love of the wild, could also be a passionate supporter of Andrew Jackson— internationally notorious for rough justice and indifference to Indian culture or the survival of wilderness. What I referred to as the third great theme of *The Pioneers*, Indian dispossession, is only tentatively sketched in the degeneracy of 'Indian John', briefly contextualised in a Heckewelderian account of the history of Chingachgooks's race. This theme will develop, in the Leatherstocking saga, into a great national threnody for the fate of what Natty unfailingly refers to as 'the rightful owners of the land'. In writing *The Pioneers*, to celebrate his roots, Cooper was it seems surprised not only by doubts but by guilt. Three successive novels, *The Last of the Mohicans* (1826) about the French and Indian Wars of 1757, *The Prairie* (1827) about American expansion after the Louisiana purchase, and *The Wept of Wish-ton-Wish* (1829) about early puritan settlements, attempt to expiate that unexpectedly focused guilt. What none of them achieves, however, is a satisfactory answer to Burke's complaint in a *Vindication of Natural*

---

[1] *Letters and Journals*, 2: 33.
[2] James Grossman, *James Fenimore Cooper* (Stanford: Stanford UP, 1967), 207.

Society: 'In vain you tell me that Artificial government is good, but that I fall out only with the Abuse. The Thing! the Thing itself is the Abuse!' Rather, his novels, as the Leatherstocking saga proceeds, endorse Burke's surprisingly Nattyesque utterance: 'we will not place the State of Nature, which is the Reign of God, in competition with Political Society, which is the absurd Usurpation of Man' (*A Vindication*, 68, 87). Taken as a whole they never quite escape the anxiety he seems to have uncovered in *The Pioneers*, when contemplating the strangulation of liberty in the infant republic. That anxiety was most famously expressed by Coleridge in his 1798 'France: an Ode', just nine years into the life-cycle of another republic, in his despairing cry that liberty never yet did breathe its soul 'in forms of human power'.

Chapter 5:

'The Reign of Nature'; or, Mr Bryant's Wordsworth

In Cooper's most Wordsworthian novel, *The Deerslayer* (1841), the young hero stands admiring Lake Glimmerglass, through a screen of trees:

> The spot was very lovely, of a truth, and it was then seen in one of its most favourable moments, the surface of the lake being as smooth as glass, and limpid as pure air, ... while the bays were seen glittering through an occasional *arch* beneath, left by a *vault* fretted with branches and leaves. It was the air of deep repose, the solitudes that spoke of scenes and forests untouched by the hands of man, the reign of nature, in a word, that gave so much pure delight to one of his habits and turn of mind. Still, he felt, though it was unconsciously, like a poet also. He .... felt a portion of that soothing of the spirit which is a common attendant of a scene so thoroughly pervaded by the holy calm of nature.[1]

The narrator adds drily, that the overall effect is 'precisely that at which *the lover of the picturesque* would have aimed, had the ordering of this glorious setting of forest been submitted to his control'.

As Tony Tanner pointed out in the opening pages of his brilliant *Scenes of Nature, Signs of Men* (Cambridge, 1987), the architectural terms in Cooper's description—the way the lake is perceived 'through an occasional *arch*' or 'a *vault* fretted with branches and leaves'—suggest one of William Cullen Bryant's best-known poems, his 'Forest Hymn', the *locus classicus* of religious feeling escaped

---
1 *The Deerslayer*, ed. H. Daniel Peck (Oxford UP, 1993), Ch. 2, 46–7.

into the wilds:

> The groves were God's first temples. Ere man learned
> To hew the shaft, and lay the architrave,
> And spread the roof above them,—ere he framed
> The lofty vault, to gather and roll back
> The sound of anthems; in the darkling wood,
> Amidst the cool and silence, he knelt down,
> And offered to the Mightiest solemn thanks
> And supplication.[1]

The character of Cooper's Leatherstocking is at its most Wordsworthian in this last of the Leatherstocking series. Viewing nature as 'the anchor of his purest thoughts', Natty has habitually found time to impress such scenes upon his mind, and to attach to them his deepest feelings; so

> He rarely moved through [the vast woods] without pausing to dwell on some peculiar beauty that gave him pleasure ... never did a day pass without his communing ... with the infinite source of all he saw, felt and beheld. (Ch. 16, 278)

The primary thesis of the novel might come straight from *Peter Bell*, contrasting as it does the moral life of the Deerslayer with that of his savage white associates, who, Cooper writes,

> knew no feeling of poetry, had lost their sense of natural devotion in lives of obdurate and narrow selfishness, and had little other sympathy with nature, than that which originated in her lowest wants (Ch. 19, 324).

Cooper had his own Romanticism, but the fact that both hero and plot are so configured surely owes much to sixteen years of friendship with 'the American Wordsworth'—as the world knew him—William Cullen Bryant, America's first Romantic poet.

---

1 Frank Gado, *William Cullen Bryant: An American Voice* (Antoca Press, 2006), 67. This book is primarily a good selection of Bryant's poems.

Mr Bryant's Wordsworth 161

IN 1825, William Cullen Bryant arrived in New York as reviews editor for the *New York Review and Athenaeum Magazine*, already a man with a mission. Seven years earlier, aged 24, he had informed readers of *The North American Review* that poetry in the new world was hopelessly moribund: Timothy Dwight's ponderous *The Conquest of Canaan* (1785) was 'remarkable for its unbroken monotony', Joel Barlow's *Columbiad* (1807) was 'utterly destitute of interest', and Philip Freneau was 'a writer of inferior verse'. All three exemplified a poetic culture addled by 'sickly and affected imitation'.[1] As indeed (in all candour) they did. Now, aged 31, Bryant delivered four authoritative lectures on poetry at the New York Athenaeum, lauding the new poetry of the old world. His mission was the reformation of American poetry and his campaign theme, in effect, 'close thy Pope, open thy Wordsworth'. The poetry of 'Wordsworth, Scott, Coleridge, Byron, Southey, Shelley and others', he told his new audience, is 'bold, varied, impassioned, irregular, and impatient of precise laws, beyond that of any former age'. It exhibits 'the freshness, the vigor, and perhaps also the disorder, of a new literature' (Bryant, 5: 31–2). Twelve years later, Emerson's 'American Scholar' lecture will demand a new poetry with 'an original relation to the universe', which (Emerson implies) would necessarily be American. Bryant by contrast, acknowledged—at least in private—how *Lyrical Ballads* liberated him from what Emerson would call the 'courtly muse'. 'I shall never forget', Richard Henry Dana famously writes, in Hazlittian vein:

> with what feeling my friend Bryant, some years ago, described to me the effect produced upon him of meeting for the first time with Wordsworth's ballads. He said that upon opening the book, a thousand springs seemed to gush up at once in his heart, and the face of Nature, of a sudden, to change into a strange freshness and life. He had felt the sympathetic touch from an according mind, and ... instantly his powers and affections shot over the earth and through his kind.[2]

---

1 *The Life and Works of William Cullen Bryant*, ed. Parke Godwin, 6 vols (New York 1883). 5: 50, 51, 54. Hereafter, Bryant.
2 Richard Henry Dana, *Poems and Prose Writings* (Boston, 1833), 148.

One recalls Peabody's pupils (twenty-five years later) experiencing the same awakening.

Bryant's father gave him a copy of *Lyrical Ballads* in 1810, a year or so before Bryant Jr began to produce his and America's first authentically Romantic poems. When some of these—including 'Thanatopsis', 'Inscription for the entrance to a wood' and 'Waterfowl'—were published together in the *North American Review* in 1817 the effect of a new language was comparable to that of the debut of Ted Hughes with *Hawk in the Rain* in 1957. One editor told another: 'you have been imposed upon; no one on this side of the Atlantic is capable of writing such verses'.[1]

Bryant, who acknowledged Wordsworth as 'a sort of poetical master',[2] absorbed more thoroughly than anyone the principles of the Prefaces, and went on to formulate the most succinct of Romantic manifestos: 'the elements of poetry', he decided retrospectively in 1876, 'lie in natural objects, in the vicissitudes of human life, in the emotions of the human heart, and the relations of man to man' and what characterised the Romantic renovation of poetry was that poets 'learned to go directly to nature for their imagery, instead of taking it from what had once been regarded as the common stock of poets' (Bryant, 5: 158). He read Wordsworth voraciously, read him with a recurring sense of 'awe', and defended aspects of his own poetic practice by appealing to Wordsworth's example. Rhyming 'blossom and bosom'—he tells Dana in 1833—is acceptable because Wordsworth does so, and 'his rhymes are generally exact' (*Letters*, 1: 385; the touchstone in this case is 'Foresight', possibly the least regarded poem in *Poems, in Two Volumes*).

According to Fenimore Cooper, while some writers reaped some praise once in a while, Bryant was lauded as '*the* author of America' (not quite, as the title of Gilbert Muller's admirable biography seems

---

[1] Bryant, 1: 150. In 1817 the *North American Review* was conducted by three eminent Wordsworthians, Richard Henry Dana Sr, Edward Tyrell Channing and Willard Phillips.

[2] *The Letters of William Cullen Bryant*, ed. William Cullen Bryant II and Edward G. Voss, 6 vols (Fordham U P, 1975), 1: 235 (to Charles Folsom, March 1827). Herefafter, Letters.

to suggest, the author of *America*).[1] A fellow journalist, Walt Whitman, wrote in the *Brooklyn Daily Eagle* (1846) that Bryant as a poet 'to our mind, stands among the first in the world'. Margaret Fuller said of him in 'American Literature' (also 1846) that he stood alone at the head of American poetry. According to Martineau and Dickens, he was America's one great poet; Mathew Arnold and Hartley Coleridge adjudged his 'To a Waterfowl' the most perfect short lyric in the language.[2] Emily Dickinson named him in her poems. In Harold Bloom's judgment Bryant was 'a superb poet, always and still undervalued';[3] and in an apt comparison by Gilbert Muller, from whom these citations are culled, he was a nineteenth-century Robert Frost.

Not everyone agreed with such high estimates. Henry Crabb Robinson observed sagely, during Bryant's visit to England in 1845, that having read through numerous poems he had 'met with nothing that will tax my memory to remain. There are no striking thoughts or even expressions that will give *life* to the poems. They are chiefly descriptive and sentimental—all quite moral & pure'—with which honest judgment Nathaniel Hawthorne, Harriet Martineau and Edgar Allan Poe concur.[4] 'Sweet', was Martineau's limiting epithet, as in 'smooth, sweet, faithful descriptions of nature' (Muller, 183). The problem with Bryant's 'The Yellow Violet', 'The Rivulet', 'Summer Wind', 'After a Tempest', 'Lines on Revisiting the Country' is that although these lyrics are outwardly modelled on Wordsworth, nothing happens in them by way of change or insight, and they lack linguistic energy. Even Bryant's 'Inscription for the Entrance to a Wood', important for its sentiment, accumulates redundantly: 'Stranger, if

---

1 Gilbert H. Muller, *William Cullen Bryant: Author of America* (SUNY Press, 2008), 2. Most of my data on Bryant's life comes from this excellent biography.

2 'Seekst thou the plashy brink / Of weedy lake? ... the abyss of heaven / Hath swallowed up thy form' and 'Guides ... thy certain flight'. The same Heaven will also 'lead my steps aright'. The poem was composed nine years after 'The Leech-Gatherer' but 'plashy' according to the *OED* might equally come from Goldsmith or Gilpin (who applied it respectively to a spring and a fen).

3 Harold Bloom, *The Ringers in the Tower* (1971), cited Muller vii.

4 *Letters*, 2: 338n, quoting a typescript diary in Dr Williams's Library. Martineau agreed that he showed a 'higher degree of power' in 'Thanatopsis' and 'The Past' (Muller 183). Poe praised some poems in the 1837 collection, including 'Thanatopsis', without placing him with Shelley, Wordsworth or Keats (Muller 136).

164   Romantic Dialogues

thou hast learned a truth which needs / No school of long experience, that the world / Is full of guilt and misery.../...enter this wild wood / And view the haunts of Nature. The calm shade / Shall bring a kindred calm, and the sweet breeze / That makes the green leaves dance, shall waft a balm / To thy sick heart.' The more lyrical poems might be written by a Moore or a Rogers and like all American nature poetry before Whitman, sometimes contain little to suggest (as London reviewers periodically complained of literature from the new world) that they were not written beside the Thames.

Nor is this surprising: Bryant was little more than a part-time poet. What he was, for some fifty years, was America's most influential journalist, proprietor and editor of the *New York Evening Post*, brilliant writer of trenchant, tightly argued, punchily expressed editorials—his style is the absolute antithesis of Wordsworth's in *Concerning the Convention of Cintra*—and the confidant of successive Presidents, from Andrew Jackson to Abraham Lincoln.

And yet it was undoubtedly the poetry that accounted for the veneration in which he was held. Eclipsed for most of the 20th Century by his greatest admirers, Whitman and Dickinson, along with his protégés, Whittier and Longfellow, he really does deserve better. And 'Thanatopsis', which Yvor Winters adjudged 'the only truly great poem written in America in the first half of the 19th century' (Muller, 22), is the place to begin.

1. 'THANATOPSIS'

Bryant composed 'Thanatopsis' (meaning, loosely, his vision of the daemon of death) over roughly a decade, from 1811 to 1821 (i.e. between the ages of 17 and 27), and published its first version at 24. Its posture is perhaps halfway between theism and materialism—a half-way house that Bryant (like Wordsworth) manages to occupy for much his poetic career. Blair and Young were among the favourite poets of Bryant's morbid adolescence—he was a sickly youth and much obsessed with death—and stylistically, the poem is somewhere between Blair's *Grave* and the kind of solemn exposition of thoughts about death and nature that Wordsworth *could* have written but

Mr Bryant's Wordsworth   165

on the whole never quite did. With its 'thees' and 'thous', and its opening keynote—'Go forth, under the open sky, and list / To Nature's teachings'—it is the work of someone who has been fired by 'Expostulation and Reply', but is still trapped in the sermonising tone of the poets who first nurtured his sensibility. Yet Bryant has caught the spirit of the Lucy poems, and the enlightenment daring they crystallise, and he isn't afraid to spell out what is implicit in Wordsworth's sublime epitaph 'A slumber did my spirit seal'.

> Earth, that nourished thee, shall claim
> Thy growth, to be resolved to earth again
> And, lost each human trace, surrendering up
> Thy individual being, shalt thou go
> To mix for ever with the elements,
> To be a brother to the insensible rock
> And to the sluggish clod, which the rude swain
> Turns with his share, and treads upon. The oak
> Shall send his roots abroad, and pierce thy mould.

Note the mingling of registers there, an unsurprising intrusion of eighteenth century diction ('the rude swain') as if Bryant has one foot in his father's literary world, one in the new.

Nobody in transcendental America seems to have noticed or objected to the poem's apparent argument that there is no afterlife except in the material life of nature from which we arise and to which it is our destiny to return. But then, nobody in England thought that Wordsworth's 'Ode Intimations of Immortality' (set on the shore of 'that immortal sea / Which brought us hither') argued that human life originated in the primal ooze. Perhaps this is because both poems couch their disconcerting insights in such a rich musical brocade. And there is certainly grandeur in the way Bryant develops, through the next forty or more relentless lines, his wondering response to the trite but awe-inspiring thought that at almost any stage in imaginable human history the overwhelming majority of those who have ever existed are already among the dead—and, as Bryant puts it, that the hills and vales and woods and oceans of this beateous world are but 'solemn decorations / Of the great tomb of man':

All that tread

> The globe are but a handful to the tribes
> That slumber in its bosom ...
> > the dead reign there alone (Gado 33)

Bryant is almost always prone to a mild tone of exposition, a poetry of statement, rather than the recreation of emotion and vision in 'The Wye', or anything comparable to, say, the tragic vision of 'The Ruined Cottage', yet this poem's vision is exceptional, making the homage of Whitman and Dickinson entirely comprehensible. 'Approach thy grave', the poet advises at the close of his poem (Gado 34),

> Like one who wraps the drapery of his couch
> About him, and lies down to pleasant dreams.

'*Like* one': and that's it. Let's all imagine that death is like sleep, as the child does in 'the great Ode', that child to whom the grave

> Is but a lonely bed without the sense or sight
> > Of day or the warm light,
> A place of thought where we in waiting lie. (*CWRT*, 1: 715)

Neither poet, intriguingly, finds it necessary to spell out what exactly, as we lie on our 'lonely bed', or 'couch', we are waiting *for*, or for how long. It is really, as Cicero cheerfully argued in Book I of his *Tusculan Disputations*, none of our concern: it doesn't trouble us that a while ago we were not; nor should it trouble us that in a little while we will be as we were (or weren't) before.

If 'Thanatopsis' declines to acknowledge the promise of resurrection, Bryant rectified this omission both strikingly and amusingly in 'The Two Graves', written in 1825, a decade after *The Excursion*. Adding playfully to Wordsworth's graveyard stories, 'The Two Graves' treats the history of a buried couple whose graves are now barely perceptible even to one who knows they are there. There is much to be said for burial away from a churchyard, the poem suggests, for a graveyard has no privacy—the ties of village life-in-death are stricter and closer than those of village life. Its mordant humour reminds one of the Solitary's remark on Grasmere's 'subterraneous magazine of souls'. In Bryant's vision of buried villagers in a communal graveyard:

> Without a frown or a smile they meet,
> Each pale and calm in his winding sheet;
> In that sullen home of peace and gloom,
> Crowded, like guests in a banquet room. (Gado 75)[1]

This *rural* couple are not villagers, however. Their souls are imagined roaming 'in the yellow sunshine and flowing air' where they listen still to the brook that watered their fields, and Bryant concludes his piece with an apt theological twist—they linger about their dwelling place, already 'beyond vicissitude', patiently awaiting the last trump:

> Patient, and peaceful and passionless,
> As seasons on seasons quickly press,
> They watch, and wait, and linger around
> Till the days when their bodies will leave the ground.
> (Gado 76)

Merely to hint at this authorised mode of resurrection draws attention to the greater attractions of the pantheistical kind of renewal that is sometimes explicit, usually implicit, in all of Bryant's best work— poems in which he avoids relaxing into more conventional pieties.[2] Bryant's letters are almost wholly devoid of philosophical reference, so it is hard to identify him with any tradition of thought, but one can hardly avoid the evidence of the poetry. The grave may well be 'a place of thought where we in waiting lie', but Bryant customarily

---

[1] One might unwarily associate Bryant's humour with the moment in *Peter Bell* (1819) in which the narrator wonders what hellish vision Peter sees in the stream below him—'Is it some party in a parlour, / Crammed just as they on earth were cramm'd—/ Some sipping punch, some sipping tea, / But as you by their faces see / All silent, and all damn'd?' (*CWRT*, 1: 504)—but Bryant claims not to have read *Peter Bell* (which he then enjoyed, and defended thereafter) until 1827.

[2] Where Wordsworth's 'Surprized by Joy', on the loss of his daughter, ends in the harrowing conviction 'That neither present time, nor years unborn / Could to my sight that heavenly face restore' (*CWRT*, 3: 49), Bryant's 'Consumption' on the impending death of his sister ends more comfortably: 'Close thy sweet eyes, calmly, and without pain; / And we will trust in God to see thee yet again' (*Poems by William Cullen Bryant*, Katz Brothers (1854) ,109).

168 Romantic Dialogues

makes it a more satisfying fate to participate in 'the life of things', and an even grander one to share in 'earth's diurnal course'.

2. 'THE PRAIRIES'

One of Bryant's most intriguing poems, 'The Prairies' (1832/33) has been distinguished in fine recent discussions as what Joel Pace in a double-edged remark calls Bryant's 'most Wordsworthian poem'.[1] The poem is based on Bryant's tactical conversion to the idea that 'the red man' dispossessed a prior race of more civilized Mound-Builders. This archaeological fiction was promoted by one Josiah Priest in his *American Antiquities* and seized upon by Bryant who had recently switched from exploiting Native Americans for poetic purposes to writing enthusiastic editorials justifying Andrew Jackson's policy of cultural apartheid, driving 'the red man', especially the Cherokees, into the less hospitable West.[2] Pace argues that Bryant's conscience found support at this time in Wordsworth's ambivalence (or his Solitary's ambivalence) about native Americans. These are presented in *The Excursion*, you may recall, as 'primeval nature's child' yet also as 'squalid, vengeful, and impure; / Remorseless, and submissive to no law / But superstitious fear, and abject sloth'. As the Solitary concludes (in lines that might have been written by Bryant) 'the Intelligence of social Art / Hath overpowered his Forefathers, and soon / Will sweep the remnant of his line away' (*Excursion*, 3:934–6). Fenimore Cooper, too, did rather well out of celebrating the noble savage, or at least some noble savages (Mohicans but not Mingoes), but believed in the inevitable disappearance of the red man when in

---

[1] Joel Pace, 'William Wordsworth, William Cullen Bryant, and the Poetics of American Indian Removal', in *Native Americans and Anglo-American Culture, 1750–1850*, ed. Tim Fulford and Kevin Hutchings. Cambridge UP, 2009), 197–216.
[2] '"The Prairies" entertains the condescending idea that the mounds "must have been the work of a 'pre-Indian civilization' driven out or destroyed by historic Indians"' (Colin G. Calloway, *One Vast Winter Count: The Native American West before Louis and Clark* [Lincoln/London: University of Nebraska Press, 2003], 96). Calloway is quoted in Eric Lindstrom, 'The Command to Nature in Wordsworth and Post-Enlightenment Lyric', *Literary Imagination* 13:3 (November 2011) 325–344, (n.28).

Mr Bryant's Wordsworth   169

conflict with the superior culture of the white. The one line that best epitomises Bryant's (and Cooper's) position is the self-exculpating fabrication expressed in Bryant's poem 'The Disinterred Warrior': 'A noble race! *but they are gone*' (*Poems*, 124, my emphasis).

Both Joel Pace and Eric Lindstrom have seen 'The Prairies' as a poem in dialogue with Wordsworth's great poem 'On revisiting the Wye' (1798). For Lindstrom, 'The Prairies' is 'a blank-verse poem about nature, culture, and historical memory of a scope comparable to "Tintern Abbey".' For Pace, Bryant's poem 'draws on Wordsworth's verse in its form (pastoral elegy in blank verse pentameter) and content (verse that endows the landscape with personal, familial, and cultural histories).' 'In Wordsworth's verses', Pace continues, 'Bryant found the spiritual, the natural, and the political blended thoroughly, elements he sought to combine in 'The Prairies'. I think there are two problems with that ascription. First it rather assumes that Bryant saw Wordsworth's 'Poem upon the Wye' as a poem about 'historical displacement'—reading it with benefit of McGann and Levinson, as it were—which seems highly unlikely. Second, as I have implied, Bryant's response to 'On revisiting the Wye' occurs a decade earlier, in 'A Forest Hymn' (that perfect encapsulation of what Victorians thought of as Wordsworthian nature feeling) and 'The Rivulet', where Wordsworth's snapshots of former being that pass like a procession of ghosts in the 'Lines on the River Wye' are flattened into Bryant's summative 'thou changest not, but I am changed / Since first thy pleasant banks I ranged' (*Poems*, 49): This is Wordsworth without the passion or the angst. If 'The Prairies' *is* emulating 'The Wye' it subjects its model to the kind of transformation Tim Fulford has argued for in his recent study, *The Late Poetry of the Lake Poets*, whereby Wordsworth himself in the 1820s set about appealing to a broader audience by converting the private 'egotistical sublime' into public, ethnographic, historical snapshots.

So 'The Prairies' does indeed engage with Wordsworth, but surely less with 'The Wye' than with the poetry of the early 1820s in which Wordsworth contemplates ethnological changes throughout national history. Bryant, born two years after Shelley and a year before Keats, is rarely more than a decade assimilating and responding to what new directions Wordsworth takes. Wordsworth first published his 'Long Meg' sonnet in the *Guide* in 1822. He raises the broader issue of tribal supersession in *The River Duddon* (1820)—'What aspect bore the Man who roved or fled, / First of his tribe, to this dark dell?' (*CWRT* 3: 352)—and he wrote, most magisterially of all, a great lament for vanished peoples in *Ecclesiastical Sketches* (1822):

> Mark! how all things swerve
> From their known course, or pass away like steam;
> Another language spreads from coast to coast;
> Only perchance some melancholy Stream
> And some indignant Hills old names preserve,
> When laws, and creeds, and people, all are lost!
> (*CWRT* 3: 373–4)

What Bryant does with this elegiac theme in 'The Prairies'—a decade after all three of these sonnets—is symptomatic of the relationship. Whatever debt there may be is repaid with interest. Just as Emerson distilled in *Nature* an argument Wordsworth never quite articulated, but left implicit, so Bryant makes a sustained and artful poem out of a recurring Wordsworthian theme that Wordsworth allows to flicker suggestively on the periphery of vision. And interestingly, as Joel Pace's treatment shows, the conflictedness that is often implicit in Wordsworth's treatments—his laments over the vanished Celt, or Druid, or Ancient Briton in his wolfskin vest are always qualified by the sense of cultural inevitability—seems to be amplified rather than muted in Bryant's poem, perhaps by conscience.

'The Prairies' is nonetheless one of his best poems for the celebration of life and movement in nature:

> The clouds
> Sweep over with their shadows, and, beneath,
> The surface rolls and fluctuates to the eye;
> Dark hollows seem to glide along and chase
> The sunny ridges (Gado 77)

In which lines there is a rare sense of the subjective eye—the experience and the mind experiencing rendered at once—that is indeed redolent of Wordsworth (as, maybe, is the 'rank grass' a little later in the poem). The sonnet to Long Meg, with its dramatic opening ('Speak! Giant Mother') surfaces in Bryant's invocation of the mound Builders. 'Are they here, the dead of other days?', he asks:

> Let the mighty mounds
> That overlook the rivers, or that rise
> In the dim forest crowded with old oaks,
> Answer. (Gado 78)

When the mounds reply, what they speak of is the mound builders, 'A race that long has passed away / ...a disciplined and populous race' but extinguished when, in the poem's self-exculpating mythology,

> The red man came—
> The roaming hunter tribes, warlike and fierce,
> And the mound-builders vanished from the earth.

This voice emanating from the mounds conveniently suggests that there is nothing one can do, or should do, to arrest the disappearance of 'the red man', for it manifests a law of nature:

> Thus change the forms of being. Thus arise
> Races of living things, glorious in strength,
> And perish, as the quickening breath of God
> Fills them, or is withdrawn. The red man too.... (Gado 79)

As those beautifully various lines show (setting aside 'The red man, too', which seems slipped in as if an afterthought and not the motive for the poem) Bryant has been listening intently to the great cadences of the Wanderer lamenting how 'man grows old, and dwindles, and decays; / And countless generations of Mankind / Depart; and leave no vestige where they trod' (*Excursion*, 4: 577–9)—listening to the sentiment, of course, but to the music, too. Which brings me (sort of) to William Cullen Bryant's projected masterpiece, his 'Recluse'.

3. Bryant's 'Recluse'

If there is conscious discipleship in Bryant's loyalty to Wordsworth's example; his acknowledgment of Wordsworth as 'a sort of poetical master of mine' has practical outcomes that may not preclude a sense of competition. Shortly before visiting Wordsworth at Rydal Mount in 1845, Bryant very nearly assumed the burden of *The Recluse*. Pressed by Dana to embark on a major work, he conceived the notion of a great poem in blank verse whose theme would be America itself, its nature and its human life, but told in the poet's voice, and given an autobiographical frame which Parke Godwin (Bryant's first biographer) associates with Wordsworth's Pedlar (Bryant, 3: 354). Its tone may be deduced from a remarkable piece of 1840, 'The Old Man's Counsel'. In this poem, a figure startlingly reminiscent both of Wordsworth's Mathew and of the early conception of the Pedlar, is introduced as tutoring the young poet:

> One such I knew long since, a white-haired man,
> Pithy of speech, and merry when he would;
> A genial optimist who daily drew
> From what he saw his quaint moralities.
> Kindly he held communion, though so old,
> With me a dreaming boy, and taught me much
> That books tell not, ... (Gado 84)

Its verse is such as one rather wishes Wordsworth had emulated in the less speakable portions of *The Excursion*; the poet's sensations in this poem are also more vividly rendered than those of Wordsworth's lacklustre 'Poet', and the transitions into the old man's speech, while recognizably similar, are less creakily accomplished. For those unfamiliar with the Pedlar/Wanderer, the effect of Bryant's poem may still seem Wordsworthian, because this short prelusive poem's farewell to the long-buried counsellor-figure takes one back irresistibly to 'The Two April Mornings' and to another Wordsworthian elder—Mathew—with his 'bough of wilding in his hand'. 'For still', the poet-acolyte confesses at the close of the poem, whenever the 'flower-buds crowd the orchard bough'

> his venerable form again
> Is at my side, his voice is in my ear. (Gado 86)

Mr Bryant's Wordsworth 173

One can easily, with Bryant and Wordsworth, forget whose lines are whose: those are Bryant's, but one needs to doubletake.

Among other poems known to have been part of the shadowy design for this 'long, elaborate work' are two from Bryant's 1842 collection, 'The Fountain' and 'An Evening Revery'. Both of these show Bryant solving technical problems that the author of *The Excursion* on the whole did not. 'The Fountain' (1839) gives an extended taste of a promising method, whereby on the canvas of a single spot, a series of pastoral sketches depict the changes American life has seen, and will see. It concludes with an overtly Darwinian recognition (I am thinking of the geological Darwin of *The Voyage of the Beagle*, first published in 1839) that ages hence in the earth's liquid evolutions, this fountain might by engulfed by ocean or wasted on the barren ridges of a new mountain range. That's eleven years before Tennyson's wonderful expression of the same idea in *In Memoriam*.

'An Evening Revery' (1840) exhibits with great grace, how best to conduct 'a philosophical Poem, containing views of Man, Nature, and Society' and 'having for its principal subject the sensations and opinions of a Poet living in retirement': it seems clear that Bryant's 'Recluse' would have been a poem made of many poems, each of which, as episodes in *The Excursion* tend not to, offer the satisfactions of form. Beginning with a thesis statement—'the summer day is closed'—'An Evening Revery' develops in bivalve form. Its first paragraph is a beautifully cadenced catalogue of events in the natural and human worlds, from grass growing and seeds falling, to fledging of birds and plightings of troth.

> The green blade of the ground
> Has risen, and herds have cropped it; the young twig
> Has spread its plaited tissues to the sun;
> Flowers of the garden and the waste have blown
> And withered; seeds have fallen upon the soil,
> From bursting cells, and in their graves await
> Their resurrection. Insects from the pools
> Have filled the air awhile with humming wings,
> That now are still for ever; ... (Gado 87).

The naturalistic sensibility is patent (one would not be surprised to find a line from Ted Hughes's *Season Songs* commending the earthworms for 'doing a good job'). The imagistic catalogue is also strongly suggestive of Whitman's staple method (according to Frank Gado, 165–7, it probably inspired it). Yet it seems to me more progressive than Whitman's somewhat static accumulations: there is a deepening of emotional timbre as the account proceeds and a dramatic sharpening of tone on the final image in the series: 'This day hath parted friends / That ne'er before were parted; / ... and it hath heard, from lips which late / Were eloquent of love, the first harsh word, / That told the wedded one her peace was flown.'

The poem's thirty lines evoking life are balanced by a thirty-line hymn to death. Entirely Bryantesque, this meditation nonetheless marshals numerous Wordsworthian *topoi*. It fuses the organising metaphor of the *River Duddon* sequence—in 'I feel the mighty current sweep me on' (that's Bryant, not Wordsworth, though again it might be either)—with the personal note of Wordsworth's 'Extempore Effusion' when Bryant asks 'Who next, of those I love, shall pass from life...?'. Most significantly perhaps, it gestures at Wordsworth's inability in 'Intimations' or elsewhere, to envisage the end of life other than in images of the renewal of life. And it comes to rest in one of the major statements of Bryant's pantheism (a pantheism that has to co-exist with Calvinist reflexes until he enrols as a Unitarian in 1857):

> Oh! beyond that bourne,
> In the vast cycle of being which begins
> At that broad threshold, with what fairer forms
> Shall the great law of change and progress clothe
> Its workings? Gently—so have good men taught—
> Gently, and without grief, the old shall glide
> Into the new; the eternal flow of things. (Gado 88)

4. Common Ground

Why do phrases like 'the vast cycle of being', 'the eternal flow of things' and the treatment of supersession in 'The Prairies', suggest

Wordsworth? If we all knew *The Excursion* as we ought, we would not need to ask. Listen for a moment to this passage, beloved of John Ruskin, in which the Wanderer, meditating on the yearnings of mankind from the beginning of time, thinks of votive offerings to a river God. Rhythmically it is without parallel. The last three lines of the quoted passage subtly mirror the extraordinary line breaks in the opening three, either side of the urgent drama of thought at the centre of the passage, where the very concept of a verse line seems impossibly strained by quickening phrases (which I here italicise) and urgent enjambments. Even the semi-colon of the third line and the comma that ends the fifth seem overborne by the pressure of thought:

> And doubtless, sometimes, when the hair was shed
> Upon the flowing stream, a thought arose
> Of Life continuous, being unimpaired;
> *That hath been, is, and where it was and is*
> *There shall be,—seen and heard, and felt, and known,*
> *And recognized,*—existence unexposed
> To the blind walk of mortal accident;
> From diminution safe and weakening age;
> While man grows old, and dwindles, and decays;
> And countless generations of Mankind
> Depart; and leave no vestige where they trod.
>   (*Excursion*, 4: 749–59)

Ending with a sonorous *ritartando* (three successive line-end semi-colons lead into that stately conclusion) the lines pose the great Wordsworthian question. On the one hand, there is 'life continuous, being unimpaired'; on the other, those dying generations leaving 'no vestige where they trod'; and in between—only implied here but permeating the oeuvre—the reconciling faith that to die is to become incorporate with mists, rocks, stones, trees, with other lives, perhaps with deity, and certainly with *future being*. This relocation of religious feeling is where Bryant, his disciple Whitman, and his master Wordsworth, meet.

In England, most 19th Century admirers of Wordsworth's 'Ode: Intimations of Immortality'—Coleridge, Pater, Hopkins, and Lamb's legal friend Thomas Noone Talfourd ('Serjeant' Talfourd)—admired it, like Emerson, within a transcendental framework which they took for granted. Talfourd, who called the Ode 'the noblest piece of lyric poetry in the world', was almost the only person to attempt a *summation* of what the poem 'says' and the summary is revealing. To him, the 'gift' of the ode was enabling its readers

> to feel[,] in all the touching mysteries of our past being[,] the symbols and assurances of our immortal destiny! The poet has here spanned our mortal life as with a glorious rainbow, terminating on one side in infancy, and on the other in the realms of blessedness beyond the grave, and shedding[,] even upon the middle of that course[,] sweet tints of unearthly colouring.[1]

Such may indeed be what the Ode's 19th century readers *read*. But is it what Wordsworth *wrote*? Those 'realms of blessedness beyond the grave' seem to be conjured hopefully out of Wordsworth's six word reference to 'the faith that looks through death'. What the ode demonstrably believes in is 'Fountains, Meadows, Fields and Groves' and especially the annual renewal of celandines and daisies, those joint candidates in *Poems in Two Volumes* for title of the 'the meanest flower that blows'. His fellow botanist, Bryant—who spent most of his time at Rydal Mount in 1845 discussing flowers, trees and the design of gardens, the two poets enjoying the waterfalls, the lakeshore, and each other's modest demeanour[2]—was well equipped to grasp that it was in flowers that the poet grounded those 'thoughts that do often lie too deep for tears'.

The note Bryant strikes repeatedly, with his own melancholy music and consolation, is one that can be heard most clearly in one of the elegiac poems that introduce 'Intimations' in *Poems, in Two Volumes*, the 'Lines Composed at Grasmere' on Charles James Fox:

> A Power is passing from the earth
> To breathless Nature's dark abyss;
> But when the Mighty pass away

---

1 *William Wordsworth: The Critical Heritage*, ed. Robert Woof (Routledge 2001) 870.
2 Bryant penned 1600 words to his wife on this cordial visit (*Letters*, 2: 343–4).

> What is it more than this,
>
> That Man, who is from God sent forth,
> Doth yet again to God return?—
> Such ebb and flow must ever be,
> Then wherefore should we mourn?
> (*CWRT*, 1: 707, ll. 17–24.)

There is a Bryantesque sleight of hand in this marvellous poem, in Wordsworth's deployment of that useful word 'God', a sleight of hand designed perhaps to cloak the poem's daring equation of 'breathless nature's dark abyss' with the bosom of God, and birth and death with the 'ebb and flow' of souls, of which strange metaphor more in a moment. It anticipates the Wanderer's haunting credo, the faith (once again) in 'Life continuous, Being unimpaired; / That hath been, is, and where it was and is / There shall be' (*Excursion*, 4: 751–3).

In a startling passage of *The Prelude*—one of those passing thoughts that seem to come from nowhere, lead nowhere (or nowhere the poet is entirely willing to go) and yet be too important to cut— Wordsworth assures us that if all life should perish, what he calls the 'living Presence' would yet exist, and life begin again. Bryant could have written this:

> A thought is with me sometimes, and I say—
> Should the whole frame of earth by inward throes
> Be wrenched, or fire come down from far to scorch
> Her pleasant habitations, and dry up
> Old Ocean in his bed, left singed and bare,
> Yet would the living Presence still subsist
> Victorious; and composure would ensue,
> And kindlings like the morning—presage sure
> Of day returning, and of life revived.
> (*CWRT* 3: 202; *Prelude, 1850*: 5: 29-37)

The lines are not merely superbly stoical, but Stoic. It is likely, though, that the stimulus for the passage comes not from Stoic writings as such but from their enlightenment progeny; most probably from Erasmus Darwin's *Economy of Vegetation* (1791), which is distinctly apocalyptic:

178   Romantic Dialogues

> Star after star from Heaven's high arch shall rush,
> Suns sink on suns, and systems systems crush,
> Headlong, extinct, to one dark center fall,
> And Death and Night and Chaos mingle all!
> — Till o'er the wreck, emerging from the storm,
> Immortal Nature lifts her changeful form,
> Mounts from her funeral pyre on wings of flame,
> And soars and shines, another and the same.[1]

Darwin's *The Temple of Nature* (published posthumously in 1804, just in time to inspire those children sporting on the shore) explains more fully the faith in generation:

> Organic life beneath the shoreless waves
> Was born, and nurs'd in ocean's pearly caves;
> First forms minute, unseen by spheric glass,
> Move on the mud, or pierce the watery mass;
> These as successive generations bloom,
> New powers acquire, and larger limbs assume;
> Whence countless groups of vegetation spring,
> And breathing realms of fin, and feet, and wing.[2]

Life arises 'Out of the cradle, endlessly rocking', one might say. As indeed Whitman did, in one of his great monodies; and as Wordsworth did in slightly different words in an ode he first published in *The River Duddon* volume ('Ode—1817', later called 'Vernal Ode'):

> Her procreant cradle Nature keeps
> Amid the unfathomable deeps
> And saves the changeful fields of earth
> From fear of emptiness or dearth.
> (*CWRT*, 3: 114, lines 35–8)

Wordsworth rarely lauds 'the reign of nature' quite that starkly, and it is somewhat startling to find him doing so in the 1820s, even in a little regarded corner of the *oeuvre*. But faith in that 'procreant

---

[1] Erasmus Darwin, *Economy of Vegetation* (1791), in *The Botanic Garden* (London 1825) Canto 4: 384–92.
[2] *The Temple of Nature* (1804) Canto 1, 295–302.

cradle' surely underlies those equable benedictions: Margaret 'sleeps in the calm earth'; Lucy has no individual 'force', she neither hears nor sees', but she participates, and grandly, in the diurnal course of a living globe. Think of the strange impasse in 'We are Seven', where an adult speaker's attempt to separate the spheres of life and death ('but they are dead / those two are dead / their spirits are in heaven') leaves the child tangibly unimpressed. Wordsworth's young heroine is already in full accordance with the author of the 'Lucy' poems (in fact, she is also in accord with Zeno, and Cicero, and Spinoza, and Whitman, and Bryant) and knows that *substance can suffer no diminution*. She put it less technically of course: 'Their graves are green, they may be seen', a declaration seized upon by both Bryant and Whitman and worked into highpoints of their own oeuvres. In Bryant's 'June' the dead poet's part in continuing life, Bryant promises, will be 'that his grave is green'.

The Stoics (at whose relevance to Bryant and Wordsworth I have been gently hinting) believed in a union of body and soul, and that at death the soul parts from the body; they believed in 'God'; and they believed in 'immortality'. So far so good: if that was all there was to it, Wordsworth might have found it easier to versify Coleridge's beliefs. The problem is that the soul of the Stoics was *material*; their God was both *material and immanent* in creation (one might even say *was* creation), and their concept of death, best imaged as 'dissolution', allows for numerous possibilities. The heroic soul might enjoy continued existence, like the shades of Ossianic heroes (or those of *An Evening Walk*); or it might simply pass back into 'the life of things'. There was no *ethical* element to this survival, no 'reward motive', no heaven or hell. The driving components of Coleridge's beliefs were absent.[1]

---

1 Bruce Graver, John Cole and Adam Potkay are largely responsible for the growing consensus that Wordsworth's poetry from 1797 to 1814 is rooted in ideas he absorbed from the letters of Seneca, and from Cicero's *Tusculan Disputations*, and his *De Officiis*, or *Moral Duties*—ideas found in more crystalline form in Epictetus and Marcus Aurelius. Since the Stoics were into physiology, such traces may have been reinforced by Wordsworth's interest in the physiology of mind to be found in Joseph Priestley and Dugald Stewart (on which see Gravil, *Wordsworth's Bardic Vocation*, 120–28). Bryant shows much less interest in philosophy, beyond

Wordsworth's 'ebb and flow' in the lines on Fox suggests a concept of soul that is curiously compounded, as if referring less to souls than to what might be termed Whitmanically 'the soul-stuff', the 'pneuma'. The Stoic concept of the *pneuma is* better known to Wordsworthians as that 'something far more deeply interfused' which 'rolls through all things' in the Poem upon the Wye, and perhaps survives in the thought of Karl Jaspers as 'the Comprehensive', that spirit *which* we are and *in* which we are. It also, I suggest, irradiates a remarkably imagist poem Bryant wrote some time around 1835, which Wordsworth would surely have admired. It is not one Wordsworth could have written—it seems to me to transcend both Bryant's usual manner and Wordsworth's closest approaches to imagism—but it envisages death, as 'Intimations' almost does, as a kind of dissolution. The very title—"Earth's Children Cleave to Earth"—says it all, even before the poem develops its Ossianic / Wordsworthian motif of morning mists leaving a mountain's brow.

> Earth's children cleave to earth: her frail,
>   Decaying children dread decay.
> Yon wreath of mist that leaves the vale,
>   And lessens in the morning ray:
> Look, how, by mountain rivulet,
>   It lingers, as it upward creeps,
> [...]
> Yet all in vain: it passes still
>   From hold to hold; it cannot stay;
> And in the very beams that fill
>   The world with glory, wastes away.
> Till, parting from the mountain's brow,

---

some reading of the Scottish common sense philosophers—including Dugald Stewart—but he did know his Wordsworth. Bruce Graver's 'The Oratorical Pedlar' showed that Wordsworth's Pedlar not only propounds wisdom drawn from Virgil, Cicero and Seneca, but does so in rhetorical strategies founded upon Quintilian's *De Oratore*, and Adam Potkay observes in *Wordsworth's Ethics* (173–82), that Wordsworth never succeeds in expressing a view of immortality that involves personhood, and that a Stoic, or Spinoza, or William Hazlitt or John Stuart Mill, would feel quite at home with all that Wordsworth affirms on the matter, as indeed Hazlitt and Mill both did.

> It vanishes from human eye,
> And that which sprung of earth is now
> A portion of the glorious sky. (*Poems*, 215)

—that last line wonderfully escaping the tendency of 'earth', 'decay', and 'wastes' to end in dust and ashes.

The word 'dissolution' doesn't appear in Bryant's poem, as in the title of Wordsworth's stanzas on Fox, but it is thoroughly enacted. Wordsworth's most intimate appropriation of the term is in a dream sonnet on the imagined death of Dora (*Ecclesiastical Sketches*, 3: 1), which seems to merge with Bryant's poem in the sestet:

> The bright corporeal presence, form, and face,
> Remaining still distinct, grew thin and rare,
> Like sunny mist; at length the golden hair,
> Shape, limbs, and heavenly features, keeping pace
> Each with the other, in a lingering race
> Of dissolution, melted into air. (*CWRT*, 3: 401)

Bryant's poem explores the image, with human mortality left implied. It is the perfection of imagism in that respect (quite possibly developed from the way Wordsworth employs objective correlatives in the Lucy poems and 'The Ruined Cottage'). Wordsworth's poem applies the metaphor of atmospheric dissolution to convey the dreamed dissolution of his dreamed Dora and he makes no further comment. But if that is what death means, no wonder—to return to 'Intimations'—

> The clouds that gather round the setting sun
> Do take a sober colouring from an eye
> That hath kept watch o'er man's mortality.

In such moments, Bryant and Wordsworth seem to share both a method and a world-view.

Consider two poets' homes, Rydal Mount and Cedarmere (the 'mere' of Cedarmere is an interesting choice from a poet whose poetical landscapes also boast 'brooks' and 'glens'): both distinguished by gardens landscaped by their horticultural poets, both with lake vistas, and rich in cherished flowers and specimen trees; both owners writing of fountains or of wells; both lauded as poets of 'high and sacred truths'. One of these poets, however, lived in a remote 'almost visionary republic', detached from national affairs and where others (Margaret Fuller among them) complained that he heard less clearly than he used to 'the still sad music of humanity'. The other, as Muller shows, lived just twenty miles from Manhattan, commuting several days a week, the confidant and the conscience of Presidents, dining with Andrew Jackson, counselling Martin van Buren, helping to launch Abraham Lincoln as a national figure, advising on the appointment or dismissal of this or that candidate for high office, espousing workers' rights, and (eventually, after a reluctant start) placing African Americans at the heart of his politics and making sure that Lincoln prosecuted the civil war with the utmost rigour. He could utter Jeremiads against instinctive radicals like William Lloyd Garrison and Fanny Wright, as the elder Wordsworth did against reform, but the almost daily composition of pugnacious editorials seems to have kept him in a perpetual state of political refreshment.

Both poets were 'unacknowledged legislators of mankind', but one (like George Eliot's Dorothea Brooke) through infinitely diffusive influence on the minds of men; the other, the Rupert Murdoch of his day, though mostly a benign one, indirectly manipulating the levers of power. That the American was candidly inspired and 'awed', by the poetry of the English recluse, may have had repercussions on much more than poetry. 'Thou hast great allies', Wordsworth promised a freed slave called Toussaint L'Ouverture—'Powers that will work for thee' (*CWRT*, 1: 643). One such power (if not the kind envisaged in Wordsworth's poem) was William Cullen Bryant. Bryant wrote no more than a dozen genuinely remarkable poems, but he exercised a legislative influence of which Wordsworth and Shelley could only dream. He was in short a prime instance of what Robert Weisbuch calls 'American actualism'.

Chapter 6:

Stepping Westward: *Nature* & *Walden*

> 'What, you are stepping westward?' 'Yea'
> —'Twould be a wildish destiny...
> Yet who would stop, or fear to advance,
> Though home or shelter he had none
> With such a sky to lead him on?
> —Wordsworth, 'Stepping Westward'

It is a notably American question. In another poem in the same work (*Poems, in Two Volumes*, 1807) Wordsworth asked a further question: 'Whither is fled the visionary gleam, / Where is it now, the glory and the dream?' One answer to the latter question always available to those of Jacobin persuasions—especially in the age of Price and Paine and Cartwright—was that the visionary gleam had fled Westward. Thoreau, too, adopts the notion that human progress involved a perpetual westering. His lecture on 'Walking' concludes with what seems to be an elaborate variation on Wordsworth's thought that 'stepping westward' was 'A kind of heavenly destiny'. In Thoreau's answer to the Wordsworths' evening walk the evening sky is so 'softly and serenely bright' that he seems to be sauntering towards 'the Holy Land'. It is not surprising that, according to Lorrie Smith, Thoreau was in the habit of invoking the poem when introducing his lecture.[1] To do so fits nicely with the famous Wordsworthian anecdote contained within the essay and borrowed from Christopher Wordworth's *Memoirs*—'When a traveller asked Wordsworth's servant to show him her master's study, she answered,

---

[1] See Lorrie Smith, 'Walking from England to America', *New England Quarterly*, 58:2 (1985) 221–41, 228.

184   Romantic Dialogues

"here is his library, but his study is out of doors"'. It is an engaging trait of Thoreau, as compared with Emerson's habit of prickly denial, that he can identify his precursor texts with marked congeniality. It is another, and one quite as deeply involved in Thoreau's debate with Wordsworth, that his echoes tend to highlight the millennial, not merely the celestial, intimations of the Romantic 'dawn'. But that is where I wish to end this chapter. In deference to his seniority, and his status in American Studies, I begin with Emerson.

1. THE EMERSONIAN SYNTHESIS

> This elevation of the spirit above the semblances of custom and the senses to a world of spirit, this life in the idea, even in the supreme and godlike, which alone merits the name of life, and without which our organic life is but a state of somnabulism; this it is which affords the sole sure anchorage in the storm ... the substantiating principle of all true wisdom, the satisfactory solution of all the contradictions of human nature, of the whole riddle of the world.
>
> —Coleridge, *The Friend*, 1818.

Between 1836 and 1854 Wordsworth and Coleridge became transfigured in the prose works of Emerson and Thoreau: *Nature* and *Walden*, in particular, sustain a dialogue with the poems of 1798–1802–1804–1807, namely 'Frost at Midnight', 'This Lime-Tree Bower', 'The Tables Turned' and 'On revisiting the Wye', 'Dejection: an Ode' and 'Intimations of Immortality'. For Emerson, given his personal reliance upon its consolations, and perhaps because of the prominence Coleridge gave to it in the last of his essays of method in *The Friend*, 'Intimations' has a peculiar primacy: in *English Traits* (1856) he acknowledges the Intimations ode as 'the high-water mark which the intellect has reached in this age', adding that 'new means were employed and new realms added to the empire of the muse by his courage'. Yet Emerson's implication in 'The American Scholar' that the illustrious poets of the recent past, having failed to live up to their early visions, must now be set aside, becomes the more usual stance of his public and private utterance. *English Traits* also puts Wordsworth down, fairly enough, as one who wrote longer than he was inspired, and less fairly as one 'who paid for his rare elevation by general tameness and conformity.'[1] This sour put-down of a 'narrow and English mind' may arise from personal resentment. Joel Pace notes that Emerson owned the American edition of Christopher Wordsworth's *Memoir*, which contained Wordsworth's letter of 16 August 1841 asking of Emerson's essays, 'where is the thing which now passes for philosophy at Boston to stop?'[2]

Emerson persuaded himself on his first visit to England, in 1833, before his most intent period of Coleridgean studies, that he need not look up to Landor, Coleridge, Carlyle or Wordsworth—the quartet of modern sages which represents the voice of England in Thoreau's essay, 'Thomas Carlyle and his Works'—for 'not one of these is a mind of the very first class'. In particular, 'they have *no idea* of that species of moral truth which I call the first philosophy.... You speak to them as to children or persons of inferior capacity whom it is necessary to humor; adapting ... remarks to their known prejudices'.[3] The extraordinary hubris belies an immense indebtedness. Writing to his Aunt Mary in 1829 Emerson had said of Coleridge's *The Friend* that 'there are few or no books of pure literature so self-imprinting ... so often remembered'. The Journals and Notebooks show not only his early familiarity *with Aids to Reflection, Biographia Literaria*, and *The Friend*, and later recourse *to On the Constitution of Church and State, Table Talk*, the *Treatise on Method, The Statesman's Manual*, but a habit of using these as the source of quotations from the entire Idealist tradition. Seminal entries from Coleridge long predate Emerson's conception or composition of either *Nature* (1836) or 'The American Scholar' (1837), and while his early Journals show him a

---

1 *The Collected Works of Ralph Waldo Emerson*, ed Alfred R Ferguson, et. al. (Cambridge, Mass.: The Belknap Press of Harvard University Press, 1971–2013), Volume 5, English Traits, 168, 12. Hereafter *CW*.

2 'Wordsworth in America: Publication, Reception and Literary Influence, 1802—1850' (Oxford D. Phil dissertation, 1999), 213.

3 *The Journals and Miscellaneous Notebooks of Ralph Waldo Emerson*, ed. William H Gilman et al., 14 vols. (Cambridge, Mass.: The Belknap Press of Harvard University Press, 1960), 4: 78–9. Hereafter JMN.

born Platonist, weaned on *The Phaedo* and tutored by Aunt Mary, his direct exploration of many of the figures he met through Coleridge deepens only in the 1840s. Between his visits to this man with no idea of the first philosophy, he digested his work even more thoroughly. Yet in *English Traits* Coleridge is publicly lampooned as 'a short thick old man' falling too readily 'into certain commonplaces'.[1]

That this 'short thick old man' had nevertheless played a major role in priming the American Transcendental pump is well known.[2] In a sentence, Marsh's edition of Coleridge's *Aids to Reflection* has been credited with enabling liberal New England thought to transcend both narrow Calvinism and the methods of Lockean empiricism, and, by extension, the marriage of these strains in the rationalist Puritan faith of that remarkably various man, Jonathan Edwards. Edwards is not merely the original of Joyce's fire sermon, but in his moving *Personal Narrative* is surely the most eloquent of early readers of religious meanings in the forms of nature. But his defence of

---

1 *Journals of Ralph Waldo Emerson*, edited by Edward Waldo Emerson and Waldo Emerson Forbes, 10 vols. (Boston and New York: Houghton Mifflin, 1909), 2: 227; and *CW*, 5: 5, 7.

2 For brief introductions to the Coleridge-Emerson connection see Frank T. Thompson, 'Emerson's Indebtedness to Coleridge', *Studies in Philology* 23 (1926): 55–76; Alexander Kern, 'Coleridge and American Romanticism: the Transcendentalists and Poe', in *New Approaches to Coleridge*, ed. Donald Sultana (London: Vision Press, 1981), 113–36; Mark Ledbetter, 'Changing Sensibilities: the Puritan Mind and the Romantic Revolution in Early American Religious Thought', in T*he Interpretation of Belief: Coleridge, Schleiermacher and Romanticism*, ed. David Jasper (Basingstoke: Macmillan, 1986), 176–84; and Anthony John Harding, 'Coleridge and Transcendentalism', in Richard Gravil and Molly Lefebure, eds., *The Coleridge Connection* (Basingstoke: Macmillan, 1990) 233–53. For deeper explorations see Anthony John Harding, *Coleridge and the Inspired Word* (Kingston and Montreal: McGill-Queen's University Press, 1985) and Barbara Packer, 'The Transcendentalists', in *The Cambridge History of American Literature*, volume 2, 1820–1865, ed. Sacvan Bercovitch (Cambridge: Cambridge University Press, 1995), 350–91. Recent full length treatments are Patrick J Keane's magisterial *Emerson, Romanticism and Intuitive Reason: The Transatlantic 'Light of All our Day'* (University of Missouri Press, 2005) and Samantha C. Harvey, *Transatlantic Transcendentalism: Coleridge, Emerson, and Nature* (Edinburgh University Press, 2013 both of which see Emerson as, in Harvey's words, 'a quintessential example of a writer at once deeply indebted and highly original' (3).

religious faith was based firmly upon empiricist procedures.[1] For him, Christianity, to be true must be derivable from natural science and natural rights, and to resort to human intuition is to make Christian belief untenable in an age of science. In offering a method of reflection, with claims to equal philosophical credibility, Coleridge gave Emerson and his generation a means of holding on to Edwards's insight into the language of nature which did not entail retention of the theology that went with it.

The key to this is Coleridge's famous misprision, or extension, of Kant. By making Reason the organ of spiritual and moral truth, a faculty whereby (because it dwells in us as an immanent portion of the Divine mind) we can maintain that a religious truth may be unamenable to Understanding yet accordant to Reason, Coleridge inaugurated the process whereby Puritan inner light enjoyed a renaissance in the ebullient Romantic faith of Emerson, Thoreau, Alcott and even Whitman. Reason, according to that most inviting and flattering formula in *Aids to Reflection,*

> is the Power of universal and necessary Convictions, the Source and Substance of Truths above Sense.... Reason indeed is much nearer to SENSE than to Understanding: for Reason (says our great HOOKER) is a direct Aspect of Truth, an inward beholding, having a similar relation to the Intelligible or Spiritual, as SENSE has to the Material or Phenomenal.[2]

Or, as Emerson simplifies the matter for his brother Edward, Reason 'is the highest faculty of the soul ... it never reasons, never proves, it simply perceives; it is vision.'[3] Emerson makes Reason equivalent to what Keats and Wordsworth mean by Imagination, or 'Reason in her most exalted mood', creative of essential truth. So, in a curious way, Coleridge is the agent of a metamorphosis of American puritanism into something far closer to that of Blake, himself the inheritor of

---

[1] On which aspect of the transatlantic theme see particularly Richard Brantley's *Locke, Wesley and the Method of English Romanticism* (Florida, 1984)

[2] Coleridge, *Aids to Reflection*, edited by John Beer (Princeton, NJ: Princeton University Press, 1993), 216, 223–24.

[3] *The Letters of Ralph Waldo Emerson*, edited by Ralph L. Rusk, 6 vols. (New York: Columbia University Press, 1939), 1: 412–13.

some broadly heretical enthusiasms of the Age of Milton. He inspires Emerson to rebuild, without its scriptural walls, the city on the hill.

'England', Emerson remarked patronisingly, as he approached Stonehenge with his friend Carlyle, 'an old and exhausted island, must one day be contented, like other parents, to be strong only in her children' (*CW*, 5: 155). Construing that oedipal sentiment as kindly meant—and Emerson often views America as a new chapter in the history of Saxon genius—let us examine how parental strength is reflected in his *Nature*. Early readers recognised the Wordsworthian and the more general Romantic affinities of this text. Samuel Osgood, in *The Western Messenger*, January 1837, began his review of *Nature* appropriately enough with a long quotation from *Tintern Abbey*. John A. Heraud commented in the *Monthly Magazine* for September 1839, 'The spirit of Coleridge, Wordsworth and Thomas Carlyle, has spread beyond the Atlantic and we hear the echoes thereof from afar'. Richard Monkton Milnes, the disciple of Carlyle and biographer of Keats, praised Emerson and America for responding more warmly than England had to the significance of Coleridge, Carlyle and their version of European, i.e. neo-Platonic, philosophy.[1]

Modern teaching editions of *Nature* usually stress (while greatly understating) Coleridge's presence alone. Yet while the primary theses of Transcendentalism's most Pantheistical text (especially those about language, symbol, and reason) are undoubtedly drawn from Coleridge, the rhetoric and imagery, it seems to me, are aligned less with Coleridge himself than with his more Emersonian *alter ego*, William Wordsworth. The oddest of all Romantic optimisms is Wordsworth's statement that although it was not his purpose formally to announce a system, the interested reader of *The Excursion* would have no difficulty in extracting it for himself. The reader of *Nature* must frequently suppose that in Emerson Wordsworth found such a reader, not of *The Excursion*—though in later years Emerson is said to have known this and *The Prelude* almost 'by heart'[2]—but of the

---

[1] Merton D. Sealts and Alfred R. Ferguson, eds. *Emerson's Nature—Origin, Growth, Meaning*, 2nd edn (Carbondale, IL: Southern Illinois University Press, 1979), 77, 99, 102.

[2] Robert D. Richardson, *Emerson: The Mind on Fire* (Berkeley: University of California Press, 1994), 149.

Stepping Westward: *Nature & Walden* 189

lyrical work which *Aids to Reflection*, *The Friend* and *Biographia* encouraged Emerson to study. For the objective of cultivating, as Emerson says at the start of his major essay, 'an original relation to the universe' is, of course, just such an objective as Hazlitt finds characteristic of the early Wordsworth, and indeed is the burden of Elizabeth Peabody's favourite poem, 'The Tables Turned':

> One impulse from a vernal wood
> May teach you more of man;
> Of moral evil and of good,
> Than all the sages can
> ...
> Enough of science and of art;
> Close up those barren leaves;
> Come forth and bring with you a heart
> That watches and receives.[1]

The orientation of Emerson's 'introduction' to *Nature* reflects more transparently the immediate influence of Carlyle, whose *Sartor Resartus* he has just published. Emerson fuses three of *Sartor*'s themes in his own introduction: the adjuration to escape the bondage of old clothes, the theme of the supernatural bases of the natural, which emerges in later chapters as a major thesis, and a Fichtean definition of nature as encompassing 'all which philosophy distinguishes as the NOT ME.' In the work's first and third chapters, however, the major assertions, that 'in the woods ... a man casts off his years as the snake his slough', that from vernal leaves come impulses of both reason and faith, that in this relation we both give and receive, and that 'nothing can befall me in life,—no disgrace, no calamity ... which nature cannot repair' (*CW*, 1: 10, 13) betoken a prolonged immersion in the lyrical Wordsworth, including of course 'The Poem upon the Wye'. This poem provides not only the epochal displacement of a scriptural deity with a generalised over-soul, but credits Nature most

---

1 Joel Pace points out that Emerson marked in this poem the lines 'Come forth into the light of things / Let Nature be your teacher'. 'Lifted to genius'?: Wordsworth in Emerson's Nurture and Nature'. *Symbiosis*, 2.2 (1998) 125–40, 138. This important essay reveals substantial evidence concerning Emerson's early annotations of Wordsworth.

memorably with most of the functions of the Holy Spirit. Nature herself has the power to assuage 'the fretful stir / Unprofitable, and the fever of the world' and to 'so impress'

> With quietness and beauty, and so feed
> With lofty thoughts, that neither evil tongues,
> Rash judgements, nor the sneers of selfish men,
> Nor greetings where no kindness is, nor all
> The dreary intercourse of daily life,
> Shall e'er prevail against us....

Emerson's expression 'The leafless trees ... and stubble rimed with frost, contribute to the mute music' (*CW*, 1:14) silently recalls Wordsworth's skating spot, in which

> the precipices rang aloud;
> The leafless trees, and every icy crag
> Tinkled like iron; while the distant hills
> Into the tumult sent an alien sound
> Of melancholy, not unnoticed...

He comments on this passage in his Journal, commending the truth and 'self-reliance' of Wordsworth's vision, and noting for himself the 'sound of the stars' on a snowy night (*JMN*, 5. 454).

Emerson then applies to the lover of nature, without acknowledgement, Coleridge's definition of the genius as one who has 'retained the spirit of infancy even into the era of manhood', and proceeds, cannily, to turn this perception against Wordsworth and Coleridge in a quite remarkable utilisation of the lyrics of 1798/1802. In successive paragraphs of his first chapter he passes from the heady intoxication of 'Poem upon the Wye' and 'Frost at Midnight'—'nothing can befall me in life ... which nature cannot repair'—to the sobrieties of 'Intimations' and 'Dejection': 'the same scene which yesterday breathed perfume and glittered ... is overspread with melancholy today', or as Wordsworth phrases it, 'The things which I have seen I now can see no more'. The poetic experience developed in the four great nature poems of English Romanticism—'The Wye', 'Frost', 'Dejection', 'Immortality'— is compressed into a single argument.

Stepping Westward: *Nature & Walden*   191

At times Emerson seems familiar with work he cannot possibly have known. Thus, the most striking declaration of the essay, 'The currents of the Universal Being circulate through me; I am part or particle of God' reads like a fearless restitution of Wordsworth's manuscript claim, in the Pantheistic confidence of 1798, that 'all beings live with God, themselves / Are God, existing in one mighty whole'.[1] Only the rather desperate and much lampooned metaphor which introduces this claim—'I become a transparent eyeball. I am nothing. I see all'—establishes copyright in this otherwise Protean passage. Even this mysterious figure may well be understood as referring us to that Emersonian sense of the self as deputised by innumerable other selves. Since the currents of the Universal Being must also have circulated through Tom Paine in his most Spinozistic moments, and through Wordsworth while revisiting the Wye, one who becomes what he reads to the extent that Emerson not only does but claims to do, must in some sense have participated in numerous such heady moments, including those of 1789 and 1798. In a bizarre way, the passage constitutes an acknowledgement.

It is generally recognised that the basic theory of language and of symbol, in chapter 4, and the characterisation of Reason as not ours but as something universal to which we belong, belong to Emerson's reading of Coleridge. Parts of chapter 4, however, may be read as unconsciously defending Wordsworth's rather naive theory of language from Coleridge's sophisticated critique in *Biographia Literaria*. Emerson insists, as does Wordsworth, that even words dealing with mental facts can be traced to material facts, and that simplicity of life is associated with purity of language. When Emerson writes that 'hundreds of writers may be found in every long-civilized nation who for a short time ... make others believe that they see and utter truths, who ... feed unconsciously on the language created by the primary writers of the country, those namely, who hold primarily on nature' he is elaborating on Wordsworth's devastating critique, in the 1815 'Essay Supplementary', of virtually all English poetry

---

[1] This passage from the so-called Peter Bell MS is quoted in *The Prelude 1799, 1805, 1850*, ed. Jonathan Wordsworth, M. H. Abrams and Stephen Gill (New York and London: Norton, 1979), 496.

between Milton and Thomson: 'the poetry of the period intervening between the publication of the Paradise Lost and the Seasons does not contain a single new image of external nature'.[1] The particular sense of what constitutes corruption of language, and what is entailed in the purification of 'this rotten diction', is as Wordsworthian as the insistently repeated sense (manifestly founded in 'The Poem upon the Wye') that for the man 'bred in the woods, whose senses have been nourished by their fair and appeasing changes' the light of nature will remain efficaceous 'in the roar of cities and the broil of politics' because noble sentiments are underwritten by natural forms. The murmuring pines and rolling river of infancy are the adult mind's 'keys of power' (*CW*, 1: 20, 21).

Emerson's real achievement in chapter 4 is mainly to clarify (with the aid of Plato, Plotinus and, unconsciously, Kant) what is implicit in Wordsworth: that this relation of mind and matter is not merely 'fancied by some poet', but 'stands in the will of God and so is free to be known by all men'. This claim is followed immediately by the clipped sentence 'It appears to men, or it does not appear', a curious truncation of a sentence by Plotinus as quoted by Coleridge in chapter 12 of *Biographia Literaria* (where, as it happens, it is given a Wordsworthian gloss).[2] On the next page the chapter ends by declaring that '"every object rightly seen, unlocks a new faculty of the soul"'. This is quoted (without attribution) from Marsh's edition of *Aids to Reflection* (see *CW*, 1. 249–250 nn). The next chapter, 'Discipline', is inspired in numerous points of argument and detail by the eleventh of the 'Essays on Method' in *The Friend*. Thus, throughout an essay which overtly associates England with 'sense and understanding' and Germany with idealism and imagination, Emerson derives the quotations representing the latter almost exclusively from Coleridge and Carlyle.

Chapter 6 of *Nature* opens with a manifestly Berkeleyan thesis,

---

1 W. J. B. Owen, *Wordsworth's Literary Criticism*, 203. Wordsworth's encomium on Percy's Reliques, in the same essay, constitutes the definitive banishment of the 'courtly muse'.

2 When Plotinus says that intuitive knowledge 'either appears to us or it does not appear' he is speaking, Coleridge says, of what Wordsworth meant by 'The vision and the faculty divine' (*Biographia Literaria*, 1. 241).

Stepping Westward: *Nature & Walden* 193

in questioning the outward existence of nature. It proceeds, however, by elaborating a quite remarkable synthesis of Wordsworth and Coleridge on Imagination. Emerson first offers an account of how nature assists in making the human mind aware of its own contribution to what it sees. The account is similar to that in Book 2 of *The Prelude*, which Thoreau will use, but is derived presumably—if derived at all—from the argument mounted in 'Influence of Natural Objects', 'Intimations' and 'Dejection'. Nature 'is made to conspire with spirit to emancipate us' Emerson argues, for the least change in our stance towards objects makes us conscious of the eye's shaping activity (30). Our sensory pleasures thus become mixed with awe, indeed 'a low degree of the sublime'. Having established this Wordsworthian point (compare 'the midnight storm grew darker in the presence of my eye', *Prelude* 2: 387–95), Emerson moves into a paraphrase of Coleridge on primary and secondary imagination. The poet, operating 'in a higher manner', 'unfixes the land and the sea, makes them revolve around the axis of his primary thought, and disposes them anew' or in Coleridgean terms, the imagination '... dissolves, diffuses, dissipates, in order to recreate'. Dissolving and diffusing in order to recreate, Emerson agrees, 'the Imagination may be defined to be the use to which the Reason makes of the material world' (31).[1]

Just how Emerson worked, in 1836, towards combining his reading notes into such curious syntheses, can most easily be illustrated from a single passage from the same chapter. The third section of chapter 6 runs as follows (I number the points for subsequent reference):

(1) Whilst the poet delights us by animating nature ... with his own thoughts, he differs from the philosopher only herein, that the one proposes Beauty as his main end; the other Truth. But, the philosopher, not less than the poet, postpones the apparent order and relations of things to the empire of thought. (2) 'The problem of philosophy', according to Plato, 'is, for all that exists conditionally, to find a ground unconditioned and abso-

---

[1] As Frank Thompson pointed out, Coleridge's distinction between Reason and Understanding underlies 'at least four of the seven divisions of Nature'. 'Emerson's Indebtedness to Coleridge'. *Studies in Philology* 23 (1926) 55–76, p. 71.

lute'. It proceeds on the faith that a law determines all phenomena, which being known, the phenomena can be predicted. That law, when in the mind, is an idea. Its beauty is infinite. (3) The true philosopher and the true poet are one, and a beauty, which is truth, and a truth, which is beauty, is the aim of both. (4) Is not the charm of one of Plato's or Aristotle's definitions strictly like that of the Antigone or Sophocles? It is in both cases, that a spiritual life has been imparted to nature; that the solid seeming block of matter has been pervaded and dissolved by a thought ... an informing soul.... (5) The sublime remark of Euler on his law of arches, 'This will be found contrary to all experience, yet it is true;' had already transformed nature into mind, and left matter like an outcast corpse (*CW*, 1. 33–4).

The first point modifies the use made by Coleridge, Wordsworth and Shelley, of the discrimination between the poet whose immediate object is pleasure, and the philosopher whose immediate object is truth (as in *Biographia Literaria*, 2: 13, where Coleridge writes that poem 'proposes for its *immediate* object, pleasure not truth'). In the second point a somewhat Kantian 'Plato'—it is fact Kant—is quoted from Coleridge (*Friend*, 1. 461) and the following reflection summarises Coleridge's next two pages. The third is an instantly recognisable and insightful reading of *precisely* what Keats meant by 'beauty is truth, truth beauty,' and is the essay's second echo of this phrase (he has earlier written 'truth and goodness and beauty are but different faces of the same all').[1] The fourth is a personal application of this now Coleridgeo-Keatsian point. The fifth—Euler's remark—is quoted, somewhat loosely, from Coleridge (*Friend*, 2: 476).[2] The result, like

---

[1] Emerson, I suspect, would have given short shrift to the acres of critical nonsense modern critics have devoted to distancing Keats from the benignly neo-Platonic utterance of his thoroughly Grecian urn.

[2] Some of these source identifications are mine, some appear in Sealts and Ferguson, above; some in Charles Anderson's *American Literary Masters*, vol. 1 (NewYork: Holt, Rinehart, and Winston, 1965); some in *The Norton Anthology of American Literature*, edited by Ronald Gottesman et al. (NewYork and London: Norton, 1979); some in the *Heath Anthology of American Literature*, 3rd edn., edited by Paul Lauter et al. (Boston: Houghton Mifflin, 1998). There is much to be learned by studying *Nature* with the aid of a variety of annotators.

Nature as a whole, is an argument which derives its materials from or through English Romanticism, *yet which barely acknowledges the existence of such a body of writing.*[1]

The broad strategy of *Nature* is Coleridgean: Emerson starts by seeing nature fully as the solace of our being, passes to an insistence that as the mind is spiritual nature must be transcended, and then enacts a recovery of nature as a system of spiritual signs. The grain, however, is again Wordsworthian. Nature nurtures, nature educates and stimulates the desire for beauty, but above all nature awakens imagination, it conspires with spirit to emancipate us, introduces us to the more sublime powers of the human mind, and instigates that second nature of human creativity. While we are all sentenced to a rite of passage in which we grow away from the mothering earth, and cease to understand the speech of her creatures (Thoreau, also, re-enacts this rite of passage), there is compensation in the recognition that the human mind, co-creator of earth's beauty in any case, becomes more beautiful than the earth itself. The basic argument of *Nature* is that of *The Prelude*. Since *The Prelude* was unread by Emerson, at this date, he cannot be paraphrasing it. Rather, like other great readers, Keats, Shelley and Carlyle, Emerson seems to have been able to project an ideal Wordsworth by triangulation from cognate passages in *The Excursion* (which include the life history of 'The Pedlar'), 'The Poem upon the Wye' and those fragments of *The Prelude* which were already widely known: the 'Skating' spot, 'There was a Boy', 'The Simplon Pass', and 'Bliss was it in that Dawn'. When he visited Rydal, knowing that Channing had been favoured with readings from it, Emerson expressed particular interest in the unpublished work. 'I told him how much the few printed extracts had quickened the desire to possess his unpublished poems'.[2]

Whatever led to Emerson's 'troubled refusal' of indebtedness, the

---

[1] Coleridge's famous remark on the sublimity of a Gothic church is acknowledged. Wordsworth is unmentioned. It seems pertinent to note that having read De Quincey's evidence of Coleridge's plagiarisms from Schelling, Emerson asked: 'why could not he have said generously like Goethe I owe all' (*JMN*, 5: 59).

[2] *English Traits*, *CW*, 5: 23. Apart from passages already available in *Lyrical Ballads* (1800), *Poems in Two Volumes* (1807), and collected editions, some had currency in America through *The Friend* and *Biographia*.

price is critical misconstruction of his genuine achievement. Both 'The American Scholar' and *Nature* are created by a young scholar painstakingly laminating the ideas, the experiences, the insights and quite frequently the phrases of Wordsworth, Coleridge, Shelley, Keats and Carlyle, with occasional contributions from Goethe and that other conduit of the Germanic, Mme de Stael. The result, however, is something other than plagiarism. The fact is that Emerson articulated in prose *as no English Romantic successfully did*, the high Romantic argument concerning nature. Not even Coleridge came close to crafting a satisfactory, portable and unitary exposition of what he and his contemporaries meant by nature—or even recognising that such an exposition was needed. Secondly, his prolonged apprenticeship worked: by 1841 or thereabouts Emerson became what he had read. In the greatest of the essays of Emerson's great decade—'Self-Reliance', 'The Over-Soul', 'The Poet', 'Circles'—there is very little sign of such lamination, and the arguments and phrasing are, but for the gradual infusion of Blake, increasingly self-reliant. And thirdly, for the moment at least, and with Carlyle's not inconsiderable assistance, he solved the problem of 'Dejection'.

Towards the end of *Nature* there is one of those almost uncanny echoes of Blake, when Emerson writes that for fallen humanity 'the axis of vision is not coincident with the axis of things, and so they appear not transparent but opake' (*CW*, 1. 43). Much later, in *Representative Men* (1850), Emerson will use a similar utterance in describing Swedenborg's somewhat mechanical system of symbolism: 'it required such rightness of position, that the poles of the eye should coincide with the axis of the world' (*CW* 4: 66). But if this an echo, who is it echoing? I find no such metaphor in Swedenborg himself or in Wilkinson's commentaries. Nor, in 1836, is he likely to be echoing Blake; there is no firm evidence that Emerson had heard of Blake by this date.[1] Emerson's formulation is more likely

---

1 The affinity between Emerson and Blake is the great unexplained facet of Anglo-American transactions in the period. I outlined the problem in 'Blake in Boston', *Symbiosis*, 1.2 (1997) 275–77. At an unknown date he received a copy of the Wilkinson edition of 1839 from Elizabeth Peabody, who told Wordsworth in May 1842 that she was reading Blake 'for the first time' and yearning to see 'the quarto edition with his own illustrations' (Dove Cottage MS. A/Peabody/7).

to be, as Barbara Packer has brilliantly demonstrated, a synthesis of Newtonian and Coleridgean metaphor. The 'axis' metaphor is derived from Brewster's *Life*, and 'coincidence' from *Aids to Reflection*, while transparency and opacity are used literally in the former, metaphorically in the latter.[1] The 'Blakean' fusion Emerson brings about is one of his earliest demonstrations of a talent for genuinely creative synthesis.

Whatever its derivation, the formulation has a peculiar importance in Emerson's argument. It appears in the final chapter, 'Prospects', as the solution to the problem he has expressed in chapter 1 in terms of 'Dejection' and 'Intimations', the failure of the hour of vision. 'Dejection: an Ode' (the work of a man of thirty) appears to conclude that the life of things is projected by the imaginative eye:

> It were a vain endeavour,
> Though I should gaze forever
> On that green light that lingers in the West:
> I may not hope from outward forms to win
> The passion and the life, whose fountains are within.

'Intimations of Immortality' (by the thirty-two year old Wordsworth) laments the transience of the 'celestial light' in which nature seemed apparelled, when it wore 'the glory and the freshness of a dream'. To Emerson, at thirty-three, already intimate with mortality, the melancholy questions of 'Dejection' and 'Intimations' were deeply felt. His prose ode answering theirs, arrives at an ameliorative reply:

> The ruin or the blank, that we see when we look at nature, is in our own eye. The axis of vision is not coincident with the axis of things, and so they appear not transparent but opake. The reason why the world lacks unity, and lies broken and in heaps, is, because man is disunited with himself (43).

The first proof that Emerson knew the texts which appear to leave their mark on him—the *Auguries of Innocence* and *The Marriage of Heaven and Hell*—comes in 1863 when he repeatedly borrowed Gilchrist's *Life* from the Boston Athenaeum. Mr Google informs me that Linda Freedman has a book forthcoming on the matter of Blake in America.

1 Barbara Packer, 'The Instructed Eye', in Sealts and Ferguson, *Emerson's Nature* (209–221), 213–9.

In theory, of course 'Dejection' argues the same. *Nature*, however, believes the condition can be cured.

In 1833, as Joel Pace has argued, Emerson went to Rydal Mount hoping to meet the author of 'Tintern' and 'Intimations', a fellow sailor 'on strange seas of thought', but found instead a 'conservative advocate of the religious and political status quo' no longer capable of the promised synthesis of these seminal texts in 'The Recluse'.[1] If, therefore, Wordsworth's new empires of thought were to be usefully mapped, Emerson would have to do it. He went home to immerse himself in the Wordworthian texts of 1798–1802, in Coleridge's *The Friend*, and in *Sartor Resartus*. *Nature* is the result. The essay's peroration blends optimistically the Wordsworthian celebration of the ordinary with Carlyle's 'everlasting Yea' and Shelley's prophecy of universal renovation in *Prometheus Unbound*. 'Build therefore, your own world. As fast as you conform your life to the pure idea in your mind, that will unfold its great proportions. A correspondent revolution in things will attend the influx of the spirit.'

There may be little, ethically, or metaphysically, in Emerson that cannot be found in Blake, Wordsworth or Coleridge or Shelley, save the gestalt: but the gestalt does make all the difference. Emerson's brazen declaration of independence from the authority of scriptures, underwritten by institutions, far transcends the *later* positions of Coleridge and Wordsworth. In 'Self Reliance' he records his reply to the criticism that such independence might be inspired by the devil— 'if I am the devil's child, I will live then from the Devil'—and adds, 'No law can be sacred to me but that of my nature. Good and bad are but names very readily transferable to that or this; the only right is what is after my constitution' (*CW* 2: 30). In such sublime, Niagara-like self-assertion, one sees why Nietzsche responded to him with an admiration he felt for no other Romantic. Yet even here, Emerson sounds like the Blake of *The Marriage of Heaven and Hell*—was it reading Emerson that made Nietzsche seem so Blakean?—or even Wordsworth on a good day. It was the sage of Rydal, after all, in his 'Answer to Mathetes', who advised youth 'to follow his intellectual genius through good and through evil' and drive his plough, as it

---

1 Pace, 'Lifted to Genius', *Symbiosis* 2:2 (1998), 136.

were, through the bones of parental advice. Wordsworth's essay, a cautious sketch of Emersonian self-reliance, praising the individual who can steer clear of convention, and obey 'a moral law established by himself' was, of course, published in *The Friend*.[1] The avid reader of Blake, of Wordsworth, and of Shelley, as known through their complete works, may well extract from their moments of panache, a Nietzschean ethic of the kind so resonantly elaborated in 'Self-Reliance'. But Emerson was the first Romantic to do so.

That somewhat cynical procedural ethic, 'first, one; then, another; we drain all cisterns' ('The American Scholar') has its negative expression and it becomes associated with some pettily chauvinistic repudiation of those cisterns, but it does make Emerson, like Carlyle, and in some ways more assimilably than Carlyle, a major conduit whereby Romanticism spoke not only to America but to Victorian England, the Manchester of Elizabeth Gaskell for instance. Wordsworth undoubtedly gave the primary poetic expression to the need to replace a theologically encrusted deity with 'something far more deeply interfused', and Coleridge certainly achieved a prior formulation of the difference between those who 'speak from within, or from experience, or from experience, as possessors of the fact' and those who speak 'from without, as spectators merely',[2] but it was Emerson who synthesised these insights, christened his synthesis the 'Over-Soul', and gave Romanticism a second birth. His 'orphic poet' in the final pages of *Nature*—the poet who speaks of the cycles of the universal man, of our Nebuchadnezzar existence, of infancy as a perpetual Messiah pleading with man to return to paradise, of the cosmos as an emanation of his own spirit—is startlingly like Blake. Emerson's general complaint against the Romantics he knew, including the one who had first taught him that nature 'must in act and substance be itself spiritual' and that man must learn 'to comprehend nature in himself and its laws in the ground of his own existence' (*The Friend*, 1:

---

[1] Coleridge, *The Friend*, 1: 390, 404–5.

[2] Indeed he did, and more cogently, distinguishing 'that intuition of things which arises, when we possess ourselves as on with the whole, which is substantial knowledge' from the merely abstract knowledge of those who see themselves as separate from nature (*The Friend*, 1: 520).

511), is that they failed to rise to Blake's challenge in *Milton*: 'To cast off Bacon, Locke and Newton from Albion's covering, / To take off his filthy garments & clothe him with Imagination, / To cast aside from poetry all that is not Inspiration.'

2. WORDSWORTH IN WALDEN

As everybody knows, Wordsworth was in Thoreau's ostensible opinion, 'too tame for the Chippeway'. Because this Journal entry of 1841 belongs to the myth of autonomy it is quoted in every study of Thoreau. Far more rarely quoted is this later entry, as Thoreau began life at Walden in 1845:

> To live to a good old age such as the ancients reached—serene and contented—dignifying the life of man—Leading a simple epic life—in these days of confusion and turmoil—. That is what Wordsworth has done—Retaining the tastes and the innocence of his youth—There is more wonderful talent—but nothing so cheering and world famous as this.[1]

Nothing, that is, until Thoreau's own exemplary, cheering, and world famous experiment in simplicity.

Walden, or Life in the Woods (1854) is clearly written to do rather more than give specific gravity to Emerson's general ideas, by practising self-reliance. Indeed in that regard it is open to and has received much sceptical comment, not least from James Russell Lowell who flatly declared this 'shanty life' an impossibility:

> He squatted on another man's land; he borrows an axe; his boards, his nails, his bricks, his mortar, his books, his lamp, his fish-hooks, his plough, his hoe, all turn state's evidence against him as an accomplice in the sin of that artificial civilization which rendered it possible that such a person as Henry D Thoreau should exist at all.[2]

---

1 Thoreau, *Journal* 2: 1842-1848, ed. Robert Sattelmeyer (Princeton: New Jersey: Princeton University Press, 1984), 200–1.
2 *Walden and Civil Disobedience: Norton Critical Edition*, ed. Owen Thomas (New York: Norton, 1966), 292.

Stepping Westward: *Nature* & *Walden* 201

Walden, nevertheless, invites its reader, as Wordsworth invited his readers to do, to live within 'the light of things', and it does, in exemplary fashion, take the surveyor's rod to Emerson's more abstract claims, bottoming *Nature* in nature. It has also been read by several modern critics as a vast rebirth ritual, 'the purest and most complete in our literature' says Stanley Edgar Hyman. Sherman Paul reads it as the record of an ascetic discipline aimed at 'metamorphosis', or recovery of the lost child; and R. W. B. Lewis as the record of a visit to a 'new world', and a warning to those still in 'the cave'.[1] What is intuited in such readings is *Walden*'s naturalisation, for the first time in American literature, of the classic Romantic form, variously epitomised in *The Prelude*, *Prometheus Unbound* and *Sartor Resartus*, of the bildungsroman raised to a myth of reintegration. To put it another way, when Thoreau states laconically in 'Spring' that Walden, no longer ice-bound, 'was dead, and is alive again', he is noting the emergence from its chrysalis of a new self, for 'the undecaying mind' as Wordsworth puts it (*Prelude*, 4: 155–8) can also 'thaw the deepest sleep / That time can lay upon her'.

There is considerable consensus that Thoreau's career as a writer reflects a prolonged engagement with Wordsworth, and that the writing and revision of *Walden* spanned years in which he moved from frank admiration, little short of hero-worship, to tentative distancing.[2] De Quincey's acid *Reminiscences*, Christopher Wordsworth's

1 For Hyman and Paul see *Walden* (Norton Critical Edition), 319, 336–41; R. W. B. Lewis, *The American Adam: Innocence, Tragedy and Tradition in the Nineteenth Century* (Chicago: University of Chicago Press, 1955), 21–22.
2 Numerous echoes in *Walden* and other works are recognized by Charles R Anderson, in *The Magic Circle of Walden* (New York: Holt, Rinehart and Winston, 1968), James McIntosh, in *Thoreau as Romantic Naturalist* (Ithaca: Cornell University Press, 1974); Robert D. Richardson, Jr., in *Henry Thoreau: A Life of the Mind* (Berkeley: University of California Press, 1986); Laraine Fergensen, in 'Was Thoreau Rereading Wordsworth in 1851' (*Thoreau Journal Quarterly*, 5:3, 1973, 20–23) and Lance Newman, *Our Common Dwelling: Henry Thoreau, Transcendentalism, and the Class Politics of Nature* (Palgrave, 2005). Neill R. Joy offers a detailed summary of the parallels between 'Ponds' and Wordsworth's *Guide to the Lakes*, in 'Two possible analogues for "The Ponds" in *Walden*: Jonathan Carver and Wordsworth' (*Emerson Society Quarterly: a Journal of the American Renaissance*, 24 (1978) 197-205). Joseph J. Moldenhauer, adumbrates

construction in his *Memoirs* of a soundly Tory Wordsworth, and London gossip as reported by Emerson and other visitors, may well, Joseph J. Moldenhauer suggests, have coloured Thoreau's views by 1851–53 as he revises *Walden*.[1] Wordsworth's own mind, the evidence suggested, had decayed, and was now in a disconcertingly deep sleep. Yet critical efforts to present Thoreau as irritably concerned to distance himself from Wordsworthian influence on these grounds seem to me peculiarly ill-conceived. *Walden* manifests an astonishing openness to the living Wordsworth. Given the publication of *The Prelude* in 1850, the fact that Thoreau's major textual revisions took place between one journal entry (16 July 1851) lamenting that nothing in later life 'comes up to, or is comparable with, the experiences of my boyhood', when 'life was ecstasy' and another (28 March 1857) claiming that 'Often I can give the truest and most interesting account of any adventure I have had after years have elapsed, for .... all that continues to interest me after such a lapse of time is sure to be pertinent', strikes one as more than coincidental. Both entries show a mind in accordance with Wordsworth's own.

In the midst of revising and shaping *Walden*, or to be more precise, as he was embarking on its major period of expansion and giving it its chapter form, he wrote what could be taken as a review of the first four books of *The Prelude*:

> Ah these youthful days! Are they never to return? When the walker does not too curiously observe particulars, but sees, hears, scents, tastes, and feels only himself,—the phenomena that show themselves to him,—his expanding body, his intellect, and heart. No worm or insect, quadruped or bird confined his view, but the unbounded universe was his. (30 March 1853)[2]

---

much of the evidence in '*Walden* and Wordsworth's *Guide to the English Lake District*' (*Studies in the American Renaissance*, 1990, 261–92) and points out that Wordsworth's 'Topographical Description of the Country of the Lakes in the North of England' was in Henry Reed's *Complete Poetical Works* (Philadelphia, 1837).

1 Moldenhauer maps the evidence in detail, but (I believe) exaggerates its impact on Thoreau.

2 Cited from J Lyndon Shanley, *The Making of Walden: with the Text of the First Version* (Chicago and London: University of Chicago Press, 1957), 7, 57.

Stepping Westward: *Nature & Walden* 203

The textual evidence for a profound identification greatly outweighs some five or six ambivalent signals of self-differentiation elsewhere in Thoreau's work. Thoreau's Wordsworthian criticism of American writers for using foreign rather than indigenous materials (they sang of Keatsian nightingales, Shelleyan skylarks and English hedges, for instance, instead of homely robins on American fences) is often taken as a sign of a proper 'American chauvinism' rather than what it is: a call to emulate, not imitate, the 'lakers' in whom such indigenousness is endemic.[1] His experience in 1848, on Mt Ktaadn, of a 'vast, Titanic inhuman Nature', anything but motherly—it inspired such vertiginous responses as 'I stand in awe of my body ...rocks, trees, wind on our cheeks! The *solid* earth! The *actual* world! The *common sense*! Contact! Contact! *Who* are we? *Where* are we?'—constitutes, it has been argued, a recantation of the Romantic view of Nature expressed in *Walden* six years later.[2] One might argue, rather, that Thoreau's organicism survived the experience, just as Wordsworth's survived his birdsnesting vertigo and the terrors of Ullswater, Stonehenge, and the Simplon Pass—and as Shelley's holistic philosophy synthesised the sublime terrors of Mont Blanc.

Thoreau's endlessly quoted remark that Wordsworth 'is too tame for the Chippeway' occurs in a Journal entry of 1841 asking for a wilder literature, expressive of nature's 'primeval aspects, sterner, savager than *any* poet has sung.'[3] The remark certainly announces that there is more to be done in the way of wildness, but does it not also imply, very surprisingly, that Wordsworth is, to date, the one Anglo-

[1] Lorrie Smith, 'Walking from England to America', *New England Quarterly*, 58:2 (1985), 221–41 (223–24).

[2] *The Maine Woods, The Writings of Henry David Thoreau*, 20 vols. (Boston and New York: Houghton Mifflin, 1906), 3: 70, 78. Laraine Fergensen, in 'Wordsworth and Thoreau: the Relationship between Man and Nature' in *Thoreau Journal Quarterly*, 9:2, 1979, 3–10, saw the experience as disillusioning, but argues in a later essay that it was not permitted to disrupt Walden's account of nature. Frederick Garber sees the episode as leading to a recognition in Walden that 'virgin land ... can challenge ... the professions of poems like "Tintern Abbey".' See 'Thoreau and Anglo- European Romanticism', in *Approaches to Teaching Thoreau's Walden and Other Works,* edited by Richard J. Schneider (NY: MLA, 1996).

[3] *The Journal of Henry David Thoreau,* ed. Bradford Torrey, in *The Writings of Henry David Thoreau.* 1: 273.

American poet one might conceivably nominate as bard to an Indian nation? He expands the point into a broader argument in 'Walking' (1862): 'English Literature, from the days of the minstrels *to* the lake Poets,—Chaucer and Spenser and Milton, and even Shakespeare, included,—breathes no quite fresh and in this sense wild strain.' The desire in the same essay for a poet who could 'impress the winds and the streams into his service' and transplant his words to the page 'with earth adhering to their roots' so that they would 'loom and bear fruit there for the faithful reader' establishes a model of the poet described, as Coleridge would say, 'in ideal perfection' and invites one to consider whether any poets have come close to that ideal. It is surely odd to read Thoreau's statement 'I do not know of *any* poetry to quote which adequately expresses this yearning for the Wild' as if it refers *not* to any failure by Paulding, Shelley, Bryant, Longfellow, Emerson, Whittier or indeed Thoreau, to do this, but *specifically* to Wordsworth's.

Given the pressure of Emerson's disenchantment, following his visit in 1848, the significance of this slender harvest of by no means adverse comment is surely the reverse of what might be expected. Thoreau's evident absorption of Wordsworth's poetry, and of the *Topographical Description*, constituted a bond which made his critique in *Walden* one of the most perceptive, and inward, that literature can show between two men who never met. The publication of *The Prelude* in 1850, along with De Quincey's and Christopher Wordsworth's disturbing versions of the later Wordsworth, seems to have sent Thoreau back to the *poetry*. Certainly he makes one disparaging remark in his Journal of 1851 on what he calls Wordsworth's 'coldness' in remarking of a beautiful scene that it gave him 'pleasure', and *Walden* makes a wry allusion to Wordsworth's sinecure as 'distributor of stamps': there was, he remarks in the opening chapter, little chance of the townsfolk of Concord offering *him* 'a sinecure with a moderate allowance.' What Thoreau made of the later Wordsworth and his lifestyle at Rydal Mount undoubtedly influences the strategy of *Walden*, whose sub-plot is, of course, recovery of precisely that visionary gleam which Wordsworth spends his career lamenting the loss of. But it would be as absurd to claim that criticism of this kind

Stepping Westward: *Nature & Walden* 205

constitutes a rejection, as to suggest that his claim to have 'laboured' to read Chalmer's anthology of poetry 'without skipping' constitutes a rejection of the English lyrical tradition. Thoreau openly inscribes himself in that tradition, quoting liberally, alongside conspicuously 'alien' infusions of Eastern writings, from Chaucer, Spenser, Shakespeare, Jonson, Chapman, Quarles, D'Avenant, Carew, Donne, Milton (several times), 'Ossian' and Cowper, together with Raleigh's Ovid and Pope's Homer.

Although stylistically *Walden* may appear to be a polar opposite to the major works of English Romantic Poetry, in its affectation of prosaic woodnotes wild, its relation to that art is self-conscious. It openly celebrates an American Grasmere ('This is my lake country' Thoreau says of the ponds surrounding Walden) and imagines its hut as opening onto a mountain 'tarn.' His allusiveness to his immediate precursors is, given the pressures on American writers to repudiate recent English influence, pervasive, open, and genial. Unlike Emerson, Thoreau has the confidence to post his debts, or his challenges, up front, and unlike Emerson he recognises and adapts the communicative strategies of the poets, their tonal shifts, their irony—in Thoreau's case a signally Wordsworthian trick of moving within the orbit of a single sentence from matter-of-factness to symbol and enigma—and their refusal of textual authority. Where Emerson merely claims to want an active reader, Thoreau adopts conspicuously Romantic strategies which make passivity untenable.

Along with many fainter echoes, *Walden* alludes conspicuously to Coleridge's 'The Eolian Harp', 'This Lime-Tree Bower', and 'Dejection: an Ode', and to Wordsworth's 'Goody Blake and Harry Gill', 'To my Sister', 'Tintern Abbey', the Arab Dream in *The Prelude*, 'There was a Boy', 'Influence of Natural Objects', 'Personal Talk', and *The Excursion*.[1] Indeed the work opens with an allusion to Coleridge, situating his work in relation to the lyric dialogue of 1798/1802—'I do not propose to write an ode to dejection', Thoreau helpfully offers in his epigraph, 'but to brag as lustily as

---

1 I take the sentence in 'Solitude', 'the most innocent and encouraging society may be found in any natural, even for the poor misanthrope and most melancholy man', as a reference to 'This Lime-Tree Bower'.

chanticleer in the morning, standing on his roost, if only to wake my neighbours up' (*Walden*, 1)—and manifests throughout a revised Wordsworthian riposte to Coleridge's ode. Wordsworth's critique of Coleridge's defeatism occurs principally in three texts, 'Resolution and Independence', 'Intimations of Immortality' and *The Prelude*, all of which leave rhetorical footprints in *Walden*. But as Thoreau uses Wordsworth to critique Coleridge, he is also developing an equally intimate, and more self-defining, counter-critique of Wordsworth.

The opening reference to 'Dejection' is a more complex allusion than it looks: the chanticleer may be Chaucerian, but in *Christabel*, as Robert Weisbuch points out, Coleridge's owls awaken the crowing cock. *Christabel*'s 'Tu—whit!—Tu—whoo!' is not necessarily melancholy, any more than the owlet's cry in 'Frost at Midnight', but when he is serenaded Wordsworth-fashion by owls on the lakeside Thoreau chooses to translate the owls' call as a cry of despair: 'O that I had never been bor-r-r-n!' ('Sounds'). These ostensibly Coleridgean owls are as suicidal as Wordsworth's (in 'The Boy of Winander') are jocund, and Thoreau may intend a playful reference to Wordsworth's attempts to cheer Coleridge up, while alluding wryly to Coleridge's own protestation—in 'The Nightingale'—against the alleged melancholy of literary Nightingales. In a second compound allusion, Thoreau embeds in a generally Wordsworthian approach to listening to the language of things, in the chapter 'Sounds', a Coleridgean note, suggesting that 'All sound heard at the greatest possible distance produces one and the same effect, a vibration of the universal lyre'. Echoes, he affirms, in the same chapter, partake of the nature of the reflecting element as well as the thing echoed, a striking affirmation—influenced perhaps by Emerson's—of Wordsworth's insistence that the shouts of children make crags 'tinkle' and draw from the hills 'an alien sound of melancholy' (*Prelude*, 1. 469-71). A third compounding of Wordsworth and Coleridge appears in Thoreau's Wordsworthian insistence, which he translates into Coleridgean metaphor, that the music of storms is Aeolian to a healthy ear ('Solitude'). The entire text of 'Sounds' and 'Solitude' creates a curious sense that Thoreau is participating in precisely the kind of intimately allusive dialogue that—as Lucy Newlyn has shown—Wordsworth and

Coleridge practised between themselves, interjecting his own genial variations, and defining himself in sympathetic critiques. He uses Wordsworth and Coleridge as Shelley does in 'Mont Blanc': and, like Shelley, is most himself in that mode of self-definition.

In the body of *Walden*, after Thoreau's coincidentally Wordsworthian apology that it is a thing unprecedented that a man should talk so much about himself, and equally Wordsworthian excuse that there is no one else he knows so well, a figure casting himself as a Solitary offers an account of the mind's ability to restore itself through intercourse with the wild. The text is famous among other things for its lengthy and Blakean diagnosis of 'marks of weakness, marks of woe' among his contemporaries, and for a portrait of a Canadian wood-chopper, whom Thoreau earnestly or playfully but certainly inconclusively probes for evidence of untutored genius or such spiritual strengths as are to be found in 'Michael' or the 'Leech-Gatherer'. The lure of the wild expresses itself more than once in dietary terms:

> I caught a glimpse of a woodchuck stealing across my path, and ... was strongly tempted to seize and devour him raw; not that I was hungry then, except for that wildness which I felt he represented

or, 'I could sometimes eat a fried rat with a good relish, if it were necessary' ('Higher Laws'). But these aberrations of a most ascetic man need not be taken too literally (as that pun on 'relish' signifies). Rather they point to Thoreau's need to out-savage the young Wordsworth (*Prelude*, Book 1) poaching woodcocks on the Esthwaite fells or sporting in the thunder shower, an image of Wordsworth—it is hard to remember—which was not available to Thoreau at the time he drafted *Walden*.

Thoreau's central theme is the nature of liberty, and its connection with imagination. His major symbol is the pond itself, the eye of the landscape, into which he gazes in acts of self-exploration: 'A lake', he says, 'is earth's eye; looking into which the beholder measures the depth of his own nature ('The Ponds'). Not only is this pond one of 'the oldest scenes stamped upon my memory', first known when he was four, but he has drifted upon it in youthful reverie, and consults it now—as Wordsworth consults known landscapes in *Tintern Abbey* and *The Prelude*—both as a prism of his own development, against its own unchanging purity, and as a symbol of an identical self which still exists, and with which he can reconnect. The pond itself images such stability through change: when looking through its carapace of wintry ice, he sees a sandy bottom yet unchanged. It has not acquired 'one permanent wrinkle'. Its being seems permanent, yet it responds to the changing seasons, and to the minutest variation of surroundings or of atmosphere. Living 'reserved and austere, like a hermit in the woods'—the reference perhaps associates 'Tintern' and Grasmere— the pond 'is' the unfallen self: and in all kinds of ways, both Wordsworthian and more traditional, serves to embody— as the Thoreauvian Yeats would put it—the generated soul.

In 'Where I Lived and What I Lived for' Thoreau speaks of lakes being so full of light that they become 'a lower heaven'; they 'give buoyancy to and float the earth'. It is possible that Thoreau had in mind both Wordsworth's reference in 'The Boy of Winander' to 'that uncertain heaven received into the bosom of the steady lake'—where its steadiness gives the lake a Thoreau-like priority over heaven—and a similar passage in the *Guide to the Lakes*. Since in lakes 'the heavens are ... brought down into the bosom of the earth' says Wordsworth 'the earth is mainly looked at, and thought of, through the medium of a purer element'.[1] Wordsworth's poetic descriptions rarely share the surveyor-like quality of Thoreau's writing (if we except 'I've measured it from side to side /, 'Tis three four long and two feet wide') but in the *Guide* he takes care to account for the particular colourings of bodies of water, or the outline of shores, and the effect of streams.[2]

---

[1] *Guide to the Lakes*, ed. Ernest de Selincourt (Oxford: Oxford University Press, 1970), 47. Moldenhauer (266) argues that Thoreau embarked on a substantial study of landscape writing in 1852–54 following a reading of the Guide. Alongside Wordsworth's own 'Topographical Description' Thoreau makes use of John Evelyn's *Sylva: a Discourse of Forest Trees*, and of William Gilpin and William Bartram.

[2] He notices, for instance, how 'The smallest rivulet—one whose silent influx is scarcely noticeable in a season of dry weather—so faint is the dimple made by it on the surface of the smooth lake—will be found to have been not useless in shaping, by its deposit of gravel and soil in time of flood, a curve that would not otherwise have existed', *Guide*, 35.

Stepping Westward: *Nature* & *Walden* 209

Walden, of course, is without visible streams, entering or leaving. Thoreau's stout insistence on the mysterious purity of *his* pond, despite this fact, may constitute a negative allusion to Wordsworth's own insistence that *his* are 'living lakes, *vivi lacus*' of 'crystalline purity' unlike the 'shallow meres found in flat and fenny countries', or the 'stagnant and sullen pools' formed by volcanic action.[1]

Stylistically, as I have implied, Thoreau belongs more intimately than does Emerson to the Romantic stable. It is the easy and unexpected transition from matter-of-fact observation to symbolic discourse that constitutes Thoreau's most obviously Wordsworthian trait, along with his insistence (in this text) on the inexhaustible society of nature. The opening lines of Wordsworth's poem 'On revisiting the Wye' appear to have provided Thoreau with hints towards a language of personal notation, especially when weighing the difference between the cultivated and uncultivated. Wordsworth opens with a series of rarely noticed metaphors, as he beholds a scene which images the quietude he seeks. The metaphors define his quest as an escape from cultural definition. Amid cliffs 'which on a *wild* secluded scene impress / Thoughts of more deep seclusion' he finds also:

> These plots of cottage-ground, these orchard-tufts,
> Which, at this season, with their unripe fruits,
> Among the woods and copses lose themselves,
> Nor with their green and simple hue disturb
> The *wild* green landscape. Once again I see
> These hedgerows, hardly hedgerows, little lines
> Of sportive wood run *wild*; these pastoral farms
> Green to the very door; and wreathes of smoke
> Sent up, in silence from among the trees... (my italics).

It is not merely the repeated emphasis upon seclusion and the wild that prefigures *Walden*. Wordsworth's orchard tufts which can 'lose themselves', his hedgerows which can revert to 'lines of sportive wood run wild', his farms 'green to the very door', put one in mind— with a precision much closer to allusion than to echo—of Thoreau's

---

1 *Guide*, 39. Two dozen more such similarities are detected between the *Guide* and 'Ponds' by Neill R Joy, and another dozen or more by Joseph Moldenhauer.

home where 'unfenced Nature' reaches his 'very sills' ('Sounds'), his field which serves as 'the connecting link between wild and cultivated fields', and even his beans 'cheerfully returning to their wild and primitive state' ('The Bean-Field').

Thoreau boats of a capacity to 'imbibe delight through every pore' (this overt allusion to 'To my Sister' occurs in the first sentence of 'Solitude'). He progresses from the profoundly ecological question 'What if all ponds were shallow? Would it not react on the minds of men?' to a qualifying and equally Wordsworthian recognition that 'imagination ... dives deeper and soars higher than Nature goes' ('The Pond in Winter'). Such echoes contribute to a manifestly conscious development of the lyric dialogue to which his 'dejection' epigraph alludes. The argument is informed by Wordsworth's 'Our minds shall drink at every pore' ('To My Sister'), his invitation to experience 'the light of things' ('The Tables Turned'), the expansive effects of landscape on the mind throughout 'The Wye' and *The Prelude*, and of course the latter's general argument about the supremacy of imagination in books 2, 6 and 14. As a proper transcendentalist Thoreau was naturally as alert as Wordsworth was to the inadequacy of mensuration ('I've measured it from side to side') as a means to comprehension of the realm of spirit, or indeed biological wholeness. His lament in August 1851 that his own knowledge of nature is becoming year by year 'more distinct and scientific', and 'that in exchange for views as wide as heaven's scope, I am being narrowed down to the field of the microscope' (*Journals*, 2: 406) is one of many such recognitions of the Wordsworthian question whether it was 'ever meant / That we should pry far off yet be unraised; / That we should pore, and dwindle as we pore' (*Excursion*, 4: 958-60). Consequently, the penultimate chapter, 'Spring', ascends from preposterously finicky mensuration of the ice, to a progressive revelation of 'the one life within us and abroad'. Listening Wordsworthianly to the voice of the pond—the passage seems designed to prove Wordsworth as well as Emerson on the pulses—Thoreau proclaims his pond a sensitive being, declares that 'the earth is not a mere fragment of dead history', 'not a fossil earth, but a living earth', and concludes significantly that not only the earth '*but the institutions upon it*, are *plastic* like clay in the hands of a potter'. The allusion, of course, is to Wordsworth's famous celebration of the moment of revolution. 'Bliss was it that dawn to be alive', Wordsworth said of the early 1790s, when 'the whole earth/ The beauty wore of promise' and when 'The inert were rous'd and lively natures rapt away!' and both found in human institutions a stuff 'plastic as they could wish!'[1]

Walden, as an experiment in natural living, is set consciously against Coleridge's loss of 'the natural man'. In 'Where I lived and what I lived for' Thoreau explains:

> I went to the woods because I wished to live deliberately.... Nor did I want to practice resignation, unless it was quite necessary. I wanted to live deep, and suck out all the marrow of life, to live so sturdily and Spartan-like as to put to rout all that was not life,... to drive life into a corner ... and be able to give a true account of it in my next excursion.

The moral of this epic of plain living and high thinking—the answering call of one water-drinking bard to another—is that 'That man who does not believe that each day contains an earlier, more sacred and auroral hour than he has yet profaned, has despaired of life' ('Where I lived and what I lived for'). Thoreau concludes, with the air of one who has digested Wordsworth's 'Reply to Mathetes' and unlike its author remembered it:

> I learned this at least by my experiment, that if one advances confidently in the direction of his dream ... he will pass an invisible boundary; new, universal and more liberal laws will begin to establish themselves around and within him ... he will live with the license of a higher order of beings ('Conclusion').

Walden's laconic and mysterious sentence 'I long ago lost, a bay horse, and a turtle-dove, and am still on their trail' ('Economy') has been read as trumping, less resignedly, Wordsworth in the Ode: 'But there's a tree, of many, one; / A single Field which I have looked upon, / Both of them speak of something that is gone.'[2] More strikingly,

---

1 Widely known as printed in Coleridge, *The Friend*, 1: 225–26.
2 Weisbuch, 144, makes the comparison and Emerson's essay on Thoreau

212   Romantic Dialogues

however, *Walden,* having begun with an allusion to 'Dejection', ends with its own 'Intimations of Immortality'. Thoreau's 'intimations' arise from recollections of 'a strong and beautiful bug' which, as he tells the tale, 'came out of the dry leaf of an old table of apple-tree wood which had stood in a farmer's kitchen for sixty years.' The bug

> was heard gnawing out for several weeks, hatched perchance by the heat of an urn. Who does not feel his faith in a resurrection and immortality strengthened by hearing of this?

In an implied rebuke to those poets whose faith is not strong enough to withstand dereliction and dismay, who sadly contemplate departed light, and who have given up on the revolutionary dawns of their youth, Thoreau asks:

> Who knows what beautiful and winged life, whose egg has been buried for ages under many concentric layers of woodenness in the dead dry life of society... may unexpectedly come forth from amidst society's most trivial and handselled furniture, to enjoy its perfect summer life at last!

After all, 'Only that day dawns to which we are awake' ('Conclusion', 222–3).

3. THE POLITICS OF WESTERING

Robert Weisbuch's reading of *Walden* sees Thoreau's use of Wordsworthian allusions as aggressive and ultimately dismissive. Thoreau, he argues secedes from an America which has become Anglicised, and Wordsworth and Coleridge are made illustrative of the rejected Anglicism. It seems to me, on the contrary, that the conclusion of *Walden* twines together several Wordsworthian associations, in a way which implies a fundamental integration of Thoreau's sense of Wordsworth with his sense of American possibilities, or, to use Weisbuch's own terms, a critique of American belatedness through mementos of Wordsworthian earliness.

The auroral motif of *Walden*, its constant call for an awakening, implies it.

Stepping Westward: *Nature & Walden* 213

from its epigraph to its closing paragraph is both the spinal cord of the work, its most politicised dimension, and its most significant engagement with Wordsworth's poetry. Thoreau twines three Wordsworthian tropes—of dawn, of westering, of eternal childhood—into a stance of optimism. He defines despair as the failure to believe that 'each day contains an earlier, more sacred, and auroral hour than he has yet profaned' and he counsels 'an infinite expectation of the dawn'. As he put it still more pointedly in 'Walking', in the midst of further extensive allusions to Wordsworth, 'he is blessed over all mortals who loses no moment of the passing life in remembering the past'.

Walden's last two chapters build consistently from the image of spring, via influxes of light and rain leading to a greening of the thought, through hints of widening moral boundaries, to a restatement, in the parable of the bug just quoted, of the call for an awakening to a higher life, a human *and a social* metamorphosis. That this call has a political dimension founded in philosophic anarchism is too often forgotten, despite the fact that the first literary fruit of the Walden experiment, the essay on 'Resistance to Civil Government' is regularly published alongside *Walden*.

The essay on 'Resistance' was inspired in part by Emerson's 1844 essay on 'Politics': both writers adopt an essentially Godwinian stance towards government as at best a necessary evil, and one which in an ongoing revolution would wither away. Emerson wonders why we still 'pay tribute to governments founded on force' and complains that he cannot call to mind 'a single human being who has steadily denied the authority of the laws, on the simple ground of his own moral nature'. Thoreau refuses, more literally, to pay tribute to a government upholding slavery or invading Mexico, and proclaims— exemplifying Emerson's more abstract point— that if '*one* HONEST man' were withdraw from the social compact 'it would be the abolition of slavery in America'.

Walden and 'Civil Government' are also tied together by a brief but disparaging reference to Webster in *Walden*'s 'conclusion', echoing the extended disparagement in the essay, and by the briefer essay's call for a state 'still more perfect and glorious' than has yet been seen, as symbolised in *Walden*'s 'bug'. The bug, whose primary purpose is to allude to Wordsworth's backward-looking 'Intimations', has a secondary purpose, it seems to me, in which Wordsworth's own use of the 'dawn' trope is used to challenge Thoreau's countrymen.

The bug, to recapitulate, emerges from the dry leaf of a table 'which had stood in a farmer's kitchen for sixty years', and from an egg deposited in the living tree many years before. Those 'sixty years' take us back more or less to the 'men of 87', those constitutional carpenters whose efforts, in Webster's eyes, and indeed Whitman's, transcend time and bind the living to the compacts of their ancestors. If the table they constructed contained the germ of a more perfect republic, it has yet to find its way to the light:

> Who knows what beautiful and winged life, whose egg has been buried for ages under many concentric layers of woodenness in the dead dry life of society, deposited at first in the alburnum of the green and living tree, which has been gradually converted into the semblance of its well-seasoned tomb...may unexpectedly come forth ... to enjoy its perfect summer at last!

We are not told how long ago the egg was deposited in the living wood. Nor, despite the fact that 'almost the last significant scrap of news from [England] was the revolution of 1649', is it clear to Thoreau whether 'John or Jonathan' will be the first 'to realise all this'. Republicanism, after all, has received vivid poetical expression in England as much as in America and the Chartists came close to a political reawakening it.[1] Was it still as self-evident in 1844, or 1849, or 1854, as it had been in 1776 that the portion of the Saxon race friendliest to liberty was the portion resident in America?

The life in us, Thoreau says, introducing his 'bug' parable in the tidal metaphor Emerson used in praising the Intimations ode— 'may rise this year higher than man has ever known it, and flood the

---

[1] What Wordsworth called 'the homely beauty of the good old cause' was much in Emerson's mind in his political essay of 1844. In a slavery speech of the same year, Emerson announced that 'the genius of the Saxon race, friendly to liberty, the enterprise, the very muscular vigor of this nation, are inconsistent with slavery' (*An address delivered in the Court-House in Concord, Massachusetts, on 1 August 1844, on the Anniversary of the Emancipation of the Negroes in the British West Indies*, Boston, 1844).

Stepping Westward: *Nature & Walden* 215

parched uplands'. But what guarantee is there that this will take place in America? After all, America has now converted its constitutional provisions into mind-forged manacles. Webster himself declares truculently, as quoted in Thoreau's essay,

> 'I have never made an effort, and never propose to make an effort; I have never countenanced an effort, and never mean to countenance an effort, to disturb the arrangement as originally made, by which the various states came into the Union'.

Thoreau's brave challenge to his own countrymen turns inside out the rhetoric of 1776, and asks, indeed, whether that revolution was as bourgeois as Melville and Whitman would come to suspect. What does the Boston Tea Party signify when weighed against slavery and annexation?

> All men recognise the right of revolution; that is, the right to refuse allegiance to and to resist the government, when its tyranny or its inefficiency are great and unendurable. But almost all say that such is not the case now. But such was the case, they think, in the revolution of '75. If one were to tell me that this was a bad government because it taxed certain commodities brought to its ports, it is most probable that I should not make an ado about it ... But when *a sixth of the population* of a nation which has undertaken to be the refuge of liberty are slaves, and a whole country [Mexico] is unjustly overrun and conquered by a foreign army, and subjected to military law, I think that it is not too soon for honest men to rebel and revolutionise.[1]

Just how galling Thoreau intended his phrasing to be becomes clear when one remembers the last twist in Sydney Smith's notorious challenge of 1820: 'Finally, under which of the old tyrannical governments of Europe is *every sixth man* a Slave, whom his fellow-creatures may buy and sell and torture?'[2] To be a patriot in 1849, it

---

[1] *Walden and Civil Disobedience*, 227. The question whether '75 was about anything more than 'a threepenny tax' is also raised in *Walden*'s elaborately allegorical battle of the ants ('Brute Neighbours'), which ends with a savage reference to 'Webster's' fugitive slave bill.
[2] *Edinburgh Review*, January 1820, 80. Robert Weisbuch also assumes that

seems, involves feeling almost precisely as Wordsworth felt in 1793, when his country declared war on liberty, or again in 1802: 'We have seen / Fair seed-time, better harvest might have been / But for thy trespasses / ...O grief that Earth's best hopes rest all with thee'.

That it should be America's duty to explore the 'wildish destiny' so poignantly envisaged in Wordsworth's 'Stepping Westward' is clear; that an America still enslaved to the constitutional provisions of 1787 is likely to do so, is not, to Thoreau, at all self-evident. 'There *is* more day to dawn' *Walden* concludes, and it is possible—the essay on 'Civil Government' agrees, with a backward glance at Tom Paine and his desire 'to begin the world anew'—'to take a step further towards recognizing and organizing *the rights of man*'. But the first step is to liberate that truly libertarian spirit which neither repository of 'Saxon genius' has yet permitted to enjoy its perfect Summer.

As R. W. B. Lewis noted in *The American Adam*, Thoreau's opening chapter asks whether the ancient ceremony of the 'busk', as described in Bartram's *Travels*, might well be revived in America: in this ceremony the Mucclasse Indians were wont to 'collect all their worn out clothes and other despicable things, sweep and cleanse their houses, squares, and the whole town, of their filth, which ... they cast together into one common heap and consume it with fire.'[1] The bravery of *Walden* is that from the moment it develops its lengthy variation on Carlyle's 'clothes philosophy' in the opening chapter, it is preparing to suggest that even the revolution settlement of 1787 might have passed its burn-by date. James Madison, one of the makers of the constitution appealed to public opinion in 1792 to 'guarantee with a holy zeal, these political scriptures from every attempt to add to or diminish from them'.[2] Webster and Whitman concurred. To Thoreau,

---

Thoreau was still conscious of Smith, thirty years on, but suggests that his reference to 1649 as the last real news 'from that quarter' is a riposte to Smith's question 'Who in the four quarters of the globe reads an American book?'

1 'Economy', *Walden* 46. For Lewis's of the 'busk' as emblematic of America's case against the past, see *The American Adam: Innocence, Tragedy and Tradition in the Nineteenth Century* (Chicago: University of Chicago Press, 1955), 14.

2 *National Gazette*, February 1792, cited in Robert A Ferguson, *The American Enlightenment* (Harvard University Press, 1997), 145. As Ferguson points out, five of the first seven presidents owned slaves, and all seven 'fully accept public silence

however, the meaning of life is the quest Wordsworth definitively symbolized in 'The Simplon Pass': the quest 'for something ever more about to be'.

Walden, in launching an attack on American 'luxury' (Chapter 2), cannily chose the term most in vogue in the revolutionary era to describe English corruption, and his antidote is surely informed by the prolific sonneteer of National Independence and Liberty.

> We must run glittering like a brook
> In the open sunshine, or we are unblest:
> ... Rapine, avarice, expense,
> This is idolatry; and these we adore:
> Plain living and high thinking are no more.

Walden's fresh promulgation of 'the homely beauty of the good old cause'[1] is carried out, it seems to me, in profoundly Wordsworthian mode.

---

on this issue as a price of highest office', 151.
1 Wordsworth, 'Written in London, September 1802'

Chapter 7:

Hawthorne & Poe, Romancing Romanticism

1. ALTERNATIVE POSSIBILITIES

Emerson's transcendental optimisms, based in large part on the liberal tradition of Cambridge Platonism, were subjected to considerable scrutiny by Poe, Hawthorne and Melville. These writers, like Emerson, were imaginatively engaged in the naturalization of Romanticism in America, but their deeper sense of evil, analogous to Coleridge's conviction of original sin, supply the subtlety and scepticism already implicit in the more problematical art of the English Romantics. Two peculiarly interesting instances of this, with intriguingly Coleridgean connections, can be found in Poe's 'Ligeia' (1838) and Hawthorne's 'Rappaccini's Daughter' (1844).[1] That Hawthorne's tale manifests some consciousness of Poe's, and is aware of Poe's games with Coleridge, will be assumed in my treatment. Whether as a strategic decision or not, Hawthorne and Poe reinvent the romantic narrative poem, using aspects of the art of 'The Thorn', 'Christabel', 'Lamia', in creating tales of the imagination; their tales can seem at once tonally Keatsian, philosophically Coleridgean, and in Hawthorne's case morally Wordsworthian. What Emerson did with Romantic ideology and Thoreau with Romantic naturalism, Hawthorne & Poe accomplish with the Romantic narratives of the human world.

When Elizabeth Peabody sent Hawthorne's *Twice-Told Tales* to Wordsworth in 1838 she picked out 'Little Annie's Ramble', with its

---

[1] 'Ligeia' was published in the *Baltimore American Museum*, 1838, included in *Tales of the Arabesque*, 1839 and revised for the *Broadway Journal*, 1845. 'Rappaccini's Daughter' was first published in *The Democratic Review*, 1844.

Michaelesque reference to how 'the pure breath of children revives the life of aged men', as a story likely to exert a reciprocal attraction on the poet of *Lyrical Ballads*. In 1839 she returned to her advocacy, assuring Wordsworth that a word from him would be received by Hawthorne as 'holy writ'. Hawthorne was then engaged in the Custom House, and 'When I asked him *what he did*—he said he was from sunrise to sunset quarrelling with sea captains & owners— about measuring out their cargoes of salt & coal & potatoes— according to the laws—and then he went home to his room & read *Wordsworth*. What an alternation!'[1] One poem one may imagine him reading most avidly is that remarkable experiment in dramatic narration, appealingly entitled 'The Thorn' and opening with an account of a heroic hawthorn much burdened by mosses: 'and this poor thorn they clasp it round / So close, you'd say that they were bent / With plain and manifest intent/ To drag it to the ground' ('The Thorn', lines 19–21). The evidence of his finest work, in 'Young Goodman Brown', 'Rappaccini's Daughter', and even in *The Scarlet Letter*, is that Hawthorne was this poem's first enthusiastic reader.

Both 'The Thorn' and *The Scarlet Letter* open with symbolic clusters; or, rather, with clusters of objects viewed unremittingly as signifiers. In each work the compelling imaginative centre is the artist's recognition of his own complicity in the besetting sin of his culture. Wordsworth's dramatic masterpiece in the 1798 *Lyrical Ballads* opens with an almost unique display of intentional perception, the narrator inviting the reader to share his intense over-determination of three in themselves wholly insignificant objects: a heap of moss, a little pond, and a stunted thorn. Each of these objects the narrator loads emotively. Each, or all, may betoken a dark and monstrous sin. In this innocent assemblage of ubiquitous natural objects—nowhere on any piece of elevated English moorland from Dartmoor to Hadrian's Wall, could one turn in any direction without finding within a few yards a peaty pond, a heap of moss, and a stunted thorn—the narra-

---

1 Dove Cottage MS, A/Peabody/5. In *The New Yorker* (March 1838) she spoke of Hawthorne as one who has arrived at the kind of philosophy which 'cannot be learned except in the same school of Nature where Wordsworth studied, and by the same pure light.' Cited, Scott Harshbarger, 'Transatlantic Transcendentalism: the Wordsworth, Peabody-Hawthorne Connection', *TWC* 21:3 (1990) 123–26, 124.

tor encourages his auditor to find the generating nodes of a Gothic tale. In other Wordsworth 'ballads' there is no tale unless we choose to make one. In this, there is an implied tale about a deserted woman, who may, or may not, have been pregnant, may have miscarried, or may have suffered the early death of her infant, but who is, in any case, cruelly excluded from human community and made into the stuff of legend. This tale is occluded or even displaced by a narratorially conjured Gothic tale of infanticide and mystery. What struck Hawthorne, I hypothesise, was the technique by which Wordsworth provides for each reader to construct a tale from the elements provided, while the narrator invites one, first implicitly, then explicitly, to conclude that Martha Ray killed her baby by one of several means:

> I cannot tell; but some will say
> She hanged her baby on the tree,
> Some say she drowned it in the pond,
> Which is a little step beyond,
> But all and each agree,
> The little babe was buried there,
> Beneath that hill of moss so fair (214–20).

While negotiating these alternative possibilities, before deciding what Martha is guilty of, the reader is permitted to indulge a superior sense of liberality, by demurring at the barbarity of superstitious villagers who determine to bring her to justice, set out to dig up the little infant's bones, and then allow their own superstitious dreads—of reflections in the pond, of mosses shaking in the breeze—to defeat both objects (225–39).

Wordsworth, as his 1800 note confesses, wrote the tale in part to examine the pathology of imagination, and in part to give its readers the experience of 'the general laws by which superstition acts upon the mind'. That those laws are indeed general—that is, they apply quite as much to the shapers of high culture as to unsophisticated villagers—is shown by Coleridge's apparent belief that the poem is about infanticide: his readerly skills were defeated by 'The Thorn' as his inept discussion in *Biographia Literaria* amply demonstrates. The peculiar force of Wordsworth's tale is that it holds narrative denial and narrative suggestion in such balance as to give its readers the experience of superstition acting upon the mind. It is unlikely that any reader of the poem approaching it without having first absorbed the advice of such fine readers as John Danby or Stephen Parrish—advice not available until the 1960s, so long can it take a writer to 'create the taste by which he is to be enjoyed'—would fail to conclude at some point, on a first reading at least, that Martha Ray must be guilty of some form of infanticide. What 'some say', 'they say', and ''tis said' must, surely leave some residue of certitude? Yet one is told, definitively, that even her pregnancy is the purest conjecture, and also that 'if a child was born or no, / There's no one that that could ever tell; / And if 'twas born alive or dead, / There's no one knows, as I have said' (159–62). This countermanding technique within successive phrases is a staple of Wordsworth's insinuative method: thus, in ' *'tis said* a child was in her womb, / *As now to any eye was plain*' (136–7), the line break marks an epistemological shift. One is told—repeatedly, to a point well beyond tautology— that the only facts in the case are these: that there is a thorn tree three yards from a path, that Martha Ray often climbs this path, that she sits by the thorn in all weathers, that no villager has exchanged a word with her since her desertion some twenty years back, and that she repeats by night and day her doleful cry: 'Oh misery! oh misery! / O woe is me, oh misery'.

Affected by 'the solitary anguish of her life', the narrator tells us, in his doubtful way, Hester Prynne began to suspect the worst of her neighbours. Indeed,

> it now and then appeared to Hester,—if altogether fancy, it was nevertheless too potent to be resisted,—*she felt or fancied, then, that the scarlet letter had endowed her with a new sense*. She shuddered to believe, yet could not help believing, that it gave her a sympathetic knowledge of the hidden sin in other hearts. She was terror-stricken by the revelations that were thus made. What were they? *Could they be other than the insidious whispers of the bad angel, who would fain have persuaded the strugling woman, as yet only half his victim,* that the outward guise of purity was but a lie, and that, if truth were everywhere to be

shown, a scarlet letter would blaze forth on many a bosom beside Hester Prynne's?[1]

Most readers, in defiance of the structure of this reading instruction, conclude that the sentence convicts many of Hester's neighbours, perhaps the majority, of 'hidden sin'. What reader in this accusatory age can resist the joy of indicting their forefathers of hypocrisy at all times and in all matters? That Hawthorne intends his reader to short-circuit his elaborate construction in this way, at least on a first reading, is certain. Yet the lengthy paragraph presents only one certainty: namely, that Hester's exemplary struggle 'to believe that no fellow mortal was guilty like herself' is a mark of her innocence.

Similar promptings of the Fiend are to be recognised as such in 'Young Goodman Brown' (1835): hints in the tale that what Brown sees in the woods are merely the *forms* of his fellow citizens rather than the villagers themselves, and that these forms are projections of his own, or of the devil, are too insistent to be missed. No reader is likely to suppose that when Brown walks back into the village in his stricken condition the neighbours he shrinks from have really been cavorting in the woods all night. What 'evil purpose' Young Goodman Brown purposes at the start we do not know, nor whether his companion is indeed the devil in the shape of old Goodman Brown, nor whether the 'figure' of Goody Cloyse is indeed loitering in the wilderness at nightfall. We do know, however, that Brown hears, or imagines, that the minister and Deacon Gookin are bound for a witches sabbath; that the Faithless Brown perceives 'that there is no good on earth'; that amid innumerable horrors Young Goodman Brown 'was himself the chief horror of the scene'; that although at the very moment he appeals to Faith he finds himself alone in the forest, '*some affirm,* that the lady of the governor was there. *At least, there were high dames well known to her*'; and that 'either the sudden gleams of light, ... bedazzled Goodman Brown, or he recognised a score of the church members of Salem village.' Brown and another veiled figure for whose confirmation this congregation is assembled are promised that this night they will know 'how hoary-headed elders

[1] *The Scarlet Letter*, ed. Brian Harding (Oxford & New York: Oxford University Press, 1990), Chapter 5, 86. My emphases.

of the church have whispered wanton words to the young maids of their households ... how fair damsels ... have dug little graves in the garden, and bidden me, the sole guest, to an infant's funeral' (we need hardly dwell on this amplification of 'The Thorn'), and that it shall be theirs, as initiates, 'to penetrate, in every bosom, the deep mystery of sin'.

'Satan', as Blake said, 'is the accuser of this world', and a spirit of accusation is his mark. To Hawthorne, also, the sign of original sin is the willing imputation of sin. Hester, therefore, is redeemed as much by her refusal to believe in the promptings of the scarlet letter as by her faith in Dimmesdale. The reader of *The Scarlet Letter*, I would argue, is invited precisely *not* to believe in the ubiquitous evil of Hester's community; as one is also invited to resist the narrator's description of Dimmesdale as a 'subtle, but remorseful hypocrite' (chapter 11) by attending, rather, to the presence (in the same paragraph) of the affirmation that 'by the constitution of his nature, he loved the truth, and loathed the lie'.

All that Wordsworth's narrator affirms is that Martha Ray suffers and is a victim of the frailty of Stephen Hill and of the willing suspension of humanity by the villagers. All that Hawthorne's narrator affirms is that Hester suffers and is a victim of the weakness of Dimmesdale and the remorselessness of Chillingworth. In both cases the reader is decoyed into judgement, implicated in passing judgement—on Martha and the community in Wordsworth's case; on Dimmesdale and the community in Hawthorne's. To believe Young Goodman Brown, *or to grant substance to the promptings of the scarlet letter*, is to accuse a community of witchcraft. No doubt Hawthorne felt guilt at his ancestors' complicity in the imputation of evil, but his response is not the obvious one, of distancing himself from their imputed 'hypocrisy'. Rather, he illustrates the ease with which his contemporaries and ours can be led into the same spirit of accusation while congratulating ourselves on our immunity to superstition. Nothing is more pleasing to the human mind than a belief in the wickedness of others. The art of Hawthorne and of Wordsworth is an endeavour, equally unsuccessful in most cases it appears, to make their readers aware of this process within themselves.

The Scarlet Letter, however, represents a further turn of the narratorial screw. As Swift said, satire is a glass in which the beholder generally recognises every man's face but his own: the skill of the satirist, therefore, is in so manipulating the glass as to make it likelier that his readers will see themselves therein. Dickens uses much the same technique—one he almost certainly learned from Hawthorne— in *Hard Times* and *Our Mutual Friend* where he makes it exceptionally hard for the reader not to share Mrs Sparsit's cankered perspective on Louisa, or Bella Wilfer's imputation of selfishness to Mr Boffin.[1] The events of *The Scarlet Letter* are viewed through a variety of lenses. Chapters 1, 22 and 24 are relatively straightforward in their liberalism: the perspective is humanist. So, for the most part are chapters sixteen to nineteen. The inescapable tendency of the narrative is to encourage us to believe that Hester and Dimmesdale are about to escape the gloomy system that has destroyed their happiness: in Chapter 19 the minister entertains, and the reader probably wills him to fall for, the temptation of flight. Chapters twenty and twenty-three, however, revert to a seventeenth-century framework. The minister's dream of transcendence in chapter nineteen is painfully reappraised in chapter twenty as a conscious yielding to temptation, a self-betrayal unprecedented in the minister's life. Chapter twenty-three enacts a triumph over Chillingworth that can be achieved only in the way Dimmesdale achieves it, and—ironically—precisely in the way the reader, prompted by Pearl as Wordsworth's 'Eye among the blind',[2] has throughout most of the novella desired him to effect it. The genuine brilliance of Hawthorne's irony has, really, very little to do with the mannered presentation of such endlessly discussed

---

[1] Could anyone pick up an anonymous *House of the Seven Gables*, open it randomly at the awakening of Hepzibah in chapter 2, or the description of her short-sightedness in chapter 7, or the treatment of Judge Pyncheon's polished smile and boots and benignity in chapter 8, or the antiquated family of hens in chapters 6 and 10, or the death of the Judge in the first two paragraphs of chapter 18, and not suppose that the work was by Dickens? Should the term employed for such moments of high comic or poignant style be Hawthornian rather than Dickensian?

[2] For a discussion of Pearl as a conspicuously Wordsworthian child modelled upon 'Intimations', and Hawthorne's knowing elaboration in Chapter 19 of the famous ram symbol in the closing book of *The Excursion*, see my 'Intimations in America', *The Oxford Handbook of William Wordsworth* (2015) 778–80.

matters as what the scarlet letter signifies, or the stigma, or the sign in the sky. Rather, Hawthorne is attempting to manoeuvre the reader into significant encounter with what Wordsworth called 'his pre-established codes of decision'.[1]

I would argue, then, that Hawthorne uses 'The Thorn' as his narrative prototype but adds to it the tendency of writers more 'romantic' than Wordsworth usually was—if we except *The White Doe*, which as a romance is deeply Hawthornian—to set his tales in the freedom of an imagined past and to colour as freely as did Coleridge and John Keats. 'Christabel' and 'The Thorn' show what can be done with Gothic materials by a genuine artist. Hawthorne adopts what is essentially a Wordsworthian narrative voice—strongly present along with other Wordsworthian motifs in 'The Gentle Boy' and 'Little Annie's Ramble' for instance—to mediate some powerfully erotic tales in which an assortment of male and female Geraldines, along with modified Porphyros, Madeleines and Lamias, function as his basic character types. His great and original artistry is most his own when informed most richly, sometimes simultaneously, by Wordsworth and Coleridge and Keats.

2. REASON AND IMAGINATION

Hawthorne's views of his English peers are most beguilingly presented in a tale called 'P's Correspondence', where 'P', though incarcerated in a mental institution somewhere in New England, writes to the narrator describing imaginary conversations with English literati, living and dead. In this topsy-turvy record, dated 1845, Dickens & Wordsworth are dead: the scene is dominated by the venerable Robert Burns, a paralytic Scott, the reverend Percy

---

[1] *The Scarlet Letter* appears to open and close in not merely a nineteenth-century frame but a feminist one: Hester is associated with 'the sainted Ann Hutchinson' and by implication with the equally sainted sybil, Margaret Fuller. Yet Hawthorne's early essay on Ann Hutchinson emphasises the threat posed to the unity of the colonists by her 'peculiar power of distinguishing between the chosen of man and the sealed of Heaven', that is, her sanctimoniousness and proneness to moral judgement. Hester, one might conclude, avoids both temptations to which Ann was prone: the imputation of sin, and spiritual pride.

Shelley, and 'a progiously fat' Lord Byron, reconciled to Lady Byron and to a sort of Puseyite Methodism. His Lordship is engaged in expurgating from his works all those parts which might be thought at all licentious: 'You may judge how much of [*Don Juan*] remains as hitherto published'. Keats is writing an epic treatment of Paradise Regained, set in 'an indefinitely remote futurity, in which 'man is within the last stride of perfection' and woman 'stands equal by his side, or communes for herself with Angels'.[1] P's news of Coleridge is particularly germane to my purpose, though we will return to the implications of this feminist Keats.

> Coleridge has at last finished his poem of Christabel.... The poet, I hear, is visited with a troublesome affection of the tongue, which has put a period, or some lesser stop, to the life-long discourse that has hitherto been flowing from his lips. He will not survive it above a month, unless his accumulation of ideas be sluiced off in some other way. Wordsworth died only a week or two ago. Heaven rest his soul, and grant that he may not have finished the Excursion! [2]

If this be madness, there is method in it, and the particular geniality towards Coleridge and Keats—'the best child of time and immortality'—is much to my point.

Several Coleridgean procedures can be observed in Hawthorne's famous 'Custom House' essay, particularly in the rather disingenuous claim that with more talent for reading the everyday, he might rather be a Trollope or a Thackeray, a claim which is comparable to Coleridge's equally unconvincing estimation of 'Ruth' above 'Christabel'. Like Coleridge's preface to 'Kubla Khan', 'The Custom House', of course, is not merely a prologue to *The Scarlet Letter* but a part of it, a means of focusing many of that novella's concerns, with the role of art, and of the artist, without rupturing the form and decorum of the novella itself. At the same time, Dejection-fashion, Hawthorne complains that his mundane duties are both murdering

---

[1] Hawthorne, *The Centenary Edition of the Works of Nathaniel Hawthorne*, ed William Charvat et al., (Columbus: Ohio State University Press, 1962--), 10: 366, 375–6.

[2] *Centenary Edition*, 10: 373–4.

his imagination, and producing a torpor which dulls his imaginative response to Nature: Uncle Sam, it seems (in an uncanny because impossible allusion to the unpublished version of 'Dejection'), is plucking out the wing-feathers of his mind. What the essay introduces, as I have already implied, is a striking elaboration of a topos by Wordsworth, rather than by Coleridge: an elaborate reworking of 'The Thorn', particularly as regards the pathology of perception.

Hawthorne's forte, shared with Melville, is the scrutiny of Emerson's faith in the translucence of symbol, and of what Emerson regarded as the theme of all his lectures, the 'infinitude of the private man'. Emerson's confidence that human beings can transcend themselves, or that self-assertion can safely be indulged, is examined in tale after tale. 'Rappaccini's Daughter', the finest and deepest of the shorter works, combines the theme of a young man's fatal inability to transcend his narcissism, with an examination of the human mind's besetting sin, the exercise of intelligence divorced from love. Hawthorne's residual Calvinism, his belief in the separateness of man from God, his conviction of sin and fall, make him a Coleridgean scrutineer of Emerson's simplifications—a likeness which emerges also (if we think of *Christabel*) in what has often been noted as a trait of Hawthorne's writing, his ability to manipulate almost pasteboard characters in implausible situations, in such a way as to generate psychological depth and truth.

To read 'Rappaccini's Daughter' (1844) without hearing John Keats on every page is a considerable feat, though it has been performed by many of Hawthorne's critics. Julian Smith, an early exception, provided a telling enumeration of Hawthorne's manifold allusions to 'Lamia' in an essay of 1966, including a persuasive list of verbal parallels. Norman Anderson, in 1977, tabulated considerable narrative and conceptual overlap between the two tales. Robert Weisbuch concluded that both Keats and Hawthorne are 'criticising and overturning literary traditions that appear frightened of imaginative passion as embodied in women'. But a 1998 essay by Debbie Lopez, 'Liberties with Lamia' was the first to recognise the imaginative depth of Keats's impact on Hawthorne, and the extensiveness in other tales of Hawthorne's appropriation of the young romantic, especially in his employment of the 'Lilith/Lamia' archetypes in his 'new world' but fall-prone Edens. There is considerably more to be said than that Hawthorne and Keats are concerned with the mixture of good and evil and the woes of selfishness.[1]

'Rappaccini's Daughter' concerns a young man, a stranger, introduced into the mysterious bower of a beautiful lady by a conniving old beldame. The lady is both heavily voluptuous and slightly unearthly. Her breath is perfumed and fatal, and although her influence immunises him (he is to some extent translated into her sphere, as Porphyro is etherealised in idealist readings of 'The Eve of St Agnes'), their encounter undoes them both. The young man's infatuation is detected and cautioned by a sage, one of those specialist unweavers of rainbows, whose final intervention on behalf of his protégé destroys the lady. Thus intentionally summarised the tale may appear to be made up of two parts 'Lamia' to one of 'The Eve of St Agnes', with more than a pinch of 'La Belle Dame sans Merci'. Its intense eroticism makes one wonder that nobody has yet observed that tonally, the passionate 'Eve' *is* quite as pertinent as the dryer 'Lamia'.[2] And Giovanni at the end of the tale does not die with his lover, but remains, as far as one can tell, like the equally invasive knight in 'La Belle Dame' to face a blighted future 'alone and palely loitering'.

Both in describing the garden—whether it is a garden of bliss, of delight, or of deceit—and in introducing Beatrice, Hawthorne writes

---

[1] Julian Smith, 'Keats and Hawthorne: a Romantic Bloom in Rappaccini's Garden', *Emerson Society Quarterly* 42 (1966) 8–12; Robert Weisbuch, *Atlantic Double-Cross*, 261–2; and Debbie Lopez, 'Liberties with Lamia: the Gordian Knot of Relations between Keats and Hawthorne', *Symbiosis* 2.2 (1998) 141–60. Lopez finds a fascination with Keatsian archetypes at work in 'Mrs Bullfrog', 'The Lily's Quest' and 'Fragments from the Journal of a Solitary Man' and challenges several established misreadings of Hawthorne.

[2] Hawthorne trumps Keats's sustained eroticism. Consummation is achieved in 'The Eve of St Agnes' first in the blended odours of rose and violet and then in a sleetily spermatic assault on the hymeneal window panes of Madeleine's chamber. The equally voyeuristic and urgent Giovanni has to 'thrust his head quite out of its concealment in order to gratify the intense and painful curiosity which [Beatrice] excited' and later forces his way into her garden 'through the entanglement of a shrub that wreathed its tendrils over the hidden entrance.'

with Keatsian effulgence. Here is Beatrice's entrance, summoned by her father (Rappaccini):

> 'Here am I, my father! What would you?' cried a rich and youthful voice ... a voice as rich as a tropical sunset, and which made Giovanni, though he knew not why, think of deep hues of purple or crimson, and of perfumes heavily delectable....
>
> Soon there emerged from under a sculptured portal the figure of a young girl, arrayed with as much richness of taste as the most splendid of the flowers, beautiful as the day, and with a bloom so deep and vivid that one shade more would have been too much.[1]

Though the manner Keatsian in all manner of ways (not least in the slow descriptive excess, and the quietly Shakespearean pun on 'tropical') Beatrice is nonetheless surprisingly wholesome, the anticipated Lamian gorgeousness being displaced onto the mythologically dubious garden with its bizarre forms and 'flowers gorgeously magnificent'.

Like 'Lamia' this tale is ostensibly based upon a fable of antiquity: Hawthorne using Sir Thomas Browne as Keats uses Burton's *Anatomy of Melancholy*. Hawthorne, however, uses his source as a tale within the tale, a cautionary tale, indeed, told by Dr Baglioni to young Giovanni, and concerning a beautiful woman sent to Alexander the Great as a gift, who had been nourished on poison from birth until 'she herself had become the deadliest poison in existence ... Her love would have been poison!—her embrace death!' To his source Hawthorne adds one remarkable detail. Beatrice tends one plant in the garden with almost sisterly care, a simile which is made flesh when we learn that she and it were born in the same moment, Beatrice as the natural child of her father's humanity (his emanation, as it were), and the flower as the offspring of his cold Urizenic intelligence.

In both tales we face a similar problem: what authority do we lend the Renaissance vignette as interpreter of the Romantic work? Hawthorne plays upon this problem to enrich his usual ambiguity-

---

1 Hawthorne, *Centenary Edition*, 10: 97.

laden style. The phenomenon in Hawthorne is rarely a simple guide to essence: in this respect he is the master of Kierkegaardian irony. In 'The Minister's Black Veil' for instance, we cannot know whether the minister wears his veil in token of some private sin, or to symbolise the veil of life and death, or from a perverse and damnable determination to view his fellow creatures as darkened by sin. In 'Rappaccini's Daughter' we cannot know whose innocence is the most injured, whose frailty is most to be pitied, or whose villainy is the darkest. Is Giovanni the innocent victim, Rappaccini the sole author of the woe, Beatrice his fatal accomplice and Baglioni a well-intentioned but powerless friend? The tale seems constructed so as to yield this meaning at first, but on reflection we may find Giovanni the narcissistic and loveless instrument of Beatrice's destruction, judging that his lovelessness makes him the poisonous accomplice of Baglioni's professional vengeance upon Rappaccini through his now twice-injured daughter.

Hawthorne may, or may not, be subjecting a Renaissance fable of male fearfulness and lack of faith to a liberal critique: that in doing so he uses a Keatsian tale which may or may not be doing the same thing to a parallel Renaissance text, produces a multiplication of interpretive possibilities. 'Lamia', of course, though ostensibly the tale of a young man deceived by a serpent in woman's form, who sees his fanciful love destroyed by the touch of cold philosophy, also covertly addresses the possibility that Lamia is the embodiment of ideal love, as well as the ultimate fantasy object, and Lycius a cruel and faithless Narcissus. We have, finally, no ground for rejecting the hypothesis that she has herself been entrapped, and no reason to suppose her love for Lycius to be anything but genuine. We do have grounds for feeling that Lycius, in his desire to show off his sexual trophy to his friends, is the real serpent in this garden. As ironists, Keats and Hawthorne are well matched. If we cannot know how Hawthorne read Browne, how Keats read Burton, or how Hawthorne read Keats reading Burton, 'P's Correspondence' does at least suggest how Hawthorne thought Keats *should* have read Burton, as indeed does the procession of female victims of male self-love in Hawthorne's tales.

That 'Rappaccini's Daughter' is a tale about reading, and one which accentuates (like 'Lamia' and 'The Thorn' and *The Scarlet Letter*) an awareness of what one reads *with*, is amply confirmed by Hawthorne's use of Keats. But in my reading the shade of Keats is invoked in this tale as a vehicle for a deeper Coleridgean tenor. For in asking with what faculty we may truly see Beatrice, and into what errors we may be led by reliance upon the understanding alone when addressing matters of faith, we are of course in the province of New England's most radical dependency upon old, its adoption of Coleridgean Reason.

The reader is alerted three times to this theme as Giovanni sees, or thinks he sees, first a lizard, then an insect, and finally a bouquet of flowers, die or wither in contact with juices from the purple plant or the breath of Beatrice. The narrative foregrounds the question as to whether Giovanni sees, or fancies, or indeed simply *thinks* these fatal effects of that Dantean figure in her Miltonic garden. Nowhere does Coleridge manifest himself more clearly than in Hawthorne's handling of the struggle between Understanding and Reason for control of Giovanni's perceptions—and nowhere does Hawthorne more magnificently contest Coleridge's dismissive view of allegory.

> These incidents ... dissolving in the pure light of her character, had no longer the efficacy of facts, but were acknowledged as mistaken fantasies, by whatever testimony of the senses they might appear to be substantiated.[1]

But Giovanni, whose fascination with Beatrice is from the first, manifestly voyeuristic, ignores his Reason (or, more Coleridgeanly, Reason dwells not in him) and the momentary transparency of Beatrice's virtue to the eye of love becomes occluded in his ratiocinative processes. Grovelling in earthly doubts, he puts Beatrice to the test (this witchcraft theme is a Hawthorne constant) to discover whether her physical peculiarities betokened 'some corresponding monstrosity of soul'.

But what is betokened by the Coleridgean substrate of this tale? Against Hawthorne's apparently innocent invocation of Coleridge's

---

[1] 'Rappaccini's Daughter', 10: 120.

discrimination between Reason and Understanding, perhaps as mediated by Emerson in his role as Mr Smooth-it-Away, must be set the suspicion that while Giovanni may desire to intuit in Beatrice an elevating simpleness of soul (the narrator commends all 'simple' feelings) the attentive reader is offered some grounds for supposing that she is after all a duessa figure, a willing practitioner of deceit. Invited by Giovanni to throw him a bloom from her fatal sister-shrub she declines for what appears to be a wholly disingenuous reason that her throw would not reach: does she not know that she and her sister are poisonous? The answer to this question, however, is that we simply do not know. That she observes, and mourns, the death of insects as they fly about her, we do know; that she knows her father wears protective clothing, is evident; that she knows herself to be poisonous is an assumption not (or, at least, not beyond all reasonable doubt) warranted by the tale.

The Emersonian concept of Reason as a mode of sense offers comfort for just as long as there is no direct conflict between what understanding and reason contribute to the apperception of a single phenomenon. And one may well read Hawthorne's description of Rappaccini's garden as a sceptical treatment of Coleridge's equally celebrated discrimination between modes of Imagination. Is it really possible, Hawthorne may well be asking, to *repeat* 'the eternal act of creation in the Infinite I AM' (primary imagination)? Is it possible to *modify* it (through secondary imagination) without marring it?[1] Giovanni finds the plants in Rappaccini's garden, products of this second Adam's secondary imagination, rather troubling:

> The aspect of one and all of them dissatisfied him; their gorgeousness seemed fierce, passionate, and even unnatural.... there had been such commixture, and, as it were, adultery of various vegetable species, that the production was no longer of God's making, but the monstrous offspring of man's depraved fancy, glowing with only an evil mockery of beauty.[2]

---

1 The issue is raised, though not in specifically Coleridgean terms, by David Morse, *American Romanticism* (Basingstoke: Macmillan, 1987), 186.
2 'Rappaccini's Daughter', 10: 110.

Imagination, as Wordsworth demonstrates in 'The Thorn' can be pathological in its effects. And as Hawthorne appears to say in his prelude to the tale, where he presents it as a translation from the French of M. de l'Aubepine, transcendental writings often have 'little or no reference either to time or space' and unless examined 'in precisely the proper point of view ... can hardly fail to look excessively like nonsense'.

If Hawthorne's tale is begotten by Coleridge upon Keats, Hawthorne is no passive voyeur. His creation is superbly individual, a masterpiece of allegory, whatever its genetic inheritance. Nor does he hold himself aloof. In the villainous figure of Doctor Rappaccini the artist himself is surely implicated; dissolving and diffusing given data in order to combine them into new and freakish combinations can incur atrocious guilt. Rappaccini's desire to create a supremely powerful new Eve, mother of a new race, is no excuse. Hawthorne, like Thoreau, reads Coleridge with full cognizance of Wordsworthian interrogations.

3. THE RIDDLE OF THE WORLD

Edgar Allan Poe's reading of Hawthorne was often as reductive as one might expect from one who was anxious to assert his own pre-eminence as the American Coleridge, and as a surpassing practitioner of the literary counterfeit, producing Gothic tales which turn into metaphysical inquiries. He reduced 'The Minister's Black Veil', for instance, to a tale concerning the minister's guilt over the young lady in her coffin at the opening of the tale. Such a gift for travesty might well have inspired Hawthorne to use certain motifs from Poe's most Coleridgean exercise 'Ligeia' in his own rather deeper 'Rappaccini'.

Poe's poetry I pass over in discreet silence. Aldous Huxley's essay on that sad aberration remains, to my mind, the definitive treatment.[1] But Poe, like Emerson, Thoreau and Melville, was haunted by

---

1 See 'Vulgarity in Literature', in *Poe: A Collection of Critical Essays,* edited by Robert Regan (Englewood Cliffs, NJ: Prentice-Hall, 1967), 34-5. For a creditable defence of Poe see Maria Filippakopoulou, 'Intimacy and Recoil: Huxley Reads Poe in French', *Symbiosis* 8.1 (April 2004) 77–90.

Wordsworth's 'Intimations' Ode, and what he made of Wordsworth's vision of the grave as 'a place of thought where we in waiting lie' is worthier of attention. One might, by the way, see much of Poe's oeuvre as an effort to counteract Wordsworth's effort to counteract Gothic tendencies in the treatment of particular *topoi*: the interest in border states, whether between life and death ('not all alive or dead') or normalcy and derangement; the reluctance or inability to believe in personal extinction; the deaths of young (and, in Poe's case, preferably beautiful) women. What is 'Annabel Lee', after all, but a kitsch and anapaestic Lucy?

> And the stars never rise but I see the bright eyes
> Of my Lucy who lived in the dale.
> For no force can dissever my soul from the soul
> Of my Lucy who died in the vale
> And the violets blossom and put me in mind
> Of my Lucy who lies in the dale.

My parody falls sadly short of Aldous Huxley's deadly transposition of Milton's melodic glimpse of Persephone into the 'permanent wave' of 'Ulalume': the third (truly dire) line is Poe's own.

Poe's tales tend characteristically toward death, like endless variations on that impulse of Coleridge on witnessing a flash of lightning that it might pass through him, or Shelley's myth of regression to a state of pure potentiality. Like the Romantics, Poe saw destruction as part of the rhythm of creation, the systole and diastole of 'attraction' and 'repulsion'. *Eureka: a Prose Poem* is his effort to make a positive metaphysic, part science, part prose poem, out of this principle. Coleridge had proclaimed in the thirteenth essay of *The Friend* (1: 94) that 'THERE IS, strictly speaking, NO PROPER OPPOSITION BUT BETWEEN THE TWO POLAR FORCES OF ONE AND THE SAME POWER'. Acknowledging that he is simply reformulating a law first promulgated by Heraclitus, Coleridge proceeds to elaborate the point in his note. 'EVERY POWER IN NATURE AND IN SPIRIT must evolve an opposite, as the sole means and condition of its manifestation: AND ALL OPPOSITION IS A TENDENCY TO RE-UNION.' Poe's doctrine and his tales make plain that for him, or his narrators, it is the drift towards annihilation (revealingly called 'attraction') that is the positive movement, and that whereas Melville responds with horror to the thought of nothingness, Poe, or his narrators, embrace it with an erotic fascination. That his soul-mate is Schopenhauer is, one would have thought, were it not for the refusal of Poe's commentators ever to mention him, abundantly clear from the ending of 'The Masque of the Red Death', 'The Fall of the House of Usher' and *The Narrative of A. Gordon Pym*.

Poe's systematic plagiarism and subversion of Coleridge's poetics, and indeed of much of his metaphysics, is a matter of record, since Floyd Stovall summarised the case in 1969. The peculiarly Coleridgean manner of Poe's appropriation of Coleridge, in relation to Coleridge's own appropriations, has been detailed more recently by Jonathan Bate.[1] Of all the American Romantics, Poe was the most anxious to conceal his indebtedness, while demonstrating his grasp of and indeed supersession of Coleridge. At the beginning of *Eureka* (his achieved opus maximum), which can be read as a recantation of his early scepticism about the transcendentalism of Coleridge and of Emerson, he places himself where Empedocles and Coleridge have also in imagination stood, 'on the top of Aetna' seeking 'to comprehend the panorama in the sublimity of its oneness.' In its closing pages, however, he casts Coleridge as trapped in the chamber of maiden thought. There are few more eloquent passages in Coleridge's *The Friend* than this oft-quoted premonition of Heidegger's great theme, the question of being:

> Hast thou ever raised thy mind to the consideration of EXISTENCE, in and by itself, as the mere act of existing? Hast thou ever said to thyself thoughtfully, IT IS! heedless in that moment, whether it were a man before thee, or a flower, or a grain of sand? ...The very words, There is nothing! or, there was a time, when there was nothing! are self-contradictory...
>
> Not to BE, then, is impossible; To BE, incomprehensible ... it was this ... which in the earlier ages seized the nobler minds ... with a sort of sacred horror. This is was which first caused

---

[1] See Floyd Stovall, Edgar Poe the Poet (Charlottesville: University Press of Virginia, 1969), and Jonathan Bate, 'Edgar Allan Poe: a Debt Repaid', in *The Coleridge Connection*, ed. Richard Gravil and Molly Lefebure (Macmillan, 1990).

them to feel within themselves a something ineffably greater than their own nature. [1]

Coleridge here goes on to discuss the birthplace of this idea 'in all that constitutes our relative individuality', and at the same time as revelation: 'the manifesting power - is it not GOD?'

That Poe has his sights on Coleridge in the conclusion of *Eureka* is amply signposted in his rhetoric:

> So long as this Youth endures the feeling *that we exist* is the most natural of all feelings. ...That there was a period at which we did *not* exist—or, that it might so have happened that we never had existed at all—are the considerations, indeed, which *during this youth*, we find difficulty in understanding. Why we should *not* exist, is *up to the epoch of our manhood* of all queries the most unanswerable. Existence—self-existence—existence from all Time and to all Eternity—seems, up to the Epoch of Manhood, a normal and unquestionable condition: —*seems, because it is*.[2]

The italics are Poe's. Nor is my source-hunting here merely speculative. Poe's meditation begins in fact, where Coleridge's does, with the 'Ode: Intimations of Immortality'. Coleridge quotes the ninth stanza of the ode, with its mysterious thanks and praise for

> ... those obstinate questionings
> Of sense and outward things,
> Fallings from us, vanishings;
> Blank misgivings of a creature
> Moving about in worlds not realized

and for

> Those shadowy recollections,
> Which, be they what they may,
> Are yet the fountain light or all our day.

---

1 *The Friend*, ed. Barbara E. Rooke, 2 vols., London and Princeton, 1969, I, 514–6.

2 *The Complete Works of Edgar Allan Poe*, edited by James A Harrison (1902), AMS Press Inc, New York 1965, Volume 16, p 312.

Poe paraphrases the same passage thus:

> We walk about, amid the destinies of our world-existence, encompassed by dim but ever present Memories of a destiny more vast – very distant in the by-gone time, and infinitely awful. We live out a Youth peculiarly haunted by such shadows; yet never mistaking them for dreams.

Coleridge's commentary on those 'shadowy recollections' leads immediately into a discussion of 'the idea of the common centre, the universal law, by which all power manifests in opposite yet interdependent forces', and the suggestion that 'enlightening enquiry' will lead man at last 'to comprehend gradually and progressively the relation of each to the other, of each to all, and of all to each' (*Friend*, 1: 511). His essay finds in the notion of a 'world of spirit' nothing less than 'the substantiating principle of all true wisdom, the satisfactory solution of all the contradictions of human nature, of the whole riddle of the world' (524). Poe's solution to 'the riddle of the world', is that deity spends eternity, like a cosmic Emerson, in 'perpetual variation of Concentrated Self and almost infinite Self-Diffusion'; that 'What you call The Universe of Stars is but his present expansive existence'; that what are called his creatures 'are really but infinite individualisations of himself'; that animate or apparently inanimate creatures have—as Diderot and Wordsworth and Wordsworth's friend 'Walking' Stewart all proclaim as part of their Romantic naturalism—'a capacity for pleasure and for pain'; that all such creatures are, by faint indeterminate glimpses, conscious 'of an identity with God'. As youths, therefore, Poe proclaims, we find Existence 'unquestionable' because we are God's 'Infinite Self-Diffusion' and man will 'at length attain that awfully triumphant epoch when he shall recognise his existence as that of Jehovah.'[1] Finally, therefore, 'That God may be all in all, each must become God'.

Poe's very last word in *Eureka*, that it is a consoling thought and a reconcilement to mortality, that loss of individual identity means 'neither more nor less than ... the absorption, by each individual intelligence, of all other intelligences (that is, of the Universe) into its

---

1 *Complete Works* 16: 314, 315.

own', is both a paraphrase, knowingly or not, of 'Walking' Stewart's similar argument in *The Apocalypse of Nature*, and (unlike 'Annabel Lee') a creditable gloss on 'A slumber did my spirit seal'.[1]

Poe's final position, therefore, despite his earlier quarrel with Frogpondium and all its works, is not merely a restatement of Emersonian 'Allness': it is a remarkable fusion of Wordworth's materialist Pantheism in 'The Poem upon the Wye' with Coleridge's counter-Pantheism in *The Friend*. Whether Poe is unaware that he has missed the whole point of Coleridge's intellectual career, or whether he is consciously asserting that Coleridge missed the point, and that he was a Pantheist *malgré lui*, is a moot point. That *Eureka* is dedicated to Alexander von Humboldt, brother of the Baron von Humboldt who told Coleridge of his astonishment that 'so great and original a poet' as the author of 'Intimations' could be at work in this age, is either as fine a piece of serendipity as one could wish, or an elaborately concealed acknowledgement of the significance of *The Friend* in the conception—or at least the conclusion—of *Eureka*. The combination of the dedication to Humboldt, the shared allusion to 'Intimations' and Poe's parodic and substantive use of two passages from the eleventh of Coleridge's 'Essays on the Principles of Method' is hardly fortuitous. But a full discussion of *Eureka*, and Poe's impressive insights into the implications of the scientific successors of Davy and Dalton, is well beyond my powers. 'Ligeia', on the other hand, is altogether more compassable, and plays with Coleridge in much the same ambivalent fashion.

4. Gothic Metaphyics

'Ligeia', which apart from *The Fall of the House of Usher* is the most accomplished of Poe's metaphysical yarns, concludes a series of tales ('Morella' and 'Berenice' being the others) in which three highly metaphysical narrators grapple with very Coleridgean questions. The

---

1 In *The Apocalypse of Nature* (London: J Ridgway, 1792) John Stewart argued that 'Death of existence is the dissolution of identity ... but we have an instinctive and conscious testimony, that we are immortal parts of the great integer, Nature; that we have existed from and shall continue to exist to all eternity' (2: 24).

narrator of 'Ligeia' shares with the narrator of 'Morella' a fascination with what the latter calls 'the *principium individuationis*—the notion of that identity *which at death is or is not lost for ever.*'[1] 'Ligeia' may also be read as addressing macabre variants upon such matters as the unity of the perceiver with the perceived, and the possibility that we are all one life—macabre because the tale is ostensibly concerned with migrations of consciousness from person to person, and body to body. In 1846 Poe, quite rightly, described this tale to Duyckink as 'undoubtedly the best I have written'.[2] That this is because the great Poe emerges in his closest dealings with the Romantics, as Weisbuch argues, is beyond doubt.

Poe strikingly announces his engagement with Coleridge by giving his tale an epigraph, purportedly from the Cambridge Platonist, Joseph Glanville. This is about as close a source to Thomas Burnet (whose words preface *The Ancient Mariner*) as one could reasonably find, whereby to assert one's equivalence to Coleridge in mastery of quaint and curious volumes of forgotten lore. But whereas Coleridge's (modified) Burnet speculates upon the existence of more forms of life than are dreamt of in modern philosophy, Poe's (probably invented, certainly unidentified) passage from Glanville contemplates the mystery of death:

> And the will therein lieth, which dieth not. Who knoweth the mysteries of the will, with its vigor? For God is but a great will pervading all things by the nature of its intentness. Man doth not yield himself to the angels, nor unto death utterly, save only through the weakness of his feeble will.[3]

It is easy to see how Poe has honed this text: ostensibly it is a Spinozistic utterance, glorifying the divine 'will'; latently it yields,

---

1 *Collected Works of Edgar Allan Poe*, Volume 2, *Tales and Sketches 1831–1842*, edited by Thomas Ollive Mabbott (The Belknap Press of Harvard University Press, Cambridge, Mass: 1978), 231. Morella inspires her husband-narrator, already a student of Locke, to study Fichte's pantheism, the metempsychosis of the Pythagoreans and 'above all the doctrines of Identity as urged by Schelling', 230–1.
2 *Collected Works*, 2: 306.
3 *Collected Works*, 2: 310.

Hawthorne and Poe: Romancing Romanticism 241

to a death-obsessed, annihilation-oriented mind, the lure of nirvana. God is will, yet only through attenuation of the will can the desired unity with God, who is in Poe's metaphysic as much a name for nothingness as for allness, attained. Neither the narrator nor the Lady Ligeia finds this Schopenhauer-inspired lesson easy to grasp.

If the mariner-like epigraph betokens a mariner-like theme, a meditation upon Poe's version of 'the one life', the next Coleridgean feature recalls a text concerned with a woman wailing for her demon lover, architectural extravaganzas, and the poet's desire to revive within him the haunting strains of an Abyssinian maid. Poe's opium-drenched narrator devotes several pages to recollecting the fading image of Ligeia. His attempts are introduced in a pattern of insistent alliteration and assonance, intolerable in prose and indeed almost unprecedented in English poetry. The one poetic precedent is to be found in the first five lines of *Kubla Khan*: 'In Xanadu did **Ku**bla **Kha**n / A stately pleasure **d**ome **decree** / Where Alph the sacred **r**iver **ran** / Through caverns **measure**less to **man** / Down to a **sunless sea**'. The famous terminal alliterations are merely the most obtrusive component of a sonic tapestry (the first line's vowels run i-a-a-u^i-u-a-a, and further echoes include pleasure/measure, dome/down, stately/sacred/sunless). That fine excess Poe echoes thus:

> in truth the character of my beloved, her rare learning, her **singular yet placid cast** of beauty, and the **thrilling** and **enthralling eloquence** of her **low musical lan**guage, made their way into my heart by paces so **steadily and stealthily progressive** that they have been **unnoticed and unknown**.

It is Poe in his best Vincent Price manner, rather than his Sidney Greenstreet one. Poe's major reference text in this tale is however *Christabel* rather than *The Ancient Mariner* or 'Kubla Khan' (it seems more than likely that Hawthorne's triple use of Keatsian texts allied to a Renaissance source was suggested by Poe's Coleridgean extravagances here).

Poe's narrator, obsessed by his memory of the learned Lady Ligeia betakes himself after her death (and his own return from Germany) to a reconditioned abbey in 'one of the wildest and least frequented portions of fair England'. There, more like William Beckford than Coleridge in this respect, he creates an Arabian fantasy within a Gothic shell, to which 'in a moment of mental alienation' he brings his second bride, a Scott/Coleridge amalgam, 'the fair-haired and blue-eyed Lady Rowena Trevanion, of Tremaine' (that Christabel's virginal features are oddly associated with Geraldine's father, Lord Roland de Vaux of Tryermaine, is often noticed). The luckless Rowena finds herself married to a man who loathes her (a case of Poe's art imitating Coleridge's life) and who yearns for the transcendental raptures he associates with 'Ligeia, the beloved, the august, the beautiful, the entombed'. Even the narrator has the grace to wonder how her parents let her get into this mess.

Rowena rapidly succumbs to a mysterious illness, not unprompted by the designer decor of her bridal chamber, which is pentagonal in shape, with lead-coloured stained-glass windows (a visual pun almost worthy of Keats), grotesque Gothic carvings (as in Christabel's chamber), and a giant sarcophagus of black granite in each corner. Her death is a long drawn out 'drama of revivification', each sign of returning life being countered by unspecified exertions on the part of that opium-enriched metaphysician, the narrator. At the climax of the tale, the enshrouded corpse of the blonde Rowena—which has hitherto 'exhibited all the loathsome peculiarities of that which has been for many days a tenant of the tomb' (the narrator is, as J. Gerald Kennedy suggests, a 'connoisseur of decay' and voyeur of decomposition)[1]— rises and advances, unbandages itself and reveals 'huge masses of long and dishevelled hair ... *blacker than the wings of the midnight*'. Before his eyes, or within his imagination, there stands before him the physical form of the Lady Ligeia. And so, one might observe, the critically perspicacious amalgamation of Christabel and Geraldine is accomplished: the vampirine volition of Ligeia transforms the untenanted corpse of Rowena Trevanion of Tremaine. Bearing in mind the possibility that Geraldine herself is the victim of such possession in Coleridge's uncompleted tale, the *Christabel* bearings are as tantalising as they are overt.

---

1 J. Gerald Kennedy, *Poe, Death and the Life of Writing* (New Haven and London: Yale University Press, 1987), 83.

The critical dispute engendered by this tale has undergone similar metamorphoses. At first, the contest was between those who read a simple tale of the supernatural, in which a deathless spirit takes possession of a freshly vacant corpse, and those who found an unreliably narrated tale of opium-induced hallucination. More psychologically inclined critics have diagnosed in the narrator a progress from simple erotomania (his dwelling on Ligeia's voluptuous beauty, considered inventory-fashion, body part by body part, occupies several pages of the tale) to megalomania (striving to sublime his prosaic Rowena into a transcendental Ligeia).[1] One critic has seen *Ligeia* as both a satire on Transcendentalism and an allegory of the reanimation of a lifeless English Romanticism by German *geist*.[2]

In *Fables of Mind*, a major study, Joan Dayan has seen Poe's tale as a climactic instance of his engagement with Locke, Newton, Jonathan Edwards and Jonathan Swift (more is reanimated in 'Ligeia' than meets the eye) and in particular Locke's speculations on the interchangeability of 'identity' and 'consciousness'. Not merely a demystification of the Gothic, Dayan says, 'Ligeia' is 'one of Poe's most serious counterfeits', and has serious philosophical underpinnings. It employs Gothic mannerism to entertain Locke's philosophical parable of 'a moveable soul in search of a place to think in' (thinking is Ligeia's forte).[3] If one is to believe Dayan's ingenious reading, which curiously does not mention Coleridge, either here or in its treatment of *Eureka*, or indeed at all, Poe has every reason to invoke the author of *The Ancient Mariner*. This is not merely because the mariner, too, is fated not to die, but because Poe is demonstrating simultaneously his capacity to out-philosophise the despised Frogpondians (his term for Transcendentalism), and to out-Coleridge Coleridge in the marriage of art and metaphysics. One could easily see Poe as a neo-Byron, of greater philosophical range, nostalgic for the precision

---

1 See Roy P. Basler, 'The Interpretation of "Ligeia"', *Sex, Symbolism and Psychology in Literature* (1948), reprinted in Robert Regan, ed., *Poe: a Collection of Critical Essays* (Englewood Cliffs, N.J.: Prentice-Hall, Inc., 1967), 51–63.

2 Clark Griffith, 'Poe's "Ligeia" and the English Romantics', *University of Toronto Quarterly*, 24 (1954-5) 8–25.

3 Joan Dayan, *Fables of Mind: an Inquiry into Poe's Fiction* (Oxford University Press, 1987), 135.

of the eighteenth-century wits, and capable not merely of despising his contemporaries for their 'mistical' tendencies, but of engaging—while practising an art of deceptive ease—in a rival metaphysics of comparable depth.

Clark Gifford's reading of the tale as an allegory of the Germanising of English Romanticism is ingenious, if as Jonathan Bate suggests, a little over-schematic. For one thing Rowena is Romantic only in name (though this, of course might be Poe's point, as Gifford indeed argues). For another, Coleridge, in particular, rather than English Romanticism in general is the major stylistic presence. For the narrator, Ligeia's expression has peculiar associations. Her face had the radiance of an opium dream, and her eyes, her 'large and luminous orbs' are the feature on which he dwells the most, as in most pen portraits of Coleridge. She had traversed 'all the wide areas of moral, physical and mathematical science' and 'her presence, her readings alone, rendered vividly luminous the many mysteries of the transcendentalists'. Her Hebrew nose and Greek chin (most pointed of those body parts) more than hint at a plaster cast of that English Romantic whose life's task was to reconcile Plato with the Gospel of St John.

But Ligeia is not Coleridge. If she were, we might see the tale as expressing Poe's own subjection to his master. The doubleness of Poe's writing, the construction of tales which resist closure, takes effect as we observe how Coleridgean features are distributed between the narrator (his haunts and his style), his lost love (her features and her lore) and the tale itself. G. R. Thompson has said of Poe's art that his tales change genre (from tales of horror to psychological studies, for instance, or one might say from the supernatural to the metaphysical) as the arabesque tapestries in Rowena's chamber change from grotesqueries to phantasmagoria as we shift our point of view. As he points out, Poe's creation of purely aesthetic structures which frustrate interpretation, mirrors his creation of an absurdist metaphysic in which the universe emerges from nothingness only to return to nothingness.[1]

For Poe to permit us some readerly certainty as to why he con-

---

[1] G. R. Thompson, *Poe's Fiction: Romantic Irony in the Gothic Tales*, University of Wisconsin Press, 1973, p.7.

jures the spirit of Coleridge in *Ligeia* would be a most uncharacteristic procedure. We may choose to see him as engaged competitively with Coleridge the metaphysician, rebuking him for failing to learn the attractions of nothingness, as Ligeia, for all her gorgeous learning and eloquence fails to do. Coleridge would not see that Priestley and Wordsworth were right: that matter itself is spirit, and that the absorption of identity with rocks and stones and trees, which themselves are God, was therefore to be welcomed as a mode of eternal life. We may see him, secondly, rebuking Coleridge for murdering the poet in himself by an excessive subjection to German Idealism: the narrator is out of his mind, after all; Rowena is as pretty as it gets, and like Keats, Poe critiqued Coleridge for not prioritising the principle of beauty. Or, thirdly, since Poe is an accomplished professional, who succeeded regularly where Coleridge did not, in producing creative work of high finish and teasing implication, we may read 'Ligeia' as criticising Coleridge for failing to realise in his own work either the magic idealism of the Germans or their perfection of Romantic Irony. Fourthly, 'Ligeia', which is as concrete, achieved and workmanlike a tale as Poe produced, despite the haze of opium through which its data are perceived, itself rebukes Coleridge's failure to recreate in an achieved text the ideal architecture of his own waking visions. Poe would not have left 'Kubla Khan' and 'Christabel' as the fragments he probably believed them to be; he would have done a proper professional job. All four hypotheses seem entertainable to me, as long as we recognise that Coleridge is the daemon of this tale, as Ligeia is that of its narrator.

'Ligeia' inverts the hermeneutic mystery of 'Kubla Khan'. Coleridge's poem may strike one at first as wholly resistant to interpretation: yet each prolonged meditation on it leads to a provisional sense of intelligibility as one or other form of mythological narrative takes hold. 'Ligeia', contrariwise strikes most readers as wholly transparent at first reading: meditation rapidly blurs that confidence as one comes to see its possible configurations as simple horror story, a serial murder story, a tale of hallucination, a parable of the will, each of these by turns, or all at once. Even the comparative 'completion' of 'Ligeia' is illusory. If Ligeia comes back, where is she in the narrative now? Rowena, certainly, is not reanimated: and her transfiguration is perhaps no more than a dream of metamorphosis. On one level, the impossible Ligeia comes between the narrator and his bride Rowena as Geraldine comes between Sir Leoline and Christabel. Indeed as a character, Rowena seems to exaggerate the nullity of Christabel: if Christabel, as pure goodness, is incapable of development, Rowena is a conspicuously undeveloped cipher. She is there only to be hated by the narrator, because he has married her; and subjected to the unaccountable fits of rage to which Coleridge subjects his child in the conclusion to Part 2 of 'Christabel'. There are details in 'Ligeia' which seem without any point at all, except to remind one of Coleridge.

Coleridge's presence persuades one to take seriously Dayan's strong reading of this tale:

> In *Morella* and *Ligeia* particularly, Poe attacks the vague discourse associated with idealist speculation, through the invention of a narrator who uncritically accepts the metaphysics of a lady who lives only to embody and communicate this cant of ultimates. But at the same time that Poe betrays the high cost of such transcendental idealization through the narrator's madness and the Lady's death, he writes a tale that asks serious questions about the nature of the human soul, consciousness—and of course personal identity.[1]

And with Dayan's consummate summation I leave 'Ligeia'.

Poe, in his tales, develops with all the exploitative skills of a true professional, the generative formula of the English Romantic poem. Wordsworth's 'spots of time' we have come to read as a kind of explained Gothic, in which what appears supernatural is recognised as formative or projective but beneficent illusion; his 'Thorn', which I have discussed above as germane to Hawthorne's maieutic method, is also the archetypal instance of a literary counterfeit in the Poe sense, a Gothic vehicle which embodies a study of superstition, a theory of imagination, and a philosophy of perception. Shelley's

---

1 Dayan, p. 135.

'Alastor' and 'Mont Blanc' pursue metaphysical debate in the guise of narrative and descriptive poems. Coleridge's 'divine comedy', all three components of which Poe invokes in 'Ligeia', embodies in a variety of Gothic frameworks precisely that metaphysic of transcendence which Poe seeks, in his triad of tales, to subvert, before he amends it in *Eureka*. Poe is not, of course the last American poet to rebuke an English precursor for allowing metaphysical enquiries to hijack his art, and then follow in the same reflective path. The case of one T S Eliot, *vis-a-vis* William Blake, comes to mind. But the relationship is closer in this case. Of course much of Poe, in 'Murders in the Rue Morgue', or 'The Pit and the Pendulum', despite its Inquisitional trappings and its nightmare quality, and in 'The Fall of the House of Usher', is well outside Coleridge's orbit. But in other works across his various genres—in the collocation of 'The Raven' and 'The Philosophy of Composition', in the ideas of 'the Poetic principle', in the tropes of both 'Manuscript Found in a Bottle' and *The Narrative of Arthur Gordon Pym*, in 'Ligeia' and in *Eureka*—his sense of Coleridge is formative, combative, and generative. Poe was not Coleridge's invention, but he is most himself when completing or extending Coleridge according to his own peculiar lights.

Chapter 8:

The Whale and the Albatross: Melville and the Active Universe

Completing *Moby-Dick* in 1851, Melville wrote famously to Hawthorne: 'I have written a wicked book, and feel spotless as the lamb.'[1] It is wholly impossible to imagine Coleridge making the same remark. Yet the affinities between Coleridge and Melville go to the heart of each writer's enterprise. Each began in optimism about human perfectibility; each found it impossible to allay a double sense of man as sinful and of society as self-destructive; each yearned for a world of translucent symbol. Each struggled with Pantheistical tendencies—undermined in the one case by the need for a personal God and in the other by the humane imperative for human freedom (which many would argue are the metaphysical and existential faces of the same philosophical doubloon). Each devoted much thought to the perils and prospects limitations of the body politic, in an era of revolution, treating such perils most persuasively—it can be argued—in symbolic register. Each, of course, read voraciously, in parallel fields, including metaphysics, contemporary science, comparative religions, politics, travel books ancient and modern.

A reading of their affinities, and of the dialogue between *Moby-Dick* and *The Ancient Mariner*, might choose to focus upon each text's awareness of 1793–94 and 1848. At an analogical level one can take both texts as concerned with 'objectifying the dereliction and dismay of the times in an objectively controlled nightmare'. This eloquent

---

[1] *Correspondence*, ed. Lynn Horth, *The Writings of Herman Melville*, Volume 14 (Evanston and Chicago: Northwestern University Press and the Newberry Library, 1993), 212.

formulation is David Erdman's, in *Blake: Prophet Against Empire*. The nightmare he refers to is Coleridge's, but the 'time of dereliction and dismay' is Wordsworth's phrase for Pitt's political terror, for which, of course, another analogue in Romantic writing of the 1790s, especially Coleridge's, is the Spanish Inquisition. Numerous readings of 'The Ancient Mariner' have understood the spectre bark as a slaver; death's skeleton as 'black' because of the horrors of the central passage; the dungeon grate through which the sun is perceived as a reference to the Newgate lodgings of such figures as John Thelwall on trial for 'constructive treason'; and the whole burden of guilt in the poem as occasioned by involvements, and betrayals, in the cause of humanity. The summative expression of the power of the poem to inspire such readings is Patrick J Keane's remarkable study of *Coleridge's Submerged Politics*,[1] which argues finally, that in speaking of the church 'where each to the great Father bends' Coleridge makes precisely that painful capitulation to Pitt which Wordsworth, in 1794 was unable to make. In 1805 Wordsworth could still represent himself in 1794 as praying for French successes, amid a congregation where all else were 'bending all / To *their* great father' (*Prelude* 10: 26-74).

Similarly, when Ahab sees himself as pursuing his destiny upon iron rails, one is aware that the metaphor employs an industrial-capitalist 'vehicle' to express its necessitarian 'tenor'. That Ishmael's voyage is upon an inter-racial ship, named after the first native American nation eradicated by white supremacy; that the Parsee relates to Ahab in overtly Coleridgean terms, 'still as a slave before his lord' ('The Hat'); that the theme of man versus nature is expressed, *inter alia*, in terms of capitalist industrialism (from the try-works of the whale's dismemberment to calculation by Flask of how many cigars he can buy with a gold doubloon) goes almost without saying. In both narratives the ship (of state) which has perpetrated a crime against (human) nature, sinks into the ocean, leaving a chastened nar-

---

1 Patrick J Keane, *Coleridge's Submerged Politics: the Ancient Mariner and Robinson Crusoe* (Columbia and London: University of Missouri Press, 1994) 367. Debbie Lee, in 'Yellow Fever and the Slave Trade: Coleridge's Rime of the Ancient Mariner', *ELH* 65:3 (1998) 673–700, sees the poem as *about* slaving.

rator exiled from yet intermittently devoted to domestic and humane values but unable to rise much above the most sentimental codification of those values.¹

There is, in other words, another comparative chapter to be written, than the one I offer here. But late twentieth-century readings of *Moby-Dick* purely in terms of Jacksonian America's betrayals of democracy became so pervasive that I choose to focus, rather, on the narrator's doomed quest for a somewhat Wordsworthian 'insular Tahiti' of the soul.² The two are not separated. America's discovery of Pantheism, like that of Wordsworth and Coleridge, is of course a response to historical betrayals. Nature, in modern Romantic studies, is inescapably political. My reading, in this chapter may emphasise the perversion of Nature rather than the specific political outcomes of that perversion, but is not intended to occlude the latter.

While much of Melville's experience of the Idealist tradition and its German derivatives comes from Pierre Bayle's *Historical and Critical Dictionary*, and of course from Coleridge, Carlyle and (less conspicuously) Emerson, his writing is—like Coleridge's—impregnated with that philosophical tradition represented by Plato, neo-Platonism, Spinoza, Kant and Schelling.³ The novel, published in England as *The Whale*, was received with general approbation for its poetry and its daring, but by the *Morning Chronicle* reviewer in

---

1 Michael Rogin's *Subversive Genealogy: the Politics and Art of Herman Melville* (Berkeley: University of California Press, 1985) seems to me to have said all that needs saying about the political Melville, except for Wai-Chee Dimock's *Empire for Liberty: Melville and the Poetics of Individualism* (Princeton, NJ: Princeton University Press, 1989) which is stimulating on the notion of the 'imperial self' (and Melville's self-image is much given to self-expression in terms of power) as subjectively cognate with 'manifest destiny'.

2 In *The Prelude* (1805) 11: 47–56, Wordsworth, tornadoed in historical events, ignores 'the fragrance ... of the shore / From arbours breathed of blessed sentiment and fearless love' because 'My business was upon the barren seas'.

3 Merton M Sealts, Jr, offers the fullest account of Melville's relative exposure to Emerson, Wordsworth, Coleridge and Carlyle by the time of writing *Moby-Dick*, and argues that much of what looks like Emerson in Melville's writing at this date is more likely to be Plato, or Plato disseminated by Wordsworth and Coleridge. *Pursuing Melville, 1940–1980* (University of Wisconsin Press, 1982), pp. 257, 267–8.

252   Romantic Dialogues

terms which would have suited a posthumous text by Coleridge:

> Here, however ... comes Melville in all his pristine powers ... with his imagination invoking as strange and wild and original themes as ever, with his fancy arraying them in the old bright and vivid hues, with that store of quaint and out-of-the-way information ... which he ever and anon scatters around in ... unreasonable profusion, with the old mingled opulence and happiness of phrase ...raving and rhapsodising in chapter after chapter ... and occasionally soaring into such absolute clouds of phantasmal unreason, that we seriously and sorrowfully ask ourselves whether this can be anything other than sheer moonstruck lunacy.[1]

This bizarre judgement notwithstanding, 'The Whale' is both a superlative lowering, in its own right, into the high seas of transcendental metaphysics, and—more than incidentally—one of the great readings of *The Ancient Mariner*.[2]

I make no claims, of course, for Coleridge as the onlie begetter of Melville's work. Another reading might focus upon the manner in which Carlyle's response, in *Sartor Resartus*, to Coleridge's handling of the *Naturphilosophie* and the *Pantheismusstreit*, tutors Melville's both in substance and in style.[3] In writing *Moby-Dick* Melville was undertaking to demonstrate his recent claim (in 'Hawthorne and his Mosses') that American writing was ready to rival that of England, and while creating a tale rooted in New England culture (a fact ade-

---

[1] *Melville: the Critical Heritage*, ed. Watson G Branch (London & Boston: Routledge & Kegan Paul, 1974), 287–8. Of several enthusiastic British reviews, John Bull makes the most succinct case for the work's 'true philosophy' and 'genuine poetry', 255.

[2] The importance of the Melville-Coleridge connection has been suggested in brief but pregnant sentences by Morse Peckham and by A Robert Lee. See Peckham's 'Hawthorne and Melville as European Authors', in *Melville and Hawthorne in the Berkshires: a Symposium*, ed. Howard P. Vincent (Kent, Ohio: Kent State University Press, 1968) 58 and Lee's '*Moby-Dick*: the Tale and the Telling'.

[3] An admirable essay on Carlyle is Katy McGettigan, 'Aestheticising the Marketplace: Appropriations of the Literary Industry in *Sartor Resartus* and *Moby-Dick*', *Symbiosis* 15.2. (October 2011) 173–92.

The Whale and the Albatross 253

quately recognized in several extant studies), he creates one of the most prodigiously intertextual texts in the language. All of English Literature, from *The Seafarer,* via Marlow and Shakespeare, Browne and Swift, Wordsworth, Coleridge, Byron, Shelley and Keats, to Dickens, Tennyson and Carlyle, is subsumed—thematically and stylistically—in Melville's American masterpiece. Whether Coleridge is markedly more present than Shakespeare or Browne or Carlyle is debateable: what is clear is that these four are closest to the imaginative heart and surface texture of the text, and that Coleridge is closest of all to its symbolic method, not least, of course, in their handling of the central symbol of the sea and the deeply significant topos of self-isolation.[1]

There is ample evidence that Moby-Dick is textually aware of The Rime and it may be helpful to begin with a rapid sampling of surface echoes and allusions, some of them indisputable, some less so; some noticed, some not. One of Ishmael's early meditations upon the constitution of ship and state has him concluding that the dignity of the common man is a

> democratic dignity which, on all hands, radiates without end from God; Himself! The Great God absolute! The centre and circumference of all democracy! His omnipresence, our divine equality.[2]

Others have noticed that the source for Ishmael's democratic and

---

[1] Both texts figure largely in W H Auden's *The Enchafed Flood*, though without direct comparison. Auden makes a contrast between between traditional and Romantic meanings of the sea voyage as symbol. See *The Enchafed Flood: or, the Romantic Iconography of the Sea*, Faber & Faber, 1951, 20–21. H. W. Piper in *The Singing of Mount Abora*, draws attention to Purchas's use of the symbol: 'For the naturall man that abides at home in him-selfe ... knows not the things of God, nor the great Mysteries of Godlinesse: he must leave the Land, his Earthly Wisdome..and launch into the deepe, there having sayles filled with the winde, the illumination of that Spirit, which leads unto all truth.' *The Singing of Mount Abora: Coleridge's Use of Biblical Imagery and Natural Symbolism in Poetry and Philosophy* (Fairleigh Dickinson University Press, 1987), 50.

[2] *Moby-Dick; or the Whale*, ed. Harold Beaver (Harmondsworth: Penguin, 1972), 212.

millennial belief—countering Ahab's totalitarian one—is Coleridge's line, 'There is one Mind, one omnipresent Mind / Omnific' in *Religious Musings*, where Coleridge further writes—in phrases clearly familiar to Ishmael—that it is 'the sublime of man ... to know ourselves / parts and proportions of one wondrous whole! This fraternises man.... 'tis God / Diffused through all, that doth make all one whole'.[1]

Early in the *Pequod*'s voyage Ahab sits in his cabin. While the chapter opens in a pastiche of *The Seafarer* ('I leave a white and turbid wake; pale waters, paler cheeks, where'er I sail. The envious billows sidelong swell to whelm my track; let them; but first I pass' (265)) it soon becomes clear that Ahab has also been reading *Dejection: an Ode*, for he describes a sunset, lamenting its powerlessness to lift his spirits:

> Oh! time was when as the sunrise nobly spurred me, so the sunset soothed. No more. This lovely light, it lights not me; all loveliness is anguish to me, since I can ne'er enjoy. Gifted with the high perception, I lack the low enjoying power; damned ... in the midst of Paradise. (266)

Some pages later, Ishmael, enrolled against his will in Ahab's quenchless feud, meditates on Moby-Dick and the legends of his ubiquity and immortality, and proclaims that the realities of the whale are fully equal to such wonders as the 'Arethusa fountain near Syracuse' (281) whose waters run from the Holy Land by an underground passages, thus yoking to his narrative (as Matthiessen noticed seventy years ago) the fountain of Xanadu and the mysteries of Mount Abora.[2]

In chapter 51, some forty pages after a lengthy allusion to Coleridge's Albatross, which I defer until later, we are introduced to a mysterious Spirit Spout which Fedallah descries, calling to his shipmates in an unearthly voice 'as if some winged spirit had had lighted in the rigging, and hailed the mortal crew'. Every morn-

---

[1] Coleridge's lines are cited in this respect by Leon Chai, *The Romantic Foundations of the American Renaissance* (Cornell University Press, 1987), 301.

[2] F. O. Matthiessen, *American Renaissance: Art and Expression in the Age of Emerson and Whitman* (Oxford University Press, 1945), 416.

ing the spirit spout, 'calm, snow-white, and unvarying', still directs its beckoning 'fountain of feathers to the sky' (335–7). In the very next chapter, appears another Albatross, this time a spectral ship, making its way from Coleridge to Melville via Poe's *Narrative of Arthur Gordon Pym*. The 'Goney' is 'bleached like the skeleton of a stranded walrus…. while all her spars and her rigging were like the thick branches of trees furred over with hoar-frost'. Here the shoals of fish which have followed the *Pequod* desert Ahab's death-devoted ship to follow the spectre bark as the two wakes intersect to form a cross (339).

Verbal allusions abound, also, along with compositional ones. Coleridge's startling alliteration in 'the white foam flew, the furrow followed free' is startlingly echoed in Melville's 'the foam flakes flew' as the ship rounds the Cape (336); Ahab's brow is described as 'gaunt and ribbed, like the black sand beach' (492), recalling Wordsworth's descriptive contribution to Coleridge's poem—'for thou art long and lank and brown / As is the ribbed sea-sand'. Ishmael is also marked by strangely Coleridgean qualities when we consider his narration. It is not merely his strange and curious learning, but his imitation of the organisational qualities of *Biographia Literaria*: eschewing the complete and embracing the disparactive, Ishmael proclaims that his role is 'simply to project the draught of a systematisation of cetology. I am the architect, not the builder' (229). 'God keep me from ever completing anything', Ishmael prays. 'This whole book is but a draught—nay but the draught of a draught. Oh, Time, Strength, Cash, and Patience!' (241).

In reductive sum, then, *The Ancient Mariner* is the story of a sailor who for the thoughtless crime (or thought crime) of slaying a naturally supernatural albatross, is punished by unending penance, constrained to tell his cautionary tale, with strange power of speech, throughout eternity. In still more reductive sum, *Moby-Dick* is the story of a sailor who for assisting in the intentional assault of his captain against a naturally supernatural Albino whale, is punished by a life-time of being constrained to tell his interminable tale, with equally strange power of speech, in the ports of all maritime nations.

While the poem feeds the readerly imagination in a way that has been equalled by few other texts, it often leaves the 'secondary power' struggling in the poet's symbolic wake. Who is the Mariner? Why does he go to sea? Does the ship have owners, a mission, a trade or a destination? Who is its captain? Are the crew all of the Mariner's faith (unreformed Scottish Catholicism)? To what period and culture do the events of the poetic narrative belong? The questions evaded by the poem seem to be Melville's agenda for the strikingly over-circumstantial opening chapters. Contrariwise, the poem is full of ostensible certainties: the Mariner is wrong to kill the Albatross; we live in a morally ordered universe; the natural world is governed by an ascertainable spiritual hierarchy; it is wrong to despise, and right to bless, the creatures of the deep; in short, 'he prayeth best who loveth best all things both great and small'.

The poem itself leaves us, nevertheless, with questions of dread-inspiring scope. As Leslie Stephen pointed out in 1892, 'The moral ...that people who sympathise with a man who shoots an albatross will die in prolonged torture of thirst, is open to obvious objections'.[1] Although the Mariner seems quite untroubled by the riddling inconsistencies of the moral order as displayed in his tale, the poem can be read as a nightmare expressive of deep dread and uncertainty. The Wedding Guest is a sadder and a wiser man upon the morrow morn because he has learned that bliss or woe may depend upon impulsive acts; that the thin crust of everydayness may plunge one at any moment (as Pip discovers in *Moby-Dick*) into a bizarre under-world of arbitrary and infinitely powerful punitive agencies; that one's spiritual destiny may be settled by a game of dice; and—most troubling of all—that God may regard an entire crew of ordinary men as expendable for the purpose of instructing a single chosen soul. *Moby-Dick* may be regarded as Melville's sustained commentary on the single symbolic moment which admits a radical scepticism into Coleridge's poem, the scene in which not only the fate of mariner and crew, but also our sense of epistemological and ontological security, hinge upon a game of dice.

---

1 *Hours in a Library*, 1892, cited from John Beer, *Coleridge's Poetic Intelligence* (Macmillan, 1977), 147.

One can, of course, rationalise some of these problems: it is right and fitting within a theological perspective that the Sun should express the power and vengeance of God, as well as his love (neither Calvin nor Edwards would have been troubled by this view); the crew die not merely for being in the wrong place at the wrong time, but because they ratify a crime against the natural order, and fail to revere a manifestation of Christ's presence. In both texts the crew have surrendered their freedom: and whether judged by God-centred standards, or by human-centred ones, by the ethics of Calvinism or those of Nietzsche and Carlyle, have willingly become non-entities.

The late H. W. Piper argued that among the doctrines that Coleridge set out to defend in *Aids to Reflection* (1826) are

> Arbitrary Election and Reprobation, the Sentence to everlasting Torment by an eternal and necessitating Decree; vicarious Atonement, and the necessity of the Abasement, Agony and ignominious Death of a most Holy and meritorious Person, to appease the wrath of God.

Piper comments, 'a modern reader might assume that this passage was ironical, but it was not.'[1] This view of Coleridge's theology is certainly open to question. Yet Coleridge is doing no more than summarising quite central claims of Christianity, all of which he undertakes to defend, in an adjacent passage of *Aids*, and he seems to have come fully to terms, by 1826, with what he permits himself to question symbolically in 1798. If so, Melville might well have sympathised. He was haunted—as Emerson was not—by a sense of evil as a real principle which has to be combatted. And he admired Hawthorne precisely for

> this great power of blackness in him [which] derives its force from its appeals to that Calvinistic sense of Innate Depravity and

---

1 Piper, *The Singing of Mount Abora*, 24. Other Coleridgeans dispute this reading, yet Coleridge does undertake, in the same passage, to explain why all Christian doctrine, including that which appears to offend morality, and including all thirty-nine articles of faith, is in fact both true and necessary. He defends 'election', specifically, in terms which suggest that the only reservation he makes concerns 'arbitrary'.

Original Sin, from whose visitations, in some shape or other, no deeply thinking mind is always and wholly free... [1]

But while finding Emerson's Transcendentalism intellectually inadequate, he also found Calvinism (as did his great contemporary, George Eliot) morally repugnant.[2]

Early in *Moby-Dick* Melville offers us a sermon on Jonah by Father Mapple, a sermon in which 'appeasement of the wrath of God' is recommended (chapter 9, 'The Sermon'). The force of Father Mapple's sermon is, however, to establish Ahab's credentials as one who—for all his faults, humanly considered—has at least the courage to defy even unto death a God who is in his eyes a God of brute power and vengeance. Father Mapple's God, Robert Zoellner points out,[3] uses Jonah's shipmates as a means to an end, as the God of *The Ancient Mariner* does, and indeed as Ahab himself does when he treats his crew as his limbs and threatens on the third day of the chase: 'the first thing that but offers to jump from this boat, that thing I harpoon. Ye are not other men, but my arms and my legs; and so obey me' (679). Ahab—one may feel—gets the God he deserves. In Coleridgean phrase, *quantum sumus, scimus*: hence Ahab's projection onto the whale of all that he is in himself.

Ahab is first presented to us by Captain Peleg in terms suggesting a legendary transhistorical being, like the Ancient Mariner another avatar of the Wandering Jew, or perhaps some figure of pride reserved for a final punishment after many metamorphoses:

> 'He's a grand, ungodly, god-like man, Captain Ahab .... been used to deeper wonders than the waves; fixed his fiery lance in mightier, stranger foes than whales ... he's Ahab, boy: and Ahab of old, thou knowest, was a crowned king!' (176).

---

1 'Hawthorne and his Mosses', cited from *Melville: the Critical Heritage*, ed. Watson G Branch (Routledge & Kegan Paul, London and Boston, 1974), 240.

2 As Matthiessen points out, Melville seems to have seen the Puritanic sense of evil in terms of the Manichean heresy and by making Fedallah (Ahab's harpoonist) a Parsee—a fire-worshipping follower of Zoroaster—he admits the terms of this myth into the novel. *American Renaissance*, 439.

3 Robert Zoellner, *The Salt-Sea Mastodon: a Reading of Moby-Dick* (University of California Press, 1973), 59–60.

Specifically, the biblical Ahab was a king punished by God for idolatry and other transgressions. To call Ahab 'an ungodly godlike man' appears to signify that to be godlike is to behave in ungodly fashion. He is at his most 'godlike' in his indifference to the human lot, and (as many have noted) his incapacity for dialogue. His 'ungodliness' takes the form of service to God's adversary. Father Mapple, as 'pilot of [this] living God', preaches a god who is to be obeyed without question, offering as a model of human conduct—David Morse has argued—the 'cowardly and skulking Jonah', who in returning to God's service is 'a rebel in bad faith'.[1]

Ahab combines in his complex revolt a hostility to the God of Calvin, to the stoicism of Spinoza, and of course to the sentimental optimism of Emerson—all of which positions are represented in the text. When he takes on Moby-Dick he consciously blasphemes the Gods of Calvin and of Spinoza: when he tempers his harpoon in savage blood he cries out in what Melville called the secret moral of the book: 'Ego non baptizo te in nomine patris, sed in nomine diaboli!' (600). Starbuck—most Christian of Ahab's motley crew—sees that he disobeys his God in obeying Ahab: were he a reader of Kierkegaard he would perhaps feel more firmly that a leap of faith would justify the teleological suspension of the ethical. Yet the text leaves it open, to the end, whether Ahab may not be right—may not be heroic—in defying the ungodly God of the book of Jonah. It addresses, *inter alia*, both the viability of Christianity and the riddlesome nature of ethics. In *Pierre*, Melville addresses this last problem more directly:

> 'What man who carries a heavenly soul in him, has not groaned to perceive, that unless he committed a sort of suicide as to the practical things of this world, he never can hope to regulate his earthly conduct by that same heavenly soul? And yet by an infallible instinct he knows that that monitor can not be wrong in itself.'[2]

---

1 David Morse, *American Romanticism* (Macmillan, 1987), 2: 47.

2 *Pierre, or The Ambiguities*, edited by Harrison Hayford, Hershel Parker and G Thomas Tanselle (*Writings*, 1971), 7: 213. In this novel Melville creates a minor neo-Platonist, Plotinus Plinlimmon, whose philosophy is based upon a theory that

Starbuck experiences precisely this dilemma, in finding himself unable to decide whether to mutiny. *Pierre* suggests that a life of 'virtuous expediency' is the 'highest desirable or attainable earthly excellence for the mass of men' (214). It follows that the Christian injunction 'be thou therefore perfect as thy father in heaven is also perfect' is mischievous.

So Father Mapple's Sermon on Jonah is balanced (and in a sense dialogically glossed) by Fleece's sermon to the sharks (the cook has been asked to silence the sharks so that the noise of their eating a captive whale does not disturb Mr Stubb, the second mate while he sits at supper):

> 'Dough you is all sharks, and by natur wery woracious, yet I zay to you, fellow-critturs, dat dat woraciousness -'top dat dam slappin' ob de tail! How you tink to hear, 'spose you keep up such a dam slappin' and bitin' dare?... Your woraciousness, fellow critturs, I don't blame ye so much for; dat is natur, and can't be helped; but to gobern dat wicked natur, dat is de pint. You is sharks, sartin; but if you gobern de shark in you, why den you be angel; for all angel is noting more dan de shark well goberned'. (401)

When Fleece concludes that the sharks should share and share alike, Stubbs comments 'Well done, old Fleece, that's Christianity': and Melville's remorseless probing of pietism of all kinds receives a further twist, when Queequeg almost loses his hand to a dead shark—which, according to Ishmael retains a sort of 'Pantheistic vitality after what may be called the individual life had departed', i.e. continues to twitch with particles of God. Queequeg comments: 'Queequeg no care what god made him shark ... wedder Fejee god or Nantucket god; but de god wat made shark must be one dam Ingin' (409).

Ahab's employers are Quakers, whose religion places a peculiar emphasis upon non-violence. They are also Nantucket whalers drawing a living from the most violent of predatory enterprises,

---

heavenly wisdom and earthly wisdom can be compared to two varieties of time—chronometrical time (or Greenwich time) and horological time (or local time). Both kinds of time are true, it is not that one is right and the other wrong, but it is folly to attempt to live by chronometrical time if one is not in Greenwich.

The Whale and the Albatross 261

and rewarding most highly—Robert Zoellner points out—the most shark-like of men. 'No harpooner is worth a straw who isn't pretty sharkish' says Peleg in chapter 18 (187). The Ancient Mariner does perpetual penance—we might say—for his unconscious sharkishness, and for a crime forbidden by no known statute or commandment. In a religious frame, the demand that the Mariner transcend his sharkishness is another instance of what Blake saw as human nature's inability to keep Urizen's iron (and unpublished) laws one minute. Politically, we might see Melville in transcendentalist America questioning the perfectibility of man—the attainability of the city on the hill—as Wordsworth and Coleridge and their whole generation were still questioning whether there was a radical imperfectibility in man, perhaps even some ingrained abhorrence of perfection, as Russian romanticism—in the figure of Dostoevsky's underground man—would later opine.[1]

The reader of *The Ancient Mariner* may feel an initial confidence (having closed the book) that the poem has a lucid and compound moral. It projects a sense of prayerfulness contiguous with 'The Eolian Harp' and 'Christabel', and a sense of nature parallel to 'This Lime-Tree Bower' ('no spot is barren be but nature there') and 'Frost at Midnight' (nature perceived as 'that eternal Language which thy God utters').[2] Yet one comes to suspect that the structure of the world in *The Ancient Mariner* belies such simplicity. If one then consults the neo-Platonic scholar's marginal gloss upon the medieval text one may experience the same multiple reaction: an initial sense that all is explained, followed by a growing doubt about the meaning of this anxiety-laden hermeneutic. It is a revisionary stroke of genius on Coleridge's part to propel his poetic text back into antiquity by the device of giving it a Renaissance commentary—thus creating a dialogic method which is paralleled by Melville in providing such

---

[1] While Melville develops the point much more fully of course, John Beer sees *The Ancient Mariner* in these terms, in *Coleridge's Poetic Intelligence*, p. 150.

[2] In *Pierre*, Melville seems to have parodied Coleridge's 'Frost at Midnight' directly: 'Say what some poets will, Nature is not so much her own ever-sweet interpreter, as the mere supplier of that cunning alphabet, whereby selecting and combining as he pleases, each man reads his own peculiar lesson according to his own peculiar mind and mood', 342.

a multiplicity of styles that the authority of all styles, and the very notion of authoritative discourse, is brought into question.

In Coleridge's text one finds oneself situated upon a border between Christian and quasi-pagan world views where Coleridge could indulge his imagination and speculative intelligence regarding a pantheistic 'one life' free of 'beloved Sarah's' censorious dispraise.

> And what if all of animated nature
> Be but organic harps diversely fram'd
> That tremble into thought as o'er them sweeps
> Plastic and vast, one intellectual breeze,
> At once the soul of each and God of all?
> ('The Eolian Harp', 44–48)

This memorable speculative flight seems to express, by the way, the yearnings not only of Coleridge but also of one Ishmael, for if Spinoza haunts Coleridge's early poetry: he permeates *Moby-Dick*. When, for instance, Starbuck considers Ahab guilty of blasphemy for his quest—

> 'Vengeance on a dumb brute!' cried Starbuck, 'that simply smote thee from blindest instinct! Madness. To be enraged with a dumb thing, Captain Ahab, seems blasphemous' (262)

—the charge provokes Ahab into uttering his creed:

> 'All visible objects, man, are but as pasteboard masks. But in each event – in the living act, the undoubted deed – there, some unknown but still reasoning thing puts forth the mouldings of its features from behind the unreasoning mask.... Sometimes I think there's naught beyond. But 'tis enough. He tasks me; he heaps me; I see in him outrageous strength, with an inscrutable malice sinewing it. That inscrutable thing is chiefly what I hate; and be the white whale agent, or be the white whale principal, I will wreak that hate upon him. Talk not to me of blasphemy, man; I'd strike the sun if it insulted me. (262)

Melville and Poe shared this thought, that 'sometimes I think there's naught beyond': the death-oriented Poe gladly making a nirvana out of nothingness—Melville more troubled by the thought. But Ahab's logic is clear: something in the universe is responsible for laming him, and if he can strike only the agent, he will strike the agent, in an act of vengeance symbolising metaphysical revolt. We are aware that Ahab loads Moby-Dick with symbolic weight, and so is Ahab. And Ishmael—when he finds himself enrolled in Ahab's vengeful quest—recognises in fear and trembling the pathological state of Ahab's symbol-making power.

> The White Whale swam before him as the monomaniac incarnation of all those malicious agencies which some deep men feel eating in them.... All that most maddens and torments; all that stirs up the lees of things; ... all that cracks the sinews and cakes the brain; all the subtle demonisms of life and thought; all evil, to Crazy Ahab, were visibly personified, and made practically assailable in Moby-Dick. He piled upon the whale's white hump the sum of all the general rage and hate felt by his whole race from Adam down; and then, as if his chest had been a mortar, he burst his hot heart's shell upon it. (283)

This conspicuous elaboration of motive supplies—to excess—the most striking absence in Coleridge's text: why does the Mariner kill the Albatross? Except that where the mariner appears to exhibit what Coleridge later called 'want of feeling, from want of thinking', Ahab thinks too much but with the wrong dimension of his mind.[1] Observing him, Ishmael rapidly grasps how each of us creates our own world, and the values—or, more mythopoeically, the deities—we find in it. Ahab may act compulsively but unlike the Mariner he needs no philosophic commentator. He gives every sign of being aware, as the Mariner is not, of the *Pantheismusstreit*, being at one and the same time a believer in and a rebel against the God-concept one finds in Spinoza.

Our guide on this matter is the intellectually elusive Ishmael, and while he utters the deeply disturbing meditation on the whiteness of

---

1 Several critics, including Matthiessen and Marovitz (cited below), have related the characterisation of Ahab to Coleridge's theory that the tragic character (Hamlet, especially) suffers from 'morbid excess' of one faculty—in this case, of course, the 'false secondary power' of understanding.

the whale, and the ostensibly ironic masthead scene, it is his voice, too, which gives us—and leaves us with—the novel's constructively ambivalent response to the idea of a divine spirit in nature. Like Wordsworth (who in in his most philosophical passages never lyeth because he nothing affirmeth), Ishmael is constantly asking himself whether he sees feeling in all things, or attaches to them some feeling of his own. Confessing himself a sorry lookout, with the problem of the world within him, Ishmael cautions the ship owners of Nantucket against enlisting any poetical young Platonist prone to 'an opium-like listlessness of vacant, unconscious reverie', for

> every dimly-discovered, uprising fin of some undiscernible form, seems to him the embodiment of those elusive thoughts that only people the soul by continually flitting through it.

In mesmeric tones he continues:

> There is no life in thee now, except that rocking life imparted by a gently rolling ship; by her, borrowed from the sea; by the sea, from the inscrutable tides of God. But while this sleep, this dream is on ye, move your foot or your hand an inch; ... and your identity comes back in horror. Over Descartian vortices you hover. And perhaps, at mid-day, in the fairest weather, with one half-throttled shriek you drop through that transparent air into the summer sea, no more to rise for ever. Heed it well, ye Pantheists! (257)

One recognises this sleep of the senses as both Coleridgean (dim-glimmering natural images appearing to express some inner truth of one's own nature)[1] and Wordsworthian (the hypothesized Platonist 'laid asleep in body and become a living soul'). The tone is ambivalent: that the masthead is no place to indulge such trances does not gainsay the 'inscrutable tides of God'. Nor does the pronoun 'you' disguise the fact that these are Ishmael's experiences, or that these are vicariously present on Melville's behalf. Sceptical though

---

[1] *The Notebooks of Samuel Taylor Coleridge*, edited by Kathleen Coburn et al. (Princeton University Press: New York, Princeton and London, 1957–2002), II 2546.

Melville was, he felt the pull of what in a letter to Hawthorne he called 'this "all" feeling'.

> You must often have felt it, lying on the grass on a warm summer's day. Your legs seem to end out shoots into the earth. Your hair feels like leaves on your head. That is the all feeling. But what plays the mischief with the truth is that men will insist upon the universal application of a temporary feeling or opinion.[1]

Ishmael, too, experiences contrary feelings or opinions.

In 'The Whiteness of the Whale', Ishmael pointedly recalls the whiteness of the albatross:

> Bethink thee of the albatross: whence come those clouds of spiritual wonderment and pale dread, in which that white phantom sails in all imaginations? Not Coleridge first threw that spell; but God's unflattering laureate, Nature.

And in his note on his own first sighting an albatross, treacherously snared by hook and line, Ishmael goes on:

> I remember the first Albatross I ever saw.... a regal, feathery thing of unspotted whiteness, and with a hooked, Roman bill sublime. ... Through its inexpressible strange eyes, methought I peeped to secrets which took hold of God. ...I cannot tell, can only hint, the things that darted through me then. (289–90)

Thinking the thoughts that the Ancient Mariner failed to think, Ishmael proceeds to make this the text's most substantive literary allusion, and its best joke at Coleridge's expense:

> by no possibility could Coleridge's wild Rhyme have had aught to do with those mystical impressions which were mine, when I saw that bird upon our deck. For neither had I then read the Rhyme, nor knew the bird to be an Albatross. Yet in saying this I do but indirectly burnish a little brighter the noble merit of the poem and the poet (290).

Melville as pasticheur must have noted with some glee that remarkable

---

1 *Correspondence*, 194 (June 1851).

sentence in the 9th chapter of *Biographia*: 'all the main and fundamental ideas [of Schelling's system of transcendental idealism] were born and matured in my mind before I had ever seen a single page of the German philosopher', a sentence which appropriates the leading ideas of one who is, after all, 'a great and original genius'.[1]

Through Ishmael's fantastical meditation on 'The Whiteness of the Whale' Melville turns to a Poe-like horror the very quality of the Albatross that Coleridge links to benign images of imagination—mist and moonlight and snow. Ishmael rehearses all the traditional Western associations of whiteness with the divine and the beautiful, and yet affirms that 'for all these accumulated associations, with whatever is sweet and honourable and sublime, there yet lurks an elusive something in the innermost idea of this hue, which strikes more of panic to the soul than that redness which affrights in blood'. Why, he asks, is white 'the intensifying agent in things the most appalling to mankind?'

> Is it that by its indefiniteness it shadows forth the heartless voids and immensities of the universe, and thus stabs us from behind with the thought of annihilation...? Or is it, that as in essence whiteness is not so much a color as the visible absence of colour, and at the same time the concrete of all colours; ... a colorless, all-color of atheism from which we shrink?

'Pondering all this', Ishmael concludes, 'the palsied universe lies before us a leper' (296).

Bearing in mind the communicative strategies of Melville's text it would be facile to take any moment in the text—this one included—as definitive, either for Ishmael or for Melville. Certainly it does invoke the metaphysical shudder at the notion of something all-pervasive and all-reductive, and it dramatises a revulsion from the Transcendentalist faith in the beneficence of the natural, and in the translucence of symbol, those two most fragile of Romantic blossoms. 'In all things', Ishmael seems to be saying, in answer to Wordsworth, 'I saw one life and felt that it was dread'.[2] Yet this pivotal chapter is among the

---

1 *Biographia Literaria*, I, 161-2.
2 I allude to Wordsworth's conclusion to Book 2 of *The Prelude*: 'In all things/

most elusive in the text. It can be read quite contrarily. The footnote on the Albatross, especially as it is not merely the longest such note in the novel, but one in which the experiential quality of Ishmael's entry on the albatross is contrasted immediately to the merely scholarly disputatiousness of those on the polar bear and the white shark, give the albatross a prominence it would not otherwise have, rather as Coleridge's own fiction of a 'person from Porlock' draws attention to a narrative structure which (as David Perkins has argued) 'Kubla Khan' would not otherwise possess.[1] In the brief *textual* reference to the albatross, and the 'clouds of spiritual wonderment and pale dread' in which it sails, we are told that this quality inheres in its nature, not in art: the spell is cast not by Coleridge but by 'God's great, *unflattering* laureate, Nature' (my italics). 'Pale dread', however functions partly as a reminder that the sanctified poet-figure in 'Kubla' inspires 'holy dread', and thus creates a rhetorical bridge from terror to awe.[2]

Objectively, 'The Whiteness of the Whale' offers a balanced quaternity of polar bear, white shark (terror), albatross and white steed (awe): subjectively, of course, the Albatross and the White Steed of the Prairies, with their parallel auras (one is 'imperial and archangelical', the other 'regal' and 'supernatural'), run away with the chapter. Yes, Ishmael, in the final paragraph, comes close to endorsing Ahab's 'pasteboard mask' model of creation. But numerous learned commentaries on that final paragraph of the chapter, with its learned mumbo-jumbo of colourless light 'operating without medium' upon colourless matter, including a highly subtle one by Leon Chai, may have missed Ishmael's point. The infidel and atheist for whom 'the

---

I saw one life and felt that it was joy'.

1 'The Imaginative Vision of Kubla Khan: On Coleridge's Introductory Note', in *Coleridge, Keats and the Imagination*, ed. Robert J Barth, S,J. and John L Mahoney (Columbia & London: University of Missouri Press, 1990).

2 The bridge is reinforced by the adjacent terms 'laureate' and 'clouds of spiritual wonderment', which jointly intimate 'Intimations', and the previous paragraph's reference to an 'elusive something in the innermost idea' of whiteness, which 'strikes panic to the soul' and reminds one at the same time, negatively, of numerous Wordsworthian 'somethings', ranging from the 'most strange something' seen in her child by the 'Forsaken Indian Mother', to the more sublime 'something far more deeply interfused' which 'rolls through all things' in the 'Poem upon the Wye'.

palsied universe lies before us like a leper', for whom even the hues of butterflies and maiden's cheeks are 'but subtle deceits', is compared explicitly to one who wilfully refuses optical protection from the glaring snows of Lapland and then confuses his blindness with universal darkness. The question 'Wonder ye then at the fiery hunt?' points in two directions at once: either the universe is palsied, or Ahab is morally snow-blind.

Why is it, those with a passing acquaintance with Spinoza may wonder, that a man who writes constantly about God, and has the noblest possible ideals of human conduct, should be regarded as the most subtle of inducers to atheism? Spinoza defines God as 'a being absolutely infinite—that is, a substance consisting in infinite attributes, of which each expresses eternal and infinite essentiality'.[1] But such a definition, as Thomas McFarland points out in his masterly *Coleridge and the Pantheist Tradition*, 'merely hypothesises a God' and tells us no more than that he is 'an empty pigeon-hole ... labelled Deus, ... the symbolic repository for the ultimate sum total of answers to all extensions of questions arising from the existence of things'. So,

> in this development of a 'particular thing' into the 'sum total' of all things, into the 'extended thing' that Spinoza calls 'God, or Nature' (*'Deus, sive Natura'*), the unemphasised original element – the I, the self, the wonderer – is ... ontologically demolished.[2]

Or, in Melville's similar conclusion the wonderer plunges from the masthead into nonentity. McFarland continues:

> As flies to wanton boys, as Caliban to Setebos, are men to the Spinozistic God-Nature, and all their cherished hopes of personal immortality, of the uniqueness and indestructibility of the individual soul—all the guarantees of the Christian faith—are in this sombre apprehension ... denied to them.[3]

---

[1] Spinoza, *Ethics* (Bohn's Edition) 1, Def 6.
[2] Thomas McFarland, *Coleridge and the Pantheist Tradition* (Oxford: Clarendon Press, 1969), 67
[3] *Coleridge and the Pantheist Tradition*, p. 69.

This splendid formulation underlines very well why Coleridge could feel reverence for the honesty of Spinoza, as well as terror at his conclusions. It might well stand, also, as one of the possible—indeed foregrounded—readings of the universe that are on offer in *Moby-Dick*.

Any theory which successfully demonstrates the idea of a correspondence between the divine power and human nature risks nullifying the freedom or the moral responsibility of the individual human being. The precise problem which Melville had with Spinoza (as did Coleridge and Carlyle) was the equanimity with which Spinoza accepts the logic of his system when he declares, of human freedom,

> Men are mistaken in thinking themselves free; their opinion is made up of consciousness of their own actions, and ignorance of the causes by which they are conditioned. Their idea of freedom, therefore, is simply their ignorance of any cause for their actions.[1]

Coleridge experienced this problem—of the conflict between pantheism and freedom—in the 1790s and Melville was clearly wracked by it in the 1850s. This is Coleridge wrestling with it in *Biographia Literaria*, which Melville read in 1848:

> The idea of the Supreme Being appeared to me as necessarily implied in all particular modes of being as the idea of infinite space in all the geometrical figures by which space is limited....
>
> For a very long time, indeed, I could not reconcile personality with infinity; and my head was with Spinoza, though my whole heart remained with Paul and John.[2]

Not only is this the pithiest possible summary of the issue ('I could not reconcile personality with infinity') but it is also very close to what Melville *may* mean when he writes to Hawthorne in April 1851 in this much discussed (and textually doubtful) passage:

> We incline to think that God cannot explain His own secrets....
> We mortals astonish Him as much as He us. But it is this *Being* of

---
1 *Ethics*, II, 35 Scholium.
2 *Biographia Literaria*, 1, 200–1.

the matter; there lies the knot with which we choke ourselves. As soon as you say, *Me*, a *God*, a *Nature*, so soon you jump off from your stool and hang from the beam. Yes, that word is the hangman. Take God out of the dictionary and you would have Him in the street. (*Correspondence*, 186)

Leon Chai takes this cryptic passage to mean that 'there is an element common to all things, including the individual self, God, and Nature. To speak of any one thing specifically is to isolate but one manifestation of the omnipresent element, which itself is God'.[1] However, as Chai concedes, the phrase 'the Being of the matter' (if accurately transcribed) makes interpretation hazardous, as does its context. The passage is preceded by the sceptical remark: 'And perhaps after all, there is no secret. We incline to think that the Problem of the Universe is like the Freemason's mighty secret, so terrible to all children. It turns out, at last, to consist in a triangle, a mallet, and an apron,—nothing more!' And it is followed by a further tribute to Hawthorne: 'There is the grand truth about Nathaniel Hawthorne. He says NO! in thunder; but the Devil himself cannot make him say yes. For all men who say yes, lie; and men who say no,—why they ... cross the frontiers into Eternity with nothing but a carpet-bag—that is to say the Ego' (*Correspondence*, 186.).

There is much in Melville's correspondence to make him an Ahab, yet in the heady moments of his correspondence with Hawthorne, Melville, while worried by the implications of Pantheism, could demonstrate its appeal.[2] In November 1851, after Hawthorne has

---

[1] Leon Chai, *Romantic Foundations*, 296. The passage is also discussed by Sanford E Marovitz, in 'Melville's Problematic "Being"', *ESQ*, 28:1, 1982, pp. 11–23. Marovitz considers Melville's use of the term 'Being' in the context of transcendent and immanent concepts of God, which he traces through Plato, Socrates, Proclus, Plotinus, Spinoza, Coleridge, Schelling and Carlyle.

[2] In a brilliant summation of Melville's ambivalence, Matthiessen points out that 'Ahab's savagery, not unlike that of a Hebrew prophet, has rejected the warmly material pantheism of the Greeks; but Melville's breadth has effected, not a fusion, but a unique counterpoint of both. The reason why the values of both Pan and Jehovah were not merely words to him, as they are to most men, is that he had relived them for himself in his own body and mind, and especially in his imagination'. *American Renaissance*, 466.

commented enthusiastically on *Moby-Dick*, Melville records his sense of existing pantheistically with Hawthorne and God in a single consciousness:

> I feel that the Godhead is broken up like the bread at the Supper, and that we are the pieces. Hence this infinite fraternity of feeling. (*Corespondence*, 212)

Here Melville seems to identify with Ishmael in his more expansive moments, and such identification might seem to endorse the moral of *The Ancient Mariner*, and suggest that the Whale is as unambiguous a symbol as the Albatross.

Ahab darkly parodies his author's ambivalence. Fiction's most redoubtable anti-Spinozist, in his assaults upon the whale, he clearly experiences anguish at feeling that Spinoza might just be right. The text foregrounds repeatedly the Shelleyan question whether Ahab is the master of his own destiny or the slave of some unperceived chain of Necessity going back to the beginning of time. Each move in the novel shows him to be a driven being, unable to evade the final encounter, moving inexorably closer to the whale even when he has renounced the instruments of navigation, and perhaps perceiving that that encounter is written in the woof of things. Nearing the close he cries:

> 'Is Ahab, Ahab? Is it I, God, or who, that lifts this arm? ... if the great sun move not of himself; but is as an errand boy in heaven ... how then can this one small heart beat; this one small brain think thoughts; unless God does that beating, does that thinking, does that living, and not I.' (653)

And on the second day of the chase, as Starbuck almost moves him to relent, he declares:

> 'Ahab is ever Ahab, man. This whole act's immutably decreed. 'Twas rehearsed by thee and me a billion years before this ocean rolled. Fool! I am the Fates' lieutenant; I act under orders. Look thou, underling! that thou obeyest mine.' (672)

Ahab moves, it seems, to a realisation that his defiance is obedience: and in a paradoxical move worthy of Kierkegaard (or Sartre) he chooses to be what he is, to do what he must, to work out his destiny—while clearly his act of defiance can have only one meaning, which is to prove (to Ishmael as the sole beneficiary of Ahab's learning experience) that what he does is both foolish and blasphemous. There is a further implication, again worthy of Carlyle or Nietzsche, that the crew of the *Pequod* must die because they are incapable of freedom: like some of Zarathustra's listeners, incapable of furnishing themselves with their own good and evil, they would throw off their only worth in throwing off their bondage.[1] As Ishmael perceives, they were enslaved to the hunt. 'They were one man not thirty ... this man's valor, that man's fear; guilt and guiltiness, all varieties were melded into oneness, and were all directed to that fatal goal which Ahab their one lord and keel did point to' (666). They become, as it were, a microcosm of a Spinozistic universe.

Tony Tanner is surely right to suggest that Moby-Dick's white forehead is not a sign to be deciphered, but a blank space which we inscribe. Nevertheless in this text Ishmael and Ahab seem to concur in contrary ways with Coleridge, in believing that a symbol partakes of the reality which it renders intelligible.[2] For Ahab the whale is either

---

1 *Thus Spoke Zarathustra* (Penguin Books, 1961), 89.

2 Tony Tanner, *Scenes of Nature, Signs of Men*, 16. Tanner's formulation of Melville's general position regarding symbolism is perhaps the best. Noting that puritan culture was a condition of 'rampant hermeneutical activity', a continuous excess of significance and signification, he sees in Hawthorne and Melville an anxious state of mind which can see signifiers everywhere 'without an assured belief in the fixed and anchoring transcendent signified' (p. 20). Leon Chai, however, argues that Melville is specifically concerned to contest Romantic symbolism. Commenting on Ishmael's observation that light 'if operating without medium upon matter, would touch all objects, even tulips and roses, with its own blank tinge' (296) Chai concludes, 'symbolism is produced by a medium that creates the conditions of perception: the human mind. Thus the symbol does not actually partake of the divine, and could not reveal it....' (Chai, 86). For all its sophistication, Chai's argument may come down to this: Ahab does not see divinity in the whale, therefore the Romantic theory of symbolism is annulled. The argument is faulty in two respects. Ahab does see divinity in the whale ('be the whale agent or principle' etc.), and no Romantic ever claimed that a symbol is only a symbol when every observer sees the same signified. Coleridge's claim that 'the symbol always partakes of the Reality which it renders intelligible' does of course invite the sceptical

agent or principal: Ahab's 'special lunacy' (Ishmael's phrase) makes the whale the symbol of divine malignancy, almost consubstantial with what it symbolises, and that is why, as a reversed Manichean, he makes war upon the whale. Or we might say in Wordsworthian terms that the world as seen by Ahab in his own dark light is invested with a kind of visionary dreariness which he does not know to be visionary; just as the partially redemptive visionary gleam with which the Ancient Mariner invests the creatures of the sea is at the time unconsciously bestowed by him, or just as Wordsworth's ancient mariner—the narrator of 'The Thorn'—is victim of an intentionality which he unconsciously bestows. Wordsworth's conspiratorial mosses in the opening stanzas of 'The Thorn' are a micro-botanical version of Ahab's Whale's 'unexampled malignancy', and in Melville's text we witness the temporary contamination of Ishmael's mind as the surviving guest at Ahab's wedding with death.

For Ishmael, however, on the first day of the chase, Moby-Dick is invested with 'a gentle joyousness—a mighty mildness of repose', and he calls him simply 'the grand god' (656–7). It is possible, after all, for a follower of Carlyle (which Ishmael appears to be, from his frequent allusions to him) to reconcile a philosophy of liberty with a belief in revelation. As Carlyle—or rather Professor Teufelsdrockh—puts it (and every other paragraph in *Sartor Resartus* is germane to *Moby-Dick*):

> Rightly viewed no meanest object is insignificant; all objects are as windows, through which the philosophic eye looks into Infinitude itself.... All visible things are emblems; what thou seest is not there on its own account; strictly taken, is not there at all: Matter exists only spiritually, to represent some Idea, and body it forth.[1]

---

interrogation which Melville's text provides.

1 *Sartor Resartus* (Oxford, 1987), p. 56. *Sartor* is acknowledged, of course in numerous passages of *Moby-Dick*, and not merely in such chapter headings as 'The Cassock' and 'The Hat'. Melville's passage, from baptismal sperm-squeezing to the sacrilegious investiture of 'the mincer' in 'The Cassock', inverts Carlyle's transition on the first page of 'Church Clothes' from the symbolism of 'Cassocks and Surplices' to mutual love as the foundation of social being. In the larger Romantic progression from 'A Squeeze of the Hand' through 'The Grand Armada' to 'The

Carlyle's 'window' is the positive view of Ahab's negative: the 'paste-board mask'.

If English Romantic poetry has its set pieces of pantheistic vitality, or celebrations of 'the one life', Melville's great response is the chapter of *Moby-Dick* called 'The Grand Armada', in which Ahab, pursued by pirates, himself pursues an immense herd of whales. Ishmael's boat is dragged by a harpooned whale into 'the innermost heart of the shoal' where the cows and calves are protected by revolving outer circles of whales. For a while they are imprisoned in the whale nursery, permitted to gaze into the tranquil depths of the sea they have turned to a slaughterhouse:

> Here the storms in the roaring glens between the outermost whales, were heard but not felt. ... we were now in that enchanted calm which they say lurks at the heart of every commotion. But far beneath this wondrous world upon the surface, another and still stranger world met our eyes as we gazed over the side.

Here Ishmael sees infant whales trailing clouds of glory, leading a double life, feeding at their mother's breasts, while 'still spiritually feasting upon some unearthly reminiscence':

> And thus, ... did these inscrutable creatures at the centre freely and fearlessly indulge in all peaceful concernments; yea, serenely revelled in dalliance and delight. But even so, amid the tornadoed Atlantic of my being, do I myself still for ever centrally disport in mute calm; and while ponderous planets of unwaning woe revolve round me, deep down and deep inland there I still bathe me in eternal mildness of joy. (498)

Like the tornadoed Wordsworth, however, or the tornadoed Teufelsdrockh, Ishmael is unable to land.[1] The chapter ends with a

---

Symphony', Carlyle's *Sartor* is again the intermediary text. And when Ishmael says (at the end of 'The Funeral') that 'far deeper men than Doctor Johnson' believe in ghosts he is alluding to *Sartor*'s climactic celebration of the spirit horde of humanity, which climax is itself keyed to Dr. Johnson and his Cock Lane ghost.

1 The inland sea and tornado metaphors in this wonderful passage again reflect Wordsworth as transfigured by Carlyle. They combine a metaphor from Carlyle's chapter on 'Pure Reason' concerning the 'high Platonic mysticism of our author

description of the wasteful carnage caused by the crew of the *Pequod*.

Certainly the passage is broadly redolent of the Eolian Harp's 'one life' lines, as Chai has suggested, and indeed even more so of 'The Dungeon' in which Coleridge imagines the tranquillising effects of nature, caressing the prisoner 'Till he relent and can no more endure / To be a jarring and a dissonant thing / Amid this general dance and minstrelsy'. But there is surely a more general complex of underlying text for the passage. The inland peace of 'The Poem upon the Wye', the doctrines of pre-existence dallied with in the Intimations Ode, and most deeply of all the words of *The Excursion* are conjured by Melville's orchestration of primary precursor texts. More familiar to Melville than to most moderns would be this passage from *The Excursion*, Book 4, about a child listening to a shell, whose interior murmurings express 'Mysterious union with its native sea':

> Even such a shell the universe itself
> Is to the ear of faith; and there are times,
> I doubt not, when to you it doth impart
> Authentic tidings of invisible things;
> Of ebb and flow, and ever-during power;
> And central peace, subsisting at the heart
> Of endless agitation (*The Excursion*, 4: 1140–47)

One might make a case on the rhythms alone for this text having been central to Melville's conception, even without the broader context in Book 4 which constitutes the prime Romantic attack upon the analytical frame of mind which views all objects 'in disconnexion dead and spiritless' and in which we 'pore and dwindle as we pore', waging thus 'An impious warfare with the life of our own souls' (960–68). Of this pathologically limited condition Flask, the sadistic third mate of the *Pequod*, is the embodiment: a man 'so utterly lost ... to all sense of reverence for the many marvels of their majestic bulk and mystic ways; ... that in his poor opinion, the wondrous whale

---

[Teufelsdröckh], which is perhaps the fundamental element of his nature', in which 'we seem to look into a whole inward Sea of Light and Love' ('Pure Reason', *Sartor* 52) with another from 'The Everlasting No' picturing him quite shut out from hope, looking into 'a dim copper firmament, pregnant with earthquake and tornado' (123).

was but a species of magnified mouse' (214). The *Excursion* passage concludes that:

> The estate of man would be indeed forlorn
> If false conclusions of the reasoning power
> Made the eye blind, and closed the passages
> Through which the ear converses with the heart.

'And of all these things', we might say with Ishmael, 'the Albino whale was the symbol'.

Ishmael's textual strategy demonstrates the futility of every kind of mensurative, analytical activity if one's object is to 'own' the whale—a paradoxical expression suggesting the need to acknowledge its majesty freely in order to take full possession of it conceptually and phenomenologically. *Moby-Dick* is structured to counterpoise every form of ineffectual analysis and rhetoric with scenes of instruction which take place at the level of primary or indeed protoconsciousness. The fact that the Ishmael who 'writes' *Moby-Dick* is also the one who creates these mind-numbing exercises in analytics may mean either that he is a poor reader of his own text, or that he is a sufficiently conscious ironist to build such counterpointing into his text in recognition both of the Coleridgean hermeneutic maxim—that while the short way may give us the knowledge best, the long way makes us more knowing[1]—and of the Romantic scepticism which in all of the major Romantic poets recognises the necessity and the unsustainability of vision. One may see the Whale as completing a Romantic synthesis, in which the Tyger and the Albatross become one flesh, neither benign, nor malign, but simply there, in a realm beyond the human, his scale and significance exceeding human grasp. But for all this, the whale provides no token of a filial bond between man and his world, no assurance of love as the medium of the 'one life'. Moby-Dick remains a cipher.

In the doubloon chapter (in which officers and harpooners puzzle over the meaning of a doubloon nailed to the mast) all the readings are possible readings of one text: as different myths and value systems are possible readings of one world. Similarly the whale's skele-

---

[1] *Anima Poetae* (London, 1895), 173.

ton is contemplated also as a religious icon, a splendid natural object, a loom for the weaver-god, and a pile of bones. The sea itself is a cetacean bower of bliss; but it is also the place where half-drowned Pip sees 'God's foot upon the treadle of the loom' and passes into an idiocy in which only Ahab can find—Lear-like—instruction and companionship. It can image the calm that Ishmael seeks, or (in 'Brit') display the terrors he wishes to allay: 'Consider once more the universal cannibalism of the sea; all whose creatures prey upon each other, carrying on eternal war since the world began'. And Ishmael's ambivalence seems inspired by this reversibility of things. He can in the chapter on 'The Lee Shore', argue that in landlessness alone resides the highest truth, shoreless, indefinite as God' and—in 'Brit' again—argue that 'as this appalling ocean surrounds the verdant land, so in the soul of man there lies one insular Tahiti, full of peace and joy, but encompassed by all the horrors of the halfknown life. God keep thee! Push not off from that isle, thou canst never return.'

This reversibility, licensing all of the text's major symbols in a double sense, applies most of all to the polarisation of Ahab and the Whale. Are Ahab and the whale antipodes, or are they—as Ishmael comes to suspect—interchangeable? It is Ahab, rather than Moby-Dick, Ishmael finally makes clear, who is blind, vengeful, destructive, with an unfathomable malignancy. Yet he is also heroic, in his sharing in the whale's grandeur. In one of the most striking of the many ways in which Melville uses metaphor and metonymy he writes as follows of a whale: 'So vast is the quantity of blood in him, and so distant and numerous its interior fountains, that he will keep thus bleeding and bleeding for a considerable period; even as in a drought a river will flow, whose source is in the well-springs of far-off and undiscernible hills.' In writing of Ahab on the first day of the chase he says: 'the long tension of Ahab's bodily strength did crack, and helplessly he yielded to his body's doom…. Far inland, nameless wails came from him, as desolate sounds from out ravines.' When Ishmael observes of the whale that 'Out of the bottomless profundities the gigantic tail seems spasmodically snatching at the highest heaven. So in dreams have I seen majestic Satan thrusting forth his tormented colossal claw from the flame Baltic of Hell' the image serves, simultaneously, and more aptly, to image Ahab's own defiance of omnipotence.

Whether Nature is or is not benign need not affect our judgement of Ahab. He may be at war with 'the all-parenting, all-potentiating power of nature', but what enables us to judge Ahab's stance, as Tanner concludes, is his human failure: he represents 'a refusal, a dismissal, a blasphemy, of every belief, aspiration and commitment which nourish the democratic ideal'.[1] His solution to human isolation is to bind the crew to expression of his will, and sacrifice them to his own purposes: he *chooses* what the mariner unwittingly accomplishes. His touchstone is the remarkable Queequeg, whose authenticity as one who 'stands the most upon himself' seems to embody Coleridgean and Carlylean and Emersonian and Nietzschean aspects of heroic existence,[2] but who nonetheless shows Ishmael the possibilities of a loving connectedness and transcendence of self. Ahab—wedded to Thanatos—recognises no bond between men except bondage by his own will. Contrariwise, in 'A Squeeze of the Hand', Ishmael is baptised into 'the very milk and sperm of kindness' (527), a phrase which offers an androgynous as well as communitarian ideal to this masculine and rapacious world. The Romantic theme of universal love has not received a more exemplary or more bodily expression, and the placing of this comradely vision (after the rebirth of Tashtego, and after The Grand Armada, and before the disastrous diversion of all the *Pequod*'s energies into the fatal hunt for the whale) seems curiously to retell a familiar plot: the union of divine and human love, or the love of nature leading to the love of man. Both kinds of love Ahab rejects, thereby turning his back upon both of the Mariner's explicitly enunciated ideals. It is easy to underestimate the significance of Ahab's rejection of the domestic and the social, but in this particular echo the deep ambivalence of Romanticism towards metaphysical adventure—one hears it even in *Childe Harold, Manfred* and *Prometheus Unbound*—comes through most strongly. *The Ancient Mariner* pointedly concludes its dark night of the soul with an apotheosis of the ordinary, in the mariner's

---

1 Tony Tanner, introduction to *Moby-Dick* (OUP, 1988), xx-xxi.
2 Coleridge's *Hints towards the Formation of a More Comprehensive Theory of Life,* ed. Seth B Watson (London, 1848), 86.

yearning to be at one with 'Old men, and babes, and loving friends / And youths and maidens gay'. This note is twice echoed in *Moby-Dick*: first in Ishmael's recognition that man must place his 'conceit of attainable felicity' in the domestic and the ordinary, 'in the wife, the heart, the bed, the table, the saddle, the fireside, the country' ('A Squeeze of the Hand'); and subsequently when Starbuck brings Ahab close to repenting 'the desolation of solitude' and giving ear to 'all natural lovings and longings' ('The Symphony').

The prose poem which opens the 'The Symphony' by composing an androgynous harmony of sky and sea leads into a scene in which the sentimentally inclined reader is offered the momentary illusion that the snow-blind Ahab will learn to see things in their 'true' colours and will abandon his quest. The 'step-mother' world throws her affectionate arms around his neck, yearning 'to save and to bless': momentarily, as that 'step-mother' makes clear, we are back with the Wordsworthian-Teufelsdröckhian world-view of 'The Grand Armada'.[1] That no conversion of Ahab's purposes will be effected (we have waited a hundred and thirty chapters for the chase, after all, and are fully entitled to one) is amply signalled by the exquisitely sentimental fall of Ahab's solitary tear—'nor did all the Pacific contain such wealth as that one wee drop'—and by the ironic framing of the touching dialogue that ensues between Ahab and Starbuck. The momentary rapprochement is introduced by Ahab's 'In such a night'[2] and—by power of serendipity—closed by Starbuck's solo rendition of 'O Captain! my Captain!'. Clearly, rapprochement is impossible: but this does nothing to lessen the implication that the androgynous dream of 'A squeeze of the hand' is as close as Ishmael comes to dis-

---

1 The preliminary moral act, Teufelsdröckh says, is 'Annihilation of Self', after which comes the realisation that the earth is 'my needy Mother, not my cruel Stepdame' ('The Everlasting Yea, 142, 144), and the related belief in mutual love as the foundation of social being. Ahab's plea to Starbuck, 'let me look into a human eye', suggests that Carlyle is haunting Ishmael once again: 'Gaze thou in the face of thy Brother' says Teufelsdröckh, 'in those eyes where plays the lambent fire of Kindness, or in those where rages the lurid conflagration of Anger' and then say 'what miraculous virtue goes out of man into man' (162).

2 'On such a day', in fact, but openly allusive to Lorenzo and Jessica, *Merchant of Venice* 5.1.24.

tilling a truth from crazy Ahab's quest.

What Ishmael has learned, though quite as imperfectly as the Ancient Mariner, is what 'A Squeeze', 'The Grand Armada', 'Brit', and 'A Symphony' express. Like Wordsworth's own assertions, Ishmael's assertions are provisional, tentative, almost cancelled out. What the 'ear of faith' hears in *The Excursion*, and what Ishmael perceives, are equally qualified as conditioned by the subjectivity of the perceiver, and the nursing whales with their baby's ears 'newly arrived from foreign parts' and still feeding on celestial reminiscences may parody, rather than endorse, Wordsworth's equally provisional 'intimations', but Melville is more than capable of doing both at the same time (as Wordsworth himself does by denying any notion that myths of pre-existence can be more than suggestive figures, or by celebrating an active principle which is nonetheless—like a harpooner's hemp tangled with an umbilical cord—'with evil mixed').

What makes the work ultimately a Romantic one is Melville's depiction of Ahab as one who, in blaspheming against human brotherhood as well as against nature and spirit (not Pan alone, but pantisocracy), rejects the entire Romantic trinity. He is a demonic potentiation of the Ancient Mariner: a mariner who would knowingly and willingly transgress against his shipmates, against the albatross and against the Polar spirit. Or a Teufelsdröckh stranded in the Everlasting No.[1] Yet Melville allows us to rest neither with Ahab nor with Ishmael: his text offers a variety of intimations rather than certainties. Like Wordsworth in 'Intimations' his forte is 'fallings from us, vanishings, blank misgivings of a creature moving about in worlds not realised'. So Moby-Dick, regarded metaphysically, is the

---

1 Ahab's indomitable defiance seems pointedly contrasted to that of Professor Teufelsdröckh. Carlyle asks of his intellectual hero, 'do not a certain indomitable Defiance and yet a boundless reverence seem to loom forth, as the two mountain-summits, on whose rock-like strata all the rest were based and built?' (*Sartor Resartus*, 175). Against this touchstone of integrated Romantic wisdom, Ahab is, we might say, fixated in the anal stage: rejection. More generally, Melville's general narrative strategy parallels Carlyle's. In *Sartor*, the conflict between scepticism and wonder is dramatised both in the dark night and rebirth of the Professor, and in the ambivalence of the editor; in *Moby-Dick* it is expressed both in the increasing polarisation between Ahab and Ishmael and in the bewildering inconsistencies within Ishmael. I am indebted here to a perceptive essay by Trish Dann.

most assured expression of Negative Capability, and regarded aesthetically is a masterpiece of the vertiginous, the greatest achievement of Romantic Irony in English or American Romanticism. It embraces Spinozistic yearnings and a variety of epistemologically rather than theologically inspired correctives to those yearnings and presents a whole which corresponds more to the ironist's conception of an infinitely full chaos than to a unitary world view. It may be Romanticism's greatest challenge to the soul 'to keep the open independence of her sea, while the wildest winds of heaven and earth conspire to cast her on the treacherous slavish shore', yet humanistically it requires one to do so while mindful of the categorical imperative toward a humane community. And the irony which Queequeg exemplifies in so unique a way, as a man tattooed with a hermetic hieroglyph encapsulating the mysteries of the universe, is what the Mariner and Ishmael—fated to tell for ever tales they barely comprehend—also exemplify. Yeats, another last Romantic, put it this way: 'Man can embody truth but he cannot know it'.

Chapter 9:

A Discharged Soldier and A Runaway Slave

In his essay 'A Backward Glance o'er Travel'd Roads' (1888), Whitman observed that in 1850–52 after years of normal aims and pursuits, he found himself 'possess'd'

> at the age of thirty-one to thirty-three, with a special desire, ... a feeling or ambition to articulate and faithfully express ... my own physical, emotional, moral, intellectual and aesthetic Personality, in the midst of, and tallying ... current America - and to exploit that Personality ... in *a far more candid and comprehensive sense* than any hitherto poem or book .[1]

'Leaves of Grass', he concludes, was:

> an attempt to put a Person, a human being (myself, in the latter of half of the Nineteenth Century) freely, fully and truly on record. I could not find any similar personal record in current literature *that satisfied me* (573).

I have added emphases to illustrate what seems to me to be the fundam ental proposition of 'A Backward Glance o'er Travel'd Roads', and indeed one implication of the metaphor 'travelled roads'. A more candid Whitman might have written: 'I read *The Prelude*, and I saw that this work had changed the nature of and the programme of poetry. Yet I thought he went about it the wrong way. He sounded defeated. He sounded superior. He wasn't democratic

---

1 *Walt Whitman: Leaves of Grass*, ed. Sculley Bradley and Harold W Blodgett (New York and London: W W Norton, 1973), 563. Subsequent references to 'A Backward Glance', the 1855 Preface, and 'Song of Myself' (the 'deathbed' edition except where noted) are from this edition, hereafter, *Leaves*.

enough, inclusive enough, honest enough, or experimental enough. Why couldn't he see that the epic form was part of the lumber, or that fidelity to changing experience needs an open form? Why *not* "make/ A present joy the matter of a song"?'

Whether those thoughts passed through Whitman's mind or not, it is the case that, at the age of 37, as a journalist with no track record in poetry, he published, within five years of the first, the second personal epic of the nineteenth century. The second is distinguished from the first by its lack of narrative, the absence of metre or discernible structure; by the replacement of Wordsworthian memory by Whitman's immediacy, of loss by fullness, of vision by sensation; and by the unashamed adoption of an intensified egotistical sublime as the appropriate mode of an American Bard. *The Prelude*—posthumously published, formal, ostensibly sexless,[1] memorial—summoned Whitman to a celebration of self which would be truly celebratory, in which the sense of vision would be more sustained, the personality larger, guiltless and more inclusive, the voice more demotic, and Paradise—Wordsworth's prospective theme for *The Recluse*—would be not merely trailered but enacted as 'the simple produce of the common day'.

If it was possible for an American poet of mid-century to have a Jacobin upbringing, Whitman had one: parented and mentored by admirers of Tom Paine, taken to hear the Quaker Elias Hicks and the abolitionist Fanny Wright, growing up with younger brothers who had been christened Andrew Jackson, George Washington and Thomas Jefferson he was weaned on the rhetoric of new beginnings. Politicised in adolescence in a Brooklyn printing milieu, where his heroes were those of William Blake, he was re-politicised—rather as Blake himself had been in 1789—by the simultaneous emergence of slavery as an issue in the 1840s, and a new wave of revolutions in Europe in 1848. For all the democratic bravado of the first *Leaves of Grass* in 1855 it is now accepted by Whitman scholars that it, like *Songs of Experience* and *The Prelude* and indeed *Paradise Lost*, was inspired less by optimism than by defeat.

Whitman became a poet by accident: he took up poetry because

---

[1] At least to those who do not notice Wordsworth's frequently erotic register.

direct engagement in politics and political journalism had become increasingly difficult for him by the late 1840s. His political allies were making compromises that he could not accept, particularly with reference to two pieces of slave-related legislation, the Wilmot Proviso of 1846 (designed to prevent the extension of slavery into new territories) and the Fugitive Slave Law of 1850 (which legitimised federal enforcement of the return of slaves to their owners, and which Whitman, whatever sentimental readers may prefer to suppose, saw less as an injustice to slaves than as an infringement of state autonomy). His response was that of Wordsworth and Coleridge in 1798: he snapped his squeaking baby trumpet of sedition, and began to construct a poetic persona free of his own political contradictions, and disillusionments. Mid-way between the introduction of the Wilmot Proviso and the passage of the Fugitive Slave Law Whitman penned in his notebooks the curiously non-aligned germ of 'Song of Myself':

> I am the poet of the body
> And I am the poet of the soul
> I go with the slaves of the earth *equally with the masters*
> And I will stand *between* the masters and the slaves,
> *Entering into both* so that both will understand me alike.[1]

From then on, according to Betsy Erkkila 'his notebooks and scrapbooks in (1848/49) indicate that he was engaged in an extensive program of self-education—reading, annotating, and taking notes on books and articles on literature, language, history, science, astronomy, geography, foreign countries, and world events.'[2] He was also intently perusing the British literary journals and regularly marking and cutting passages related to the work of the modern British poets, particularly Wordsworth, Coleridge, Keats and Tennyson.[3]

---

[1] *Notebooks and Unpublished Prose Manuscripts*, ed. Edward F Grier, 6 vols (New York: New York University Press, 1984), 1:67, hereafter *NUPM*. Italics added.

[2] Betsy Erkkila, *Whitman the Political Poet* (New York and Oxford: Oxford University Press, 1989), 53.

[3] See Walt Whitman, *Notes and Fragments*, ed Richard Maurice Bucke (1899), Part 6, for a list of cuttings made by Whitman from magazines and newspapers.

This list is hardly surprising. Consider this fragmentary inquisition, jotted down in an early notebook.

> Do you not know that
> your soul has brothers
> and sisters, just as
> much as the body has?[1]

The likeliest explanation for this jotting, which seems from its layout to be on the threshold of poetic form, is that Whitman had already pondered Wordsworth's 'We are seven' and its adult inquisition of a child about her brothers and sisters and their status in life or death. Whitman never refers overtly to this poem but the child's triumphant assertion of her siblings' immortality—'Their graves are green, they may be seen'—germinates eventually in what may be Whitman's most characteristic passage, his answers to a child's question, 'What is the grass'.

> And now it seems to me the beautiful uncut hair of graves.
>
> Tenderly will I use you curling grass,
> It may be you transpire from the breasts of young men,
> It may be that if I had known them I would have loved them,
> It may be you are from old people, or from offspring taken
>   soon out of their mothers laps,
> And here you are the Mothers' laps.

Similarly, one does not need to know that Whitman thought Coleridge akin to Adam to see how Coleridge's astonishing sunset imperatives from 'This Lime-Tree Bower my Prison'— 'Shine in the

---

His literary cuttings around the period 1848 to 1856 are dominated by the names of Emerson, Wordsworth, Tennyson, and Keats, with individual entries on Chaucer, Sidney, Marvell, Shakespeare, Cowper, Goldsmith, Southey, Clare.

1 Walt Whitman, *Day Books and Notebooks*, ed. William White, (NY: New York University Press, 1978) 3: 785. For a further imitation of 'We are seven' that Whitman published in the *Brooklyn Daily Eagle* in 1846 (without acknowledging Wordsworth) see Karen Karbiener, 'Intimations of Imitation: Wordsworth, Whitman and the Emergence of *Leaves of Grass*', in Pace and Scott, ed., *Wordsworth in American Literature Culture* (Palgrave 2005) 144–59. Karbiener's essay pursues the line of thought explored in this chapter.

slant beams of the sinking orb, / Ye purple heath-flowers! / Richlier burn ye clouds! / Live in the yellow light, ye distant groves! / And kindle, thou blue Ocean!'—germinate in the climactic strophe in 'Crossing Brooklyn Ferry':[1]

> Flow on river! Flow with the flood-tide, and ebb with the ebb-tide!
> Frolic on, crested and scallop-edg'd waves!
> Gorgeous clouds of the sunset! Drench with splendor me, or the men and women of countless generations after me...
> Stand up, tall masts of Mannahatta! Stand up, beautiful hills of Brooklyn

Nor does one need to know that Whitman thought Tennyson 'indispensable', to realise that his own most commanding lyric, 'Tears! tears! tears!' constitutes a beautiful rhythmic set of variations on Tennyson's 'Tears, idle Tears' to the tune of Tennyson's 'Break, break, break' (on which see my Epilogue). All in all, Whitman may well have given T. S. Eliot the idea that in a poet's maturity, 'not only the best, but the most individual parts of his work may be those in which the dead poets, his ancestors, assert their immortality most vigorously'.[2]

The little that is known of Whitman's well-concealed interest in these poets comes from his annotations.[3] Most quoted is his response to Keats's remark that 'a Poet is the most unpoetical of any thing in existence; because he has no Identity'. Whitman annotated this in 1848 as if mediating in the 'egotistical sublime' debate: 'The great poet absorbs the identity of others, and experiences of

---

[1] For a discussion of such imperatives see Eric Lindstrom, 'The Command to Nature in Wordsworth and Post-Enlightenment Lyric', *Literary Imagination* 13:3 (November 2011) 325–344.

[2] 'Tradition and the Individual Talent', *Selected Prose*, ed. John Hayward (Harmondsworth: Penguin Books, 1953) 22.

[3] As Kenneth Price observes in *Whitman and Tradition*, whereas criticism has seen Whitman 'as a primitive genius' outside literary tradition, the 'sheer energy of Whitman's denials of connectedness with literary high culture, ... suggests that more attention should be paid to his defensive strategy.' Kenneth M Price, *Whitman and Tradition: The Poet in his Century* (New Haven and London: Yale University Press, 1990), 4.

others, and they are definite in him or from him; but he perceives them all through the powerful press of himself ... his own masterly identity'.[1] Somewhat improbably, the poet who would soon write 'I loafe at my ease', and adopt a supremely indolent stance throughout 'Song of Myself', rebuked Wordsworth for his neglect of society in another lyrical ballad, 'To my Sister', one of Wordsworth's most Whitmanesque productions ('No joyless forms shall regulate / Our living calendar ... / Our minds shall drink at every pore / The Spirit of the season').[2] Reading *Blackwood's Edinburgh Magazine* (1849), he developed this critical stance, noting that 'Wordsworth lacks sympathy with men and women—that does not pervade him enough by a long shot' (Price 20) and elsewhere recorded that 'Of the leading British poets many who began with the rights of man abjured their beginning and came out for kingcraft, priestcraft, obedience and so forth—Southey, Coleridge, and Wordsworth did so' (*NUPM* 5:1778).

What is happening, clearly, in these jottings, is that Whitman is both informing himself about the state of the art in British poetry and criticism, and beginning to define himself as a poet. Once he had decided on the bardic stance he then set out, in 1855, to prepare himself for it by doing something quite extraordinary. He made page after page of notes on ancient British history, in the Geoffrey of Monmouth version, emphasising Caractacus and the importance of the orders of bards and druids.[3] Some sixty years after Wordsworth rather more plausibly set himself such a course of then fashionable druidic studies in Racedown, preparatory to enrolling himself 'by Nature's side among the men of old' (*Prelude* 13:298), Whitman—perhaps stimulated by one or other of Wordsworth's visions on Salisbury Plain—decides to enrol himself belatedly in the same bardic order. Not that the little poetry he wrote in the years 1848/1854 shows any traces of his own future style, or indeed of Keatsian or Wordsworthian epic. Indeed nothing in his output of the time (mostly topical satires in a rather journalistic vein) suggests that Whitman would, within five

---

1 Cited from Gay Wilson Allen, *The Solitary Singer* (New York: Macmillan, 1955), 131.
2 According to Price, Whitman slipped a copy of this poem into an 1851 review of Wordsworth in the *American Whig Review* (156 n).
3 *Notes and Fragments*, 181–92.

years of *The Prelude* and *In Memoriam* produce a work that would combine the personal profile of the one and something of the lyric structure of the other while emulating the cultural project of both— that is, a work of consolation addressed to those whom recent developments had disinherited of their best hopes.

'Song of Myself' is a message of succour to the future. It is Whitman's *Paradise Lost*, his *Prelude*, his *Ode to the West Wind*. Only its sheer 'go', Tennyson's word for it (Price, 74), disguises the fact that this poem a belated contribution to the Romantic genre of political poetry inspired by failure and defeat, and indeed taking its energies from political activism sublimated into poetry. When Whitman wrote it he was witnessing the crumbling of the ideals of the Republic, aware as he said in one of his anti-slavery lecture notes that 'Nations sink by stages, first one thing and then another' (Erkkila 66). Harriet Martineau, chronicler of what she termed 'the martyr age of the republic', was similarly anguished. 'I regard the prospects of the republic of the United States', she wrote in her *Autobiography* (1855) 'with more pain and apprehension than those of any other people in the civilized world. It is the only instance, I believe, of a nation being inferior to its institutions'. In her *History of the American Compromise*, the following year, she explained: 'Idolatry of the Constitution has lowered the republican spirit and sapped the political virtue of the North'.[1] Her history looks back, as did Thoreau, on the failures of the 'men of '87', on the Missouri Compromise of 1820 (which prohibited slavery within the Louisiana Purchase north of latitude 36.3 while admitting Missouri to the union as a slave state), and on spineless politicians absenting themselves during crucial votes, such as the Nebraska Bill of 1853 which effectively abrogated the prohibition. On the Missouri Compromise, which also embittered Jay and Adams, she cites a deeply troubled Jefferson:

> The momentous question, like a fire-bell in the night, awakened and filled me with terror. I considered it at once as the knell of the union. It is hushed, indeed for the moment. But this is a reprieve

---

[1] Harriet Martineau, *Autobiography,* 3rd edn., 2 vols (London: Smith, Elder, 1877), 2: 456; *A History of the American Compromises* (London: John Chapman, 1856), 6.

only, not a final sentence. A geographical line, coinciding with a marked principle, moral or political, once conceived ... will never be obliterated (*American Compromise* 12).

This 'knell of the union' sounded repeatedly for Whitman before and after the first *Leaves of Grass*. Despite the ebullient stance of the work, he was in a mood remarkably close to that described in the closing lines of *The Prelude* itself:

> Then, though (too weak to tread the ways of truth)
> This age fall back to old idolatry,
> Though men return to servitude as fast
> As the tide ebbs, to ignominy and shame
> By nations sink together, we shall still
> Find solace ... (14: 435–40)

The ground of hope for Wordsworth is that we may be faithful 'in forwarding a day / Of firmer trust' and that if we witness truly, 'what we have loved / Others will love, and we will teach them how' (*Prelude*, 14: 442, 448–9). Whitman, however, was determined that the mind of 'Walt' would not, as Wordsworth's did '[give] way to overpressure from the times / And their disastrous issue' (*Prelude* 12: 51).

There is, according to Robert Weisbuch, no textual evidence whatever that 'Song of Myself' answers *The Prelude*, but Weisbuch, like myself, is in no doubt that it does. He sees it as an answering poem, alike as 'an epic in which the poetic self is hero', and implicitly 'but exuberantly competitive, a brash show of the American advantage in freeing time and self from linear history' (Weisbuch, 178). Where *The Prelude* can offer only a message of hope, 'Whitman refuses Wordsworth's hope, for hope is a historical emotion based on a present lack and a future good.' 'Song of Myself' sees hope 'as utterly unnecessary to an American present filled to joyful bursting' (193). Whitman not only resolves to 'make / A present joy the matter of a song' (*Prelude* 1: 47) but makes such making the staple method of the poem. As John Lynen puts it: 'Whitman's poetry is above all a poetry of the now, a poetry which not only depicts the present moment but makes the poem itself exist as that moment and portrays all events, objects, and thoughts as things now appearing to consciousness', and indeed 'the whole of "Song of Myself" is a picture of Whitman's state of mind as he loafs on a bank contemplating a spear of grass.'[1]

Weisbuch claims that 'Song of Myself', while competitive, makes no allusion to *The Prelude*, yet his own comments—like my own procedure so far—may suggest that such a claim involves too narrow a definition of allusion. Certainly the opening motifs of 'Song of Myself', which Weisbuch himself cites, echo those of *The Prelude*. Both poems, he points out, celebrate the liberated self. Wordsworth, 'escaped / From the great city', invokes as his epic muse a natural breeze, whose action renovates the creative spirits of the poet. Whitman, rejecting 'Houses and rooms ... full of perfumes', invokes the anima, secure in his own relaxation and liberation:

> I loafe and invite my soul,
> I lean and loaf at my ease ... observing a spear of summer
>   grass. (1:4–5)

'Spear ... grass'? If, despite its absence of direct allusion, the opening of 'Song of Myself' reads like a palimpsest of echoes, this is surely because it reaches back through the opening of the recently published *Prelude*, to other great Wordsworthian openings, that of 'The Poem upon the Wye', reclined under 'this dark sycamore', and that of 'The Ruined Cottage' where the travelling poet desires the relaxation which Whitman's persona and the Pedlar already claim—limbs stretched on the earth—which poem ends with a consolatory image of spear-grass 'By mist and silent rain-drops silver'd o'er'.[2] It reinforces Weisbuch's general case, while using a broader model of 'allusion', to note that each of these Wordsworthian openings represents as a gift, or as desire, or as remembrance what Whitman represents as simply his. If we do not see the allusions, it is surely because we are inside them, looking out.

Take for instance the compound allusion in Whitman's passage

---

1 John Lynen, *The Design of the Present: Essays on Time and Form in American Literature* (New Haven and London: Yale University Press, 1969), 292.

2 The later poem known to Whitman (as to Bryant, Emerson, Hawthorne and Melville) as Book 1 of *The Excursion* (*CWRT* 2: 335).

about hunting things to their hiding places (section 31 of 'Song of Myself'), that list which concludes:

> In vain the razor-bill'd auk sails far north to Labrador,
> I follow quickly, I ascend to the nest in the fissure of the cliff.

Lynen, making a direct comparison of the style of Whitman and Wordsworth, quotes this and calls it 'such an un-Wordsworthian example of merging' (Lynen 330). Yet Whitman is surely engaged here in appropriating data from John James Audubon, to perform a conspicuous usurpation of the birdsnesting 'spot of time'.[1] The conclusion of Whitman's passage trumps, gargantuanly, the young Wordsworth's accidental experience of transcendence of ordinary perception ('the sky seemed not a sky of earth, and with what motion moved the clouds') by converting it into habitual and willed transcendence of space and time. Of course there is a contrast: Wordsworth descends to his raven's nest using ordinary hands and feet on a literal rock-face, 'by knots of grass / And half-inch fissures in the slippery rock / But ill sustained'. Whitman ascends to his—or rather Audubon's—auk's nest by spanning a continent and aeons of geological time. In vain the mother raven builds her nest so high, Wordsworth implies. In vain, says Whitman, hide anything from me:

> In vain the mastodon retreats beneath its own powder'd bones,
> In vain objects stand leagues off and assume manifold shapes...

For Wordsworth a local rock and a familiar nest will suffice: for Whitman's bardic soul nothing less will suffice than the auk, or nearer than Labrador.

Near the beginning of 'Song of Myself' Whitman expostulates, as Emerson has done before him, in the voice of 'The Tables Turned': 'You shall no longer take things at second or third hand ... nor look

---

[1] I am grateful to Donald Madison for pointing out that Whitman's immediate source for the auk is Audubon's *Ornithological Biography* of 1831–39. The Chadwyck-Healey *English Poetry Full-Text Database* offers only one other nineteenth-century English poem in which the words 'nest' and 'fissure' appear in such close juxtaposition, namely Doyle's 'The Eagle's Nest'. Audubon, incidentally, was in Wordsworth's library at Rydal Mount.

A Discharged Soldier and a Runaway Slave 293

through the eyes of the dead .... nor feed on the spectres in books.' For a man working wholesale with bookish experiences—and on the whole doing less with them than Wordsworth does with his Cartesian Arab Dream, or Joanna Baillie's mimic hootings to the lakeside owls, or Cowper's dandified preacher—this is a somewhat ironic pretension. Whitman, it seems to me, perceiving primal poetic possibilities in the attenuated form of *The Prelude* seeks to liberate them, intensify them, making a poem which is all (as one reviewer of *The Prelude* wanted it to be) 'trances of thought and mountings of the mind'. In part, of course, he does this by adopting Tennyson's strategy in *In Memoriam,* constructing his poem of independent lyrical passages, working mainly with image rather than scene, and with a thematic rather than narrative organisation. Whitman's poetry disperses the Wordsworthian narrative topoi into a collage of images and briefly sustained tableaux, in which, nevertheless, we recognise the bildungsroman motifs of escape from the city, adventures in landscape, the public road as one's Yale and Harvard, impressions of the city, moments of vision and consecration, historic tableaux (the revolutionary terror in Wordsworth's case, battle and massacre in Whitman's), elaborated encounters and fleeting ones—shepherds or clam-diggers, artificers or frame builders, a blind beggar with his placard, the voice of prostitutes. This is not imitation: rather, it is the most intimate collaboration in the refinement of a nineteenth-century democratic yet bardic 'I'.

More deeply, however, we see a competitive doubling of fundamental modes of self-presentation or bardic delineation. Wordsworth's strengths are intensified, his disclaimers cancelled, his wants supplied. Wordsworth's poem presents the history of a self in process of creation; Whitman's deploys the ecstasies of a present self of transcendental reach. Wordsworth's 'myself' encounters numerous concrete others—Louvet, Beaupuy, Coleridge, Dorothy—where Whitman's tends to merge others into himself, or into what has been called an intersubjectivity. Wordsworth's self is capable of doubt and indirection; Whitman's, affecting to be transhistorical, is a power like one of nature's and knows no backsliding. Wordsworth's listens quietly to the language of things, while Walt's gorges itself upon the sublime American continent. Wordsworth is led by Nature, his mind (in a repeated metaphor) impregnated by her: Walt jets the 'father stuff' far and wide. Whitman, I suspect, even adapted Wordsworth's characteristic rhetoric of transubstantiation, whereby nature and the human mind seem to share one substance and to occupy each other, to the frequencies of his own poetry. Both habitually question the duality of body and soul, but Whitman (in section 5) is not laid asleep in body to become a living soul—his soul awakens in bodily form to explore a body which become as pliant and translucent as soul.[1] 'I mind', he says to his soul,

> I mind how once we lay such a transparent summer morning,
> How you settled your head athwart my hips and gently turn'd over upon me,
> And parted the shirt from my bosom-bone, and plunged your tongue to my bare-stript heart,...

Thus the wedding of mind and world becomes the consummation of soul and body.

Eroticism is not monopolised by Whitman, but there is certainly a difference. In Book 2 of *The Prelude* Wordsworth is on the lake at nightfall:

> Oh then the calm
> And dead still water lay upon my mind
> Even with a weight of pleasure, and the sky,
> Never before so beautiful, sank down
> Into my heart and held me like a dream.
> Thus were my sympathies enlarged, and thus
> Daily the common range of visible things
> Grew dear to me: already I began
> To love the sun....
>   I had seen him lay
> His beauty on the morning hills, had seen
> The Western mountains touch his setting orb,

---

[1] For this perception (without the Wordsworthian parallel) see Karen Sanchez-Eppler, *Touching Liberty: Abolition, Feminism and the Politics of the Body* (Berkeley: University of California, 1993), 81.

A Discharged Soldier and a Runaway Slave 295

> In many a thoughtless hour, when, from excess
> Of happiness, my blood appeared to flow
> For its own pleasure, and I breathed with joy.
>   (2: 170–189)

This is what Whitman does with similar material:

> Press close bare-bosom'd night – press close magnetic
>   nourishing night!
> Night of south winds – night of the large few stars!
> Still nodding night – mad naked summer night.
>
> Smile O voluptuous cool-breath'd earth!
> Earth of the slumbering and liquid trees...
> Smile, for your lover comes. (21)
>
> ...Something I cannot see puts upward libidinous prongs,
> Seas of bright juice suffuse heaven (24)

Elsewhere in the first *Leaves*, in 'I Sing the Body Electric', the delicate eroticism of Wordsworth's Western hills 'touching' the orb of the sun explodes into spectacular metaphor (the more spectacular for Whitman's sparing use of metaphor):

> Limitless limpid jets of love hot and enormous, quivering
>   jelly of love, white-blow and delirious juice,
> Bridegroom night of love working surely and softly into the
>   prostrate dawn,
> Undulating into the willing and yielding day,
> Lost in the cleave of the clasping and sweet-flesh'd day.

Wordsworthian is not the first epithet that springs to mind. Nevertheless, excepting the magnitude of this 'procreant urge', one can feel that if what occurred between Wordsworth and Coleridge was symbiosis, what occurred between Wordsworth and Whitman was closer to metamorphosis: there are few elements of Wordsworth which do not appear *either intensified or inverted* (one *can* have it both ways) in Whitman.

That Wordsworth's programme is in Whitman's mind is confirmed, it seems to me, by one of the most creative allusions of the nineteenth century. For where Wordsworth ends *The Prelude* by claiming, in lines I have already quoted,

> What we have loved, others will love,
> And we will teach them how,

Whitman opens 'Song of Mself' by claiming

> I celebrate myself, and sing myself
> And what I assume, you shall assume,
> For every atom belonging to me as good belongs to you.

The manoeuvre is at once imitative and corrective. For all its apparent egotism (leaving the reader no freedom to assume something else) the Whitman formulation perhaps presumes rather less. For what he 'assumes', as Whitman scholars have argued, is a bardic voice, a visionary stance, and a prophetic agenda—that of a prophet of nature and of human possibilities. *The Prelude* asks 'what one is, / Why may not millions be? (13: 88–9) and its poet lays claim to 'a sense that fits him perceive / Objects unseen before' (13: 304–5). 'Song of Myself' claims, in the dissenting language of Transcendentalism, that all the Lord's people are prophets.

Both poets project a self who is our representative, and whose experiences are offered as normative (the 'I' of *The Prelude* frequently modulates into the normative 'we'): the hero of each poem is a human spirit. But whereas the poet in Wordsworth's 1800 preface is a man speaking to men, the voice at the conclusion of *The Prelude* has become hieratic. Whitman sniffed a sense of election. The 'I' in 'Song of Myself' is at first anonymous, from the outset ordinary, and when identified, identified as 'one of the roughs'. That this is a strategic decision brought about by a critical response to *The Prelude* I have no doubt.

As Weisbuch notes, there has been a critical consensus from Matthiessen in 1941 to Lynen in 1969 that Whitman's poetic of 1855 echoes Wordsworth's of 1800 in terms of 'their shared respect for common language and common objects as potentially poetic, their notion of poetry as the underpinning of science, and their deep sense of the interpenetration of human thoughts and apparently inanimate objects' (Weisbuch 179). M. H. Abrams, in 1987, offered a rather broader set of perspectives. Wordsworth and Whitman, Abrams argues, take for their subject 'the common people'; stress reformation of the hereditary forms of poetry and rejection of language 'distilled from other poems'; include as fit for poetry 'all shunned persons' (Wordsworth's beggars, convicts and idiots become Whitman's onanists and prostitutes). They see the poet and the man of science as joint labourers; they realise that the poet has to create the taste by which is enjoyed, and undertake to *politicise* the literary taste of educated middle class reader; their own manifestos (of 1800 and 1855) deconstruct prevalent poetics as a politics of class in the guise of aesthetics.[1]

Even this understates the case, however. Read in slow motion, and setting aside its opening and closing conjurations of America, the 1855 Preface enunciates a series of major theses about poetry, which can be seen as developing from Wordsworth's 1800 Preface, from *The Prelude*, and from Shelley's *Defence*. The first of Whitman's critical theses is, in fact, specifically Shelleyan: American 'Presidents shall not be their common referee so much as their poets shall ....He [the poet] is the arbiter of the diverse ....the equalizer of his age and land'. Shelley's 'unacknowledged legislator' has become democratized (*Leaves*, 714). But the rest are primarily Wordsworthian. As samples, unmentioned by Abrams or Weisbuch, I would cite first his claim that 'The known universe has only one complete lover and that is the greatest poet' (717), or in Wordsworthian terms, the poet is the bearer of relationship and love. According to Whitman, again, 'Past and present and future are not disjoined but joined. The greatest poet ... drags the dead out of their coffins and stands them again on their feet' (718) or, in Wordsworth's almost equally memorable phrasing, the poet binds together in one society the living and the dead. (The phrase 'the living and the dead' recurs in Whitman's poetry almost as frequently as in Wordsworth's and constitutes a major and little recognised facet of their joint vision). When Whitman proclaims as a principle that 'In

---

1 M. H. Abrams, 'Afterword', in *The Cast of Consciousness: Concepts of the Mind in British and American Romanticism*, ed. Beverley Taylor and Robert Bain (New York: Greenwood Press, 1987), 217–8.

the ... great masters the idea of political liberty is indispensable ....
the attitude of great poets is to cheer up slaves and horrify despots....
Liberty is poorly served by men whose good intent is quelled from
one failure or two failures or any number of failures'(722), it is clear
whose failures Whitman is adverting to, and equally clear that the
poet of *Lyrical Ballads*, or indeed the 'Poems Dedicated to National
Independence and Liberty' is the model as well as the warning. The
related assertion (723) that poetry concentred 'in the real body and soul
and in the pleasure of things' is superior to 'all fiction and romance',
intensifies Wordsworth's commitment to portraying 'men as they are
men within themselves', looking 'steadily at my subject' and keeping
his reader 'in the company of flesh and blood'.

Something more intrinsic to the whole enterprise must be noted
also. While the rhetoric seems most unlike Wordsworth's sober prose,
and makes the argument at times painfully difficult to follow (you
can die many times in a Whitman sentence) it seems to me that this
very rhetoric may derive from Wordsworth in two senses: first it proclaims by demonstration that 'there neither is nor can be any essential difference between the language of poetry and that of prose' to
put the matter in Wordsworth's terms, or 'Verse and Prose, on some
occasions, run into one another, like light and shade' in Hugh Blair's
more figurative expression.[1] Secondly it practises (even to excess)
two of Wordsworth's most idiosyncratic stylistic signatures, the proliferating predicate (of the kind that enacts the visionary moments in
'Tintern Abbey' and *The Prelude*) and the classical periodic sentence.

'The Poem upon the Wye' drew from Whitman one of his crucial
self-definitions: on Wordsworth's 'laid asleep in body and become
a living soul' Whitman comments that 'high exalted musing' needs
'a trance, yet with all the senses alert ... the senses not lost or counteracted'[2] The poem also introduced Whitman to what I would call

---

[1] Hugh Blair, *Lectures on Rhetoric and Belles Lettres* (1783), ed. Harold F. Harding, 2 vols (Carbondale: Southern Illinois University Press, 1965), 2: 313. Blair's subsequent remark that 'It is hardly possible to determine the exact limit where Eloquence ends and Poetry begins' is often cited in reference to Whitman's theory and practice.

[2] *Walt Whitman's Workshop*, ed. Clifton Joseph Furness (Cambridge, MA: Harvard University Press, 1928), 21

the proliferating predicate, the ur-sentence, as it were, of both *The Prelude* and 'Song of Myself'. In the sentence I have in mind, the verb 'I have felt' takes four objects, each developed with parallels and with surprising variations (magnificently analysed by the linguist H. G. Widdowson),[1] refusing to make linear progress, suspended—levitating almost—in time. Relineated, Wordsworth's sentence reads:

> And I have felt—
> *a presence* that disturbs me with the joy of elevated thoughts;
> *a sense sublime* of something far more deeply interfused,
> whose dwelling is the light of setting suns, and the round
>   ocean, and the living air, and the blue sky, and in the
>   mind of man
> *a motion* and *a spirit*,
> that impels all thinking things, all objects of all thought, and
>   rolls through all things.

Oner sees why Herbert Read once claimed that Wordsworth was writing free verse. To the ear, his prosody is quite unchained.

As for the periodic sentence, let me align Wordsworth's most remarkable example (perhaps the closest he ever came to writing a Whitman poem) with the most complex (and most Wordsworthian) sentence in Whitman's preface. Whitman claims, in outline, that:

> All the best actions of war and peace ... all help given to relatives and strangers and the poor and old [...] and all shunned persons .. all furtherance of fugitives and of the escape of slaves [...] all that has at any time been well suggested out of the divine heart of man [...] these singly and wholly inured at their time and inure now and will inure always to the identities to which they sprung or shall spring.

It is not simply that Whitman's sentence appears to be grounded in the 'Tintern Abbey' suggestion that 'little unremembered acts of kindness and of love' are likely to save your soul. Rather it is the syntax and even more deeply the rhythm of thought, which reminds

---

1 H. G. Widdowson, *Stylistics and the Teaching of Literature* (London: Longman, 1975), 43–5, 61–2.

one of Wordsworth when he is trembling on the brink, as it were, of free verse. Comparing Whitman's with a sentence from the *Concerning the Convention of Cintra,* I find that the sentences mount in the same way from image to image, express the same wonder, and gather themselves through the same rallentando effect, for syntactically parallel resolution.[1] Wordsworth's sentence suspends its resolution even more artfully than Whitman's and runs as follows (the sentenced is a page long, so I illustrate its curve very selectively):

> The history of all ages; tumults after tumults; wars, foreign or civil, with short or with no breathing spaces, from generation to generation; [...] the senseless weaving and interweaving of factions—vanishing and reviving and piercing each other like the Northern Lights; public commotions, and those in the bosom of the individual; [...] the slow quickening but ever quickening descent of appetite down which the miser is propelled; the agony and cleaving oppression of grief; [...] the life distemper of ambition;—*these inward existences,* and the visible and familiar occurrences of daily life in every town and village; the patient curiosity and contagious acclamations of the multitude in the streets of the city and within the walls of the theatre; a procession or a rural dance; a hunting or a horse-race; a flood or a fire; [...] *these demonstrate incontestibly that the passions of men* [...] in all quarrels, in all contests, in all quests, in all delights; in all employments which are either sought by men or thrust upon them—*do immeasurably transcend their objects.*[2]

Nor is this the only instance of such cataloguing convergence. It is, as Robert Weisbuch points out (224), rather startling that as Wordsworth embarks on his depiction of London he adopts what at first seems to be a Whitmanic syntax (though that syntax denotes plenitude in Whitman's case, bedlam in Wordsworth's, and is in *The Prelude* self-consciously Juvenalian). Where Wordsworth writes:

---

[1] Did Whitman know Wordsworth's 'pamphlet'? As both their CVs are strong on comradeship with Spanish heroism it does seem not improbable.

[2] *Concerning the Convention of Cintra: A Bicentennial Critical Edition,* ed. Richard Gravil and W. J. B. Owen (Humanities-Ebooks, 2009) 217–8.

'What a shock / For eyes and ears! What anarchy and din, / Barbarian and infernal' and proceeds to note,

> those that stretch the neck and strain the eyes,
> And crack the voice in rivalship, the crowd
> Inviting; with buffoons against buffoons
> Grimacing, writhing, screaming—him who grinds
> The hurdy-gurdy, at the fiddle weaves,
> Rattles the salt-box, thumps the kettle drum,
> And him who at the trumpet puffs his cheeks,
> The silver-collared Negro with his timbrel,
> Equestrians, tumblers, women, girls and boys,
> Blue breeched, pink-vested, with high towering plumes.
> (7: 685–705)

Whitman counters with:

> The blab of the pave, tires of carts, sluff of boot-soles, talk of the promenaders,
> The heavy omnibus, the driver with his interrogating thumb, the clank of the shod horses on the granite floor,
> The snow-sleighs, clinking, shouted jokes, pelts of snow-balls,
> The hurrahs for popular favourites, the fury of rous'd mobs,
> The flap of the curtain'd litter, a sick man inside borne to the hospital,
> The meeting of enemies, the sudden oath.[…]
> I mind them or the show and resonance of them – I come and I depart.

Agreeing with Weisbuch that 'Whitman's is an inclusionary vision while Wordsworth's is exclusionary' (227) one might yet conjecture that this reversal is programmatic rather than coincidental. It is part of that general revisionary remaking which can also take Wordsworth's sense of shock at hearing 'The voice of woman utter blasphemy' and turn it (however self-applaudingly) into an act of inclusion:

> The prostitute draggles her shawl, he bonnet bobs on her tipsy and pimpled neck,

> The crowd laugh at her blackguard oaths, the men jeer and
>   wink to each other,
> (Miserable! I do not laugh at your oaths nor jeer you).

This aspect of the dialogue between Wordsworth's poetry and Whitman took a further turn in 1871. By then, Whitman was in his 'Milton! Thou shouldst be living at this hour' phase and in 'Democratic Vistas' America is evidently a stagnant fen. 'The official services of America, national, state, and municipal, in all their branches and departments, except the judiciary, are saturated in corruption, bribery, falsehood, mal-administration; and the judiciary is tainted.' The city, too, had changed:

> these cities, crowded with petty grotesques, malformations, phantoms, playing meaningless antics. Confess that everywhere, in shop, street, church, theatre, barroom, official chair, are pervading flippancy and vulgarity, low cunning, infidelity – everywhere an abnormal libidinousness, unhealthy forms, male, female, painted, padded, dyed, chignon'd, muddy complexions, bad blood, the capacity for good motherhood deceasing or deceas'd, shallow notions of beauty, with a range of manners, or rather lack of manners ... probably the meanest to be seen in the world.[1]

By 1871, clearly, either Wordsworth's vision of Bart's Fair has triumphed over 'the blab of the city pave' or Whitman's general distaste for humanity has reasserted itself. Brooklyn has become Bedlam.

Moreover Whitman is by this date dabbling in eugenic fantasies, appealing for scientific parenting to 'raise up and supply throughout the States a copious race of superb American men and women', perfect in their *clear-blooded, strong-fibred* physique.'[2] The strange closing image of 'Song of Myself', in which Walt offered himself as a posthumous guide to humanity—

---

1 Whitman, *Prose Works 1892*, edited by Floyd Stovall, 2 vols. (New York: New York University Press, 1964), 2: 370, 372.

2 *Prose Works*, 2: 395, 397, emphases added.

A Discharged Soldier and a Runaway Slave 303

> You will hardly know who I am or what I mean,
> But I shall be good health to you nevertheless,
> And *filter and fibre your blood*—

has turned decidedly macabre. Indeed on the evidence of 'Democratic Vistas' one might feel inclined to say of Whitman, as David Ferry memorably said of Wordsworth, that 'his genius was his enmity to man, which he mistook for love.' But then, Whitman's mood while writing 'Song of Myself' was already in many respects as despondent as it became in 1871. At either date he could have echoed Wordsworth's cry in the sonnet 'August 1802': 'Shame on you, feeble heads, to slavery prone.' And his attempts to assume an inclusive and democratic stance always had a disturbing quality of ambivalence. Which brings me, at last, to my set texts: Wordsworth's 'The Discharged Soldier' and Whitman's 'The Runaway Slave'.

Wordsworth's discharged soldier exemplifies the kind of encounter in which his poetry specialises, but is much the most complex such case. As a figure he marries the Godwinian social art of Wordsworth in the mid 90s (like the Female Vagrant and the sailor she encounters on Salisbury Plain, he is a victim of national policy and social irresponsibility) with the earliest and latest instances of Wordsworth's habit of turning people into archetypes as he does in all his poetry from *The Vale of Esthwaite* to *Resolution and Independence*. The soldier is so transumed, though he manifests considerable resistance: he becomes an Anchises figure, just as he did when more Gothically manifested in Wordsworth's schoolboy poem, 'The Vale of Esthwaite'. Like other powerful Wordsworthian passages this one works simultaneously as an expression of reverence for men as they are men within themselves, *and* as an exhibition of imagination creating its own sustenance. It also leaves unanalysed the psychological dynamics on which it is based.

At the time of the supposed encounter (assigned to Wordsworth's first university vacation in 1788) Wordsworth (the narrative has suggested) felt guilty at having allowed Cambridge affectations to tamper with his better self. 'It seemed the very garments that I wore preyed on my strength'. At the time of writing (the longest version of the passage belongs to 1798) Wordsworth had acquired deeper historical guilts through his still recent identification with practitioners of terror. The soldier, too, has long been 'parted from his better self', by his trade of soldiering, which to Wordsworth (as to Godwin and Shelley) meant being trained to murder on behalf of the state. He still appears in 'military garb, / Though faded yet entire' as if unable to free himself from the insignia of his trade. Knowing that he has served in 'the Tropic islands' Wordsworth questions him about what he has endured of 'war, battle and pestilence': one associated in whatever way with slavery will know all about fever—felt by some at this date to be divine punishment for engagement on slaving.[1] In 1793–98 such a soldier's duties might have included putting down slave revolts. An estimated 40,000 British and 40,000 French died of Yellow fever while so engaged. In the early version of the poem he appears thus topically dehumanised, 'cut off / From all his kind, and more than half detached / From his own nature', while in the 1850 text, structured so as to play upon the Charon allusion at the start of Book 4, he appears to Wordsworth as belonging more to Hades than to Hawkshead. The apologist for terror confronts the veteran of Caribbean wars, and learns from him (as Marmaduke learns from Oswald in Wordsworth's *Borderers*), that in the 'after-vacancy' of action, 'we wonder at ourselves like men betrayed', that 'Suffering is permanent, obscure and dark, / And shares the nature of infinity' (*Poetical Works*, Philadelphia 1852, p.62). Yet the soldier also meets one who exhibits how guilt is to be borne. Like Aeneas, after confronting his father's shade, the poet repasses the portals and reascends:

> And so we parted. Back I cast a look,
> And lingered near the door a little space,

---

[1] Thomas Clarkson published his *Essay on the Slavery and Commerce of the Human Species* in 1786 and founded the Society for Effecting the Abolition of the Slave Trade in 1787, the year Wordsworth went up to Cambridge, so such associations would not be unlikely in 1788. Joan Baum associates the 1798 poem directly with Southey's 'The Sailor Who Had Served in the Slave Trade' (and flogged a female slave to death) and 'The Ancient Mariner' as a symbolist treatment of the guilt incurred by those who worked 'the middle passage'. Joan Baum, *Mind-Forged Manacles: Slavery and the English Romantic Poets* (North Haven, Conn: Archon Books, 1994), 53-4.

> Then sought with quiet heart my distant home.

Whitman's 1855 preface, we noted, appears to make behaviour towards a discharged soldier and a runaway slave, or indeed 'all shunned persons', the arbiter both of eternal salvation and of poetic immortality. Until *Drum-Taps*, however, encounters with actual and realised human beings are surprisingly rare in his poetry—long processions of images pass before our eyes but we barely have time to ponder their significance. But certain kinds of being do recur, and of these the slave is (in the 1855 *Leaves*) the most recurrent.

> The runaway slave came to my house and stopt outside,
> I heard his motions crackling the twigs of the woodpile,
> Through the swung half-door of the kitchen I saw him limpsy and weak,
> And went where he sat on a log and led him in and assured him,
> And brought water and fill'd a tub for his sweated body and bruis'd feet,
> And gave him a room that enter'd from my own, and gave him some coarse clean clothes,
> And remember perfectly well his revolving eyes and his awkwardness,
> And remember putting plasters on the galls of his neck and ankles;
> He staid with me a week before he was recuperated and pass'd north,
> I had him sit next me at table, my fire-lock lean'd in the corner.

The 'discharged soldier' in the form in which Whitman would have read it is the climax of Book 4 of *The Prelude* and the encounter has been prepared for throughout that book, which is about the poet's need of such an encounter to resolve certain disquietudes in himself. The soldier is the first realised human being in the poem, exemplifying that there was now 'a human-heartedness about my love'. The 'runaway slave' is the first social exemplification of what Whitman means by announcing in lyric 5 that 'a kelson of the creation is love'.

Whitman sidles up to this subject in lyric 10 via clam-diggers and a trapper's wedding breakfast just as Wordsworth is on his way home from a country dance, and it may be appropriate to observe, though it is differently indicated, there is a certain apprehension about both encounters. Other than the voyeuristically imagined lonely woman (whom we never see and who may symbolise Whitman's sexual identity) the slave is the closest approach to a realised figure in the poem, and one of very few in *Leaves of Grass*. Nor did Whitman do the realising. Needing a humane encounter to focus the democratic spirit of his poem Whitman adapted a story told in Audubon's *Ornithological Biography*.[1]

At an obvious level Whitman does the sort of thing literal-minded readers criticise Wordsworth for *not* doing. He invites the guy in, shares his house, his table, his food, which hospitality, by the way, reverses the roles in Audubon's narrative. Rather than merely noting the man's sufferings 'Whitman' (again rather self-applaudingly) tends his visitor's sores, creating a sense of day-to-day practical caritas which Wordsworth's passage leaves implied. He also inverts the Wordsworth narrative in a manner consistent with his general strategy of reversal, but inconsistent with his democratic programme: for whereas *The Prelude* presents the poet as *debtor*, aggrandising the soldier, 'Song of Myself' represents the slave as silent recipient of the bard's largesse. To see the slave as in any sense an agent, one has to coalesce this passage with the closely related passages in 'Song of Myself' in which a kind of collage of transfiguration is enacted: the hunted figure in section 33 crucified by his pursuers and with whose passion the speaker identifies; and the superb figure of the black drayman in section 13, in command of his horses and himself—which (if we except the highly problematic 'Black Lucifer' in a cancelled text of 'The Sleepers') is Whitman's only representation (of an African American as a figure of self-command.

The 'firelock' is the most obviously ambivalent item (except perhaps the room entered through Whitman's own) in the passage. Whitman scholars have generally assumed that the Bard keeps it at the ready in case he needs to defend the slave from pursuers.

---

1 *Ornithological Biography*, 2: 27–32.

Whitman, however, seems to leave it lying carelessly in the poem so that we can make of it what we wish. It might signify Walt's self-assurance (trusting his guest not to use it, just as Audubon allows the runaway to clean and grease the writer's gun), or his insecurity (he needs to keep it in view), or his disdain (never knew of one of 'em look a white man in the eye), but the poem invites us to read the passage in the terms created for us by the Walt persona. Obediently, we construe a passionate commitment to the liberty of the slave.

In prose, however, Whitman gives little support to such commitment. Just a year later, in the strangely tortured essay on 'The Eighteenth Presidency' (1856) Whitman invites the young men of America to realise that 'you are either to abolish slavery or it will abolish you'. Yet in the same essay he gives to the headlined question 'MUST RUNAWAY SLAVES BE DELIVERED BACK?' the simple answer, 'They must'. And why, pray?

> For by a section of the fourth article of the Federal Constitution, These States compact each with the other, that any person held to service or labor in one State under its laws, and escaping into another State ... shall be delivered up to the persons to whom such service or labor is due.

The architects of the Constitution, Whitman claims without apparent irony, were 'mighty prophets and gods': their work is 'a perfect and entire thing'. Not a brick may be removed from the edifice. Unlike the organically evolving Constitution of Burkean theory, the American Constitution is 'the covenant of the Republic from the beginning, now and forever.'[1] On the other hand (though such hieratic, one might even say feudal, language appears to leave little room for another hand) it may be one's duty to resist by force of arms federal enforcement of what each State is bound by its own will to do.

Whitman's firelock, therefore, is ambivalently placed—floating in an undetermined syntactic space—because Whitman (having found it in Audubon) was deeply ambivalent about what he wanted to do with it. Despite the empathy with the 'picturesque giant' in lyric 13,

---

1 *Poetry and Prose*, edited by Justin Kaplan (New York: Library of America, 1996), 1318–19.

and 'the hounded slave' in lyric 33, the preponderance of analogous references even in 'Song of Myself' suggests a negativity towards black Americans falling well short of ambivalence. While in lyric 33 Walt shares the pain of 'the hounded slave', and indeed makes this the climax of his rhetoric of 'merging'—'I am the hunted slave' and 'All this I not only feel but am'—the poem has shown the distance to be bridged: in lyric 15 the 'woolly pates' in the field remind us of Whitman's more usual stereotyped vision of slaves; in lyric 19 the 'heavy-lipped slave' shares a line with 'the venerealee' exemplifying a none-too-cordial inclusiveness. Even in 1854 Whitman could write of slaves by the roadside as 'clumsy, hideous, black, pouting, grinning, sly, besotted, sensual shameless' in which the word 'black' appears to be glossed by every other term in that catalogue.

Yet in that year, Martin Klammer has argued, Whitman conceived the idea of becoming the poet of national unity *at precisely the right historical moment for the question of slavery to form a focal point for such a project*, and found himself needing to rethink his own acceptance up to that date of racial stereotypes. In Klammer's thesis:

> *Leaves of Grass* portrays African Americans as equal partners with whites in a democratic future and as beautiful and dignified people ... African Americans are seen as essential to the speaker's—and the reader's—own humanity; Whitman repeatedly shows his white readers that to be a whole and fully realised human being in mid-nineteenth-century America is to participate in the experience of, and even identify with, black people.[1]

All this is persuasive. The poem is marked with that intent from the outset: even the grass in the opening lines is perceived as 'Growing among black folks as among white'. Black Americans, Klammer argues, are conspicuous in the central strategy of the poem, which is to depict a development in the self from observer to participant; from identifying with those most like himself to those who are most 'other' (121). Symbolically, 'the perfect human form is realized not, as one might suspect, in the image of a white laborer or farmer but in the

---

1 Martin Klammer, *Whitman, Slavery, and the Emergence of 'Leaves of Grass'* (University Park, PA: Pennsylvania State University Press, 1995), 113.

description of an African American drayman' (125).

Read in this way, the Runaway Slave—however exceptional as a realised figure in 'Song of Myself'—becomes a figure far more central to 'Song of Myself' than is any *single* figure among the range of human beings who thread their way through *The Prelude*. Yet the evidence is that Whitman could not have created him at any earlier point, or at any later point in his career. Two years after the first *Leaves*, in an 1857 editorial in the *Brooklyn Daily Times* Whitman writes that 'the institution of slavery is not at all without its redeeming points', arguing that 'no race ever can remain slaves if they have in them to become free. Why do slave ships go to Africa only?' In 1858 in another editorial on Oregon's exclusion of all blacks, free or slave, he argues approvingly: 'Who believes that the Whites and Blacks can ever amalgamate in America? Or who wishes it to happen? Nature has set an impassable seal against it. Besides is not America for the Whites?'. Looking back in 1890, by when he has found succour in Carlyle's white supremacism, he observed:

> I never went full on the nigger question—the nigger would not turn—would not do anything for himself—he would only act when prompted to act. No! no! I should not like to see the nigger in the saddle—it seems unnatural; for he is only there when propped there, and propping don't civilize.[1]

So the runaway slave of 1855 must be read in the context of a ambivalence which is quite clearly manifest in 1854 and 1856, and amply confirmed in retrospect. We know that the Wordsworth who in 1802 celebrated the life (or, arguably, death?) of Toussaint l'Ouverture, the black Jacobin who led a guerrilla army of four thousand men, found himself in 1840 less than sanguine about over-hasty abolition, though he continued to welcome a stream of abolitionist visitors and received pro-slavery visitors very differently.[2] But Whitman's doubleness on the matter of slaves is rather as if Wordsworth in 1797

---

[1] Cited by Arthur Golden in *Walt Whitman: the Centennial Essays,* ed. Ed Folsom (Iowa: University of Iowa Press, 1994), 92, 100n. See also M. Wynn Thomas, 'Whitman and the Dreams of Labor', in the same collection.

[2] Wordsworth's 'Toussaint' was included by John Greenleaf Whittier in his *Antislavery Poems: Songs of Labor and Reform* (Boston and New York: 1848).

and 1799, either side of 'The Old Cumberland Beggar', had argued journalistically for incarcerating beggars in work-houses.

The ambivalence in the 'Runaway Slave' has usually passed unnoticed by Whitman's readers. Betsy Erkkila's sentimental reading of 1989 did not confront these questions: for her the firelock is quite unproblematic. Recent readings have recognised the brevity of Whitman's anti-slavery passion, and Karen Sanchez-Eppler, at least, finds the 'runaway slave' as problematic as I do.[1] But these more sceptical readings raise another question. Was it simply the historical moment—the accident of starting 'Song of Myself', as the grand democratic national American poem, at the moment of national outcry over the case of Anthony Burns—or was there also a rhetorical determinant? Do poems call forth poems? Did the Discharged Soldier, also, give rise to the Runaway Slave?

For if it is indeed Whitman's strategy to achieve in the 'Runaway Slave' and the 'hounded slave' passages a climactic 'merge' with what he conceives as most opposite to himself, and if it is his democratic purpose to compel the reader into a similarly heroic act of identification, and if his 'drayman' is a symbol of African Americans endowed with respect and self-command—and I find these suggestions convincing—is one not in familiar rhetorical territory? I return to the inadequacy of the term allusion, or one's failure to recognise that something like allusion works at the deepest levels of structure and rhetoric.

It is not enough for the great poet, Wordsworth said in his letter of 1802 to John Wilson, to 'delineate such feelings as all men *do* sympathise with': he must 'add to these others such as all men *may* sympathise with, and such as there is reason to believe they would be better and more moral beings if they did sympathise with'.[2] Behind 'the Runaway Slave' I detect a familiar compound ghost, in whom one major element—perhaps given Whitman's struggle with racial stereotypes, the major element—is the Idiot Boy, challenging the reader to conquer his (and possibly Wordsworth's) aversion; another

---

[1] Sanchez-Eppler, 77.
[2] *Letters of William and Dorothy Wordsworth*, ed. E de Selincourt, *Early Years*, 2nd edn, (Oxford, 1967), 355.

is the Female Vagrant, taking command of her own narrative; a third is the Leech-gatherer, providing the poet with a figure of power at the extremes of endurance; and a fourth is the Discharged Soldier in whom Wordsworth seems to recognise what he later calls 'human nature faithful to herself under worst trials' yet who also symbolises the perhaps inescapable involvement in one's country's guilts. One component in Whitman's fugitive hour of identification with black America is, I would suggest, that the poet of democracy felt pressured by *The Prelude* into a demonstrative act of comradeship with one actual, rather than merely itemised, piece of human jetsam. As it happens, one of four fragmentary pictures Whitman sketched of black Americans in 1854, and the most sympathetic of them, takes this form, rather familiar to readers of Book 7 of *The Prelude* where a blind beggar wears a placard on his chest to tell his story: 'And here an old black man', Whitman writes, 'stone-blind, with a placard on his hat, sits low at the corner of a street' (*NUPM* 4: 1304).

Nor, perhaps, is Wordsworth's own stance on race far distant from the analysis. Whitman might have noted Wordsworth's sonnet to 'Toussaint L'Ouverture' (little suggests that Whitman could have conceived of a black general leading an insurrection), the Calais sonnet on Napoleon's expulsion of the negroes from France, and indeed *The Prelude*'s unambivalent rejection of slavery as *self-evidently* incompatible with liberty. It is pertinent, I suggest, to Whitman's gathering suspicion that the Federal Constitution's compromise with slavery might prove to have been fatal to American democracy, that Wordsworth's poem not only celebrates 'the stir'

> Of that first memorable onslaught made
> By a strong levy of humanity
> Upon the traffickers in negro blood;

but lays claim to an absolute conviction

> That, if France prospered, good men would not long
> Pay fruitless worship to humanity,
> And this most rotten branch of human shame…
> Would fall together with its parent tree.

That is, a true Revolution (which Whitman, like Thoreau, was beginning to suspect that the American Revolution may not have been) is simply not compatible with slavery.

Whitman, I believe, inherited from the Romantics in general, but from Wordsworth in particular, a model of the poem as self-creation. That model, particularly as found in the posthumous *Prelude*, determined him to write the democratic poem of America in the mode of a celebration of the self, or rather an apotheosis of the self, in a persona which would chant its songs democratic as if it were always 1789, or 1776, or 1848. He shared with Wordsworth a poetic programme which stressed the refreshment of poetic language, nakedness of personality, the embrace of science, the celebration of nature, and the pursuit of liberty. But writing half a century later, Whitman 'makes of *The Prelude* a prelude, "Song of Myself" its fulfilment' (Weisbuch 232). The compound poem thus achieved is filled with echoes and intensifications. It tells of the consolations hidden in a spear of grass, and of loafing and inviting the soul; it deals with the mating of earth and sky, and delicious pleasures in the motions of the blood; with labourers going forth into the fields, and poets called to a sense of consecration; with exuberant horseriding, and birdsnesting, and forays in the fissures of the crags; with the embracing of all shunned persons, who are as good as you or I, maybe better than you or I; with house framers and shepherds and artificers and their lives of hazard, not in Arcadia but here and now.

The 'fulfilment', in Weisbuch's term, is marked less by the achievement of an unprecedented vision, than by Whitman's solution to the problem of the long poem in the nineteenth century. For all Wordsworth's struggle against tradition, tradition overwhelmed him: he became mired in uncompleted epics, increasingly Horatian odes, virally proliferating sonnet sequences. Whitman pursued the revolution in ways that Wordsworth could not conceive: he overthrew Milton, loosened traditional metres (making possible both the *vers libre* of Eliot, and the genuinely free verse of Williams and Lawrence) and disposed of the two classical genres which the Romantics merely reformed—the ode and the epic. Having broken the ground, of course, he completed neither of these tasks. His verse often exhibits prosaic flatness and oppressive rhythmic repetitions, and is surprisingly burdened with traditional rhetorical figures.[1] It took Lawrence in free verse to write wholly without rhythmic cliché. And it took Eliot, with Tennyson's assistance, to find an adequate continuous form as musical as Whitman desired his to be.[2] The symbiotic experiment did not end with 'Song of Myself'. But between them Wordsworth and Whitman renovated poetry from the ground up: audience, programme, voice, diction, cadence, form.

---

1 See Gary Schmidgall, *Containing Multitudes* (Oxford University Press, 2014) chapter 2, for a comprehensive treatment of renaissance figures in Whitman.

2 The last two sentences would require a book to illustrate. That book, *Crossing the Bar: Tennyson, Whitman, Dickinson, Lawrence*, exasminng the invention of free verse, the poetry of death, and the birth of modernist poetics, is one I shall never, now, write.

Chapter 10:

Emily Dickinson's Imaginary Conversations

> You inquire my Books—For Poets—I have Keats—and Mr and Mrs Browning. For Prose—Mr Ruskin—Sir Thomas Browne and the revelations....You speak of Mr Whitman—I never read his Book—but was told that he was disgraceful—
>
> —Emily Dickinson to T. W. Higginson, 25 April 1862

1. A Dialogic Imagination

She was dissembling, of course. For poets she did indeed have Keats and Mr & Mrs Browning. She also had the entire 17th century, Blake, Wordsworth, Coleridge, Bryant, Shelley, Byron, and above all, every word of Tennyson. I shall emphasise the Romantics in this chapter, alongside her contemporaries, attempting to distil in Dickinson's peculiar chemistry, traces of the poets she blended in her poetic laboratory, returning to Tennyson (and Whitman and Dickinson) in a Victorian Epilogue.

It was once thought that Emily Dickinson was the least literary of poets, a wholly autochtonous Emersonian being, and that one half-line in her poetry—'I see New Englandly'—justified the assumption that her cultural horizons ended at Boston. For many readers and many of her critics Emily Dickinson is still the least literary of poets, though recent studies have addressed Dickinson's peculiar intimacy with the lyrical canon.[1] Numerous of her poems, perhaps half of

---

1 Ruth Miller, *The Poetry of Emily Dickinson* (Middletown, Conn: Wesleyan UP, 1968), Joanne Feit Diehl, *Dickinson and Romantic imagination* (Princeton:

those which are anthologised and regularly attract readings, have been identified as originating in a response (however slant) to poems by Wyatt, Donne, Southwell, Vaughan, Thomson, Wordsworth, Coleridge, Byron, Shelley, Keats, Moore, the Brownings, Longfellow and Christina Rossetti, making her perhaps the most assiduous and creative recycler of mostly imported literary materials since Sidney and Shakespeare. She also made innumerable poems, both wry and sentimental, from the lived experience of characters in Dickens, George Eliot, the Bronte sisters and Stowe, and from the prose of Sir Thomas Browne, De Quincey, Ruskin and Emerson. It would indeed be dangerous to underestimate the range, as Richard Sewall vividly expressed it, 'of that prehensile mind and burr-like memory'.[1] Moreover, the scholarly recovery of her sewn 'fascicles'—essentially, ordered meditative sequences which create a situational matrix for a high percentage of her poems—enables her work to be reassessed in relation to seventeenth-century devotional sequences, especially those of Herbert and Quarles, and to such contemporary poetic structures as Whitman's and Tennyson's.[2] It is arguable that, thanks

---

Princeton University Press, 1981) and Dorothy Huff Oberhaus, *Emily Dickinson's Fascicles: Method & Meaning* (University Park, PA: Pennsylvania State University Press, 1995), have done most to restore Dickinson to a poetic tradition. Judith Farr's *The Passion of Emily Dickinson* (Cambridge, MA: Harvard University Press, 1992) recognises Tennyson and the Pre-Raphaelites. Barton Levi St Armand, *Emily Dickinson: the Soul's Society* (Cambridge: Cambridge University Press, 1984), a brilliant study of Dickinson's immediate intellectual context, extends to a consideration of the Spasmodics and Ruskin. Major studies since this chapter first appeared include Richard E. Brantley's *Experience and Faith: The Late-Romantic Imagination of Emily Dickinson* (Palgrave Macmillan, 2004), and Patrick J. Keane in *Emily Dickinson's Approving God* (University of Missouri, 2008).

1 Richard B. Sewall, *The Life of Emily Dickinson* (NY: Farrar, Straus & Giroux, 1974), 671.

2 The fascicles appear in Ralph W. Franklin's The Manuscript Books of Emily Dickinson (Cambridge, MA and London: The Belknap Press of Harvard University Press, 1981). While Sharon Cameron, in *Choosing Not Choosing: Dickinson's Fascicles* (Chicago & London: U of Chicago Press, 1992), has offered a somewhat sceptical verdict on the interpretive value of the fascicle organisation of the poems, Miller and Oberhaus both perceive in the evidence made available by Franklin's edition a poet capable of large and consistent structures, and whose thought within those structures tends to exhibit a consistent teleology. Ruth Miller argues that it

to her 'frightful isolation' in Victorian Amherst (Heathcliff's characterisation of the situation of Catherine Earnshaw in Thrushcross Grange is not inapposite to a poet who dramatised herself in Brontean terms), Dickinson is necessarily the most *bookish* poet in the Anglo-American tradition and even that she is in a strict sense unreadable without some awareness of the precursor texts on which many of her major poems are meditations.

Whether it was reading Wordsworth's arguments for arranging his poems, in the later lifetime editions, as Miller first suggested, or a fascination with the devotional series of the 17th century (which Dorothy Wordsworth, coincidentally, was also reading at about the same time) or the example of Blake, or of Tennyson, or even of the 'disgraceful' Mr Whitman that persuaded Dickinson to write her poems for, or edit them into, sequences of twelve to twenty-five poems (more such sequences, incidentally, than any poet has ever undertaken) cannot be known. I mention Blake partly because Blake's dialectic, whereby the soul passes from innocence through experience to 'organiz'd innocence', is suggested by Miller's view of the essential and recurring fascicle plot. In Miller's words: 'Each is a narrative structure designed to recreate the experience of the woman as she strives for acceptance or knowledge, is rebuffed or fails because of her limitations, but then by an act of will, forces herself to be patient in order to survive, fixes her hopes on another world where Jesus and God await her, and remains content meanwhile with herself alone'.[1] Oberhaus,

---

was Dickinson's habit to use her poetry to issue challenges to other writers. 'One could gloss much of Browne's *Religio Medici* and *Christian Morals* with poems by Emily Dickinson, echoing his language, challenging his ideas'. Her reading of what is now known as the 16th fascicle (Fascicle 32 in her numbering) illustrates a deep imagistic thematic and structural relation to Francis Quarles's *Emblems, Divine and Moral*. Dorothy Huff Oberhaus has made similar claims for this devotional poet's intimate dialogue with Herbert's *The Temple*.

1 Miller 248–9. Weisbuch's summary of Miller's position, that each fascicle narrates the passage of a protagonist from orthodox faith, through doubt, to toughened faith is particularly and no doubt deliberately suggestive of Blake (Robert Weisbuch, *Emily Dickinson's Poetry,* Chicago and London: U of Chicago P. 1975, xii). There is an erroneous supposition among some Dickinson scholars that she could not have known Blake: the fact is that she could have known the *Songs of Innocence and Experience* at any time after Elizabeth Peabody starting selling the

similarly, sees all forty fascicles linked by a narrative thread: 'the inner drama of the meditator/ protagonists's variegated progression from the first fascicle's vow to the fortieth fascicle's plateau of confidence'. The much anthologised poems of scepticism or outright denial thus acquire, in their fascicle context (which may, we have to remind to remind ourselves, be both *post facto* and provisional), a role in a drama with a conversion and salvation teleology. The jury is out on this matter, but Dickinson may emerge as a poet whose loyalty is so much to the next world, rather than to this, that to use criticism to persuade one otherwise would involve serious deception.

The recognition that Dickinson's isolation was not a literary one—that she lived a life of the mind comparable to that lived at Haworth—began not surprisingly with poems which refer directly or indirectly to the Brontes or to the Barrett Brownings. Some twenty individual poems have been traced to Barrett's influence by Jack L. Capps and Diane S. Bogus, while Ellen Moers confirmed the suspicion of J. E. Walsh that a further sixty or so may have taken their origin from individual lines or passages in the verse novel, *Aurora Leigh*.[1] Walsh, notoriously, offered this as evidence of plagiarism, while Moers developed the altogether more promising notion that read alongside their 'source' in Barrett, 'the Dickinson poems serve almost as arias in rhyme to break up the onrushing blank verse recitative of *Aurora Leigh*'. 'I rather suspect', she concluded, 'that Emily Dickinson sometimes wrote a verse or two with just that complementary function in mind—that is, to underline and elaborate the emotional content of something that happened in *Aurora Leigh*, rather than in her own life' (Moers, 59).

Wilkinson edition of the songs in 1837. The great book on Emily Dickinson will need to relate her dialectic to his. Dickinson's 1755 poems include many that fall well below the ironies of Blakean 'simplicity', but at her frequent best she specialises in structures as open-ended as Blake's 'The Clod and the Pebble', or as wholly non-referential as 'the Blossom', while her bees, flowers, volcanoes and stars are as emblematic—as much 'outside nature'—as his lambs, flowers, tygers and stars.

1 Jack L. Capps, *Emily Dickinson's Reading 1836–1886* (Cambridge, MA: Harvard UP, 1966), Diane S. Bogus, 'Not so Disparate: An Investigation of the Influence of Elizabeth Barrett Browning on the work of Emily Dickinson' (*Dickinson Studies* 49 (1984) 38–46); Ellen Moers, *Literary Women* (London: The Women's Press, 1978).

In *Aurora Leigh*, for instance, Marian Erle, led by Aurora towards a scene of confession,

> Turned round and followed closely where I went,
> As if I led her by a narrow plank
> Across devouring waters, step by step;
> And so in silence we walked on a mile.[1]

In J 875 this situational image is first expanded—'I stepped from plank to plank / A slow and cautious way / The stars above my head I felt / About my Feet the Sea. // I knew not but the next / Would be my final inch'—and then generalised: 'This gave me that precarious gait / Some called Experience'. Similarly, to Capps and others, the prosaic moment in *Aurora Leigh*, in which Aurora records that the departing Romney 'touched, just touched / My hatstrings tied for going (at the door / The carriage stood to take me)' generates (inter alia, the image recurs in several poems) this piece of eschatological bravura which culminates in a downhill ride to 'Judgement':

> Tie the Strings to my Life, My Lord,
> Then, I am ready to go!
> Just a look at the Horses –
> Rapid! That will do! (J 279).[2]

Novels, too, contribute to her art. A reader of *Uncle Tom's Cabin* who remembers the 'little boat' going down exultantly in Poem J 30 can feel sure that Dickinson hovered over Stowe's chapters 26 and 28, where the angels sound for break of day, and the waves of life settle over Eva's 'little bark'. The fiction of all three of the Bronte sisters as well as her beloved George Eliot would, if read slowly enough, account in a similar way for the generative moments of many dozens of Dickinson's poems. 'All overgrown with cunning Moss' overtly

---

[1] Elizabeth Barrett Browning, *Aurora Leigh*, Book 6 (London: Chapman & Hall, 1857), 246, (lines 481–4 in modern editions).

[2] I usually cite Dickinson's poems from *Emily Dickinson: the complete Poems*, ed. Thomas H. Johnson (London: Faber and Faber, 1975), as the edition most widely available, and use his numbering, with J prefixes, though I have also consulted Ralph W. Franklin's *The Poems of Emily Dickinson: Variorum Edition*, 3 vols. (Cambridge, MA and London: The Belknap Press, 1998).

elegises Charlotte Bronte. It is only a shade less obvious that the woman who named her dog after the one in the Rivers household in *Jane Eyre* should find it appropriate to write a poem about her experience of allowing human love to come between herself and God (or about Jane Eyre's or her own persona doing so), as in J 765:

> You constituted Time –
> I deemed Eternity
> A revelation of Yourself –
> 'Twas therefore Deity
>
> The Absolute – removed
> The Relative away –
> That I unto Himself adjust
> My slow idolatry –

Nor is it surprising that the landlocked poet whose Brontean imagination uses the unseen 'moor' and 'sea' to assure herself of the co-ordinates of heaven (poem 1052) should also wonder, in a mood reminiscent of Catherine Earnshaw the elder, whether a Calvinistic heaven and one's own feistiness might prove somewhat ill-assorted:

> I never felt at Home – Below –
> And in the Handsome Skies
> I shall not feel at Home – I know –
> I don't like Paradise –
>
> Because it's Sunday all the time – (J 413)

Given the extraordinarily reclusive life Dickinson elected to lead, it is not surprising that a substantial part of her poetry should arise from her reading. In one way or another, poems as characteristic of Dickinson's at her best as 'I felt a funeral in my brain', 'I died for beauty', 'You've seen balloons set, haven't you?', 'Because I could not stop for death', and 'I heard a fly buzz when I died' have been attributed to Dickinson's profound and intimate absorption in the work of 'Mr and Mrs Browning'. Capps saw 'Because I could not stop for death' as a transgendering of 'The Last Ride Together' ('the basic metaphor in both poems is that of a chivalrous gentleman riding in the company of a congenial feminine companion'), attributed 'Tell all the Truth but tell it slant' to *The Ring and the Book*, and traced three of Dickinson's 'pearl' poems to a passage in *Paracelsus*.

Perhaps because he was looking for direct phrasal allusion, Capps found rather little to link Dickinson with the Romantics.[1] He found, predictably, a trace of Wordsworth in the daffodil image in 'Absent Place – an April day', noted the clear and indirect allusion to Keats in 'I died for Beauty' (where Dickinson alludes to Barrett's own allusion in 'A Vision of Poets' to 'Ode on a Grecian Urn'), but despite her knowledge of Moore and her fascination with De Quincey, Capps found little more to link her with the second generation of Romantics than the certainty that Byron's 'The Prisoner of Chillon' gave rise to 'A prison gets to be a friend', and to the conclusion of 'Talk with prudence to a Beggar'. It is not that she ignored the Romantics: rather, he suggested, she was so much in consonance with Romantic attitudes that she barely registered them as stimuli (Capps, 82).

Since then, however, Joanne Feit Diehl's study *of Dickinson and the Romantic Imagination* has changed that conclusion radically. It does not require an enormously accomplished reader to guess that 'The Frost was never seen' might owe something to Coleridge, or 'His mind of Man, a secret makes' to Wordsworth, or 'The name of it is Autumn' to Keats, or 'The duties of the wind are few' to Shelley's 'Ode to the West Wind', or 'I taste a liquor never brewed' to Emerson. What Diehl hypothesised, however, with reference to many dozens of Dickinson's poems, including whole clusters of poems to do with Autumn, or cocoons and butterflies, or bees and flowers, or spiders, or volcanoes or lightning, is a habit of dialogic composition: perhaps the most extraordinary instance of a mind in persistent dialogue with a broad range of other poets in the history of Anglo-American lyricism.

As Diehl has shown, such deeply characteristic poems as 'It was

---

1 My 'method', such it is, assumes, along with some theoreticians of intertextuality, that given the shared medium of language, all utterance embodies prior utterance, and that in literary art, 'allusion' can only be avoided as the cost of extreme impoverishment and may exists even at the level of metrical echo. For Dickinson, who shared her reclusive life with writers living and dead, this law would have been especially operative.

not death for I stood up', 'Further in Summer than the birds', 'As imperceptibly as Grief', and 'There's a certain slant of light' are products of dialogue with the romantics. Diehl's approach is most persuasive in examining the extraordinary extent of Dickinson's dialogue with Keats and Shelley, whose most characteristic themes and tropes seem to provide Dickinson with a rich vein of materials for transmutation.[1] Dickinson exhibits, as one might expect of so chilly a writer, some scepticism towards Keats's consolatory use of natural imagery.[2] Whereas Keats's Autumn has its own music, Dickinson experiences Summer's end as betrayal:

> As imperceptibly as Grief
> The Summer lapsed away –
> Too imperceptible at last
> To seem like Perfidy –
> A Quietness distilled
> As twilight long begun,
> Or nature spending with herself
> Sequestered Afternoon – (J. 1540)

Like numerous Dickinson poems, J 1540 requires to be read against Keats's optimistic sense of natural cycles, which of course reaches its greatest triumph in 'To Autumn.' The images here, while in no obvious sense echoing Keats's 'last oozings' in its distillation of quietness, or his sleeping reaper in the personification of sequestered nature, belong to the extensive category of her variations on this classic treatment of reconciliation with endings, the Keatsian adjustment to Lear's 'ripeness is all'.

This by the way, seems to me as it did to Yvor Winters, one of

---

[1] One cannot read Diehl's chapter on Shelley (122–160) without feeling how profoundly Dickinson influenced him: a signal instance of Bloomian apophrades. Shelley moves toward Dickinson, even more than Diehl is prepared to claim, remaking himself into a poet of the solipsistic imagination, as Dickinson raids him for images that conduct towards the imageless.

[2] Diehl (68–121) compares not only poetic figures but some that suggest familiarity with Keats's letters, for instance their use of the spider as a figure of precarious poetic self-sufficiency, and the sense of soul-making as the formation of 'atoms of perception' (Keats's epistolary phrase, echoed in J 664).

Dickinson's very finest poems. It has an unmistakable music, here registered in the manner in which the initial tetrameter sets up an expectation of common metre, but the initial line of each of the following quatrains (marked by the half rhymes) drops a beat. 'A qui–et–ness di–stilled' expands to fill the space of the anticipated fourth foot. The remaining diminished quatrains read:

> The dusk drew earlier in –
> The morning foreign shone –
> A courteous, yet harrowing Grace,
> As guest, that would be gone –
> And thus, without a Wing
> Or service of a Keel
> Our Summer made her light escape
> Into the Beautiful.

Diminished beats, lightened punctuation, images of negation, the most faintly implied metaphor—Summer sculls herself across the bar, as it were, into 'the Beautiful'—lead to the counter-Keatsian turn from the consolations of Autumn into a lament that perfidious Summer has reached the bourne where the poet cannot follow.

In Poem 130, to which Diehl does not refer, the choice of Keatsian encounters being so wide, Dickinson's wonderfully melodic celebration of the 'sacrament of summer days, / Oh last Communion in the Haze', sets out with a marked acknowledgement:

> These are the days when Birds come back –
> A very few – a Bird or two –
> To take a backward look.
> These are the days when skies resume
> The old – old sophistries of June –
> A blue and gold mistake.
> Oh fraud that cannot cheat the Bee –
> Almost thy plausibility
> Induces my belief.

'Almost'. The third stanza, patently, offers a reversal of Keats's bees who are gently ironised in their perception that 'warm days will never cease': Dickinson's speaker, despite the recurrent warnings of 'sophistries', 'mistake' and 'plausibility' seems half in love with deceit, but the 'almost' warns us to remember the cheating fancy of 'Ode to a Nightingale'. She seals the dialogic quality of her meditation with 'softly thro' the altered air / Hurries a timid leaf', a cold sign of departure which fuses Keats's wailful choir of gnats 'borne aloft / Or sinking as the light wind lives or dies' with his 'gathering swallows' whose gathering portends departure. But her speaker is left on the outside, half isolated in a chill irony, half supplicating for inclusion in that 'Last Communion in the Haze' and its 'immortal wine'.

Diehl argues that for Dickinson the problem was not, in the Bloomian mode, that of being chosen by a single strong precursor, as Wordsworth is chosen by Milton, and Shelley by Wordsworth for instance, but in clearing herself a space given her status as a woman for whom all the voices of the lyric tradition constitute a single composite perilous precursor. But the same problem existed, it seems to me, for the poets whose contemporary she was, and those who felt it most strongly were not, as it happens, Elizabeth and Christina, but Alfred, Robert and George. Dickinson's early poems are full of melodic echoes; in the later ones they tend to be suppressed. She has, it seems to me, three strategies for accomplishing this suppression. One of these is a spareness and leanness of tone, allied with that surreal imagistic quality which her most unique achievements display. Another is the increasing indulgence in those famous dashes (partly one imagines, as a desperate defence against the echoes which start to swarm whenever a belated poet permits some lyric expansiveness). Dickinson's 'stiff sing-song', as Yvor Winters called it,[1] and Robert Browning's spasmodics, are both, perhaps, ways of making space for oneself in a poetic isle which is already full of noises. A third strategy is to create strange new harmonies out of a multiplicity of echoes, in what seems to me a very contemporary mode. While sometimes she takes her Wordsworth, her Keats, her Tennyson, singly, more often their essential oils are indescribably blent.

Coming to maturity well after the simultaneous appearance

---

[1] Yvor Winters, *In Defence of Reason* (New York: Swallow Press, 1947), 283.

of Coleridge, Keats and Shelley in the Galignani edition of 1829, and during the dominance of Barrett, Tennyson, and Browning, Dickinson's subtle music is peculiarly Victorian-Romantic. She grew up on the Romantics and I have no doubt that the lyric dialogue of Wordsworth and Coleridge was as clear to her as it was to such modern scholars as Paul Magnuson or Lucy Newlyn. Among her contemporaries, Meredith and the Brownings, poetic kleptomania (or, more politely, compound allusion) remained the fashion. She shared with George Meredith not only a proto-Modernist difficulty and elision, but his own habit of multiple allusion. In the third sonnet of his magnificent *Modern Love* (1862) which she cannot have read at a formative date (and may not have read at all), Meredith's tormented husband, no longer sure of his wife, ponders kissing her:

> It cannot be such harm on her cool brow
> To put a kiss? Yet if I meet him there!
> But she is mine! Ah, no! I know too well
> I claim a star whose light is overcast:
> I claim a phantom-woman in the Past.
> The hour has struck, though I heard not the bell![1]

The resonances of these lines depend upon the fact that Meredith's form combines the naturalist novel with the Elizabethan sonnet sequence. The dialogue with himself, in broken half-lines, recalls the dramatic fracturing of pentameters in the struggles of Sidney's star-lover Astrophel, while his star image refers also to Shakespeare's idealist bluster in casting love as 'an ever-fixéd mark that looks on tempests and is never shaken'.

By the time Meredith picks up this image, subjecting it to numerous ironic twists throughout *Modern Love*, Keats has already inverted the 'Bright Star' image into a measure of the poet's incapacity for steadfastness, and done so with such authority that Browning's speaker in 'Two in the Campagna' can invoke *both* Shakespeare's romantic idealism *and* Keats's sceptical revision merely by lamenting that his love is 'fixed by no friendly star'. Meredith's 'star', therefore, is freighted with the perceptions of Shakespeare, Keats and Browning.

---

[1] *The Poetical Works of George Meredith* (London: Constable, 1912), 134.

He frequently relies on such tropical histories to create complex effects from simple images, and the method is capable of astonishing amplitude of suggestion. The melancholy close of *Modern Love* is announced in sonnet 47 in a rich blend of Keats and Shakespeare and Wordsworth:

> We saw the swallows gathering in the sky,
> And in the osier-isle we heard them noise.
> We had not to look back on summer joys,
> Or forward to a summer of bright dye:
> But in the largeness of the evening earth
> Our spirits grew as we went side by side.
> The hour became her husband and my bride,
> Love that had robbed us so, thus blessed our dearth!
> The pilgrims of the year waxed very loud
> In multitudinous chatterings, as the flood
> Full brown came from the West, and like pale blood
> Expanded to the upper crimson cloud....

The musical complexities here, in this Indian Summer of a doomed relationship, severed by recriminations and by impending suicide, derive from Macbeth's 'multidinous seas incarnadine', Timon's 'pale fire', Keats's 'To Autumn', Wordsworth's 'spousal consummations' and 'hour of glory in the grass', and his 'Stepping Westward'. The effect is to orchestrate guilt, sorrow, remorse and regret of every conceivable timbre.

Tennyson, whose work Dickinson knew intimately, tends to offer one poet at a time, as an amplifier of particular resonances. His nineteenth lyric in *In Memoriam* famously borrows Wordsworth's 'sweet inland murmur' of the Wye some miles upstream from Tintern Abbey to express the tides of sorrow:

> There twice a day the Severn fills,
> The salt sea-water passes by,
> And hushes half the babbling Wye,
> And makes a silence in the hills.[1]

---

[1] Tennyson, *In Memoriam, Maud and Other Poems,* edited by John D. Jump (London: Dent, 1974), 86.

But in certain poems, including 'Tears, idle Tears…', he will use a Keatsian motif, barely present in the combination of 'gather' and 'Autumn' (there isn't a swallow in sight) to amplify a consciously Wordsworthian theme, of the irretrievability of the past:

> Tears, idle tears, I know not what they mean,
> Tears from the depth of some divine despair
> Rise in the heart, and gather to the eyes,
> In looking on the happy Autumn fields,
> And thinking of the days that are no more…

Without a swallow in sight, the combination of 'gather' and 'Autumn' casues Keats (as Seamus Heaney would say) to rise in the pool of the ear. This poem, 'unsurpassed by any piece of the same length in the language', according to Poe, was among the best known lyrics of the poet lauded by both the *Southern Literary Messenger* and the *Presbyterian Quarterly* 'the poet of our age'.[1] It certainly spawned some of Dickinson's finest poems.

By 1862 Dickinson had perfected this symbiotic habit. 'I heard a Fly buzz – when I died' (J 465) achieves such a startle with its opening and its closing wit that even the Keatsian synaesthesia of the fly's 'Blue – uncertain stumbling Buzz' may not register as a genial technical borrowing. Her more significant borrowing seems to have gone wholly unremarked. The second stanza of 'Tears, idle Tears' runs:

> Fresh as the first beam glittering on a sail,
> That brings our friends up from the underworld,
> Sad as the last which reddens over one
> That sinks with all we love below the verge;
> So sad, so fresh, the days that are no more

This association of memory and death, more domestically and uncannily troped by Dickinson in terms of the cemetery as a local 'underworld', a township where tombs are roofs, and the meek await their resurrection, is of course her primary territory.

But it is Tennyson's third stanza that calls to her most:

---

1 John Olin Eidson, *Tennyson in America: His Reputation and Influence from 1827 to 1858* (Athens, GA: University of Georgia Press, 1943), 70, 94–5.

> Ah, sad and strange as in dark summer dawns
> The earliest pipe of half awakened birds
> To dying ears, when unto dying eyes
> The casement slowly grows a glimmering square;
> So sad, so strange, the days that are no more

In her own meditation on dying ears and dying eyes, in which Tennyson's elaborate trope for memory becomes the substantive theme of a deeply sceptical meditation on death itself, the famous 'Buzz' interposes

> Between the light – and me –
> And then the Window failed —and then
> I could not see to see –

To 'fail' is a code-word, in Mr and Mrs Browning, for death, but Dickinson's intensification of Tennyson's casement image for the perceptual limits of dying eyes is the more generative moment; she used it in numerous liminal poems.

2. Sundered Things: Dickinson's Lucy Poems

> A slumber did my spirit seal;
> I had no human fears:
> She seem'd a thing that could not feel
> The touch of earthly years.
>
> No motion has she now, no force;
> She neither hears nor sees;
> Roll'd round in earth's diurnal course
> With rocks, and stones, and trees!

Tennyson's poems also explain why Dickinson's long engagement with Wordsworth's 'Lucy poems' is sometimes so hard to see: Dickinson perceives Wordsworth through Tennyson. Bryant, Poe and Whitman were also devout Lucyans, but Dickinson's oeuvre represents the most prolonged encounter—in twenty or more poems—with this quintessential body of Wordsworthian poetry. All four Lucy poems seem to have mattered to Dickinson: 'Strange fits of passion' with its alarming premonition of death, 'She dwelt among the untrodden ways' with its lament for the loss of a girl-woman almost unknown to her kind, 'A slumber did my spirit seal', with its sublime intimations of life in nature, and 'Three Years she Grew' with its drama of early mortality. 'Lucy Gray', vanishing into the snow like a fleeting premonition of Dickinson, is a lesser presence (Wordsworthians tend to regard the balladic 'Lucy Gray' as set apart from the Lucy poems and Dickinson may have agreed).

Her first celebration of a silently sleeping Lucy figure, unknown and unremembered except by the speaker, responds as the speaker of *Maud* imagines he would respond to the foot of Maud 'had I lain for a century dead':

> She slept beneath a tree –
> Remembered but by me.
> I touched her cradle mute –
> She recognized the foot –
> Put on her carmine suit
> And see! (J 25)

The tell-tale foot returns in Poem 28:

> So has a Daisy vanished
> From the fields today –
> So tiptoed many a slipper
> To Paradise away –
>
> Oozed so in crimson bubbles
> Day's departing tide –
> Blooming – tripping – flowing –
> Are ye then with God?

The association of daisies with crimson is, of course, part of the erotic language of both Charlotte Bronte (St. John Rivers, in *Jane Eyre*, signals his own passional renunciation in crushing the daisies with his foot as he thinks of Miss Oliver) and of Tennyson. Maud's lover knows which way she went, for 'her feet have touched the meadows / And left the daisies rosy'. Here, however, the passage from daisies to crimson bubbles is figurative. The vanishing daisy, the tip-toeing slipper (a personified flower?), the bubbling tide are metaphors for the passage of the soul, and the poem works by enormously impacting a structure associated less with Tennyson (though he used it with subtle variation in 'Tears, idle Tears') than with Coleridge's apostatic 'France: an Ode' and Shelley's libertarian riposte in 'Ode to the West Wind'. Both Coleridge and Shelley image liberty in a triad of natural images subject to the winds, which are first individually developed and then brought together in a reprise ('O lift me as a leaf, a wave, a cloud' is Shelley's activist response to Coleridge's quietist 'O ye loud Waves! And O ye Forests high! / And O ye Clouds'). Dickinson's allusion to this history is confirmed, of course, not just by the three successive couplets but by the reprise of 'Blooming – tripping – flowing – ' in line seven.

Dickinson's miniature triad thus presses into the service of private loss a structure employed in the two most famous—and famously dialogic—expressions of historical dereliction. But not necessarily her own dereliction. 'Blooming – tripping – flowing' may, as I have suggested, function as an odal reprise, magnifying the miniature form, but the three verb-images belong to a homelier poetry. In 'The Fountain' Wordsworth's Mathew reconciles himself to the irreparability of loss by contemplating Whitmanesque / Dickinsonian / Lawrentian birds, ('With nature never do they wage / A foolish strife') and by calmly juxtaposing the perpetual vigour of the fountain with his own seventy-two years: ''Twill murmur on a thousand years, / And flow as now it flows'.

One might not associate this 'flows' with Dickinson's 'flowing' were it not for the subsequent Mathew poem, 'The Two April Mornings', in which the disconcerting Mathew is reminded by dawn's 'crimson' light of a similar morning some thirty years before, when he stopped short beside his nine-year-old daughter's grave.

> Six feet in earth my Emma lay,
> And yet I loved her more,
> For so it seemed, than till that day
> I e'er had loved before.
>
> And, turning from her grave, I met

> Beside the church-yard Yew
> A blooming Girl whose hair was wet
> With points of morning dew
> ...
>
> No fountain from its rocky cave
> E'er tripped with foot so free,
> She seemed as happy as a wave
> That dances on the sea.

But the poem focuses a chill epiphany (compare 'Renunciation is a piercing virtue'; J 745):

> There came from me a sigh of pain
> Which I could ill confine;
> I looked at her and looked again;
> —And did not wish her mine.

From 'The Two April Mornings' Dickinson at some level remembers 'Crimson', crossed with Tennyson's, 'blooming', 'trip[ping]', 'foot' (also fused with Tennyson), and—implied by wave but specified in 'The Fountain'—'flow[ing]'. Poem 28, therefore, is a Lucy poem combining the two-stanza form of 'A slumber did my spirit seal' with the rhetorical form of two major romantic odes, working with, and germinated by, a figures from *Maud* and *Jane Eyre*, yet using metre in a characteristic spasmodic alternation between iambic and trochaic, and using metaphor in a way which is already distinctly Dickinsonian. However juvenile this poem of 1858, it is a fairly characteristic piece of Dickinson: a babel of 'quotation' in barely fifty syllables (and I mean that as a compliment to her poetic maturity: only major poets can do this), finding room for surprise and uncertainty.

However aware of their difference—'His mind of man a secret makes / I meet him with a start / He carries a Circumference / In which I have no part' (J 1663)—Dickinson's Wordsworth forms a large part of the quarrel over Nature out of which her poetry is born.[1] Accepting Wordsworth's view that 'the brain is wider than the sky',

---

[1] Or Emerson of course, but Dickinson surely has the source, not the conduit, in mind.

as she puts it in Poem 632, and his view that there are two natures, that given by God, and that other nature created by the poets, she makes the human mind the main region of her song and mines, chiefly, that 'second Nature' of the poets. Poem 308 is her delightfully whimsical comment on Wordsworth's sublimer sense of competition: she can finish two 'sunsets' while day is making one, and while 'His own was ampler ... / Mine – is the more convenient / To carry in the hand'. Like Wordsworth her solitude was not one, primarily, of situation, but a recognition of tragic and inescapable isolation: 'Points have we all of us within our souls / Where all stand single', said Wordsworth, to which Dickinson concurred, speaking of the 'depths in every consciousness from which we cannot rescue ourselves – to which none can go with us'.[1] Like Wordsworth, too, though with a melancholia more often akin to Tennyson, she lived *on* as well as *in* memory, chewing the cud of intense experience in variations of deeply, sometimes impenetrably, ruminative verse. David Porter has justly called her the poet of 'afterwards' (Porter, 9).

Poem 652, confidently identified by Jack L Capps as an exercise rooted in Byron's 'The Prisoner of Chillon'—it begins 'A Prison gets to be a friend'—has more recently been interpreted by Daria Donnelly as a rewriting of the poem upon the Wye. Donnelly suggests persuasively that Wordsworth's 'abundant comparatives' ('more deep', 'purer', 'coarser', 'remoter', 'warmer, 'deeper', 'holier') 'argue strenuously for personal progress in vision and understanding, doing so against an undercurrent of anxiety that the speaker's affective life has diminished over time.'[2] She notes that Wordsworth's invocation of 'the coarser pleasures of my boyish days', is echoed in Dickinson's 'plashing in the Pools – / When memory was a Boy', and argues that Dickinson's reference to achieving 'a demurer Circuit – / A Geometric Joy – ', comments upon, and exposes, Wordsworth's exchange of vivid affective experience for creative power. Perhaps, too, there is a hint of Keats's 'A thing of beauty is a joy forever'

---

[1] David Porter, *Dickinson: The Modern Idiom* (Cambridge, MA: Harvard University Press, 1981), 6.

[2] Daria Donnelly, 'Emily Dickinson and the Romantic Comparative', in *Romanticism and Gender*, edited by Anne Janowitz (Cambridge: D. S. Brewer, 1998), 116–139,126.

with his melancholy implication that art and life exist in antithetical modes. One reason for concurring with Donnelly's suggestion that this poem compresses Wordsworth's argument is its range of reference, its burrs of 'Resolution and Independence' ('plashing'), *The Prelude* (the five-year-old in the pools of Derwent), and above all, surely, the Ode, in which 'shades of the prison-house begin to close upon the growing boy'. It is not that Capps was necessarily wrong to identify the poem with 'The Prisoner of Chillon'. Rather, I would suggest, Dickinson associates the two, using and reversing Byron's meditation on imaginative liberty, in her critique of Wordsworth's own natural 'prison' and his 'slow exchange of Hope – / For something passiver'. Nor is Coleridge's redefinition of liberty in 'France: an Ode' entirely excluded: it seems present in Dickinson's perception of liberty as something 'too wide for any Night but Heaven'.[1]

Joanne Feit Diehl's scintillating treatment of Dickinson's dialogue with the Romantics is by no means exhaustive. Although noting Dickinson's radical transformation of the Wordsworthian inscription poem, and her tendency to annex the landscape to self-depiction, performing 'a solipsistic usurpation of nature' at odds with Wordsworth's reciprocity, she barely notes this sceptical response to 'She dwelt among th'untrodden ways':

> She laid her docile crescent down
> And this confiding Stone
> Still states to dates that have forgot
> The news that she is gone –
>
> So constant to its stolid trust,
> The Shaft that never knew –
> It shames the Constancy that fled
> Before its emblem flew – (J 1396)

If 'docile Crescent' is not a reference to that moon-associated Lucy,

---

[1] Dickinson's familiarity with *The Prelude* (in her copy of Reed's 1852 *Poetical Works*) comes out also in the allusions to Furness Abbey and the Discharged Soldier in Poem 670. Poem 757 (and others) suggest, also, Wordsworth's various treatments of the setting sun's 'fellowship' with morning hills, which she would also have encountered in Hazlitt's 'My first Acquaintance with Poets'.

whose knowability is so problematic, yet whose death in the two-stanza 'A slumber did my spirit seal', shares the immutability of 'rocks and stones and trees', and makes all the difference to an all-too-mutable speaker, there is no such thing as poetic allusion. One can be quite as certain that Poem 1396 does relate to at least three of the Lucy poems, and that the form of 'A slumber did my spirit seal' has much to do with seven or eight of Dickinson's eight-line meditations on death, as that Poem 106, 'The Daisy follows oft the Sun', relates to none of the Lucy poems.

Poem 106, however, is chosen by Margaret Homans to represent a Dickinsonian reply to Wordsworth's 'Strange fits of passion have I known'. The poem begins,

> The Daisy follows oft the Sun –
> And when his golden walk is done –
> Sits shyly at his feet –

and uses the image of flower-heads turning toward the west, conventionally enough until the wonderfully elliptic penultimate line, to suggest the soul stealing closer to God:

> Forgive us, if as days decline –
> We nearer steal to Thee!
> Enamored of the parting West –
> The peace – the flight – the Amethyst –
> Night's possibility!

According to Homans, however, this poem is actually a love lyric contesting 'the woman's place in the traditional plot of romantic desire'. The poem 'critiques the perspectivism of an earlier group of love lyrics also about a powerful male lover and a female figure whose name makes her a mirror of the sun, Wordsworth's 'Lucy' poems'.[1]

---

[1] Margaret Homans, 'Syllables of Velvet', *Feminist Studies* 11:3 (1985), 576-9. 'In actuality', Homans believes, 'neither Sun nor daisy moves' (this doubtful grasp of both cosmology and botany might give one pause about other aspects of the critique). The daisy wishes to hasten the sun's departure, anxious to enjoy 'Night's possibility' which holds promise of female sexual desire liberated from the imperious phallus. In 'Enamoured of the parting West' the term 'parting' signifies, if I follow the argment successfully, anticipatory labial easement. The possibility of a

One might object that considered as a group, the Lucy poems happen to be elegies rather than love lyrics, and that nothing in the poems supports the claim that Lucy dies (in those in which she does die) because she is lacking in subjectivity: one of them is precisely about her unrecognised subjectivity; another observes that subjectivity growing rampantly. One might point out, also, that the enchanted lover in 'Strange fits of passion' does *not*, as Homans suggests, see himself reflected in the moon (the poem won't work very well for a reader who does not grasp that the speaker identifies Lucy with the moon, possibly because she, not he, is called Lucy). But the poem has to be subjected to such occlusions and eclipses if it is to support Homans's conclusion that 'the Dickinson poem exposes what the daisy would consider to be the absurd egotism of Wordsworth's speaker's belief in the omnipotence of his thoughts' (576–8). Whatever daisies may think, Wordsworth's speaker is palpably experiencing precisely the reverse of what Homans alleges; namely the impotence of his thoughts, given the threat which mortality represents to what he holds most dear. Like numerous other Wordsworth poems of this date, including the other Lucy poems and the Matthew poems, this one handles a particularly characteristic Dickinsonian preoccupation, that of coming to terms with the mortality of others and of oneself. If Dickinson's hypercritical daisy does see error in Wordsworth's speaker—and given that Dickinson's nature poems are often based upon sceptical interrogation of Wordsworthian nature it is certainly arguable that she (the daisy) might—the error is in being overly attached to 'June', or life.

Frances Ferguson's reading of the Lucy poems in *Wordsworth: Language as Counter-Spirit* takes account of the fact that when

---

late Romantic/early Victorian writer using erotic symbolic notation of this kind is of course amply attested by the writings of Charlotte Bronte, Elizabeth Browning, Christina Rossetti, Tennyson, Robert Browning, Meredith and Melville, but this reading surely strains credulity? For a finer feminist reading see Sandra Gilbert and Susan Gubar, *The Madwoman in the Attic* (New Haven: Yale University Press, 1979): Dickinson wrote to Susan Gilbert in 1852 comparing the wife to flowers at noon, which 'pine for the burning noon, though it scorches them' and 'even at the age of twenty-two when she wrote this letter, she had begun apprehensively to define herself as an ambivalently light-loving / sun-fearing flower' (596).

Wordsworth classified his poems he placed 'Strange fits' and 'She dwelt' among the Poems founded upon the Affections, and 'Three Years' and 'A Slumber' as Poems of the Imagination. In the 'Poems founded upon the Affections', Ferguson suggests, Wordsworth presents the mind at war with the mortality which nature inflicts, and the mind loses the struggle, but in the 'Poems of the Imagination', we find depicted 'the mind's survival of the numerous symbolic deaths which it has experienced'.[1] If in the Lucy poems there is such a progress towards calmness and towards a form of triumph, it is at a great cost, but a cost which is a necessary part of the process of maturation. It is that cost, and its payability, which account for the length and the variety of Dickinson's prolonged and varied encounters with the theme. It may well be, and it has been suggested by numerous readers of Dickinson, that this particular mode of maturation was one of many rites of passage at which Dickinson baulked. Nevertheless, imaginatively, Dickinson makes even Browne, Wordsworth, Tennyson and Whitman seem amateurs in the dying business, and Larkin an interloper in the realm of aftermath. Where William Cullen Bryant merely echoes Lucy, Dickinson ('I felt a funeral in my brain'; 'I heard a fly buzz when I died') becomes her.

In Wordsworth's 'Strange fits', the poet-lover is presented as wholly enwrapped in an illusory dream into which mortality does not come. So rapid is the drop, so abrupt the loss of the illusion of immortality, when 'at once the bright moon dropped', that Lucy's mortal passage into nothingness is momentarily supposed to have taken place. Love, and the beloved, are suddenly known to be subject to the waning of the moon, and to all sublunary exigencies including mortality, but not at the remote end of some infinitely extensible natural cycle: death—to adopt the Heideggerian formula—is my possibility now. The task is to become 'certain' of one's death, and capable of contemplating it, of anticipating it, in resoluteness. That anticipation Wordsworth makes the task of the Lucy and Mathew suites. As he plays his variations upon the images of transient humanity and intransigent mortality, each poem contrasts, to develop an insight of

---

[1] Frances Ferguson, *Wordsworth, Language as Counter-Spirit* (New Haven: Yale University Press, 1977), 177.

John Danby's concerning the Matthew Poems, 'the moment of the rose and the moment of the yew':[1] Wordsworth pairs the moon and the rose in 'Strange fits', the violet and the star in 'She dwelt', and the dew and the yew in 'The Two April Mornings' where even the oak spells mortality. The Lucy suite takes Wordsworth towards the moment in the 'Piel Castle' stanzas when Wordsworth will make the strangely deliberate claim, 'the feeling of my loss will ne'er be old. / This, which I know, I speak with mind serene' as he bids farewell to 'the heart that lives alone, / Housed in a dream, at distance from the Kind!'.

If one is in doubt whether the Lucy poems are songs of innocence or of experience, this doubt is resolved in 'A slumber did my spirit seal', the poem which, formally, Dickinson seems most drawn to (she tackles the theme over and over in some twenty eight-line two-stanza poems of the same metre but without the a-rhymes). The poem has, in some readings, the laconic irony of Experience exposing the illusions of Innocence. What Lucy seems in the first stanza she becomes in the second: she 'seemed' a thing, she becomes a thing; his spirit slumbers, hers is still. The language of the poem works remorselessly towards neutralising the expected consolations. With no motion, no force, neither seeing nor hearing, Lucy is rolled round, a passive entity in the Newtonian universe of death. There is no sense—in the state of the soul here represented—that one might understandably sit beside her grave with one's little porringer, as in 'We are seven': or that the grave is a comfortable, satin-lined space where 'sleep the meek members of the Resurrection' (Dickinson) or 'a place of thought where we in waiting lie' ('Intimations'). The lines represent an engagement with extinction comparable to Wordsworth's meeting with the Absurd, and his sense of cosmic Abandonment, in the meeting with the Blind Beggar in *The Prelude*—whose blindness and paper label are an emblem 'of the utmost we can know/ Both of ourselves and of the universe' (*Prelude* 7: 645–6). Nevertheless, 'A Slumber' has a complex counter-movement. The subject of the epitaph is the speaker's illusion, his dream, from the poem awakens

---

1 John F. Danby, *The Simple Wordsworth* (London: Routledge and Kegan Paul, 1960), 79.

him, and it achieves an almost pantheistic consolation in the close. Coleridge called it 'a sublime epitaph', that is one which raises the reader (having looked through death) to a surpassing joy or peace. One may recall that Wordsworthian rocks mutter, and his stones speak; or that Lucy in 'Three Years she Grew' has felt the breathing balm of mute insensate things. One may remain sceptical about the power of stones to participate in the one life, yet still hear 'and trees' as an up-beat caveat.

> Rolled round in earth's diurnal course
> With rocks and stones and trees.

Between the null and the consolatory reading of 'A Slumber', Dickinson dwelt. By and large, the 'one life' option was not available to her, as it was to Bryant and Whitman, but as a devotional Victorian, preoccupied in much of her poetry with last things, and endlessly reconfiguring the soul's passage to eternity, she has her own chill version of faith in its stead. What Dickinson shares most with Wordsworth's Lucy poems is their preoccupation with the 'difference', and as in 'Surprized by Joy', loyalty to the dead. In this emphasis, Wordsworth, Tennyson and Dickinson are most in tune.

Poems 25 and 28, I suggested earlier were Tennysonian Lucy poems, in which either the dead remain conscious of us, or they have tip-toed to Paradise: like the 'linnet' in Poem 27 (linnet is one of Tennyson's feathered personae in *In Memoriam*) they have flown in 'transport' to a fair repose. In J 149/150 the Dickinsonian Lucy is both 'dew' and 'star' and has slipped from the speaker's 'eve'. In J 671, another half-rhyming eight-liner, she lives with the Daffodils, with the universe for her maid, to fetch her 'Grace – and Hue'. In J 1396 the shaft that never knew her, 'this confiding Stone', upbraids the inconstant mind, while in J 1666 the grave is again an empty nest for the flown spirit, but its 'impassive stone' records the 'Act' (of dying) and makes available the haunting allusion to the play upon 'know' and 'unknown' in Wordsworth's 'She dwelt' ('She liv'd unknown, and few could know / When Lucy ceas'd to be'):

> I *know* thee better for the Act
> That made thee first *unknown*.

Stone may not be living in Dickinson's universe, as it is in Wordsworth's, but it can be either 'confiding' or 'impassive': it can also, in Dickinson's more surreal extensions, as the speaker merges with Lucy, become her own expressive 'Granite lip' (J 182). In 'I felt a funeral in my brain' (J 280) Lucy still 'hears', though whether her 'And Finished knowing – then' is an attainment of the Emersonian 'All' or a total loss of knowing hangs in doubt. Both 'The quartz contentment, like a stone' and 'the Hour of lead' in Poem 341 belong to the *living*, whose ongoing life is compared to the 'letting go' of those dying in snow.

Wordsworth's resolution in 'Piel Castle' is reaffirmed in 'Surprized by Joy' along with a grim certainty, in Wordsworth's case, that 'neither present time, nor years unborn / can to my sight that heavenly face [the face of his child Catherine] restore'. The sufferer in Dickinson's Poem 686 determines, too, that 'time never did assuage.' Many of Dickinson's meditations entertain this strangely divided mind in which all that is certain of the 'heavenly' pertains to earth. The realisable factor is loss: and on this theme her meditations (as in J 49, 'I never lost as much but twice', and J 73, 'Who never lost are unprepared / A coronet to find') inevitably interrogate the relatively jaunty consolations of Tennyson's ''Tis better to have loved and lost / Than never to have loved'.

As in Tennyson's poetry of inconsolability, however, the vitality of the dead in Dickinson's poems can serve mainly to mock the living. In Poem 607 ('Of nearness to her sundered Things'), where 'the Shapes we buried, dwell about, / Familiar in the Rooms – / Untarnished by the sepulchre, / The Mouldering Playmate comes' the tone combines the chilly moonlit vault which glimmers in *In Memoriam* LXVII with the powerful and restorative haunting of his XCV, in which 'the dead man touched me from the past'. The association tends to nullify the Tennysonian joy.

A similar deflation occurs in J 1764. Here Dickinson revisited 'Tears, idle Tears' yoking its evocations of 'the days that are no more'—'So sad, so fresh', 'So sad, so strange', and 'wild with all regret'—to the theme of the dead returning with the springtime:

> The saddest noise, the sweetest noise,

> The maddest noise that grows, –
> The birds, they make it in the spring,
> At night's delicious close.

But spring brings resentment, and thoughts of 'the dead / That sauntered with us here'. Where Tennyson's music assuages his own thought, in the paradox of 'and My regret / Becomes an April violet / And buds and blossoms, like the rest' (*In Memoriam*, CXV), Dickinson's complaint is robustly unsaccharined:

> An ear can break a human heart
> As quickly as a spear,
> We wish the ear had not a heart
> So dangerously near. (J 1764)

Dickinson, in meditating her deepest and most recurrent *topoi*, moves in on Wordsworth and Tennyson, arguing with each instance of the Romantic vision, endorsing, rejecting, amending, testing, probing.

Poets (to theorize for a moment) profoundly modify the expressive capacities of language. In particular, they impress themselves into tropes so that echoes proliferate of themselves, and can only with great labour be avoided (most of what any of us say is replete with ineluctable quotation). Perhaps in writing of such themes as Dickinson habitually chose, all that happens is that the confident poet relaxes his or her genetic vigilance and permits language to echo. Or perhaps the poetic collective stamps particular themes so that sincerity is inescapably mutual. Dickinson, for whatever reason, presents one with numerous instances of appearing to share in a collectively, transatlantically generated language. She enacts, as perhaps no English poet did—at least until Thomas Hardy—the birth of post-Romantic tristesse. She also demonstrates the incontrovertibility of Elizabeth Palmer Peabody's conviction that no Treaty of Paris, no constitutional convention, no shading of the map, can actuate poetic secession. In the republic of writing the Atlantic *is* 'the pond'.

Epilogue:

The Escape from 'Locksley Hall'

> Friends shall drop in, a very few—
> Shakespeare and Milton, and no more.
> When these are guests I bolt the door
> With Not at Home to anyone
> Excepting Alfred Tennyson
> —*Thomas Bailey Aldrich*[1]

Americans, says Cecilia Tichi in her Introduction to Edward Bellamy's *Looking Backward* (1888), 'have never abandoned the mission to transform a gilded nation into an exemplary golden one'.[2] The hero of Bellamy's novel goes to sleep in 1887 and awakes to find himself in the year 2000. Ensconced in a library, he names as his circle of literary immortals a visionary tradition in which there are just two Americans, and some writers not often thought of as visionaries at all: 'Shakespeare, Milton, Wordsworth, Shelley, Tennyson, Defoe, Dickens, Thackeray, Hugo, Hawthorne, Irving' (*Looking Backward*, 119). Of these, he praises Dickens as overtopping all writers of his age in opening men's eyes to 'the necessity of change', and Tennyson as the one writer who 'beheld in a vision the world I looked on' in the fictional time of the novel (121–2).

The lines that inspired this eulogy are from 'Locksley Hall', which is the only literary text found worthy of substantial quotation in Bellamy's future world:

---

1 'The Menu', *The Sisters' Tragedy* (Boston: Houghton Mifflin, 1890).
2 Edward Bellamy, *Looking Backward*, ed. Cecilia Tichi (Harmondsworth: Penguin, 1982), 27.

> For I dipped into the future, far as human eye could see,
> Saw the vision of the world, and all the wonder that would be; ...
> Till the war-drum throbbed no longer, and the battle-flags were furled,
> In the Parliament of man, the Federation of the world.

It is all very visionary and uplifting no doubt, but where, one might ask, the year of publication being 1888, are the exemplary texts of Emerson, Melville, Thoreau and—above all—Whitman?

TENNYSON AND WHITMAN / WHITMAN AS TENNYSON

The disappearance of Tennyson from modern reckoning, his decline from the culture hero status he enjoyed in Bellamy's day, is of course the legacy of the Modernists, who all conspired—Hopkins, Joyce and Eliot particularly—to patronise him. Harold Bloom's aversion to the cultural status of T. S. Eliot, in poetry and in criticism, has something to do, no doubt, with his repeated, if still unusual, insistence on Eliot's indebtedness to the Victorian and Romantic voices of Tennyson and Whitman:

> Eliot ... can promise to show us 'fear in a handful of dust' only because the monologist of Tennyson's *Maud* already has cried out: 'Dead, long dead, / Long dead! / And my heart is a handful of dust'. Even more poignantly, Eliot is able to sum up all of Whitman's extraordinary 'As I ebb'd with the Ocean of Life' in the single line: 'These fragments I have shored against my ruins'[1]

If Bloom does not pursue his insight into Eliot's dual 'encumbrance' in equitable detail (as Carl Plasa noted in *Symbiosis* 2.1) but rather relies on extensive quotation from Whitman, there is perhaps a very simple explanation. *Maud* and late Whitman—in mood certainly, and at times even in prosody—are at times not easy to distinguish, especially when Whitman is most himself. If, as Eliot claimed, poets are most themselves when the dead assert themselves most vigorously

---

1 Harold Bloom, 'Reflections on T. S. Eliot', *Raritan* 8:2 (1988) 70–87.

in their work, it may also be true that poets are even more themselves when they can permit the living the same apophraditic rights as the dead. Shelley did so, with Wordsworth and Coleridge; Whitman likewise with Wordsworth, Shelley and Tennyson.[1] Consider this remarkable poem, opening and closing with epizeuxis and climaxing with ecphonesis (some of Whitman's 750 declamatory 'O's):[2]

> Tears! tears! tears!
> In the night, in solitude, tears,
> On the white shore dripping, dripping, suck'd in by the sand,
> Tears, not a star shining, all dark and desolate,
> Moist tears from the eyes of a muffled head;
> O who is that ghost? that form in the dark, with tears?
> What shapeless lump is that, bent, crouch'd there in the sand?
> Steaming tears, sobbing tears, throes, choked with wild cries;
> O storm, embodied, rising, careering with swift steps along the beach!
> O wild and dismal night storm, with wind—O belching and desperate!
> O shade so sedate and decorous by day, with calm countenance and regulated pace
> But away at night as you fly, none looking—O then the unloosened ocean,
> Of tears! tears! tears!

This exemplary poem (exemplary of Whitman's prosody) begins, incontrovertibly, with the rhythmic signature of Tennyson's 'Break, break, break, / On thy cold gray stones O sea'. The first line is prosodically identical, and in the second line the only difference

---

[1] Whitman cited here from *The Works of Walt Whitman*, ed. David Rogers (Herts: Wordsworth, 1995).

[2] Epizeuxis is the repetition of single words with no other words intervening. For a fine analysis of Whitman's employment of such renaissance rhetorical figures see Gary Schmidgall, *Containing Multitudes: Walt Whitman and British Literary Tradition* (Oxford University Press, 2014) 38–48.

is that Whitman's third foot is either elided or anapaestic, making a faint variation of tempo on a conspicuously Tennysonian base. The poem then develops through a set of variations based upon the storm lyrics of *In Memoriam* (lyrics XV, XXVI), exploring the contrast between the parnassian grace of the Tennyson manner and its passional material. Its last line returns, in homage, to the opening note, which, as it happens, itself married the rhythm of 'Break, break, break' to the burden of 'Tears, idle tears'. In accordance with the creative laws of Whitman's prosody, his 'Tears' shows formal trimeter mutating into triple phrase, so that 'bent' in the seventh line occupies the same prosodic time as the two phrases it separates. The exclamatory 'O's—just conceivably there to amplify the alliterative and sonorous *exclamatio* of Tennyson's second line—and the 'But', curiously recalling the famously associative 'But' of 'Break, break, break', introduce lines of variable phrase before the penultimate line returns to triple phrase. The last line echoes the broken trimeter with which both poems began—broken in that both lines require a pause, or ictus, after each monosyllabic beat: / (x) / (x) / (x).

Something of the same technique underlies what may be Whitman's greatest single lyric, the elegy for Lincoln, 'the most sweet and sonorous threnody ever chanted in the church of the world', as Swinburne called it,[1] a poem that begins with Whitman at his most Eliotian in the handling of metre. He opens by establishing an iambic base, with occasional funeral-march anapaests:

> 1
> When lilacs last in the dooryard bloom'd,
> And the great star early drooped in the western sky in the
>   night,
> I mourned, and yet shall mourn with ever-returning spring.
> Ever-returning spring, trinity sure to me you bring,
> Lilac blooming perennial and drooping star in the west,
> And thought of him I love.
>
> 2
> O powerful western fallen star!

---

[1] Algernon Swinburne, *William Blake* (1868), 303.

> O shades of night—O moody, tearful night!
> O great star disappeared—O the black murk that hides the star!

The opening trope, obviously enough, is a sombre variation upon that of *In Memoriam*'s most surprising lyric, substituting lilac for Tennyson's violet:

> and in my breast
> Spring wakens too; and my regret
> Becomes an April violet,
> And buds and blossoms like the rest.[1]

More importantly, one notices that characteristic feature of Whitman's prosody, a tendency in his greatest poems to depart from and return to metrical cadences. The three lines of the opening sentence are a tetrameter (iambic, with an anapaestic third foot); a very mixed hexameter (pyrrhic, spondee, amphimacer, anapaest, iamb, anapaest); and a hexameter (iambic, with an anapaest in the fifth). The three lines opening the second section are pure iambic tetrameter, pentameter, and heptameter (with minor variations in the last). The remainder of the poem develops increasingly free cadences but returns always to formal pentameters and hexameters, in its refrains (*'And life, and the fields, and the huge and thoughtful night'* or *'I float this carol with joy, with joy to thee O death'*) and in the final, and as it happens, overtly Tennysonian, hexameters:

> Lilac and star and bird twined with the chant of my soul,
> There in the fragrant pines and the cedars dusk and dim.

Surprisingly, much though not all of 'Lilacs' might be adduced as corroborating T. S. Eliot's famous pronouncement, that he could not imagine a line of verse that would not scan at all, rather than D. H. Lawrence's surely self-descriptive insistence (though it occurs in his essay on Whitman) that free verse is something altogether different from metrical verse, eschewing rhythmical 'clichés' altogether.[2] In

---

1 *In Memoriam*, CXV, *The Poems of Tennyson*, ed. Christopher Ricks ((London: Logman, 1969).

2 T. S. Eliot, 'Reflections on vers libre', in *Selected Prose*, ed. John Hayward

any case, in some other respects, to invoke Whitman is to invoke Tennyson also. Harold Bloom ('Reflections', 78) plausibly cites these lines from the 14th section of 'Lilacs' as haunting the T. S. Eliot of *The Waste Land*:

> Then with the knowledge of death as walking one side of me,
> And the thought of death close-walking the other side of me,
> And I in the middle as with companions, and as holding the hands of companions,
> I fled forth to the hiding receiving night that talks not,
> Down to the shores of the water, the path by the swamp in the dimness,
> To the solemn shadowy cedars and ghostly pines so still.

And, according to Bloom again ('Reflections', 79) Whitman's 'darker intensities' occasion Eliot's repressed 'agon' with Whitman, intensities such as those in the *Sea-Drift* elegies (which include 'Tears') and these from 'Crossing Brooklyn Ferry':

> It is not upon you alone the dark patches fall,
> The dark threw its patches down upon me also,
> The best I had done seem'd to me blank and suspicious,
> My great thoughts as I supposed them, were they not in reality meagre?
> Nor is it you alone who know what it is to be evil,
> I am he who knew what it was to be evil,
> I too knotted the old knot of contrariety,
> Blabb'd, blush'd, resented, lied, stole, grudg'd,
> Had guile, anger, lust, hot wishes I dared not speak,....

But by the time both of these passages were composed, the dark intensities of Tennyson's *Maud*—identified by John Heath-Stubbs as a primary structural influence upon *The Waste Land*—were being read in America.[1] Whitman, who reviewed *Maud* in 1855, knew that

---

(Harmondsworth: Penguin, 1953) 88; D. H. Lawrence, *The Complete Poems*, ed. Vivian de Sola Pinto and F. Warren Roberts (Harmondsworth: Penguin, 1977) 184.

1 John Heath-Stubbs, 'Structure and Source in Eliot's Major Poetry', *Agenda*,

The Escape from Locksley Hall

Tennyson's often Parnassian voice was also capable of such effects as these, in which, despite the erratic rhyme, metre is subject to as much passional solvent as it is in 'Lilacs':

> Dead, long dead,
> Long dead!
> And my heart is a handful of dust,
> And the wheels go over my head,
> And my bones are shaken with pain,
> For into a shallow grave they are thrust,
> Only a yard beneath the street,
> And the hoofs of the horses beat,
> Beat into my scalp and my brain,
> With never an end to the stream of passing feet,
> Driving, hurrying, marrying, burying,
> Clamour and rumble, and ringing and clatter,
> And here beneath it is all as bad,
> For I thought the dead had peace, but it is not so;...

It was the opening lines of this passage, Bloom remarks in his *Raritan* essay, that enabled Eliot to show us 'fear in a handful of dust'; but *Maud* gave Eliot a good deal more than that, precisely because one can hear its intensities in the more psychotic passages of late Whitman. If a dual 'agon' is possible, the alienated voice of 'The Fire Sermon' and 'What the Thunder Said' is burdened by both precursors. Perhaps it is this dual creation of a poetry to express modern dislocation that enables Harold Bloom, having claimed that Eliot was the ephebe of both Tennyson and Whitman, to illustrate the matter almost wholly from the latter.

DICKINSON, TENNYSON AND THE BROWNINGS

But at least the strange love affair between Tennyson and Whitman is a matter of record. That between Tennyson and Dickinson has ever been consigned to the bottom drawer.

In reality, as I argued in chapter 10, Dickinson is the most *bookish*

1985,22–35.

poet in the Anglo-American tradition. Her compositional method, in an extraordinarily high percentage of her poems, perhaps the majority of her very finest poems, is to take a cutting from a longer poem, plunge it in the rooting compound of her mind, and allow it to grow; or perhaps, since the genetic order of the new composition is of course radically modified in the process, graft it to the stock of her own experience.

Connections with 'Mr and Mrs Browning', reviewed in Chapter 10, have, not unnaturally, been more recognised than others: Dickinson's famous remark, 'for Poets—I have Keats—and Mr & Mrs Browning' authorises this sense of priority. Jack L. Capps, who traced many such connections, saw Robert as the more generative partner in Dickinson's work, and denied any such interest in Tennyson. All he found was a hint of 'Locksley Hall' (not at all audible to me, I must confess) in 'This – is the land – the sunset washes' (J 266). That, he said, 'appears to be the extent of Tennyson's influence on her poetry'.[1]

Few of Dickinson's critics have disagreed. Yet when Dickinson began her own lyric intimations of immorality Tennyson's Lincolnshire sound was the loudest and most seductive voice in poetry. *The Princess* (1847), *In Memoriam* (1850) and *Maud* (1855), published when Dickinson was seventeen, twenty and twenty-five, offered her the most palatable model of a mode of production in which she could reconcile an essentially lyric gift with a meditative weighing of loss. It is surely significant that Tennyson is the most fully represented poet (and, after Emerson, the most represented author) in the Dickinson library: this held not only *The Princess*, *In Memoriam* and *Maud* in their first editions, but three successive collections, those of 1853, 1862 and 1871 (the 10-volume edition). The first three works made the greatest impact upon Dickinson's art, and again almost certainly (though this requires an argument well beyond the scope of this book) inspired her fascicle experiments.

These works not only offered her highly palatable models of a structured lyricism but they also constituted emotional landmarks.

---

[1] Jack L Capps, *Emily Dickinson's Reading 1836-1886*. Cambridge, MA: Harvard UP, 1966.

Susan Gilbert and Emily both 'feasted' (Dickinson's own word) on *The Princess*, which was Sue's school-leaving present, and as Judith Farrar has recognised, they read *Maud* together: the pearls, roses and lilies of *Maud*, published during Austin Dickinson's courtship of Sue, giving Dickinson a frequently utilised erotic code. If Laura Ingalls Wilder is to be believed, such application of Tennyson was not unusual: in Wilder's 'Little House' books, published in the 1930s and 40s but depicting frontier and prairie life in the last quarter of the nineteenth century, a crimson velvet Tennyson, concealed in the linen drawer, serves a similar purpose for the adolescent heroine.[1]

Maud, incidentally, was better received in America than in England. James Russell Lowell broke down while trying to read it aloud, and at an open air reading in Newport, Rhode Island, also in August 1855, when George William Curtis manfully persevered to the end, Julia Ward Howe found herself seduced by its music, while Longfellow was rather alarmed by its 'spirit of ferocity').[2] Now one of the most under-rated poems of the nineteenth century, the proto-Modernist *Maud* (I believe) deserves much of the credit for two apparently contrary arts: the fascicle meditations of Emily Dickinson and, as hinted earlier, the mature style of Walt Whitman. Compared with the standard dramatic monologue the reader of *Maud* is plunged into uncertainly psychotic territory without any trace of the usual placing 'notes' which instruct Browning's reader, for instance, how to view the speaker. Its importance for Dickinson cannot be overstated: to risk a rather heady statistical generalisation, which someone may one day validate, while only one in six of the *In Memoriam* lyrics seeded Dickinson variations, she grafted one in four of those in *Maud*.

Unlike Wordsworth and Keats, Dickinson was both a quasi-Calvinist and a Victorian. Her treatment of death was therefore inescapably bound up, as theirs was not, with such Victorian preoccupations as the soul's preparedness for Heaven, and with—at times—surprisingly confident treatment of spiritual reunion. In such treatments Elizabeth Barratt, Robert Browning and Tennyson are recognisably

---

1 Elizabeth B. Teare made this point in a paper delivered at Stirling in 1997.
2 John Olin Eidson, *Tennyson in America: his Reputation and Influence from 1827 to 1858* (Athens, GA: University of Georgia Press, 1943), 132, 133.

her chosen partners, and she is often in advance of them. Poem 616, for instance—in which

> I cheered my fainting Prince –
> I sang firm – even – Chants –
> I helped his Film – with Hymn
> ...
>
> And so with Thews of Hymn ...
> And ways I knew not that I knew – till then –
> I lifted Him –

seems to me best read alongside two poems in which Browning treated the moment of death as heroic quest. The encounter with the round squat turret in 'Childe Roland' is one of Browning's versions of this moment; the other, more personal version is the strange love poem, 'Prospice'. Whereas Childe Roland's end is witnessed only (as he sees it) by those met 'to view the last of me', the questing knight as he pantingly nears the place in 'Prospice'—'when the snows begin, and the blasts denote, / I am nearing the place'—strives towards a light which becomes the breast of Elizabeth Barrett (whose penultimate line in 'How do I love thee' he echoes with his last):

> For sudden the worst turns the best to the brave
>   The black minute's at end,
> And the element's rage, the fiend-voices that rave,
>   Shall dwindle, shall blend,
> Shall change, shall become first a peace out of pain,
>   Then a light, then thy breast,
> O thou soul of my soul! I shall clasp thee again,
>   And with God be the rest!

Dickinson lived the death of Barrett so intensely that in J 312, as we shall see, she merges with Browning as chief mourner at Barrett's funeral. It is impossible, however, if estimates of Dickinson's dates are correct, that J 616 (written late 1862) could be a response to 'Prospice' (composed c. 1861, published 1864) though it may well imagine an Elizabeth persona witnessing and aiding the arrival of her knight—not a rewrite but a prewrite of 'Prospice' from Elizabeth

Barrett's point of view.[1] There can be no question of 'influence' unless Dickinson had long-forgotten access to manuscript circulation between the Brownings and the Lowells and their publishers. Poem 615, however, which immediately precedes it both in the Complete Poems and in Fascicle 21, is certainly, as Weisbuch has recognised, a Dickinsonian treatment of the Roland motif:

> Our journey had advanced –
> Our feet were almost come
> To that odd Fork in Being's Road –
> Eternity – by Term –
>
> Our pace took sudden awe –
> Our feet – reluctant – led
> Before – were Cities – but Between –
> The Forest of the Dead –
>
> Retreat was out of Hope –
> Behind a Sealed Route –
> Eternity's White Flag – Before –
> And God – at every Gate –

These twelve lines superimpose the opening of *Childe Roland* on its close, the sense of entrapment on the plain which has only just been entered by a path no longer there, and the panoramic audience replaced by divine ambush. Whereas Browning's poem might be read as implying no certitude at all, Dickinson's appears to enjoy too much certainty: in many of her poems she harbours no little resentment of the ambush she knows to be in store. But Browning's poem dramatizes, perhaps, the underlying dread of both, that at the moment they both knew would come, they would lack the faith that alone would carry them through. The final encounter with the tower of unbelief is Browning's nightmare: suppose that in the moment of the final test, for which one has been in training all one's Christian life, one cannot summon the faith required if one is to blow a stout metaphysical raspberry in the face of unbelief? Dickinson's nightmare

---

[1] Both poems eventually appeared in *The Atlantic Monthly,* but Browning's in 1864 and Dickinson's not until 1929.

has more to do, it sometimes seems, with the expected deity turning out to be a little more on Calvin's lines than one might altogether like to believe. She prepares to do battle with divinity.

In Fascicle 36, finding that 'Behind Me – dips Eternity – / Before me – Immortality – ' Dickinson writes of such a predicament in Tennysonian rather than Browningesque manner. Defining death in somewhat *In Memoriam* tones as 'but the Drift of Eastern Gray / Dissolving into Dawn away' she celebrates it in Tennyson's Balaclava spirit of 1854:

> With Midnight to the North of Her –
> And Midnight to the South of Her –
> And Maelstrom – in the Sky – (J 721)

Into the valley of death rides the woman in white. Such robust simplicities apart, Dickinson's poetry presents itself in terms of genuine and Blakean difficulty, whether one sees this as her proto-Modernity or the inevitable privacy of someone without an audience. She may have elected, like Tennyson, to run her 'widowed race' from a similarly early age, but her oeuvre clearly emulates the strenuous qualities in Romantic poetry which she found wanting in her contemporaries, especially, perhaps, in Elizabeth Barrett who, she seems to have felt, pandared too much to audience. The rare elusiveness and enigma of the Blakean or Wordsworthian poem, which uses its ending only to avoid a sense of ending, and to send one back into the poem in pursuit of meaning, seems almost to have struck Dickinson as the norm for properly modern poetic acts. Robert Weisbuch summarises the challenge of Dickinson's more cryptic work in ways that suggest to me that Dickinson was aware of, and determined to pursue, the 'writerly' art of the Romantics rather than the more 'readerly' structures of most Victorian poetry on either side of the Atlantic. One may cavil at the assumption that Dickinson ever gave much thought to 'audience' while concurring with Weisbuch's primary point that 'Dickinson's poems are not reader friendly in the conventional ways, though, like callisthenics, they may have the reader's health in mind'.[1]

---

1 In *Dickinson and Audience*, ed. Rober Weisbuch and Martin Orzeck (Ann

The Music of 'Locksley Hall'

That Capps, echo-hunting in the sixties, should prefer to concentrate on 'Locksley Hall', is not surprising. The lines may look vaguely like traditional fourteeners (seven-foot iambic lines), which had a long history in British North America, but they are in fact catalectic *octameters,* and with their insistent end-stopped trochees, they sound unlike anything else in poetry:

> Comrades, leave me here a little, while as yet 'tis early morn:
> Leave me here, and when you want me, sound upon the bugle-horn
> 'Tis the place, and all around if, as of old the curlews call,
> Dreary gleams about the moorland, flying over Locksley Hall; ....

As long ago as 1943 (an excellent year for Anglo-American relations, as it was for American cinematic recreations of English classics in aid of the war effort) John Olin Eidson claimed that 'No creation of Tennyson's can be traced so clearly through American poetry as the rhythm of "Locksley Hall" during the twenty years after the publication of the poem'(Eidson, 105).[1] This no doubt, accounts for the splendid parody in Phoebe Cary's poem 'Granny's House' (1855):

> Comrades, leave me here a little, while as yet 'tis early morn,
> Leave me here, and when you want me, sound upon the dinner-horn.
> Tis the place, and all about it, as of old, the rat and mouse
> Very loudly squeak and nibble, running over Granny's house;—

Cary gave Poe's 'Annabel Lee' (deservedly) much the same treatment. Her point, I suppose, was that few, if any, young poets in America in the 1850s could avoid sounding like cancelled drafts of Tennyson:

Arbor: University of Michigan Press, 1996), 68.
  1 I am indebted to this fine book for several of the imitations of 'Locksley Hall' cited in the next few pages. Such rich material deserves to be put back in circulation.

his cadences swamped the ear as ineluctably as those of Eliot and Yeats in the 1930s and 40s.

The mood and matter of Tennyson's poem—melancholic, sensuous, social, prophetic—as well as its melody, saturated new world production. Henry Wadsworth Longfellow, less alarmed by 'Locksley Hall' than he was by *Maud*, caught a very Tennysonian visionary dawn in 'The Belfry of Bruges' (1842):

> As the summer morn was breaking, on that lofty tower I stood,
> And the world threw off the darkness, like the weeds of widowhood.[1]

William Wetmore Story (the sculptor-poet of the Browning circle in Italy) found a silver lining in his 'Light and Shadow' (written 1843; published in *Poems* 1847):

> Life is never quite unclouded, nor its circle wholly fair—
> But the morn of Hope still creepeth on the Shadow of Despair.[2]

James Russell Lowell, arguing for abolition in 'The Present Crisis' (1845), converts Tennyson's couplets into a five line stanza (aabbb) and his crepuscular imagery into an uplifting westering motif:

> When a deed is done for Freedom, through the broad earth's aching breast
> Runs a thrill of joy prophetic, trembling on from east to west,
> And the slave, where'er he cowers, feels the soul within him climb
> To the awful verge of manhood, as the energy sublime
> Of a century bursts full-blossomed on the thorny stem of time.[3]

---

1 Henry Wadsworth Longfellow, *Poetical Works,* 6 vols (Boston and New York: Houghton Mifflin, 1886–91).

2 William Wetmore Story, *Poems* (Boston: Little, Brown & Co, 1856).

3 James Russell Lowell, 'The Present Crisis', first published in the *Boston Daily Courier* (1845), cited from Eidson.

Thomas Buchanan Read, in 'Christine' (*Poems*, 1847), has his sculptor-persona relieve his manly heart in fine Tennysonian gloom—

> Come my friend, and in the silence and the shadow wrapt apart,
> I will loose the golden claspings of this sacred tome—the heart.[1]

—and fills the poem with literal glooms that seem equally Tennysonian in more than one sense:

> I was standing o'er the marble, in the twilight falling gray,
> All my hopes and all my courage waning from me like the day.

After *In Memoriam* was published in 1850, some 'Locksley' imitations combine the seductions of both texts, as in Bayard Taylor's 'The Birth of the Prophet' with its rhyming triads:

> For the oracles of nature recognise a Prophet's birth—
> Blossom of the tardy ages, *crowning type* of human worth—
> And by miracles and wonders he is welcomed to the earth.[2]

Taylor had recognised, presciently, after reading *The Princess* in 1848 that it was dangerous for him to read Tennyson: 'his poetry would be the death of mine' because 'his intense perception of beauty haunts me for days and I cannot drive it from me' (Eidson 62).

Thomas Holley Chivers, too, in 'The Queen of my Heart' (*Virginalia,* 1853), combines the metre of Locksley Hall with the matter of *In Memoriam,* while anticipating the motif of 'Crossing the bar':

> By what Beacon shall my spirit reach the peaceful Port of Heaven,
> From the Valley of Dark Shadows where so many men are lost?[3]

---

1 Thomas Buchanan Read, *Poems*, 1847, cited from Eidson.

2 Bayard Taylor, *The Poet's Journal* (Boston: Ticknor and Fields, 1863). The last of Taylor's triads, incidentally, has a truly Boston rhyme: 'balm / calm / am'.

3 Thomas Holley Chivers, *Virginalia* (Philadelphia: Lippincott, Grambo & Co,

Similarly, Richard Henry Stoddard's 'The Burden of Unrest' (*Songs of Summer*, 1857), from Tennyson's American publisher, combined the 'Locksley' tune (converted into a rhyming stanza) with the matter of the recently published *Maud* (1855):

> Thrilling with my youthful longings, which anticipated thee,
> Dreams were mine of bridal chambers, and they coloured all my song.[1]

Charles E. Havens simply plagiarised the tone of social prophecy, and patriotized it, under the equally plagiarised title, 'Bugle Song':

> Lo! Its echoes dying, dying, down the mystic vale of time,
> Tell us that the sword shall cease to be an instrument of crime
> ...
> And the banner of our Union, emblem of the reign of love,
> Shall be hoisted o'er the ramparts, overshadowed by the Dove[2]

That this poem was published in the *Pioneer, or California Monthly Magazine* (1854) reminds one that as Walt Whitman had the grace to admit in 1887 his 'great and ardent nation' had absorbed all of Tennyson's songs and 'he has entered into the formative influences of character here ... inland and far West, out in Missouri, in Kansas, and away in Oregon, in farmer's house and miner's cabin'.[3] In their different ways, Longfellow, Lowell and Havens, like Whitman, find no great difficulty in grafting progressive republican sentiment onto Tennyson's supposedly aristocratic stock.

1853). Here the metre is allied to an eight-line stanza, ababcdcd. Chivers's gift for pastiche extended to Poe in the quite wonderful 'The Vigil in Aiden' from *Enochs of Ruby* (New York: Spalding and Shephard, 1851): 'In the rosy bowers of Aiden / With her ruby lips love-laden / Dwelt the mild the modest maiden / Whom Politian called Lenore' and another 660 delicious lines.

1 Richard Henry Stoddard, *Songs of Summer* (Boston: Ticknor and Fields, 1857).
2 Charles E. Havens, cited from Eidson.
3 Whitman, 'A word about Tennyson', *Prose Works*, ed. Floyd Stovall (New York: New York University Press, 1964), 2: 572.

Most of these poets used this line in several poems.[1] Sometimes they produced stanzaic variants, without changing the metre: Story broke each line at the caesura making a four-line stanza. One of the earliest and most creative variants is by Elizabeth Barrett Browning. Her 'Lady Geraldine's Courtship' (1844) employs the Tennyson metre in a four-line stanza, rhyming abab, instead of in couplets, but with a feminine ending on the a-rhyme, i.e. she cancels the catalexis. As Tennyson did, she also allowed some of the trochees to disappear in almost anapaestic swirls (a welcome relief to the ear in a poem of 405 lines):

> And there evermore was music, both of instruments and singing,
> Till the finches of the shrubberies grew restless in the dark.

Edgar Allan Poe, inevitably, attempted to go one better in 1845. He took the Barrett Browning variation, spliced it with Ancient-Marineresque repetitions and internal rhymes, and sustained the b-rhyme for another line and a half, to produce such preposterous effects as:

> Back into the chamber turning, all my soul within me burning,
> Soon again I heard a tapping somewhat louder than before.
> 'Surely,' said I, 'surely that is something at my window lattice;
> Let me see, then, what thereat is ...'

Dickinson is guilty of no such crudities, and her work is as far as can be imagined from the wholesale imitations of Tennysonian rhythms I have been illustrating from the work of more impressionable poets. Yet (to repeat the argument with which I concluded the last chapter) poets impress themselves into tropes so that echoes pro-

---

[1] See, inter alia, Longfellow's 'Nuremberg' and 'A Psalm of Life', divided into stanzas; Lowell's 'The Captive' in six-line trochaic stanzas, with the rhyming lines catalectic; Chivers's 'Apollo', also in *Virginalia*, using a nine-line stanza; Bayard Taylor's 'My Mission' (*The Poet's Journal*, 165–66), a satire on 'the transcendental crew'; Story's 'Prologue: spoken at the inauguration of Crawford's Bronze Statue of Beethoven, etc' (*Poems*, 296).

liferate of themselves, and can only with great labour be avoided. Dickinson presents one with numerous instances of appearing to share in a collectively, transatlantically, generated language, and in many such instances it is absolutely clear that one is mistaken in supposing that any theory of influence, beyond a kind of consanguinity, can account for the effect.

Indeed, Dickinson's poetry is full of man-traps for echo hunters. One of her very first productions, Poem 4 in Johnson's *Collected Poems,* shares both theme and trope with a poem composed by the laureate three years after her death. In old age, after an illness, Alfred Lord Tennyson delivered one of his most spontaneous and most widely loved productions, 'Crossing the Bar':

> Sunset and evening star,
> And one clear call for me!
> And may there be no moaning of the bar,
> When I put out to sea,
>
> But such a tide as moving seems asleep,
> Too full for sound and foam,
> When that which drew from out the boundless deep
> Turns again home.
>
> Twilight and evening bell,
> And after that the dark!
> And may there be no sadness of farewell,
> When I embark;
>
> For tho' from out our bourne of Time and Place
> The flood may bear me far,
> I hope to see my Pilot face to face
> When I have crost the bar.

'Crossing the Bar' was published in 1889. The unwary reader of these lines by Dickinson, published in 1896—

> On this wondrous sea
> Sailing silently
> Ho! Pilot, ho!
> Knowest thou the shore

> Where no breakers roar –
> Where the storm is o'er?
>
> In the peaceful west
> Many the sails at rest –
> The anchors fast –
> Thither I pilot thee –
> Land Ho! Eternity!
> Ashore at last!

—might be excused for exclaiming, 'Ah! Tennyson!'. Her poem shares with Tennyson's, a pan-Victorian, hymnal sense of the soul as Bark and Christ as its Pilot towards a breakerless, barless, shore. But there is no question of 'influence': Dickinson's imitation was written some thirty six years *before* its so obvious original. Not 'influence' but 'confluence' is at work: in reality, a shared eschatology and traditional hymnal tropes of the soul as bark and Christ as one's pilot explain the serendipity. Tennyson attracted condemnation for employing Christ in this way as a sort of helmsman (adding to his skills in carpentry and fishing); and Dickinson anticipates his guilt.

But once in a while, even in literary studies, truths emerge, however slant. And I end this book with an indubitable metrical truth.

'Her "Last Poems"'

In commemorating Elizabeth Barrett, in a poem called 'Her "last Poems"', Dickinson was fully aware of Tennyson's proprietorship in this elegiac territory. This is one of several poems in which Dickinson writes about Barrett Browning directly, as opposed to the many poems in which, as Ellen Moers pointed out long ago, she makes poems out of suggestions from *Aurora Leigh*. It was her habit to take an image or metaphor barely noticed in Barrett Browning's rushing verse and make it into a poem, so the ideal edition of *Aurora Leigh,* Ellen Moers hinted, would have the resulting Dickinson poems set in it as interleaved arias to break up the 'headlong recitative' of the verse novel.[1]

---

1 Moers, *Literary Women,* 59.

One manuscript of Johnson 312 (Poem 600 in Franklin) begins:

> Her – last Poems –
> Poets – ended –
> Silver – perished – with her Tongue –
> Not on Record – bubbled other,
> Flute – or Woman – so divine – [1]

Thomas Johnson has been criticised for quietly regularising the poem's lineation. He was clearly uneasy with the apparently random line breaks as she reaches the paper's edge, isolating 'Tongue' and 'other' or 'Other'. On the other hand he recognised that the manuscript indentation of the first line, 'Her "Last Poems"' (referencing Barrett's *Last Poems*, 1862) makes it into a title, and that it should not—therefore—be linked up with what seems metrically the other half of a tetrameter, 'Poets ended'. Moreover, one has to tread very slowly, because the grammar linking the first five or six phrases is barely 'there'. So his editing of J 312 offers a poem which, with its four-beat, two-beat irregular alternation is, if not free verse, certainly half way towards that very different thing, 'vers libre':

> Her – "last Poems" –
> Poets – ended –
> Silver – perished – with her Tongue –
> Not on Record – bubbled other,
> Flute or Woman –
> So divine –
> Not unto its Summer – Morning
> Robin – uttered Half the Tune –
> Gushed too free for the Adoring – ['free' reads 'full' in ms.C]
> From the Anglo-Florentine –
> Late – the Praise –
> Tis dull – conferring
> On the Head too High to Crown –
> Diadem or Ducal Showing

---

1 *The Manuscript Books of Emily Dickinson*, ed. R. W. Franklin, 3 vols (Cambridge, MA & London: The Belknap Press of Harvard University Press, 2001), 2: 597–8.

Be its Grave - sufficient sign –
Nought – that We – No Poet's Kinsman –
Suffocate — with easy woe –
What , and if, Ourself a Bridegroom –
Put Her down – in Italy?

One can certainly question, as Dickinson scholars have been prone to do, whether such lineation significantly mars Dickinson's intentions, however sensitively Johnson treats what he supposes her metre to be. Incidentally, Johnson's decision to give 'So divine' a line to itself, despite the probability that it concludes a metrical line, is confirmed by only one of the three transcripts in Franklin's Variorum. The fascicle 26 text (MS.C) is clearly a poem in four quatrains with the stanza breaks on the rhyme-words 'divine', 'Florentine' and 'Sign'.[1]

Her – last Poems –
Poets ended –
Silver – perished – with her Tongue –
Not on Record – bubbled Other –
Flute – or Woman – so divine –

Not unto it's Summer Morning –
Robin – uttered half the Tune
Gushed too full for the adoring –
From the Anglo-Florentine –

Late – the Praise – 'Tis dull – Conferring
On the Head too High – to Crown –
Diadem – or Ducal symbol –
Be it's Grave – sufficient Sign –

Nought – that We – No Poet's Kinsman –
Suffocate – with easy Wo –
What — and if Ourself a Bridegroom —
Put Her down — in Italy?

---

1 *The Poems of Emily Dickinson: Varorum Edition*, ed. R. W. Franklin (Cambridge, MA & London: The Belknap Press of Harvard University Press, 1998), 2: 597–8. I convert Franklin's irreverent-looking hyphens into the more usual en-dashes. Dickinson's 'dashes' actually range from smudged stops to hyphens, to en-dashes and occasional em-dashes, which makes editorial fidelity a dream.

One can sympathise with these editors' problem: the second stanza appears to offer a four-line tetrameter model to which one is tempted to make the others conform, even though it is the only one that actually occupies four manuscript lines. Franklin's Variorum text, however, does follow Johnson's judgements regarding such isolated words as 'tongue' and 'other', 'Crown' and 'Sign', treating each word, though isolated in the manuscript he is working from, as a final foot. He also ignores the initial indent, which effectively centres the line as a title. This may be sacrilege. Critics have expended much energy discussing such minutiae, and pleading for the fascicle mss as a sacrosanct form of 'private publication' (Sharon Cameron's famous oxymoron) not to be edited, like the work of other poets, in conformity to usual prosodic practice, whether such editorial practice is right or wrong. That anyone should argue for the sanctity of isolated half feet is a tribute to the passion she inspires. In this case, however, it is the effect of Dickinson's effective camouflage.

The real question is not whether Johnson and Franklin are chaining Dickinson's free verse, but how far was Dickinson prepared to go—and why, exactly—to disguise her artful theft. As one's eye struggles with the forest of dashes and splintered feet which became Dickinson's hallmarks around 1862, one's ear faintly catches a familiar tune. A hymn perhaps? Well, no. The half-heard metre is, of course, Tennyson's unmistakably catalectic trochaic octameter. The tune of 'Her – last Poems' is neither a variation on, nor an adaptation of, nor an approximation to the tune of 'Locksley Hall'. Accent by accent, foot by foot, caesura by caesura, and period by period, it is *precisely* that of 'Locksley Hall'. Only the logically necessary period after the title phrase (especially when in MS. B the dash is replaced by an exclamation mark) disguises its start. The rhyme scheme is relaxed. Otherwise the lines might be (I do so in fear and trembing) relineated and ruthlessly un-dashed so as to complete a ten line poem beginning with, and enormously complicating, two of Tennyson's own (here italicized):

> *I remember one that perished: sweeter did she speak and move:*
> *Such a one do I remember; whom to look at was to love.*

> Her "last Poems"! – Poets ended, Silver perished with her
>   Tongue;
> Not on Record bubbled other, Flute or Woman, so divine.
>
> Not unto its Summer Morning, Robin uttered Half the Tune;
> Gushed too free for the Adoring, from the Anglo-Florentine.
>
> Late the Praise, 'tis dull conferring, on the Head too High
>   to Crown,
> Diadem or Ducal Showing – be its Grave, sufficient sign.
>
> Nought that We, no Poet's Kinsman, suffocate with easy
>   Wo:
> What, and if, ourself a Bridegroom, put her down in Italy?

The coalescence of Emily and Robert in the final line (as Emily imagines herself transgendered into the chief mourner) begins a period in which she writes a number of poems about death in the persona of one or the other within that poetical marriage, a subject treated in definitive depth by Ann Swyderski.[1]

So: why *does* Amherst's Woman in White choose to commemorate 'that foreign lady', the Anglo-Florentine, in this most famous and (during her entire adolescence and apprenticeship) ineluctable Tennysonian metre? One answer, perhaps, is that having come of poetic age in the Age of Tennyson she had no choice. Another is that, since Barrett Browning was the only poet to have done something genuinely creative with the metre of 'Locksley Hall' it is an apt if somewhat oblique, not to say arcane form of tribute. In 'Lady Geraldine's Courtship' one sees Barrett's borrowing, from the layout of the lines, and hears her emendation of Tennyson, in the restored syllable in alternate lines. You may or may not hear Dickinson's borrowing beneath the expert visual camouflage. She makes less change; yet more. Simply by relineation she takes herself further

---

[1] 'Dickinson's Enchantment: The Barrett Browning Fascicles', *Symbiosis* 7.1 (April 2003) 76–98. For the fullest treatment of this theme to date, see the same author's brilliantly assiduous Ph.D dissertation, 'Emily Dickinson and Elizabeth Barrett Browning: "The outer – from the Inner / Derives its magnitude"', University of Exeter, 2000.

from Tennyson's original than her illustrious precursor managed by changing the rhyme scheme, the stanza and the rhyming foot. A third answer is that the elusive means of double allusion signals in a peculiarly graceful way the kind of freedom Dickinson sought: her means of escape from 'Locksley Hall'. Another Protestant rebel, of similar vintage, Soren Kierkegaard, expressed his own ideal of authenticity, that of 'the Knight of Faith', as that of working incognito, as it were, within the everyday: and at this date 'Locksley Hall' was almost as 'everyday' a medium as Dickinson's more usual common or hymn-book metre. A fourth, related possibility is that she intends to critique Barrett's headlong metrical freedom (as in she 'gushed too free') as sharing too much the sweep of Tennyson's form. Her own poetry characteristically occludes syntax and breaks the metre to isolate the image for contemplation. 'Tongue' is, without doubt, the final catalectic foot of a tetrameter. Yet, paradoxically, knowing that in this case she is engaged in artful relineation might support what is otherwise a very weak case for separate lineation of 'Tongue' and 'other'. Dickinson's first line of defence against an offshore isle too full of poetic noises is a poetry full of silences.

Whatever the reason for her decision to fracture Tennyson in this way, it is salutary, I think that this hotly defended experiment in free verse (and that is what such manuscript lineations have been claimed to be—by Ruth Miller, Susan Howe and Sharon Cameron among others) should turn out to be a simple but surprisingly effective relineation of Tennyson. Charles Anderson's fine study of Dickinson aptly calls itself Emily Dickinson's 'stairway of surprise'. This is, perhaps, one of the odder twists in that surprising stairway, and one that shows Dickinson struggling alike with master and mistress in the very act of employing the art of one to memorialise the other.

Seeing 'New Englandly' in any case implies no abrogation of the kind of elective affinities implied in her famous remark that 'For poets – I have Keats – and Mr and Mrs Browning'. One might imagine her adding, somewhat in the vein of Thomas Bailey Aldrich (quoted in the epigraph to this epilogue), 'Lord Tennyson calls – yet – I do not admit – his tune'.

Some Recommended Reading

Brantley, Richard E. *Experience and Faith: The Late-Romantic Imagination of Emily Dickinson.* Palgrave Macmillan,. 2005

Chai, Leon. *The Romantic Foundations of the American Renaissance.* Cornell University Press, 1987

Harvey, Samantha C. *Transatlantic Transcendentalism: Coleridge, Emeron and Nature.* Edinburgh University Press, 2013

Keane, Patrick J. *Emerson, Romanticism, and Intuitive Reason : the Transatlantic 'Light of all our Day'.* University of Missouri Press, 2005

——. *Emily Dickinson's Approving God: Divine Design and the Problem of Suffering.* Univrsity of Missouri Press, 2008

Giles, Paul. *Transatlantic Insurrections: British Culture and the Formation of American Culture, 1730-1860.* University of Pennsylvania Press, 2001

——. *Atlantic Republic: The American Tradition in English Literature.* Oxford University Press, 2006

Gordon, George Stuart. *Anglo-American Literary Relations.* Oxford University Press, 1942.

Gravil, Richard, 'Intimations in America', in *The Oxford Handbook of William Wordsworth* ed Richard Gravil and Daniel Robinson (Oxford University Press, 2015)

McKusick, James. *Green Writing: Romanticism and Ecology.* St. Martin's Press, 2000

Manning, Susan. *Fragments of Union: Making Connections in Scottish and American Writng.* Palgrave, 2002

——. *Poetics of Character: Tansatlantic Encounters, 1700–1900.* Cambridge University Press, 2013

Newman, Lance. *Our Common Dwelling: Thoreau, Transcendentalism, and the Class Politics of Nature.* Palgrave Macmillan, 2005

Nemwan, Lance, Joel Pace, and Chris Koenig-Woodyard, eds. *Sullen Fires Across the Atlantic: Essays in Transatlantic Romanticism.* Online. *Romantic Circles*, 2006

Pace, Joel. 'Wordsworth and America: Reception and Reform', in Stephen Gill, ed. T*he Cambridge Companion to Wordsworth.* Cambridge University press, 2003

Pace, Joel and Matthew Scott, eds. *Wordsworth in American Literary Culture*, ed. (Palgrave, 2005). Includes essays by Bruce Graver on Whittier, Richard Gravil on Cooper, Karen Karbiener on Whitman, Lance Newman on Thoreau, and Adam Potkay on Wordsworth and Bishop Doane.

Price, Kenneth. *Whitman and Tradition: the Poet in his Century.* Yale University Press, 1990

Schmidgall, Gary. *Containing Multitudes: Walt Whitman and the British Literary Tradition.* Oxford University Press, 2014

Swyderski, Ann, 'Dickinson's Enchantment: The Barrett Browning Fascicles', *Symbiosis* 7.1 (April 2003) 76–98

——. 'Emily Dickinson and Elizabeth Barrett Browning: "The outer – from the Inner / Derives its magnitude"'. Doctoral dissertation, University of Exeter, 2000

Tovey, Paige. *The Transatlantic Eco-Romanticism of Gary Snyder.* Palgrave Macmillan, 2013

Weisbuch, Robert. *Atlantic Double-Cross: American Literature and British Influence in the Age of Emerson.* University of Chicago Press, 1989

Some Romantic-era Essays in
Symbiosis: a Journal of Transatlantic Literary Relations

Underlined titles are available in PDF from humanities-ebooks.co.uk

Adams, Amanda. 'Recognized by My Trumpet': Celebrity and/as Disability in Harriet Martineau's Transatlantic Tour. 14.1 (April 2010) 3–18.

Andrews, Stuart. Fellow Pantisocrats: Brissot, Cooper and Imlay. 1.1 (April 1997) 35–47.

Blake, David and Elliot Gruner. Redeeming Captivity: the Negative Revolution of Blake's Visions of the Daughters of Albion. 1.1 (April 1997) 21–34.

Boelhower, Bill. Mnemohistory: the Archaeological Turn in the Humanities from Winckelmann to Calvino. 9.2 (October 2005) 99–116.

Bracewell, Joy. Bodies of Evidence: Illustrated British Editions of Harriet Beecher Stowe's Uncle Tom's Cabin. 13.2 (October 2009) 159–188.

Brantley, Richard E. From Loss to Gain: Aftermath in the Late Romantic Poetry of Emily Dickinson. 10.2 (October 2006) 93–114.

____. Emily Dickinson's Empirical Voice. 15.1 (April 2011) 105–32.

Burrus, Jessica. Entering the Past: Grace Greenwood and Nathaniel Hawthorne in Stratford. 17.2 (October 2013) 97–115

Burwick, Frederick. Wordsworth and Frost: 'The Real Language of Men' 18.1 (April 2014) 43–59.

Castillo, Susan. Imperial Pasts and Dark Futurities: Freneau and Brackenridge's 'The Rising Glory of America'. 6.1 (April 2002) 27–43.

Chandler, David. 'Home Sweet Home' and Popular Anglo-American Romanticism. 16.1 (April 2012) 21–36.

Clark, Jennifer. Poisoned Pens: The Anglo-American Relationship and the Paper War. 6.1 (April 2002) 45–68.

Collins, Michael. Republicanism and the Masonic Imagination in Edgar Allan Poe's 'The Cask of Amontillado'. 12.2 (October 2008) 149–66.

Filippakopoulou, Maria. Intimacy and Recoil: Huxley Reads Poe in French. 8.1 (April 2004) 77–90.

Finnerty, Páraic. The Daisy and the Dandy: Emily Dickinson and Oscar Wilde. 9.1 (April 2005) 65–90.

Flynn, Christopher. 'No Other Island in the World': Mansfield Park, North America and Post-Imperial Malaise. 4.2 (October 2000) 173–86.

_____. Dismembering Anglo-America: The Body Politic and the First English Novel about the American Revolution. 9.2 (October 2005) 193–208.

Fulford, Timothy. Romantic Indians and Colonial Politics: the Case of Thomas Campbell. 2.1 (October 1998) 203–224.

Gaull, Marilyn. 'Conjecturing a Climate': The Discovery of Transatlantic Weather. 15.1 (April 2011) 17–28.

Grant, Robert. Anti-Americanism in Nineteenth-Century British Literature of Emigration: Global Contexts. 14.2 (October 2010) 159–78.

Gravil, Richard. Blake in Boston. 1.2 (October 1997) 275–277.

_____. Regicide and Ethnic Cleansing; or, Edmund Burke in Wish-ton-Wish. 4.2 (October 2000) 187–204.

Hall, Julie. Nathaniel Hawthorne's 'Wild' Wales. 13.1 (April 2009) 3–20.

Hannah, Daniel. 'Panting Struggling': William Blake's Transatlantic Erotics'. 16.1 (April 2012) 57–72.

Hardie, Tony. 'Imago Christi': Hopkins and Whitman. 6.1 (April 2002) 1–26.

Harvey, Samantha. Coleridge's American Revival: James Marsh, John Dewey and Vermont Transcendentalism. 15.1 (April 2011) 77–104.

Hayes, Kevin J. Henry J. Coke's Ride Over the Rocky Mountain: A Journey from Leatherstocking to Lear. 12.1 (April 2008) 3–16.

Holman, Rupert. Nathaniel Hawthorne at Greenwich. 5.1 (April 2001) 69–76.

Hutchings, Kevin. Romantic Niagara: Environmental Aesthetics, Indigenous Culture and Transatlantic Tourism, 1776–1850. 12.2 (October 2008) 131–48.

Hsu, Li-Hsin. Thomas De Quincey's 'Serpentine' Writings and Emily Dickinson's Reptiles. 18.1 (April 2014) 3–22.

Hull, Simon. A Transatlantic Cockney in Babylonian London: Washington Irving and the Problem of Pleasure. 18.2 (October 2014) 157–73

Jarvis, Robin. Contesting the 'Secret Grudge': The Image of America in The Edinburgh Review, 1803–1829. 13.1 (April 2009) 45–60.

Jones, Catherine A. Hawthorne's Scotland: Memory and Imagination. 4.2 (October 2000) 133–51.

———. The Transatlantic Beethoven Hero. 14.1 (April 2010) 103–122.

Karbiener, Karen. Cross-Cultural Confessions: America Passes Judgement on Thomas De Quincey. 3.2 (October 1999) 119–130.

Kaufman, Will. 'Our rancorous Cousins': British Literary Journals on the Approach of the Civil War. 4.1 (April 2000) 35–50.

Lawson-Peebles, Robert. Fenimore Cooper's First Novel, Family Property, and the Battle of Waterloo. 8.2 (October 2004) 124–39.

———. The Revolutionary Legends of Jane McCrae and Lady Harriet Acland. 18.2 (October 2014) 111–32.

Lee, Sohui. The Guillotine and the American Public: A Godwinian Reading of The Scarlet Letter. 4.2 (October 2000) 152–72.

Logan, Deborah. Harriet Martineau and the Martyr Age of the United States. 5.1 (April 2001) 33–49.

Long, James Weldon. A Romance of the Revolutionary Atlantic: James Fenimore Cooper's *Lionel Lincoln*. 15.1 (April 2011) 63–76.

Lopez, Debbie. Liberties with Lamia: the 'Gordian Knot' of relations between Keats and Hawthorne. 2.1 (October 1998) 141–160.

McCoppin, Rachel. Sympathy for the Other: British Attempts at Understanding the American Indian. 14.2 (October 2010) 237–56.

McGettigan, Katy. Aestheticising the Marketplace: Appropriations of the Literary Industry in *Sartor Resartus* and *Moby-Dick*, 15.2. (October 2011) 173–92.

McGuire, Ian. Culture and Antipathy: Arnold, Emerson and Democratic Vistas. 5.1 (April 2001) 77–84.
Manning, Susan. Why does it matter that Ossian was Thomas Jefferson's favourite poet? 1.2 (October 1997) 219–36.
Mason, Nicholas. Blackwood's Magazine, Anti-Americanism and the Beginnings of Transatlantic Literary Studies. 14.2 (October 2010) 141–58.
Morzé, Leonard von. A Massachusetts Yankee ... Charles Brockden Brown's Ormond. 15.1 (April 2011) 45–62.
Nardini, Nicholas. Henry Reed's American Wordsworth: Romantic Universality Across the Atlantic. 15.2 (October 2011) 155–72.
Oliver, Susan. Periodical editing: from Francis Jeffrey to Horace Greeley. 9.1 (April 2005) 45–64.
Pace, Joel. 'Lifted to genius?' Wordsworth in Emerson's Nurture and Nature. 2.1 (October 1998) 125–40.
_____. 'A Publisher's Politics: Lyrical Ballads (Philadelphia 1802). 7.1 (April 2003) 35–55.
Peacock, James. Who was John Bartram? Literary and Epistolary Representations of the Quaker. 9.1 (April 2005) 29–44.
Perkins, Pam. Writing Republican Femininity: The Letters of Eliza Southgate Bowne. 5.2 (October 2001) 121–37.
Pethers, Matthew J. Transatlantic Migration and the Politics of the Picturesque in Washington Irving's Sketch Book. 9.2 (October 2005) 135–58.
Ready, Katherine. Dissenting Sociability and the Anglo-American Context: The Correspondence of William Ellery Channing and Lucy Aikin. 9.2 (October 2005) 117–34.
Reilly, Susan. 'A Nobler Fall of Ground': nation and narration in Pride and Prejudice. 4.1 (April 2000) 19–34.
Richardson, Robert D. Jr. Liberal Platonism and Transcendentalism: Shaftesbury, Schleiermacher, Emerson. 1.1 (April 1997) 1–20.
Robertson, Fiona. British Romantic Columbiads. 2.1 (April 1998) 1–23.

Sagar, Keith. Lawrence's debt to Whitman. 7.1 (April 2003) 99–117.

Shannon, Ashley E. Lydia Maria Child's Romantic Revolution. 16.1 (April 2012) 73–94.

Swyderski, Ann. Dickinson and 'that Foreign Lady – '. 4.1 (April 2000) 51–65.

_____. Dickinson's Enchantment: The Barrett Browning Fascicles. 7.1 (April 2003) 76–98.

Templeton, Peter. 'Different Instincts, different appetites, diffgernt morals and a different culture': Dickens, Trollope and the Pastoral Sekf-Image of the Antebellum South. 18.1 (April 2014) 23–42.

Thorn, Jennifer. Violence, Piety, Enlightenment and Charles Brockden Brown's *Wieland*. 17.2 (October 2013) 139–58.

Turner, Deanna C. Shattering the Fountain: Irving's Re-Vision of 'Kubla Khan' in 'Rip Van Winkle'. 4.1 (April 2000) 1–17.

Vallins, David. Self-Reliance: Individualism in Emerson and Coleridge. 5.1 (April 2001) 51–68.

Vericat, Fabio L. Hawthorne Revisited in Henry James's The American Scene. 12.2 (October 2008) 191–208.

Wind, Astrid. 'Adieu to all': The Dying Indian at the Turn of the Eighteenth Century. 2.1 (April 1998), 39–55.

_____. Irish Legislative Independence and the Politics of Staging Indians in the 1790s. 5.1 (April 2001) 1–16

Wood, Sarah F. Refusing to R.I.P.; or, Return of the Dispossessed: the Transatlantic Revivals of Irving's Rip Van Winkle. 10.1 (April 2006) 3–20.

Worth, Timothy. 'An Extraordinary Species of Tyranny': Fanny Trollope's Domestic Manners of the Americans. 5.1 (April, 2001) 17–32.

INDEX

Abrams, M. H., 297
Adams, John Quincy, 146
Adams, John, 29, 32, 40,
    42, 49, 61, 131 n.
  Defence of the Constitutions, 49, 51
  Thoughts on Government, 50
  and Jefferson, 42 n., 50, 131 n., 155
Adams, Samuel, 43, 50
Aldrich, Thomas Bailey, 341, 364
Allusion, 9, 17, 117, 120, 205–6,
    210–13, 252, 265, 273, 291,
    310, 321, 325, 334, 338
America, *see* American Revolution,
    British North America, colonies,
    American Constitution, slavery,
    United States of America
American Civil War, 95n, 122, 182
American exceptionalism,
    90, 98, 117, 121
American expansionism, 56, 157, 213
American literary renaissance,
    15–18, 85, 92, 94, 123
  as restatement of English
    Romanticism, 19–20
American Literature, 92
American perfidy, 95, 122
American Revolution, 11, 39, 48–50,
    53, 55, 59–60, 66, 97, 116, 124,
    130, 132, 146, 214–6, 312;
  as an English event, 12, 27–31,
    48–50, 53–4, 61–2, 67
  see also Cartwright, Price, Franklin,
    Paine, Jefferson, Pownall,
    Raynal, War of Independence
American 'Romantics, 77–89
Andrews, Stuart, 69, 78 n
Anglo-American relations, as
    parent and child, 43–4
  mental emancipation, 90,
    107–13, 116, 123–6;
  political alienation, 28–33
Anglo-American republicanism, 38–48
Anglo-American 'special
    relationship', 100
Arbella, the, 36
Atlantis, 61, 70
Auden, W. H., 253 n.
Audubon, John James, 292, 306, 307
automobile emissions, 50 n

Barbauld, Anna Letitia, 68, 73–75
Barlow, Joel, 36, 54, 57,
    71–2, 75, 94, 161
Barrett-Browning, Elizabeth,
    315, 318–9, 325, 350–1,
    352, 357, 359–64
Browning, Robert, 92, 315,
    325, 348, 350–1
Bartram, William, 36, 80, 216
Bate, Jonathan, 236
Baum, Joan, 304 n
Beer, John, 256 n., 261 n
Bellamy, Edward, *Looking
    Backward*, 341
Birkbeck, Morris, 42 n., 96
Blair, Hugh, 14, 83, 115, 164;
  and Whitman, 298
Blake, William, 14, 19, 36, 54, 78,
    113, 133, 187, 196, 317
  America, 20, 54, 57–67
  *Marriage of Heaven
    and Hell*, 59, 62
  and Barlow, 36, 63
  and Dickinson, 317–8 and n.
  reception in America, 21, 196–7,
  and writers on America, 59
Bloom, Harold, 17, 59, 125,
    163, 324, 342, 346–7

Boone, Daniel, 78, 85, 145–6
Bradstreet, Anne, 71
Brissot, J-P de Warville, 69, 79
Bristed, John, 96 n., 103–4
British calumnies of America, *see*
    British periodicals, Sydney Smith
British North America, 28, 32, 39, 353
    autonomy of, 28–33, 39
    democracy of, 39 nn., 217
    arguments for continuance of, 45–8
British periodicals, 18, 92–106
See also *Edinburgh Review*, *Monthly*
    Magazine, *Quarterly Review*
Bryant, William Cullen, 16, 24, 71, 76,
    85, 92, 118, 143, 159–82, 338
    'Thanatopsis', 164–6
    'The Prairies', 168–71
    and Cooper 159–60
    and *Lyrical Ballads,* 161–2
Burgh, James, 12; *Political*
    Disquisitions, 30–1, 34, 37
Burke, Edmund, 129, 143,
    144, 148, 150–3
    Reflections on the Revolution
    in France, 129, 131, 136–7,
    148–9, 150, 153–6
    Vindication of Natural Society,
    137–9, 151, 158
    on America, 32–3, 43–4,
    50, 54, 131, 147
Burrows, Edwin G, 43, 44
Byron, George Gordon, Lord, 14,
    21, 54, 68, 69, 76, 86, 123,
    125, 145, 148, 161, 227,
    253, 315, 321, 332–3

Calhoun, John C., 153
Calvinism, 157, 174, 186, 228,
    257–8, 259, 320, 349, 352
Campbell, Thomas, 71, 75,
    98, 104–6, 123
Capps, Jack L., 318, 319,
    320, 321, 332, 348
Carlyle, Thomas, 14, 19, 21,
    124, 188, 215, 253, 309
    and Coleridge, 19
    and Emerson, 113, 114, 115, 116,
    185, 188–9, 192, 196, 198, 199,
    On Heroes, 21–22
    in *Moby-Dick*, 251, 252–3, 257,
    269, 272, 273, 279 n., 280 n.
    and Romanticism, 14, 21–2
    Sartor Resartus, 21–22,
    116, 189, 216, 273–4
Cartwright, Major John, 12, 34, 46,
    48, 50, 52, 53, 54, 117, 183
    American Independence, 44–5
    Take Your Choice! 34, 58
    and Jefferson, 34, 48, 135
Cary, Phoebe 353
Chai, Leon 13, 18, 254 n.,
    270, 272 n., 275
Channing, William Ellery, 77,
    82–5, 103, 122, 123
    as Romantic, 82–5
    in Grasmere, 118–9,
    hears *The Prelude*, 119, 195
    and the war of 1812, 99 n.
Chartism, 34, 54
Chateaubriand, René de, 78, 117, 130
Chatham, Earl of [Pitt the
    Elder], 25, 44, 50, 101
Chivers, Thomas Holley, 355–6
Cobbett, William, 81, 98 n.
Coleridge, Hartley, 163
Coleridge, Samuel Taylor, 14, 16,
    18, 19, 20, 21–2, 24, 36, 56,
    68, 76, 83, 84, 108, 123, 127,
    156, 161, 179, 184–99, 204,
    205–6, 219, 221, 227, 228,
    223, 233, 235–47, 249–72,
    288, 315, 321, 325, 330, 333
    Aids to Reflection, 185, 187, 257
    The Ancient Mariner, 240, 249–66,
    Biographia Literaria, 191, 194, 266
    Christabel, 206, 226, 227, 242
    'Dejection: an Ode', 205
    'The Eolian Harp', 205, 262,

'France: an Ode', 158
The Friend, 83, 185, 194, 235–9;
   and Wordsworth's reception in
   America, 184, 195 n., 199, 211 n.
'Frost at Midnight', 190,
'Kubla Khan', 227, 241, 245, 267–9,
'Religious Musings', 69, 254,
and Emerson, 113–4, 184–99
and Melville, 249–69, 276,
and pantheism,
and pantisocracy, 68–9, 79–81, 84
and Poe, 235–47,
and Whitman, 285, 286–7
see also, Coleridge: Works, Reason
   and Imagination, Pantheism
colonies, diversity of, 25–6
Committees of Correspondence
   and Corresponding
   Societies, 53–4, 69
Constitution, American, 14, 61–62,
   81, 96 n., 152, 214–6,
   French critiques of, 49
   idolatry of, 56, 214–6, 289, 307
Constitution, British, 29, 30,
   34, 47, 51, 150–53
   Adams on, 49, 51
   see also, De Lolme, equality
Constitution, French, 154–5, *and*
   see French revolution
Constitution, Saxon, 33–34
constitutions of American
   Colonies, 34, 35–6
Cooper, James Fenimore, 75,
   81–2, 85, 91, 99 n., 101, 102,
   107-112, 123, 125, 129–
   The American Democrat, 150–5
   Gleanings in Europe, 91, 108–11
   Notions of the Americans, 108
   The Pioneers, 129–46
   The Wept of Wish-ton-Wish,
      112, 141 n., 156
   and Burke, 131, 136–9, 144, 148–58
   and Jefferson, 144, 146, 147
   disillusionment with America, 148
   on national independence,
      102, 107–112
   on politics, 146–58
Cooper, Thomas, 69, 79
Cressy, David, 96 n.
Crèvecoeur, Hector St John
   de, 36, 79, 117, 130

Dana, Richard Henry, 118, 161, 162
Danby, John F., 222, 337
Davie, Donald, 136, 142, 144
Dayan, Joan, 243, 246
De Lolme (Swiss
   constitutionalist), 49 n.
De Quincey, Thomas, 195 n.,
   201, 204, 316, 321
De Tocqueville, Alexis, 130, 153
Decatur, Stephen, 97
Declaration of Independence, 28,
   33, 40, 53, 65, 66, 105, 113
Dekker, George, 129, 149
democracy versus republicanism,
   49–50, 147–9, 151–2, 154–5
'Demophilus', 48, 134
Despotism in America (1840), 55
Dickens, Charles, 22, 95, 98,
   225 and n., 226, 341,
Dickinson, Emily, 315–40,
   347–52, 357–64
   'Her "Last Poems"', 359–64
   'So has a Daisy vanished', 329–30
   and Blake, 317 and n., 352
   and Elizabeth Barrett Browning,
      318–9, 321, 350, 352, 359–64
   and Robert Browning, 320–1,
      324, 348, 350–1,
   as devotional poet, 316–8
   and English lyric tradition, 315–7
   the fascicles, 316–8
   and fiction, 319–20
   and immortality, 350
   and Keats, 315, 321, 322–4
   and multiple allusion, 325–8
   and Shelley, 316, 321, 325, 330

and Tennyson, 315, 326–8, 338–40, 362–4
and Wordsworth, 328–39
Dickinson, John, *Letters from a Farmer in Pennsylvania*, 29–30, 32, 40, 44, 48–9
Diehl, Joanne Feit, 315 n., 321–2, 324, 333
Dimock, Wai-Chee 251 n.
Donnelly, Daria, 332, 333
Doskow, Minna, 60

Edinburgh Review, 28–9, 70, 86, 93, 96, 97–101, 102, 103, 107, 215, 288
Edwards, Jonathan, 102, 186–7, 243, 257
Eidson, John Olin, 353, 354, 355, 356
Eliot, George, 24, 92, 157, 182, 258, 316, 319
Eliot, T. S., 23, 247, 287, 312, 313
Emerson, Ralph Waldo, 102, 107, 124, 161, 184–200,
  'The American Scholar', 102, 112-8, 199
  English Traits, 186
  Nature, 170, 184–200
  and Blake, 196–7, 198, 200
  and Carlyle, 112, 116, 185, 188
  and Coleridge, 113, 184–97
  and Keats, 113
  use of sources, 191–96
  and Wordsworth, 113–6, 121–2, 125, 170, 184–5, 195–9
  and Young, 114
emigration, 28 n., 41, 42, 68–9, 79, 81–2, 99–100
England, revolutionary prospects, 3, 7, 21, 53
English republicanism, 7–8, 10–11, 17, 18–20, 53, 113–4
English Revolutions, (1649) 50, 214, (1688) 38, 50
Equality, rejected in American Revolution, 52, 56, 152–3,
Erdman, David V., 60, 250
Erkkila, Betsy, 285, 289, 310
Evans, Estwick, 24, 53, 77, 86–9, *A Pedestrious Tour of Four Thousand Miles*, 86–9
Everett, Edward, 96, 104–6, 106

Faux, William, *Memorable Days in America* (1820), 106
Fearon, Henry, 93, 105, *Sketches of America*, 95–6
Federalism and *The Federalist*, 52, 102, 130, 147, 150, 154
Fergensen, Laraine, 201 n., 203 n.
Ferguson, Frances, 334–5
Ferguson, Robert A, quoted 216 n.
Fiedler, Leslie, 140, 145
Franklin, Benjamin, 12, 35, 39, 41, 44–5,48, 50, 57, 61, 63, 69, 70, 85, 94, 97, 104
French Revolution (1789), 12, in *The Pioneers*, 130–1, 143, 146–9
  Adams and Jefferson on, 155 n.
  and the Burke-Paine controversy, 136–7, 139, 143, 146–9
  Mackintosh on, 155
  Wollstonecraft on, 155 n.
Freneau, Philip, 71, 72, 75, 76, 161
Freud, Sigmund, 144–5
Fuller, Margaret, 20, 82, 92, 107, 123, 163, 225 n.

Garber, Frederick, 203 n
Gardner, Charles Kitchell (later Adjutant General), 101–7
Gilbert, Sandra M and Susan Gubar, 334 n.
Giles, Paul 18
Glanville, Joseph, 239
Godwin, Parke 172
Godwin, William, 79, 81, 83, 84, 86, 131, 146, 213, 302, 303
  meets Fenimore Cooper, 108

Index 377

government, classical forms
  of, 51, 151–2
Grasmere, 118, 166, 205, 208
Graver, Bruce, 180 n.
Greene, Jack P., 28 n., 35–6,
Griffith, Clark, 242
Grossman, James, 157

Hall, Francis, 93, 105
Halleck, Fitz-Greene, 71, 76, 123, 148
Harrington, James, *The Commonwealth
  of Oceana*, 27, 35–6, 37–9,
  51, 52, 53, 101, 147
Harshbarger, Scott, 220 n.
Harvey, Samantha C. 21 n., 186 n.
Havens, Charles 356
Hawthorne, Nathaniel, 14, 16, 18, 19,
  21, 22, 55, 123, 125, 163, 219–34
  'P's Correspondence', 226–7
  'Rappaccini's Daughter',
    219–20, 238–34
  The Scarlet Letter, 221–3, 224–6,
  'Young Goodman Brown', 223–4
  alternative possibilities, 219–221
  and Coleridge, 227–8, 232–4
  invents Dickens, 225 n.
  and Emerson, 228, 233
  on Ann Hutchinson, 226 n.
  as ironist, 224–6
  and Keats, 238–32
  and Poe, 219, 234
  and Wordsworth, 122,
    219–22, 224–6, 228
Hazlitt, William, 20, 108 n., 114, 116,
  123, 151, 180 n., 189, 333 n.
Heckewelder, John Gottlieb
  Ernestus, 157
Heidegger, Martin, 236, 336
Holmes, Isaac, *An Account of the
  United States of America*, 25
Homans, Margaret, 334–5
Hulme, Obadiah, 33, 54, 57; An
  Historical Essay on the English
  Constitution (1771), 33–4, 47–8,
  52, 58, 101, 134–5, 135 n.
Huxley, Aldous, 234-5
Hyman, Stanley Edgar, 201

Imagination, 77, 187, 193, 195,
  207, 210, 219, 221, 228,
  233–4, 242, 246, 303
  see also Reason
Imlay, Gilbert, 69, 78–80, 86
  and Burke, 138
  and Jefferson, 79
  in 'Ruth', 80
  Topographical Description
    (1792), 78–9
Irving, Washington, 94, 102, 127, 341

Jackson, Andrew, 51, 56, 86–7,
  97, 103, 148, 155–6, 157,
  164, 168, 182, 251, 284
Jaspers, Karl, 180
Jay, John, 147, 150, 289; *Address
  to the People of Great
  Britain* (1774), 44
Jefferson, Thomas, 29, 32, 40–1, 44,
  47, 48, 50, 55, 56, 67, 75, 79,
  94, 95, 116, 134, 138 n., 144,
  146, 149–50 and n., 284, 289
  Notes on Virginia, 67, 79, 138 n.
  *Summary View of the Rights of
    British America*, 30, 44–45
  and Adams, 42 n., 50, 131 n., 155
  and Cartwright, 45, 48
  and Imlay, 79, 138 n
  and Madison, 116, 149
  on Missouri Compromise, 289–90
  and Price, 45, 67
Jeffrey, Francis, 85, 99, 100–1
Joy, Neill R., 201 n., 209 n.

Kant, Immanuel, 13, 113,
  187, 192, 194, 251
Keane, Patrick J., 21 n., 186
  n., 250, 316 n.
Keats, John, 14, 15, 16, 22, 113,

187, 194, 219, 242, 253,
  285, 287–8, 321–4, 326–7
'Eve of St Agnes', 229 and n.
'Lamia', 228, 229, 230–1
and Emily Dickinson, 315,
  321–4, 325, 326, 327
and Hawthorne, 219,
  226, 227, 228–31
Kennedy, J. Gerald, 242
Kentucky, 20, 78, 88
Kierkegaard, Soren, 231, 259, 272, 364
Klammer, Martin, 308

L'Ouverture, Toussaint, 56,
  182, 309, 311
Lafayette, Marquis de, 108, 110,
  112, 130, 137, 146, 148
Lawrence, D. H., 23, 144–5,
  312–3, 345
Lewis, R. W. B., 201, 216
Liberty, 28, 30, 31, 33, 34, 40–9
  passim, 51, 52, 59, 61 and n.,
  62, 66–8, 70, 83–4, 88–9, 95,
  99–100, 117, 129, 131, 133, 135,
  137, 140, 143, 152–4, 158, 207,
  214, 215, 273, 298, 311, 333
Lincoln, Abraham 14, 182, 344
Literary and Scientific Repository
  (New York), 99 n., 101–6
Locke, John, 29–30, 36, 39–41,
  47, 49, 50, 52 n., 83, 136
London Corresponding Society, 54
Lopez, Debbie, 228–9
Louisiana Purchase, 157, 289
Longfellow, Henry Wadsworth 11
  n., 164, 204, 349, 354
Lowell, James Russell 92, 200,
  349, 354, 356, 357 n.
luxury and dissipation, 31,
  43, 46, 53, 217
Lynen, John, 117, 290

Macaulay, Catherine, 31, 47
McCord, James, 60

McFarland, Thomas, 131, 268
Mackintosh, Sir James, 108, 109, 155
McWilliams, John P, 11 n.,
  111–2, 147 n
Madison, Donald, 292,
Madison, James, 49, 101,
  116, 149, 150, 216
Marovitz, Sanford E., 263 n., 270 n.
Martineau, Harriet, 53, 55–6, 62
  n., 95, 98, 106, 163, 289
Matthiessen, F. O., 12, 16, 254,
  258, 263 n., 270 n., 296
Mayflower, the, 36, 53
Melville, Herman, 55, 114, 125,
  215, 219, 228, 236, 249–81
  Moby-Dick, 114, 249–81
  Pierre 259–60, 261 n
  and Carlyle, 251–3, 269, 272,
  273–4, 278, 279 n., 280 n.
  and Coleridge, 249–75
  and pantheism, 251–2, 260,
  262, 263–4, 268–71, 274
  and Wordsworth, 274–81
  as Romantic ironist, 280–1
Meredith, George, 325–6
Miller, Ruth, 315 n., 316 n., 317, 364
Milton, John, 13, 15, 27, 35, 40, 51,
  63, 112, 121, 204, 302, 341
Missouri Compromise, 289
Moers, Ellen, 318, 359
Moldenhauer, Joseph J., 82 n.,
  201 n., 202, 208 n.
Monthly Magazine, 93, 104, 188
Morse, David 17, 233 n., 259,

Native Americans, 45, 75–6, 78, 81–2,
  87, 103, 140–1, 141 n., 168,
nature and Nature, 30, 78, 83, 85,
  86, 87, 88, 113, 114, 115,
  137, 143, 158, 159–60, 162,
  165, 177–8, 203, 264, 278
  and Liberty, 40, 57–8, 78, 85
  see also Emerson, *Nature*;
  and pantheism

Newlyn, Lucy, 206–7, 325
Newman, Lance, 18, 201 n.
Neussendorfer, Margaret, 118 n.,
Newton, Sir Isaac 97, 114, 116, 243
Nietzsche, Friedrich, 23,
    198, 199, 257, 272
North American Review, 76,
    96, 103, 106, 161

Oberhaus, Dorothy Huff,
    316–7 nn., 317–8
oligarchy, 52, 55–6, 70, 155–6
'one life', see Pantheism
Otis, James, *The Rights of the British
    Colonies* (1764), 32–3

Pace, Joel, 121 n., 168, 169,
    170, 185, 189 n., 198
Packer, Barbara, 13, 197
Paine, Thomas, 31, 40, 45, 49, 50,
    52, 53, 57, 80, 81, 85, 101,
    116, 130, 131, 132, 135,
    137, 139, 144, 146–7, 149,
    153, 183, 191, 216, 284
    Agrarian Justice, 38
    Common Sense, 42, 43, 47
    The Rights of Man, 54, 59, 143
Pantheism or the 'one life', 167,
    174, 188, 191, 210, 239–41
    262, 266, 274, 275, 338
    see also Melville and Pantheism
Paul, Sherman, 201
Paulding, James Kirke, 71,
    72, 102, 204,
Peabody, Elizabeth Palmer, 12,
    91, 107, 118, 317 n., 340
    letters to Wordsworth,
    118 n., 119–25
    on Hawthorne, 122, 219–20
Penn, William, 36, 63, 140
Piper, H. W., 253 n., 257
Plato, Platonism, neo-Platonism 113,
    116, 186, 188, 192, 193–4,
    219, 240, 251, 259 n.,
    261, 264, 274 n.,
Poe, Edgar Allan, 215, 353, 357
    Eureka, 237–9
    'Ligeia', 239–47
    and Coleridge, 235–9, 239–47
    and Hawthorne, 215, 235
    and Tennyson, 327, 357
    and Wordsworth, 235
Power, Julia, 12, 13
Pownall, Thomas, 35, 42,
    59, 74, 116, 117
    To the Sovereigns of America, 118
    To the Sovereigns of Europe,
    42, 57, 59, 118
Price, Kenneth M., 287 n., 288 n.
Price, Richard, 12, 32, 40, 42, 50,
    52, 53, 54, 57, 61, 63, 66,
    67–8, 70, 74, 77, 83, 89,
    98, 101, 116, 117, 183
    *Observations on the American
    Revolution*, 42, 61
    *Observations on Civil
    Liberty*, 34, 45–6
    *Discourse on the Love of
    Our Country*, 34, 42
Priestley, Joseph, 42 n., 66, 68,
    69, 73, 83, 179 n., 245
property qualifications, 52, 154
Quakers and Quaker values,
    36, 138, 140, 260, 284
Quarterly Review, 93, 96,
    102, 103, 106, 111

Raynal, Abbé [Guillaume Thomas
    François], 31–2, 44, 116, 117
Read, Thomas Buchanan 355
Reason and Imagination,
    193, 197, 226–34
Reason and Understanding, 187,
    197, 232–3, 275–6
representation, 29–30, 34,
    38, 40, 47 n, 71
revolutions, see American,
    English, French

Robertson, Fiona, 64 n.
Rogin, Michael, 251 n.
Romantic ideology, 19, 77, 219
Romantic irony, 20, 225, 231, 245, 281
Romanticism 12, 13, 14, 19, 20,
    22, 24, 54, 77, 83, 85, 113,
    190, 195, 199, 243–4

Sartre, Jean Paul, 58, 272
Saxon Constitution, 33, 47–8, 51–2
Saxon Diaspora, 47, 48, 143,
    188, 214, 216
Scott, Sir Walter, 98, 108–9,
    132, 145, 156, 226, 242
Sealts, Merton M, Jr., 194 n., 251 n.
Sharp, Granville, 34, 52 n., 66
Shelley, Mary, 68
Shelley, Percy Bysshe, 13, 16, 21,
    68, 71, 102, 113, 161, 182,
    194, 196, 198, 203, 207, 227,
    246, 271, 304, 322, 343
  Defence of Poetry, 15, 297
  'Ode to the West Wind',
    14, 70, 89, 321, 330
  *Philosophical View of
    Reform*, 68, 70
Sidney, Algernon, *Discourses
    Concerning Government*
    (1698) 27, 47, 50, 51, 53,
    54, 57, 58, 69, 101, 149
Sidney, Sir Philip 316, 325
slavery, 14, 36, 52, 53, 55, 65, 67, 86,
    88–9, 101, 105, 122, 284, 304
  abolition, 52, 53, 106, 182,
    213, 284, 309, 354
  compromises concerning, 79, 289
  entailed upon America, 106
  incompatible with liberty, 311
  Sydney Smith on, 95, 98
  Thoreau on, 213, 215
  Whitman on, 285, 307–9, 311
Slotkin, Richard, 78 n.
Smith, Adam, 39, 41, 45, 130

Smith, Henry Nash, 139–40 n.
Smith, John (Captain), *Description
    of New-England* 36
Smith, Julian 228
Smith, Lorrie, 183
Smith, Sydney 12, 51, 86, 92–9,
    102, 105, 106, 215
Society for Constitutional
    Information, 54
Southey, Robert, 54, 68, 71, 75,
    78, 79, 81, 84, 161
Spiller, Robert E., 92, 94
Spinoza, Benedict de, 179, 251,
    259, 262, 263, 268–9, 271
Stafford, Fiona, 68 n., 140–1
Stewart, Dugald 179–80 n.
Stewart, John ('Walking
    Stewart'), *The Apocalypse
    of Nature* (1792), 238–9
Stiles, Ezra, *The United States
    Elevated to Glory and Honor*
    (1783), 39, 48, 54, 57, 59
Stoddard, Richard Henry 356
Stoicism, 177, 179, 180, 259
Story, William Wetmore 92, 354
Swedenborg, Emanuel, 113, 115, 196
Swyderski, Ann 363
Symbiosis: *A Journal of Anglo-
    American Literary
    Relations*, 21, 367–70
symbolism, 22, 70, 77, 188,
    191, 207–8, 220, 228, 231,
    249, 253, 263, 271, 272
    and n., 277, 310, 311

Tanner, Tony, 159, 272
Taylor, Bayard 355, 357 n.
Tennyson, Alfred Lord, 22–3, 116,
    173, 326–8, 338, 340–64
  In Memoriam 173, 344, 345
  'Locksley Hall' 348, 353–7,
  Maud 329, 342, 346–7, 349
  'Tears, idle Tears' 287, 327–8, 344

and Dickinson 315, 317,
324, 328, 332, 336, 339,
348–9, 350, 352, 358–64
and Whitman 285, 287,
289, 293, 342–7
and Wordsworth 326–7, 328
Thelwall, John 34, 71
Thompson, Frank T., 186 n., 193 n.
Thompson, G. R., 244
Thoreau, Henry David, 11 n.,
14, 16, 18, 19, 20, 21, 53,
95, 112, 120, 185, 195
'Resistance to Civil
Government', 120, 213–6
Walden 200–17
'Walking', 183, 204, 213
and English lyric tradition, 204–5
and Wordsworth, 16, 125,
183–4, 193, 200–17
Towers, Joseph, *A Vindication of
the Political Principles of
Mr Locke* (1782). 40–1, 52
transatlantic time-lag, 71
Trollope, Frances, 53,
Tucker, Josiah, Dean of
Gluicester 412 n., 66
Turgot, Baron de, 49

United States of America: as
the future of English
republicanism 41–4, 100–1
as refuge of liberty, 43, 46, 53–4
United States of the British
Empire, 45–6

Vane, Sir Henry, 27, 35, 37, 51, 101

Wallace, James D., 78 n.,
93 n., 94 n., 129
Wallace, Michael, 43, 44
Walsh, Robert, *An Appeal from the
Judgements of Great Britain
Respecting the United States of
America* 96, 99–101, 104, 108
War of 1812, 18, 74 and n.,
75, 93, 99 and n, 101
War of Independence, 11, 39, 48,
52, 54, 57, 59, 75, 99, 100,
101, 135; in Blake 57–62
Wars, French and Indian, 32, 75, 157
Washington, George, 29, 48, 50, 59,
60, 63, 69, 97, 104, 124, 284
Webster, Daniel, 38, 213–4, 215, 216
Weisbuch, Robert 13, 17, 18, 19, 24,
117, 182, 206, 212, 228, 229,
240, 290, 291, 296, 297, 300,
301, 312, 317 n., 351, 352,
Welby, Adlard, *A Visit to North
America and the English
Settlements in Illinois,* 96 n.
Whitman, Walt 13, 21, 22, 23, 53,
55, 85, 95, 124, 127, 283–313,
315, 316, 330, 336, 342
'Song of Myself' 291–313
'Tears! Tears! Tears!' 343–4
'When Lilacs last in the
Dooryard Bloomed' 344–5
on American Constitution 214,
216, 307
and Bryant 162–3, 166, 174
and English poetry 17,
125, 285, 287,
and eroticism 295
prosody of 298–9, 313, 342–4
on slavery 304–11
and Tennyson 342–6
and Wordsworth 125, 175,
178, 180, 283–313
Widdowson, H. G., 299
Williams, Samuel 32, 77–8, 85, 86
*A Discourse on the Love of
Our Country* (1774) 39
n., 42, 46–7, 78
*Natural and Civil History of
Vermont* (1794) 39, 78
Winters, Yvor 144, 145, 164, 322, 324

Winthrop, John (1587–1649; Governor) 28 n., 36, 61, 96
Winthrop John (1714–1779, Professor and Astronomer) 61
Wollstonecraft, Mary, 78, 79, 83–4, 155 n.
  An Historical and Moral View of the French Revolution, 155 n.
Wood, Gordon S., 49 n., 52 n.
Wordsworth, William 12, 14, 15, 16, 20, 22, 24, 27, 28, 35, 36, 55, 56, 76, 78, 79–80, 84, 85, 112, 136, 145, 161, 326, 343, 352
  on America 80–2, 122
  and Bryant 161–2, 164–82
  and Coleridge 190–2, 195, 236–8
  and Dickinson 315, 317, 321, 324, 328–38
  and Emerson 113–6, 121–2, 184–93, 195–9
  and Hawthorne 122, 219–27
  and Melville 251, 265, 273–6, 280
  and Peabody 118–24
  and Poe 234–9, 246
  reception in America 76–7, 118–9
  republican sonnets of 26–7, 216-7, 302,
  on slavery 53, 182, 309, 311
  and Thoreau 183–4, 200–17
  and Whitman 283–312
Wordsworth, individual works:
  Concerning the Convention of Cintra 61, 164, 300
  The Excursion 81–2, 167, 171, 172–3, 175, 210, 291
  Guide to the Lakes 201 n., 208
  'Lines written a few miles above Tintern Abbey' 169, 190, 209, 298–9
  'Lucy Poems' and 'Matthew Poems' 173, 328–39
  'Ode: Intimations of Immortality' 118, 121, 166, 175–6, 181, 197, 280
  The Prelude 177, 190, 283, 290, 292, 294–5, 301, 303–6
  'The Tables Turned' 120, 189
  'The Thorn' 125, 220–21, 225
  'We are seven' 125, 179, 286
Wright, Frances, 36, 39 n.,48, 53, 70, 89, 105, 182, 284
Wright, Julia M., 66
Wylie, Ian, 69

Young, Edward 164; *Conjectures on Original Composition* (1759) 114

Zoellner, Robert, 258, 261

Pre-Publication Comment on Romantic Dialogues

'An impressive achievement. Gravil has a compelling thesis—that the American Renaissance actualized the political and aesthetic tropes of British Romanticism—and he argues it with freshness and learning. This book adds an indispensable chapter to the narrative of Anglo-American cultural relations.'

—*Michael T. Gilmore, Brandeis University*

'A brilliant book, illuminating on almost every page, and written with a rare clarity, charm and humour. It should be of fundamental interest to anyone interested in the cultural relations of England and the young United States. For anyone teaching or seeking to understand American literature, especially the canonical works of the 19th century, this book is indispensable and will remain the standard work for a long time to come.'

—*Norman Fruman, Professor Emeritus, University of Minnesota*

'Through his astonishingly thorough command of British and American Literature and his brilliant insight into the constituent ideas, images and tropes that struck vibrant chords in authors and readers on both sides of the Atlantic, Richard Gravil vastly extends our awareness of a persisting complexity of shared concerns and literary interconnections. His interweaving of cross-connections is managed with such a sure and subtle touch that readers will find hemselves frequently surprised that obvious parallels have so long escaped critical scrutiny.'

—*Frederick Burwick, University of California, Los Angeles*

From Humanities-Ebooks

John Beer, *Coleridge the Visionary* [PDF]
John Beer, *Blake's Humanism* [PDF]
Richard Gravil, *Wordsworth and Helen Maria Williams; or, the Perils of Sensibility* †
Richard Gravil, *Wordsworth's Bardic Vocation, 1787–1842* †
Richard Gravil and Molly Lefebure, eds, *The Coleridge Connection: Essays for Thomas McFarland* [PDF]
John K. Hale, *Milton as Multilingual* [PDF]
Simon Hull, ed., *The British Periodical Text, 1796–1832* [PDF]
John Lennard, *Of Sex and Faerie: Essays on Genre Fiction* †
C W R D Moseley, *Shakespeare's History Plays: 'Richard II' to 'Henry V', the Making of a King* †
W. J. B. Owen, *Understanding 'The Prelude'* [PDF]
Pamela Perkins, ed., *Francis Jeffrey: Unpublished Tours.*†
Keith Sagar, *D. H. Lawrence: Poet* †
Trudi Tate, *Modernism, History and the First World War* †
Irene Wiltshire, ed. *Letters of Mrs Gaskell's Daughters 1856–1914* †

Wordsworth Editions

The Cornell Wordsworth: a Supplement, edited by Jared Curtis ††
The Fenwick Notes of William Wordsworth, edited by Jared Curtis, revised and corrected †
The Poems of William Wordsworth: Collected Reading Texts from the Cornell Wordsworth, edited by Jared Curtis, in 3 volumes †
The Prose Works of William Wordsworth, Volume 1, edited by W. J. B. Owen and Jane Worthington Smyser †
Wordsworth's Convention of Cintra, a Bicentennial Critical Edition, edited by W. J. B Owen, with a critical symposium by Simon Bainbridge, David Bromwich, Richard Gravil, Timothy Michael and Patrick Vincent †
Wordsworth's Political Writings, edited by W. J. B. Owen and Jane Worthington Smyser. †

† Also available in paperback, †† in hardback
http://www.humanities-ebooks.co.uk
all available to libraries from MyiLibrary.com

www.ingramcontent.com/pod-product-compliance
Lightning Source LLC
Chambersburg PA
CBHW020941230426
43666CB00005B/111